Criminal Justice
in Canada
a reader

Fourth Edition

Criminal Justice
in Canada
a reader

Fourth Edition

Julian V. Roberts, Ph.D.
University of Oxford

Michelle G. Grossman, M.A., M.S.W.
University of Oxford

NELSON / EDUCATION

NELSON / EDUCATION

Criminal Justice in Canada: A Reader, Fourth Edition
Julian V. Roberts and Michelle G. Grossman

**Vice President,
Editorial Director:**
Evelyn Veitch

**Editor-in-Chief,
Higher Education:**
Anne Williams

Senior Acquisitions Editor:
Lenore Taylor-Atkins

Marketing Manager:
Terry Fedorkiw

Developmental Editor:
Kamilah Reid Burrell

Permissions Coordinator:
Melody Tolson

Production Service:
Integra

Copy Editor:
Matthew Kudelka

Proofreader:
Integra

Indexer:
Integra

Manufacturing Manager:
Joanne McNeil

Design Director:
Ken Phipps

Managing Designer:
Franca Amore

Interior Design:
Johanna Liburd

Cover Design:
Jennifer Leung

Cover Image:
Patricia Brown/Superstock

Compositor:
Integra

Printer:
Transcontinental

Library and Archives Canada
Cataloguing in Publication Data

Criminal justice in Canada:
a reader/Julian V. Roberts,
Michelle G. Grossman.
— 4th ed.

Includes bibliographical
references.
ISBN 978-0-17-650228-7

1. Criminal justice, Administration
of—Canada. I. Roberts, Julian V
II. Grossman, Michelle G

HV9960.C2C75 2011
364.971   C2010-907721-0

ISBN 13: 978-0-17-650228-7
ISBN 10: 0-17-650228-9

The editors dedicate their work on this book to the memory of Mary K. Roberts (1917–2005)—a scholar in all but name.

CONTENTS

PREFACE

Julian V. Roberts, Ph.D., and Michelle G. Grossman, M.A., M.S.W.

Welcome to the new, improved *Criminal Justice in Canada*. A decade ago, teachers in the field of criminology and criminal justice who sought a text for their students had few Canadian works from which to choose. That has since changed: several excellent books are now available. Finding a collection of readings, however, remains a challenge. Though several good readers exist, they deal with crime rather than criminal justice or specific topics, such as crime control policy. Instructors looking for a more general collection of primarily introductory readings are often forced to cobble together a collection of readings and package them through commercial or university print shops.

Our reader simplifies this task. The fourth edition is aimed at any course with a primary or secondary focus on the criminal justice system. We have designed this book to accompany standard criminal justice and criminology texts by providing a diversity of views: some articles take a critical approach to criminal justice; others report findings from a more "mainstream" perspective. Many readings have been commissioned especially for this new edition. The readings have been selected to achieve three goals: (1) to provide some basic information on the structure of criminal justice; (2) to hear from people who are working in or who have passed through the criminal justice process, because the voice of practical experience has greater value than mere theory; and (3) to draw upon empirical research that sheds light on the way that the justice system functions in Canada.

ACKNOWLEDGMENTS

First and foremost, we thank the contributing authors whose work is represented here and the copyright holders for their permission to reprint material. We would also like to acknowledge the important contributions of all the individuals involved in the production of this volume at Nelson Education Ltd.

Julian V. Roberts and Michelle G. Grossman
At Oxford, August 15, 2010

A Note from the Publisher

Thank you for selecting *Criminal Justice in Canada*, eds. Julian V. Roberts and Michelle G. Grossman. The editors and publisher have devoted considerable time to the careful development of this book. We appreciate your recognition of this effort and accomplishment.

ABOUT THE CONTRIBUTORS

EDITORS

Julian V. Roberts holds a Ph.D. from the University of Toronto and is currently a professor of criminology in the Faculty of Law at the University of Oxford. His recent books include *The Role of Previous Convictions at Sentencing* (Oxford: Hart, 2010); *Principled Sentencing* (with von Hirsch and Ashworth; Oxford: Hart, 2009); *Punishing Persistent Offenders* (Oxford: Oxford University Press, 2008); *Understanding Public Attitudes to Criminal Justice* (with M. Hough; Maidenhead: Open University Press, 2005); and *The Virtual Prison: Community Custody and the Evolution of Imprisonment* (Cambridge: Cambridge University Press, 2004).

Michelle G. Grossman has graduate degrees in criminology and social work from the University of Toronto. In addition, she has worked in a clinical capacity at the Toronto Child Abuse Centre. Most recently, she has worked in a policy/research capacity for the Government of Canada, at the Department of Justice and Solicitor General, with a particular focus on the issue of victims. She has published a number of articles in the area of sexual aggression. She is currently completing a doctoral thesis at the Centre of Criminology, University of Oxford.

CONTRIBUTING AUTHORS

Nicholas Bala has been a law professor at Queen's University in Kingston since 1980. His research and teaching focus on families and children involved in the justice system. Much of his work is interdisciplinary and collaborative, addressing young offenders, post-separation parenting and alienation, family violence and high-conflict separations, familial support obligations, and child witnesses. The Canadian courts frequently cite his work.

Shereen H. Benzvy Miller, M.A. LL.B, is a human rights lawyer by training and inclination. She has taught courses in law, criminology, and sociology at Carleton University, the University of Pennsylvania, and York University. She is a trained mediator and has written on restorative justice and governance. Previously a criminologist and criminal defence lawyer, she worked on a multitude of law reform files, including development of the statement of purpose and principles of sentencing for inclusion in the *Criminal Code of Canada*, and with the Correctional Law Review, which drafted the *Corrections and Conditional Release Act*. While her focus has been on criminal justice and human rights, she views the essence of her work as contributing to the support of democratic processes and values that improve Canada for Canadians.

Gillian Blackell is Senior Legal Counsel with the Family, Children, and Youth Section of the Department of Justice Canada. She has worked on legal policy issues related to violence against women and children for ten years, has been involved in the development of legislative reforms, and has had the privilege of participating in negotiations at the United Nations.

Paul Burstein started his own practice in 1992 specializing in criminal and constitutional litigation. He has argued appeals before the Supreme Court of Canada, the Ontario Court of Appeal, and the Federal Court of Appeal. Paul has appeared before parliamentary committees dealing with various criminal legislative proposals and has been the Director of Osgoode Hall Law School's Criminal Law Intensive Programme since 1999. He is also involved with the Trial Advocacy courses offered by the Law School to both students and practitioners and is an Adjunct Professor at Queen's Law School, teaching both trial and appellate advocacy.

Kathryn M. Campbell is a faculty member in the Department of Criminology at the University of Ottawa. She is an expert in the field of youth justice and editor of *Understanding Youth Justice in Canada*, published by Pearson Canada in 2005.

Peter J. Carrington is a professor of sociology at the University of Waterloo and has been a member of the Sociology and Legal Studies Department at the University of Waterloo since 1984. He is interested in the interplay between criminal careers and criminal networks, and in social networks and the juvenile and criminal justice systems. He is editor of *Canadian Journal of Criminology and Criminal Justice* and coeditor of *Sage Handbook of Social Network Analysis*.

Carla Cesaroni is an assistant professor at the Ontario Institute of Technology. She received her Ph.D. from the Centre of Criminology, University of Toronto. Her interest in youth in custody began while she was a volunteer at a secure custody facility for high-risk, violent youth. She has worked with and interviewed over 300 male youth in facilities throughout the province of Ontario. Her current research is on the stress and adjustment of youth in detention.

Judge David P. Cole was appointed to the Ontario Court of Justice in 1991. He currently presides at Metro West court in Toronto. From 1992 to 1996, he was seconded to the Commission on Systemic Racism in the Ontario Criminal Justice System. He teaches the law of sentencing and penal policy at the Faculty of Law and the Centre of Criminology, both at the University of Toronto. He is the coauthor of *Release from Imprisonment: The Law of Sentencing and Parole,* and the coeditor of *Making Sense of Sentencing.* He also is a member of the editorial board of the *Canadian Journal of Criminology and Criminal Justice.*

Mia Dauvergne is the manager of the Analysis Unit at the Canadian Centre for Justice Statistics, a division within Statistics Canada. She holds an M.A. in Criminology from the University of Ottawa and has worked in the field for more than a decade. Her research has focused on the incidence and nature of crime in Canada, including homicide and other violent crime, motor vehicle theft, drug-related crime, and hate crime.

Myriam Denov is currently an Associate Professor in the School of Social Work at McGill University. She holds a Ph.D. from the University of Cambridge, where she was a Commonwealth Scholar. Her current research and teaching interests lie in the areas of human rights, war and political violence, and at-risk youth. She has recently published a book on child soldiers with Cambridge University Press.

Liz Elliott is Assistant Professor and Co-Director of the Centre for Restorative Justice in the School of Criminology at Simon Fraser University. Her teaching and research interests are in restorative justice, prisons, crime prevention through social development, and criminological theory.

Robin T. Fitzgerald is currently a postdoctoral research fellow at the Key Centre for Ethics, Law, Justice, and Governance at Griffith University in Queensland, Australia. She received her M.A. from the School of Criminology at Simon Fraser University and her doctorate from Carleton University. Her research interests include neighborhood and community effects on crime, policing social (dis)order, and disproportionate minority contact with the justice system.

Holly Johnson is an associate professor of criminology at the University of Ottawa. She was principal investigator on Statistics Canada's national surveys on crime victimization and violence against women and is the author of many publications in that field. She also provides advice to community-based researchers and governments internationally on the development and design of surveys to measure violence against women. She acts as adviser to the International Violence Against Women Survey, a multicountry project coordinated through the UN. She received her Ph.D. from the University of Manchester.

Catherine Kane is Director General and Senior General Counsel, Justice Canada, Criminal Law Policy Section. She joined the Department of Justice, Criminal Law Policy Section, in 1982. In addition, she was the first Director of the Policy Centre for Victim Issues at the Department of Justice, Canada. Her work in the department has focused on a range of criminal law reforms, particularly those dealing with sexual assault, victims and witnesses of crime, impaired driving, and mentally disordered offenders. She is actively involved in many intra- and inter-departmental committees; federal, provincial, and territorial committees; and the Uniform Law Conference of Canada. She has served as secretary to the Criminal Section since 1996 and served as chairperson of that section in 2004.

Barry N. Leighton is a criminologist specializing in policing in Canada. He teaches or has taught at a number of universities, including Carleton University and the University of Ottawa.

Brian Manarin is an assistant Crown attorney prosecuting criminal matters in Windsor, Ontario, after many years of practice with the Ministry of the Attorney General in the Greater Toronto Area. He was called to the Ontario Bar in 1988, and his prosecutorial experience has run the gamut of matters criminal. An internationally published author, he has written numerous articles on various legal topics.

Marie Manikis is currently pursuing her graduate studies in law at the University of Oxford. She previously completed an LL.M. at Osgoode Hall Law School, where she taught a course on the *Charter of Rights and Freedoms*. Prior to this, she practised law in Montreal, completing her law degree at the University of Montreal while clerking for a Superior Court Justice.

Anthony Matarazzo is a project manager and senior research analyst at the Canadian Centre for Justice Statistics. He recently obtained his Ph.D. from the University of Waterloo, where he studied the criminal careers of a birth cohort of Canadian offenders. His research interests include youth crime and youth justice, delinquent and criminal careers, and research methods and statistics.

Susan McDonald is Principal Researcher with the Research and Statistics Division of the Department of Justice Canada. She is a lawyer and has a doctorate in Adult Education. In her position with the Department of Justice she is responsible for all sociolegal policy research on victims of crime. She also works on issues such as public confidence in the justice system, access to justice, and gender and diversity.

Peter McKnight is an award-winning columnist and editorial writer with the *Vancouver Sun* and an adjunct professor in the School of Criminology at Simon Fraser University. He holds a B.A. in psychology, a law degree, an M.A. in journalism, and an M.A. in philosophy, all from the University of Western Ontario, and has held fellowships at the University of Cambridge and MIT. A member of the Ontario Bar and a former probation and parole officer, he writes and speaks on a wide variety of topics, including law and justice issues, science and medicine, and philosophy, religion, and ethics.

Julius Melnitzer is an author living in Toronto. His books include *Maximum, Minimum, Medium: A Journey Through Canada's Prisons* (1995); and *Dirty White Collar* (2002).

Karen Middlecoat graduated from University of Toronto with a B.A.H. with a double major in criminology and psychology and a minor in english. She started working in the Ministry of Correctional Services as a correctional officer, then spent a year at the Metropolitan Toronto Forensic Services (METFORS), working with psychiatric staff to conduct assessments on individuals to determine their fitness to stand trial. She became a probation and parole officer in 1985 and worked in the field till 1997, when she was asked to work at the Toronto courts as the administrative probation liaison.

Eugene Oscapella completed an undergraduate degree in economics at the University of Toronto (1974), obtained his law degree from the University of Ottawa (1977), and received his Masters of Laws from the London School of Economics and Political Science (1979). He was called to the Ontario Bar in 1980. From 1982 to 1985, he was Director of Legislation and Law Reform for the Canadian Bar Association. He is a founding member of the Canadian Foundation for Drug Policy, and was a former chair and member of the policy committee of the Canadian Criminal Justice Association. He lectures in criminology at the University of Ottawa.

Judge Gilles Renaud has been a member of the Ontario Court of Justice since 1995. Previously he served as a prosecutor and defence counsel. He is a prolific author, having written eight books on evidence, advocacy, and sentencing, including two in French, and a collection of humorous short stories.

Rick Sauve is in his twelfth year working for LifeLine of St. Leonards. After serving 17 years in prison he worked as a cabinetmaker, then for Toronto Boys Home as a child and youth worker with inner-city youth. While incarcerated, he finished high school as well as degrees in psychology and criminology.

He has been active in prisoners' rights and led the successful court challenge in the Supreme Court of Canada for prisoners' right to vote. He lives with his wife Michele in the countryside near Lindsay, Ontario.

Sheldon Schwartz received a B.A. from York University, majoring in economics. He worked in the field of public accounting and auditing for several years before entering the field of social work. After three years working for an agency providing supervision services under contract to the Correctional Service of Canada (CSC), he was hired by the Government of Canada for another department (Human Resources Development Canada, formerly Employment and Immigration). After six years in various HRDC roles, he transferred back to CSC in 1996, where he has been ever since. He has received a Bachelor of Social Work degree from York University and a Masters in Social Work from the University of Toronto and is now a registered social worker.

Simon Verdun-Jones is a professor of criminology at Simon Fraser University. His major interests are criminal law, mentally disordered offenders, plea bargaining, sentencing, victim participation in the criminal justice system, the International Criminal Court of Justice, and violence and aggression in mental health facilities. Among his recent books are *Introduction to Criminal and Civil Law* (2006); *Criminal Law in Canada: Cases, Questions, and the Code*, 4th ed. (2007); and *Canadian Criminal Cases: Selected Highlights*, 2nd ed. (2007).

Michael Waby is an assistant Crown attorney working for the Ministry of the Attorney General in Ontario. He is currently also the vice president of the Ontario Crown Attorneys' Association. He joined the Metropolitan Police in 1986 and worked in West London for the balance of his service. Upon qualifying as a barrister, he left the police service in 1996 and then worked as a criminal barrister in a set of chambers in Temple doing a mix of defence and prosecution work before moving to Canada in 2001. After a brief period working as a defence counsel in Toronto, he became a Crown Attorney in 2003, prosecuting those charged with criminal conduct ranging from homicide to property offences.

Richard Weisman is Associate Professor in the Law and Society Program at York University in Toronto. He is currently completing a book on the role of remorse in law, using cases and other data from Canada, the United States, and South Africa.

PART ONE
Introductory Readings

CHAPTER 1
Criminal Justice in Canada: An Overview

This introductory chapter provides context for the rest of the volume. It begins by noting two alternative models of criminal justice in Canada and then reviews the research on public opinion about criminal justice. Many Canadians believe they know how the criminal justice system works (and have strong opinions about how it *should* work); but as we shall see, there is often a considerable gap between the public's ideas about how the system works and how it actually works. One of the main purposes of any course or text in the field of criminology is to correct public misperceptions. A good place to start, therefore, is to document the extent of public knowledge of crime and justice.

Julian V. Roberts, University of Oxford

Criminal justice in Canada—as elsewhere—involves a complex system of checks and balances in which responsibility for a criminal case is divided among many different decision makers. To complicate matters further, these decision makers are guided by somewhat different mandates. Judges are guided by the *principle of proportionality* when imposing a sentence. This means they attempt to ensure that the severity of the sentence imposed reflects the seriousness of the crime committed (and the offender's level of culpability). Parole boards, on the other hand, have a different mandate. When deciding whether a prisoner should be allowed out of prison to spend the remainder of his or her sentence in the community under supervision, a parole board is concerned about whether that offender will benefit from release on parole and whether that person represents a risk to the community. The seriousness of the crime plays little role in the decision—unless it sheds light on the issues of rehabilitation or risk to the community. Thus the length of the sentence is determined largely by the seriousness of the crime, while the portion of the sentence served in prison is often determined by other criteria. This is just one example of the system's complexity.

The justice system is also complex because it must respond to a wide diversity of human behaviour. If crime comprised only a limited number of proscribed acts, the system could develop a far more focused (and predictable) response to it. But the variability in criminal conduct is immense, and the system needs to vary its responses to it accordingly. The criminal justice system must be able to respond to cases of premeditated murder, minor acts of vandalism committed by bored teenagers, and all forms of offending between these two extremes. In addition, even when they have been convicted of the same category of crime, no two offenders are ever alike. Two people convicted of burglary may have very different backgrounds, and one may be more blameworthy than the other. Consider a case of break and enter in which one offender is 35 years old and has four previous convictions for breaking into houses; whereas the other offender is 18 and has no previous convictions. Even if they have committed the crime together, their cases are very different, and it is surely appropriate that the justice system treat them differently.

MODELS OF CRIMINAL JUSTICE

Two competing perspectives underlie our criminal justice system. These perspectives give rise to alternative models of justice that are closely associated with the writings of Herbert Packer, who coined the terms ***crime control*** and ***due process*** (see Packer 1968). As the name implies, the crime control model stresses the importance of controlling crime and favours providing criminal justice professionals with considerable powers for responding to crime. Thus crime control advocates would support giving police wide powers to search suspects, enter people's houses, and detain persons accused of a crime.

In contrast, the due process model limits the powers of the criminal justice system to prosecute accused persons. Due process advocates argue that if the State—which has unlimited resources to prosecute suspects—is not subject to some limits, society will become intolerable, as people will be subjected to constant surveillance and police interventions. For this reason, we create specific rights that must be respected by the police and indeed by all agents of the criminal justice system.

How are these limits on the powers of the State established? One example is by requiring police to obtain permission from a court prior to placing a wiretap on a suspect's telephone line. Similarly, police officers cannot stop a person and search him or her without reasonable grounds for doing so. In these and many other ways the due process model prevents the State from having unlimited power over the lives of suspects and accused persons. The due process model is therefore more concerned with protecting the rights of the accused and following correct legal procedure. For almost every important issue in criminal justice, one can find crime control as well as due process approaches.

For example, when determining the limits on the powers of the police, crime control advocates argue that the police should have wide powers to gather evidence and to question and interrogate suspects and accused persons. Due process advocates, on the other hand, want such powers limited in order to ensure that individual rights are not compromised and that innocent people are not stopped and detained by the police. The conduct of criminal trials also provides many examples of the conflict between due process and crime control models of criminal justice. During a criminal trial, an accused person is not obliged to take the stand and testify in his or her own defence. The onus is on the state, through the prosecutor, to establish the guilt of the accused beyond a reasonable doubt, without any help from the testimony of the accused. The due process model defends this procedural rule by arguing that the accused should not have to cooperate with the state's case. In contrast, crime control proponents would argue that the accused *should* have to testify because this may be the only way to get to the truth.

A criminal justice system founded exclusively on one perspective or the other would be problematic. Pursuing crime control to the exclusion of due process considerations would inevitably result in an increase in the number of persons wrongfully convicted, because due process procedural safeguards provide the innocent with a strong defence against a false accusation. However, a system that stresses due process considerations to the extreme would result in a higher number of wrongful acquittals: guilty people would evade punishment because the police would be hampered in their search for incriminating evidence. For this reason, the Canadian justice system has elements of both perspectives. But even a balanced approach can result in miscarriages of justice. As we shall see later in this volume, wrongful convictions can—and do—occur, resulting in the imprisonment of innocent people, sometimes for many years.

The ultimate arbiter of conflicts between the two models of criminal justice is the Supreme Court of Canada, the decisions of which are binding upon Parliament and all courts in Canada. The Supreme Court often hears arguments regarding the constitutionality of specific pieces of criminal justice legislation and decides whether a particular law is consistent with the rights guaranteed by the *Canadian Charter of Rights and Freedoms*. A law that goes too far in the direction of controlling crime may violate one of the provisions of the *Charter*. The impact of the *Charter* on the criminal justice system is discussed in the next chapter of this book.

PUBLIC OPINION AND CRIMINAL JUSTICE

The public in Canada (as elsewhere) tends to be quite critical of their criminal justice system. Many people view the system as overly lenient and as biased more toward the interests of the accused or offender than toward those of the victim. This perception, however, is often false. The media, furthermore, increasingly report that Canadians have lost confidence in their criminal justice system. But is this true? What do the polls say about the issue? Two surveys, both conducted in 2002, asked Canadians to express their degree of satisfaction with or confidence in the justice system (see Roberts, Crutcher, and Verbrugge 2007). In one of these surveys, respondents rated the degree of confidence they had in "the justice system in Canada" using a 7-point scale, where 7 represented a great deal of confidence and 1 no confidence at all. Leaving aside the 22 percent in the midpoint category (4), 46 percent of the respondents expressed confidence in the system, while 32 percent expressed little or no confidence—a difference of 14 percent.

On balance, this poll suggests that Canadians are more positive than negative about their justice system. The other survey conducted that same year asked respondents to express their level of satisfaction with the system. The response options were "very satisfied," "satisfied," "dissatisfied," or "very dissatisfied." This range of options permits a comparison of the proportion of respondents with positive or negative views. Just over half (54%) were satisfied, and 41 percent were dissatisfied. Thus, the surveys suggest that more Canadians are positive than negative about the system.

How do confidence trends for criminal justice compare to those for other public institutions? Table 1.1 shows that compared to other public institutions, the justice system attracts lower confidence ratings. However, the proportion of respondents expressing a great deal or quite a lot of confidence in the justice system is not significantly lower than the proportion expressing similar levels of confidence in the education system. Moreover, confidence levels in criminal justice are significantly higher for the justice system than for Parliament.

Table 1.1 *Public Confidence in Selected Public Institutions, Canada, 2003*

	A great deal of confidence	Quite a lot of confidence	Not very much confidence	No confidence at all
Local business	19%	61%	11%	1%
Banks	19	49	21	6
Health care system	19	48	24	4
Educational system	17	48	21	3
Justice system	14	43	27	7
Corporations	8	38	33	10
Parliament	8	35	35	10
Welfare system	9	32	29	9

Source: Adapted from Roberts, J.V., Crutcher, N., and Verbrugge, P. 2006. "Public Attitudes to Sentencing in Canada: Some Recent Findings." *Canadian Journal of Criminology and Criminal Justice.*

We should also not lose sight of the fact that the health care and educational systems have mandates very different from that ascribed to the justice system. The health care system exists for the benefit of the health consumer: the patient. Its activities are directed toward one goal: improving the well-being of the patient, without any competing interests. In contrast, the justice system has a more complex mandate to fulfill; it must respond to the interests of multiple parties. Offenders, victims, and the families of both groups have rights and needs that sometimes conflict. It is therefore unreasonable to expect confidence levels to be comparable for the justice and health systems. In addition, the health care and educational systems share a mandate to help members of the public. In contrast, the mission of the criminal justice system is not *primarily* to help victims, but rather to promote public safety and impose appropriate punishments. Judges must discharge multiple mandates, one of which is to ensure that defendants receive a fair trial. Similarly, prosecutors must act in the public interest, which may mean discontinuing a prosecution or not launching an appeal against acquittal or sentence. Predictably, nurses, educators, and military personnel receive higher ratings from the public than lawyers, judges, or members of the parole board (see Roberts 2007). The public may lose sight of the complexity of the justice system's mandate, which may explain why justice professionals receive somewhat lower ratings of public confidence.

CONFIDENCE IN BRANCHES OF CRIMINAL JUSTICE

The public may be more positive than negative about the justice system as a whole, but people responds very differently when asked to rate the performance of or express confidence in specific branches of the justice system. In general, the public has a great deal of confidence in the police and far less confidence in other criminal justice professionals. For example, a survey conducted in 2002 found that over two-thirds of respondents rated the police as doing an "excellent" or "good" job, whereas only half expressed the same level of support for judges (Roberts 2002).

Table 1.2 summarizes findings from this survey of public ratings of four criminal justice professions. As the table shows, people rate the police more

Table 1.2 *Public Evaluations of Criminal Justice Professions in Canada*

	Excellent or good	Average	Poor or very poor
Police	67%	25%	7%
Defence Counsel	56	36	6
Prosecutors	53	40	5
Judges	50	31	17

Source: Public Safety Canada. *Public Confidence in Criminal Justice: A Review of Recent Trends 2004-05.* Table 15. Found at: *http://www.publicsafety.gc.ca/res/cor/rep/2004-05-pub-conf-eng.aspx*

positively than they rate other criminal justice professionals. Moreover, this finding is not restricted to Canada: similar trends emerge in all other countries in which such surveys have been conducted (see Roberts 2007).

Explaining Variations in Confidence Levels

Several explanations can account for this hierarchy of confidence. With respect to Packer's (1968) two models of criminal justice, the public is more sympathetic to crime control than to due process. Support for this proposition can be found in the results of a number of surveys. A British poll found that four out of five respondents agreed with changing the law to permit the state to retry individuals who have been found not guilty (*Observer* 2003). An American survey found that nearly half of those interviewed believed that the criminal justice system treats defendants better than victims (National Crime Center 1991). Although these issues have not been explored by pollsters in Canada, it is likely that many Canadians share these views.

The public is equally intolerant of obstacles to prosecuting (and convicting) defendants. The judicial system can make two kinds of "classification" errors: it can convict innocent people, and it can acquit guilty parties. The aphorism is well engrained in legal thinking that it is better to acquit ten guilty individuals than allow an innocent person to be convicted. In other words, one kind of error is considered much worse than the other. The desire to ensure that the innocent are acquitted explains the many criminal procedures designed to avoid such a judicial mistake. The public, however, appears to be less concerned about the occurrence of wrongful convictions. A British Attitudes Survey asked people whether it was worse to convict an innocent person or to let a guilty person go free. Almost half (42%) of the sample believed that letting a guilty person go free was worse (Dowds 1995). This finding reflects the crime control orientation of the public. Although it was a British survey, research on related issues makes it clear that Canadians would respond in the same way. In short, most people favour a justice system that gives police and prosecutors significant powers rather than a system that follows procedural safeguards to ensure that due process is maintained.

Thus, the police are more closely allied in the public mind with a crime control mandate and for this reason receive higher ratings. While the police have to observe constitutionally based rules regarding the surveillance of suspects and the collection of evidence, police practices are ultimately regulated by the courts through constitutional challenges. The judiciary has a more complex mandate. Unlike their counterparts in the systems of justice found on the continent of Europe, judges in common law jurisdictions such as Canada must remain neutral while the parties to the proceedings conduct the case. In the popular mind, judges are probably associated far more closely with a due process model of justice—one that, as we have seen, attracts less support from members of the public.

In popular opinion, therefore, the mandate of the police is closer to the crime control model of justice. Judges, on the other hand, must strive to protect the rights of the accused during a trial, and prosecutors must consider the interests in justice, not simply pursue the conviction of the defendant. The public is seldom aware of the true nature of the prosecutorial role. Research has shown that many people see the prosecutor as the "victim's lawyer" (Roberts 2002), and they may be disappointed when Crown counsel take a position at odds with the opinion of the crime victim. Members of the public are less familiar with and have less sympathy for these elements of justice; and this lack of familiarity may be reflected in their perceptions of the courts and prosecutors.

One final explanation for the higher public approval ratings of the police is more mundane than theoretical. From many perspectives, the police are the most visible of all criminal justice professionals: they wear uniforms, drive (usually) marked vehicles, and perform their duties in public, on the streets of the nation. The public nature of policing contrasts the work of other professionals, such as judges or lawyers, whose duties are discharged out of the public eye. A significant proportion of the population has contact with a police officer at some point; the MORI poll in the United Kingdom found that almost one-third of the respondents reported having some contact with the police in the previous year. Yet how many people have contact with a judge, a member of a parole board, or a probation officer? Higher levels of exposure to the police likely promote confidence in the policing branch of criminal justice. The movement towards community policing in recent years reflects this relationship between exposure and confidence. The premise underlying community policing is that increasing the visibility of the police in the community promotes public confidence.

PUNISHMENT AND PREVENTION

Although the news media focus on punishment as a goal of criminal justice, the system also attempts to prevent crime. The public are often described as wanting simply to punish offenders. However, polls reveal that there is widespread support for crime prevention. In fact, given a choice between punishment and prevention, Canadians have always supported prevention. A number of polls have asked respondents to choose between two responses to crime: punishment or prevention. In 2003, Canadians were asked to identify "the main goal of the criminal justice system"; their responses are summarized in Figure 1.1. As can be seen, there was more support for prevention than for punishment (41% compared to 23%). Moreover, as Table 1.3 reveals, Canadians have always expressed more support for prevention than for punishment.

PUBLIC KNOWLEDGE OF CRIMINAL JUSTICE

This section summarizes findings from a review of public opinion polls in Canada about crime and criminal justice issues. I start by discussing one of the most important public misperceptions affecting attitudes toward the justice system. For the sake of brevity, full bibliographic citations for works cited in this section of the chapter are omitted here; they can be found in Roberts and Hough (2005).

Figure 1.1 *Public Perceptions of the Primary Goal of Criminal Justice in Canada*

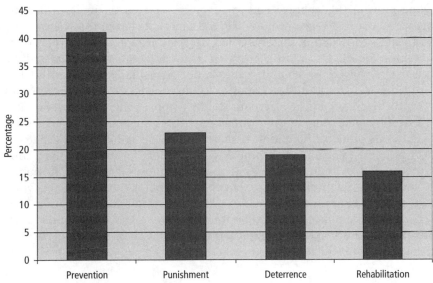

Source: EKOS Research Associates. *Canadian Attitudes Towards the Prevention of Crime,* 2000.

Public Perceptions of Crime Trends

Public opinion surveys in many nations show that the public always thinks that crime rates are rising, regardless of whether crime is going up or down or remaining stable. Public perceptions of crime trends are generally unrelated to actual trends. Thus in the 1980s, most people were correct when they responded to polls by saying that crime rates were rising. Then, throughout the 1990s, crime rates declined significantly; yet polls revealed that most Canadians still believed that crime was on the rise.

Table 1.3 *Support for Different Approaches to Crime*

(Percentage of Respondents Supporting Prevention vs. Enforcement)

	1994	1997	1997	1998
Crime prevention	73%	61%	73%	57%
Law enforcement	22	35	22	37

Source: Roberts, J.V. and Hastings, R. 2007. "Public Opinion and Crime Prevention: A Review of International Findings." *Institute for the Prevention of Crime.* Vol. 1: Pg. 199.

The most recent poll—conducted in 2010—confirmed these trends. The Angus Reid company asked a representative sample of Canadians whether crime rates in this country had increased, decreased, or remained stable over the past five years. Almost half the sample believed that crime rates had increased, when in fact they had declined (Angus Reid 2010). Police statistics and victimization surveys tend not to reach the general public because downward or stable trends are not particularly newsworthy. The resulting misperception has important consequences for public attitudes toward the criminal justice system: if most people believe that crime rates are steadily increasing, then they may well also believe that the system has failed in its principal function—namely, to prevent crime. This misperception of crime trends, then, is probably responsible for much of the public criticism of the criminal justice system. Finally, most members of the public believe that a relatively large proportion of crime involves violence when in reality violent crime accounts for a relatively small percentage of crimes reported to the police. Most crime involves nonviolent criminal conduct, but people tend to focus primarily on the most serious offences—namely, those involving violence.

Sentencing

Opinion polls often ask the public to rate the court system and, specifically, the severity of sentences imposed. The percentage of Canadians who feel that sentences are too lenient has been high for more than 20 years. In 1970, approximately two-thirds of Canadians endorsed the view that sentences were not harsh enough. In 1992, the proportion expressing this view was 85 percent. A more recent poll (conducted in 2005) found that 73 percent of Canadians felt that the justice system was "too soft" toward people convicted of crimes (Roberts, Crutcher, and Verbrugge 2007). However, this perception is often founded upon inaccurate knowledge of the actual severity of sentences imposed. People tend to underestimate the severity of sentencing practices. For example, approximately 90 percent of offenders convicted of robbery are sent to prison; yet fully three-quarters of respondents to a representative survey of the public estimated the incarceration rate for this crime to be under 60 percent (Canadian Sentencing Commission 1987). Similar results emerged for other offences. Thus, the perception of leniency in sentencing at the trial court level is based upon a misperception of the actual severity of sentences imposed.

Many people also mistakenly believe that increasing the severity of penalties will have an appreciable impact on crime rates. The reality is that such a small percentage of offenders are actually sentenced that the ability of the sentencing process to reduce crime is very restricted. This point has been made repeatedly in the sentencing literature. Ashworth (2010) notes that judges deal with no more than about 3 percent of the offences actually committed. Statistics Canada reports similar trends in this country: a sentence is imposed in fewer than 5 percent of crimes committed because of *case attrition* in the criminal justice process. The term *case attrition* simply means that cases drop out of the criminal justice system. Only some crimes are reported to the police, and of these, only some are deemed by the police to be *founded*. Of the founded incidents, some do not result in the laying of a criminal charge. Of the charges actually brought to court, some are dropped or stayed, and the remainder do not all end in the conviction of an accused. If such a small percentage of crimes result in the imposition of a penalty, the nature of the sentence will have little impact on the overall volume of crime. Clearly, then, the sentencing system is limited in its ability to reduce the crime rate.

Use of Incarceration as a Sanction

Notwithstanding how difficult it is to compare international sentencing because of the differences between criminal justice systems (e.g., offence definitions and early release provisions), statistics show that incarceration rates in Canada are high relative to those in most other countries. Even with the incarceration rates declining in recent years (see Chapter 3), in 2005 the incarceration rate in Canada was still significantly higher than in many other Western nations (Public Safety and Emergency Preparedness Canada 2005). Commissions of inquiry as well as the federal government have long acknowledged that Canada relies too heavily on imprisonment as a sanction. Yet the public is often unaware of this reality. In 1999, a poll asked Canadians whether the incarceration rate in this country was higher, lower, or the same as in most other Western countries. Only 15 percent of respondents knew that the incarceration rate was higher here than elsewhere. Most respondents believed that the incarceration rate was lower in Canada (Roberts, Nuffield, and Hann 2000).

Corrections

There is a significant gap between public perception and the reality of prison life. Many Canadians feel that an inmate's life is an easy one and are not aware of the privations and difficulties suffered by incarcerated offenders. Most people are also unaware of the high rates of homicide, suicide, and assault in correctional institutions. One Gallup survey conducted in 1991 found that half the respondents felt that conditions in penal institutions were "too liberal," although fewer than 5 percent reported any firsthand experience in a correctional institution.

In addition, many members of the public believe that if prison conditions were much harsher, prisoners would be less likely to reoffend and risk reincarceration. However, research has shown that making prisons more austere and taking away privileges may make prison life more unpleasant, but it does not result in lower reoffending rates. Simply put, making a prison a very inhospitable place to live will not mean that prisoners will be less likely to return to a life of crime. Preventing reoffending involves ensuring that ex-offenders get jobs and have a stake in the community.

Parole Grant Rates

The correctional issue that generates most public criticism concerns early release from prison. Most Canadians believe that too many inmates are released from prison too early. This view is based largely on misperceptions about the purpose of the parole system. In general, the public believes that most prisoners are granted release on parole and that parole is easy to obtain. One poll found that half the respondents overestimated the federal parole rate. In reality, less than half the applications for full parole release at the federal level are approved (Public Safety and Emergency Preparedness Canada 2005). In addition, prisoners applying for parole must convince the Parole Board that they are not a risk to the community and that their progress toward rehabilitation would be assisted by release.

Success Rates of Parolees

The gap between public perception and reality is probably greater for parole and early release issues than for any other criminal justice topic. Intense media coverage of the small number of cases in which a parolee is charged with a serious offence likely contributes to widespread public concern about prisoners released on parole. High-profile incidents influence public knowledge about parole and subsequently affect public attitudes toward early release programs. Moreover, the public tends to believe that a significant percentage of these parolees commit further offences. In fact, the failure rate of offenders on parole tends to be quite low. Public misperceptions regarding parole recidivism may also fuel public opposition toward the early release of inmates serving terms of imprisonment for violent crimes.

Costs of Incarceration versus Supervision in the Community

A Gallup survey found that fewer than 20 percent of respondents were able to accurately estimate the cost of keeping an offender in prison. Few Canadians realize that it costs over $80,000 to house an offender in a penitentiary for a year (ibid. 2005). Most people believe it costs less than this amount. At the same time, just as people underestimate the cost of incarceration, they also overestimate the cost of supervising an offender in the community. On average, it costs approximately $20,000 to supervise an offender in the community—one-fifth the cost of imprisonment (ibid. 2005). If the public knew how much money the system could save by punishing offenders in the community rather than in prison, they would probably be more supportive of community-based sentences and parole.

SUMMARY

Most people have a great deal of interest in criminal justice stories. However, this does not mean that they are necessarily well informed about the system. While expecting the public to have accurate views of all aspects of crime and justice would be naive, and while there are areas in which public awareness has increased in recent years, there remain important issues for which further public education is imperative. Crime provokes a great deal of public concern and debate over the nature of appropriate crime control policies. However, when evaluating public support for these policies, criminologists should bear in mind what people actually know about crime and criminal justice. Only when the public has a realistic understanding of crime and justice can an informed debate over crime control policies take place.

PLAN OF THE FOURTH EDITION

This fourth edition of *Criminal Justice in Canada: A Reader* contains a diverse collection of contemporary readings in criminal justice. **Part One** contains chapters dealing with general issues associated with criminal justice, while **Part Two** consists of contributions from participants in the criminal justice system. These chapters feature criminal justice professionals drawing upon their own experiences to comment on the system. Textbooks in criminal justice and even the most carefully conducted research cannot replace the experience of those actually participating in the criminal process. (This is why I always encourage students to observe the practice of the system directly whenever possible by going on "ride alongs" with the police or by sitting in court as an observer.) This section of the reader was conceived with this purpose in mind: to provide a view of the justice system drawn directly from the participants themselves.

The remaining chapters in **Part Three** address some of the most important criminal justice issues being discussed in Canada today. The contributors discuss a wide range of topics, including the successes and failures of the criminal justice system. It is important not to lose sight of the failings of the system, and for this reason one of the issues explored is the problem of wrongful convictions. All justice systems make mistakes and no error is more serious than convicting a person who is innocent. Regrettably, a number of individuals have been convicted of a crime they did not commit, and this is discussed from the perspective of research and also the individual who is victimized in this way.

FURTHER READING

Goff, C. 2011. *Criminal Justice in Canada*. Toronto: Thomson Nelson.

Griffiths, C. 2007. *Canadian Criminal Justice: A Primer*. 3rd ed. Toronto: Thomson Nelson.

Roberts, J.V. and M. Hough. 2005. *Understanding Public Attitudes to Criminal Justice*. Maidenhead: Open University Press.

REFERENCES

Angus Reid. 2010. *Americans, Britons, and Canadians Take a Harsh Stance on Crime*. Toronto: Angus Reid.

Ashworth, A. 2010. *Sentencing and Criminal Justice*. 5th ed. Cambridge: Cambridge University Press.

Canadian Sentencing Commission. 1987. *Sentencing Reform: A Canadian Approach*. Ottawa: Supply and Services Canada.

Dowds, L. 1995. *The Long-Eyed View of Law and Order: A Decade of British Social Attitudes Survey Results*. London: Home Office.

National Victim Center. 1991. *Citizens' Attitudes About Victims' Rights and Violence*. New York: National Victim Center.

Observer, The. 2003. "Crime Uncovered." April 27.

Packer, H. 1968. *The Limits of the Criminal Sanction*. Stanford: Stanford University Press.

Public Safety and Emergency Preparedness Canada. 2005. *Corrections and Conditional Release Statistical Overview*. Ottawa: Public Safety Canada.

—— . 2007. "Public Confidence in Criminal Justice in Canada: A Comparative and Contextual Analysis." *Canadian Journal of Criminology and Criminal Justice* 49: 153–85.

Roberts, J.V. and R. Hastings. 2007. "Public Opinion and Crime Prevention: A Review of International Findings." *Revue de l'Institut pour la Prevention de la Criminalite* 1: 193–218.

Roberts, J.V., 2002. *Public Evaluations of Criminal Justice Professionals in Canada*. Ottawa: Department of Justice Canada.

Roberts, J.V. and M. Hough. 2005. *Understanding Public Attitudes to Criminal Justice*. Maidenhead: Open University Press.

Roberts, J.V., N. Crutcher, and P. Verbrugge. 2007. "Public Attitudes to Sentencing in Canada: Some Recent Findings." *Canadian Journal of Criminology and Criminal Justice* 49: 75–107.

Roberts, J.V., J. Nuffield, and R. Hann. 2000. "Parole and the Public: Attitudinal and Behavioural Responses." *Empirical and Applied Criminal Justice Research* 1: 1–29.

CHAPTER 2
Criminal Justice and the *Canadian Charter of Rights and Freedoms*

Who ultimately determines the way the justice system functions? To a large degree it is Parliament, which is comprised of the elected representatives of the people. In Canada, the federal Parliament creates and amends criminal laws, while the provinces and territories administer the criminal justice system. But that does not mean that Parliament can legislate any kind of law it likes, or that the provincial and territorial governments can run the system as they like. Courts have the authority to review legislation as well as the actions of criminal justice professionals to ensure these are consistent with Canada's supreme law —the *Canadian Charter of Rights and Freedoms* (hereafter 'the *Charter*'). This chapter reviews the role the *Charter* has played in shaping the criminal justice system in Canada. It discusses how the daily decisions of criminal justice practitioners such as police officers and prosecutors have been influenced by this fundamental law, which protects our rights.

Marie Manikis, University of Oxford

The courts ensure that all criminal justice laws and practices are consistent with the *Charter*. If the judiciary finds that a particular law violates an individual's rights, it may strike the law down; Parliament should then comply with the ruling and make sure the law is consistent with the *Charter*. For instance, the Supreme Court of Canada decided to strike down the entire *Criminal Code* section that criminalized abortion, since it violated women's *Charter* right to security (see *R. v. Morgentaler*, 1988). Ever since this ruling, Parliament has avoided enacting any criminal laws on abortion in order to respect the *Charter*. The *Charter*'s impact on the criminal justice system has been and continues to be strong. For this reason, anyone interested in the Canadian criminal justice system—all readers of this book—need to know about the role of the *Charter*.

The enactment of the *Charter* substantially changed the Canadian criminal justice system. Prior to the *Charter*, Canada had a constitutional system similar to England's, based on the common law. Following the *Charter*, Canada developed into a state with an entrenched Bill of Rights similar to the American individual-rights–based model. This model depends on a system of checks and balances in which the judicial branch has the power to verify that laws and state conduct are in accordance with the rights contained in the *Charter*. This important step toward a due process model of rights has provided individuals with an instrument for addressing the power imbalances and abuses that exist between them and the State—including prosecutors and the police.

This chapter reviews the *Charter*'s impact on the criminal justice system. It then considers the objectives of certain rights and their impact on participants in the criminal justice system. Finally, it explores some of the *Charter*'s limits as well as the challenges this instrument may still need to address.

THE *CHARTER*'S IMPACT ON THE POLICE

The Right to Privacy: Modifying Police Conduct During Search and Seizure

The *Charter* has constitutionalized the right to security against unreasonable search and seizure. In so doing it has established privacy as one of the most important values in our society. According to the decision in *Hunter v. Southam Inc.* (1984), privacy rights require, in most cases, that police officers obtain a warrant before searching a house, car, or any other location where a person has a reasonable expectation of privacy.

In other words, the police cannot just walk into someone's house whenever they want and search for incriminating evidence. A search performed without a warrant is presumed to be abusive. To address such cases, the Supreme Court (in *R. v. Collins* (1987)) created an elaborate framework that requires the state to prove that the search was not abusive and was based on reasonable grounds. The police must have reasonable grounds to believe that the person is carrying an illegal object or substance on her person or inside her belongings.

Prior to the *Charter*, search powers existed but were not scrutinized, and this often led to abuses of power. Police and prosecutors sometimes obtained evidence in breach of individual rights, often without a warrant or reasonable grounds. Such evidence was then admissible in criminal court proceedings. For example, police officers were able to enter homes at any time and search people on the premises for illegal drugs. Or if they suspected that public washrooms were being used for "indecent" acts, they were permitted to hide behind air ducts and covertly observe individuals in stalls.

A notable example of a search that violated an individual's rights took place in 1974 in a Fort Erie tavern. During a "raid," the police physically searched almost all of the 115 individuals present and subjected 35 women to strip and body cavity searches. This search resulted in the discovery of six ounces of marijuana, most of it found on the tavern's floor instead of on these individuals. The Supreme Court considered this police raid to be legal. Police abuses would remain mostly out of sight until the *Charter* was enacted.

The *Charter* provides individuals with privacy protections in cases of abusive police conduct. Individuals now possess rights that are enforceable through the courts, which have the power to provide suitable remedies. Clearly, the *Charter* has increased citizens' sense of privacy as well as their security from unwarranted state interference. It has also enabled the courts to scrutinize police behaviour and contributed to the discovery of abusive situations, thereby bringing these practices out of the shadows.

Despite the *Charter's* important contribution to privacy rights, concerns remain regarding searches and seizures, particularly for certain groups. Systemic racism is a reality that the criminal justice system faces—one that has affected the exercise of all police powers, including the search power (Rosenberg 2009). Although the *Charter* is in place to ensure that minorities and youths are treated fairly by the State, evidence in the lower courts suggests that police still abuse privacy rights (Stuart 2008). In addition, constitutional guarantees against unlawful searches seem to be less effective in contexts involving the poor and the homeless. For example, it is harder to ensure an individual's privacy rights when he lives in public housing, or when she is homeless and living on the street. This remains an important challenge for future *Charter* developments to address.

The Right to Counsel: Modifying Police Conduct During Detention, Arrest, and Interrogations

The right to consult a lawyer upon arrest is one of the most frequent subjects of *Charter* appeals. Section 10(b) of the *Charter* states that "[e]veryone has the right on arrest or detention ... to retain and instruct counsel without delay and to be informed of that right." The Supreme Court has interpreted this simple sentence quite broadly and requires police to provide suspects with (a) detailed, practical information about their rights (and how they can exercise them effectively); and (b) a reasonable opportunity to talk to a lawyer by providing them with the necessary means to contact one should they express a desire to do so (Penney 2004). To ensure that these requirements of fundamental justice are met, legal aid authorities have organized facilities that provide immediate and free advice for suspects who have been detained or arrested.

The right to counsel renders the complex criminal justice system more accessible to individuals. It recognizes the importance of legal counsel as a means to achieve more just results. The purpose of the right to counsel is to give criminal suspects a fair opportunity to exercise their right to silence and to refrain from self-incrimination. This places great importance on defence lawyers, who advise individuals on their right to silence and how to exercise it. Furthermore, the police must refrain from searching for evidence when a person detained or arrested asserts the right to counsel, until he or she is given a reasonable opportunity to contact counsel (see *R. v. Bartle* (1994).

Despite the importance of the right to counsel, its impact is limited. To begin with, the police's duty to inform the individual of his right to counsel is triggered solely at the outset of an investigative detention, *immediately* as the individual is detained or arrested (see *R. v. Grant* (2009); *R. v. Suberu* (2009)). After that, most individuals must rely on their own resources, unless they qualify for legal aid, which is rather rare. Also, individuals who invoke their right to counsel must only be given a "reasonable opportunity" to do so. There is no requirement that they actually talk to a lawyer (Penney 2008). And once this opportunity has been taken, police are permitted to question the detainee, even if that person protests that she does not want to participate in the interview (see *R. v. Hebert* (1990)). In addition, police are permitted to encourage individuals to disregard their lawyer's advice, as long as they do not unduly persist or impugn the integrity of counsel.

Various commentators have expressed concerns about the police's commitment to providing the right to counsel in the context of routine, everyday police–citizen encounters (Rosenberg 2009). In some poorer neighbourhoods, visible minorities are routinely stopped on the streets for questioning. On those occasions they must rely solely on their wits and resources, *without* counsel. Administering the criminal justice system in such a manner can lead to problems, since the enforcement of justice in those circumstances relies heavily on the stopped person's ignorance of his rights and on his inequality of opportunity to assert those rights (Rosenberg, 2009). Access to justice thus remains an important societal challenge in a society in which racial profiling in the streets persists (see Rudin 2008; Tanovich 2008).

To summarize, the *Charter* has had a profound impact on police practices. The police are required to respect people's privacy rights during searches and to inform arrested or detained individuals of their right to consult a lawyer. This development deters abusive police practices; it also reduces the power imbalance between the suspect and the State by providing individuals with more information about their rights. This information empowers individuals, who enjoy greater protection from self-incrimination and from the possibility of being wrongfully convicted. Yet despite these developments, there is much room for improvement. Access to justice should be unaffected by class or social status.

THE *CHARTER*'S IMPACT ON PROSECUTORIAL CONDUCT: THE DISCLOSURE OF EVIDENCE

One of the most important contributions that the *Charter* has made to the criminal justice system involves changes to prosecutorial "disclosure" practices. At present, in order to prepare his defence, the defendant has a right to full disclosure of all the evidence against him or her. This means that the prosecutor (the Crown) must provide the accused with all relevant information gathered during the investigation, whether or not the prosecutor intends to introduce it as evidence, and whether it is inculpatory or exculpatory (see *R. v. Stinchcombe*, 1991). This obligation on the prosecution has revolutionized the process by modifying the pre-*Charter* paradigm, which held that the results of investigation in the Crown's possession belonged to the Crown to secure a conviction. The results of investigations are now considered public property that must be provided to the accused in order to achieve greater justice.

Prior to the *Charter*, disclosure issues were decided and governed by Crown counsel (prosecutors) and thus were almost entirely discretionary. Curiously, civil cases in Canada were subject to a much more generous regime of disclosure, even if the interests at stake were far less crucial to the individual than the liberty interests at stake in criminal cases. The criminal regime presumed that the accused would use this disclosure to fabricate evidence that would facilitate perjury. In rare cases, limited disclosure was provided, but the quality of disclosure varied from one jurisdiction to the next and from one prosecutor to the next. No remedy was provided in cases of insufficient disclosure, except for disciplinary proceedings, which were virtually unheard of.

This state of affairs contributed to wrongful convictions and deprived some accused individuals of the means to demonstrate their innocence (Rosenberg 2009). For example, Donald Marshall, Jr., was wrongfully convicted of murder and sentenced to life in prison. The Marshall Inquiry in 1989 revealed that the prosecutor's failure to provide full disclosure contributed to his wrongful conviction (see Nova Scotia, Royal Commission on the Donald Marshall, Jr., Prosecution). Other inquiries relating to wrongful convictions reached similar conclusions (see Ontario, Commission on Proceedings Involving Guy Paul Morin; Manitoba, Commission of Inquiry into Certain Aspects of the Trial and Conviction of James Driskell).

Since the *Charter*, Canada has become the country that provides individuals with the most generous disclosure rights in terms of content and timing. The *Charter* has revolutionized this practice and has certainly helped reduce the risk of wrongful conviction.

THE *CHARTER'S* IMPACT ON VICTIMS AND WITNESSES

The *Charter* has had an impact on participants other than the accused and criminal justice officials, mainly through the equality guarantee (Barrett 2008). Judges have recognized that vulnerable victims and witnesses, such as children and sexual assault victims, can benefit from certain constitutional protections.

It can be very difficult—sometimes traumatic—for children and sexual assault victims to testify in criminal trials. For this reason the Supreme Court has recognized the importance of several measures in the *Criminal*

Code (R.S.C. 1985, c. C-46) to facilitate victim participation in the process (see *R. v. Legoviannis* (1993) For children, Section 486.2 allows certain victims to testify outside the courtroom or behind a screen to avoid seeing the accused. The Court has stated that since child witnesses have rights and require protection from emotional harm during criminal proceedings, protective measures like these should be welcomed (see Bala 2008).

In addition, cross-examination practices by the defence counsel regarding sexual assault victims have changed. Judges have recognized that victims have security, privacy, and equality rights; as a consequence, the content of cross-examinations has been restricted. For example, in sexual assault trials, evidence and cross-examination questions based on stereotypes, such as the victim's/witness's prior sexual history and sexual reputation, are now prohibited. Furthermore, to encourage victim testimony and to avoid discriminatory conclusions based on stereotypes, the Court has recognized that victims of sexual assault have privacy rights regarding their medical and therapeutic records. Thus the accused generally does not have access to these records for his defence (*R. v. Mills* (1999)). Furthermore, the prosecution in possession of these records may not disclose them to the defence unless the victim expressly consents or the judge allows it as an exception based on the interests of justice.

In summary, victims qualified as "vulnerable"—namely, sexual assault victims and children—have been successful with their rights in court. Conversely, rights for victims who are not considered "vulnerable" are exceptional and limited. Victims' rights were never explicitly entrenched in the *Charter,* and the courts remain a less than welcoming place for them. Judicial reform and education could greatly enhance participation and access to justice for these individuals.

THE *CHARTER'S* IMPACT ON JUDGES

Charter Remedies and the Exclusion of Evidence

Arguably, one of the most important elements the *Charter* has brought to criminal law is the possibility to obtain remedies in cases of rights violations. Judges are the protectors of rights and have the ability to devise the remedies they see fit as a response to violations. For example, courts can order government officials and institutions to pay money to people whose rights have been violated. Prior to the *Charter,* the way evidence was obtained was not important; even in cases of abuse, remedies were not available, except for disciplinary sanctions, which were virtually never imposed.

The power to exclude unconstitutionally obtained evidence (also known as the exclusionary rule) pursuant to Section 24(2) of the *Charter* has been one of the most powerful and drastic *Charter* remedies in the context of criminal trials, since the exclusion of evidence often results in the defendant's acquittal. That section's main objectives include the preservation of the justice system's integrity and the protection from wrongful convictions.

Initially, this remedy was used more often, notably in cases of right-to-counsel breaches, abusive searches and seizures by police, illegal detentions, and abusive interrogations that led to confessions. In certain cases, the exclusionary rule was quasi-automatic. Many academics and civil rights activists welcomed this ground-breaking remedy, contending that it was a defining feature of any legal system committed to the protection of individual due process rights in criminal law (see Packer 1964; Stribopoulos 2008). Stuart (2008, 51) noted that "the remedy of exclusion has proved to be an important vehicle to hold agents of the State indirectly accountable and to seek to persuade police to comply with Charter standards in future cases." In the past few years, however, the public has expressed dissatisfaction with these numerous exclusions—at least when they have resulted in acquittals. Public opposition has been particularly vocal in cases where serious crimes remained unpunished.

Public discontent may have in part contributed to the Supreme Court's recent decision in *R. v. Grant* (2009), in which judges decided to exclude unconstitutionally obtained evidence less frequently. In most cases, where state officials have not intentionally breached the defendant's rights and the evidence obtained is reliable, the evidence will not be excluded.

Since that decision, the judiciary has been confronted with the difficult task of finding the right balance between the discovery of truth related to a crime in criminal proceedings and the exclusion of evidence obtained in breach of the accused's fundamental *Charter* rights. The complexity often arises when evidence that renders the accused factually guilty of a serious crime has been obtained in violation of the accused's rights. It has been argued that evidence is more easily excluded when the accused has committed a minor offence without causing injury than when the accused was in possession of a dangerous weapon such as a gun (Rosenberg 2009). For example, if the police stop an individual without a motive and discover a hidden gun, the evidence (the gun) has been obtained unconstitutionally; yet its discovery suggests that the individual is guilty of a serious crime: the possession of a gun. In such cases, to facilitate convictions, judges may be tempted to allow the evidence despite how it was obtained. Many *Charter* scholars have warned against this practice, since rights violations should be taken seriously and denounced without considering whether the individual is factually guilty or not (see Quigley (2008)).

Some claim that this new approach undermines the importance of recognizing and then imposing remedies for *Charter* breaches. Others argue that it establishes a balance between excluding unconstitutionally obtained evidence on the one hand; and on the other, admitting this evidence to promote the truth and to strengthen the public's confidence in the criminal justice system.

The *Charter*'s Impact on Sentencing

Finally, it is interesting to note that the *Charter*'s impact has been less influential in our system of punishment. Two constitutional provisions can be invoked: Section 9, which guarantees protection from arbitrary detention and imprisonment; and Section 12, which guarantees protection from cruel and unusual punishment and treatment. The *Charter*'s protections against unreasonable punishment have rarely been applied, and usually only in cases of blatant violation. For instance, Parliament since 1982 has legislated mandatory sentences of imprisonment for a number of crimes. Thus in 2008 new mandatory minimum sentences were introduced for firearm crimes and impaired driving offences.

A considerable body of literature has demonstrated that most minimum sentences of imprisonment are unfair and ineffective, as well as unduly harsh in certain cases (see, for example, Doob and Cesaroni 2001; Roach 2001). Despite this, the Supreme Court has not interfered with Parliament's plans and has refrained from considering them unconstitutional on the basis of being cruel and unusual punishment.

In the context of youth justice and sentencing, however, judges have been more active. The Supreme Court of Canada recently constitutionalized the principle of "diminished moral blameworthiness" for young offenders (see Bala 2009; *R. v. D.B.* (2009). Since youth have limited capacities and greater vulnerability (relative to adults), their moral blameworthiness is lower than that of adults guilty of similar crimes. Based on this principle, the presumption of adult sentencing for youth in cases of serious offences violates the young offender's *Charter* rights. Moreover, youths also benefit from special measures to prevent their identity from being publicly exposed even in the most serious crimes.

PRACTICAL MEASURES TO FACILITATE THE IMPLEMENTATION OF *CHARTER* RIGHTS

The *Charter*'s contribution to the advancement of individual rights constitutes a significant development in criminal justice. However, the *Charter* is not perfect and cannot solve all the problems identified in this chapter. Legal education and governmental services are important elements that need to be developed concurrently with *Charter* rights to address these systemic concerns and to ensure the *Charter*'s effective implementation.

First, despite the *Charter*'s enactment, police still engage in racial profiling of visible minorities. It has been argued that the criminal justice system has failed to address these issues in the courts or to adopt appropriate critical race standards in judicial reasoning (Tanovich 2008). Also, youth and visible minorities are subjected to proactive tactics by police that often result in *Charter* breaches. Education and police training can be good starting points to achieve the effective implementation of equality rights free from discrimination based on gender, race, age, or income. Moreover, legal education is an important measure that can contribute to meaningful legal reform. For example, it can promote recognition that marginal groups—notably, victims of crime—also deserve *Charter* protections.

CONCLUSION

It is safe to say that the *Charter* has had a profound impact on virtually every facet of the criminal justice system. Key developments since the *Charter's* enactment include changes in police and prosecution practices regarding individual rights. Police forces currently have constitutional duties to respect an accused's right to privacy and to inform that person of the right to counsel during detention and arrest. Prosecutors also have the important obligation of disclosing to the accused *all* elements of the investigation. The *Charter's* impact on victims, young offenders, and vulnerable witnesses, as well as the important remedial powers vested in courts to address *Charter* breaches, have made an important contribution to the recognition and protection of fundamental individual rights. But despite these important positive changes, systemic concerns remain. Access to justice and *Charter* litigation is harder for certain marginal groups, which are subjected to racism, discrimination, and inequalities; consequently, there is room for further *Charter* developments to address these issues. Unless *Charter* rights and developments are accompanied by education, and by governmental resources and services, systemic problems will remain and the implementation of *Charter* rights will be illusory for certain individuals.

DISCUSSION QUESTIONS

1. *Some people argue that judges should not exclude evidence from trial even if it is obtained in a way that breaches the defendant's* Charter *rights. What is your view and why?*
2. *In your view, do you think the* Charter *provides defendants with too many rights? Are the duties imposed on police and prosecutors unreasonable?*

FURTHER READING

Mandel, M. 1994. *The Charter of Rights and the Legalization of Politics in Canada*. 2nd ed. Toronto: Thompson Educational Publishers.

Roach, K., and R. Sharpe. 2005. *The Charter of Rights and Freedoms*. 3rd ed. Toronto: Irwin Law.

Stribopoulos, J. 2006. "Has Everything Been Decided? Certainty, the Charter, and Criminal Justice." 34 *Supreme Court Law Review* (2d), 34: 381-408.

Stuart, D. 2005. *Charter Justice in Canadian Criminal Law*. 4th ed. Toronto: Carswell.

REFERENCES

Bala, N. 2008. "Youth as Victims and Offenders in the Criminal Justice System: A *Charter* Analysis—Recognizing Vulnerability." *Supreme Court Law Review*, 40: 595–625.

——. 2009. "*R. v. D.B.*: The Constitutionalization of Adolescence." *Supreme Court Law Review*, 47: 211–34.

Barrett, J. 2008. "Expanding Victims' Rights in the *Charter* Era and Beyond." In J. Cameron and J. Stribopoulos, eds., *The Charter and Criminal Justice: Twenty-Five Years Later*. Markham: LexisNexis.

Doob, A., and C. Cesaroni. 2001. "The Political Attractiveness of Mandatory Minimum Sentences." *Osgoode Hall Law Journal*, 39: 287–304.

Packer, H. 1964. "Two Models of the Criminal Process." *University of Pennsylvania Law Review*, 113: 1–68.

Penney, S. 2004. "What's Wrong with Self-Incrimination? The Wayward Path of Self-Incrimination Law in the Post-*Charter Era*—Part II: Self-Incrimination in Police Investigations." *Criminal Law Quarterly*, 48: 280–336.

——.2008. "Triggering the Right to Counsel: 'Detention' and Section 10 of the *Charter*." In J. Cameron and J. Stribopoulos eds., *The Charter and Criminal Justice: Twenty-Five Years Later*. Markham: LexisNexis.

Quigley, T. 2008. "The Impact of the *Charter* on the Law of Search and Seizure." In J. Cameron and J. Stribopoulos, eds., *The Charter and Criminal Justice: Twenty-Five Years Later*. Markham: LexisNexis.

Roach, K. 2001. "Searching for Smith: The Constitutionality of Mandatory Sentences." *Osgoode Hall Law Journal*, 39: 367–412.

Rosenberg, M. 2009. "Twenty-Five Years Later: The Impact of the *Canadian Charter of Rights and Freedoms* on the Criminal Law." *Supreme Court Law Review* (2d), 45.

Rudin, J. 2008. "Aboriginal Over-Representation and *R. v. Gladue:* Where We Were, Where We Are, and Where We Might Be Going." In J. Cameron and J. Stribopoulos, eds., *The Charter and Criminal Justice: Twenty-Five Years Later*. Markham: LexisNexis.

Stribopoulos, J. 2008. "Has the *Charter* Been for Crime Control? Reflecting on 25 Years of Constitutional Criminal Procedure in Canada." In M. Beare, ed., *Honouring Social Justice: Honouring Dianne Martin*. Toronto: University of Toronto Press.

Stuart, D. 2008. "*Charter* Standards for Investigative Powers: Have the Courts Got the Balance Right?" *Supreme Court Law Review*, 40: 1–53.

Tanovich, D. 2008. "The *Charter* of Whiteness: Twenty-Five Years of Maintaining Racial Injustice in the Canadian Criminal Justice System." *Supreme Court Law Review* (2d), 40: 655–86.

CASES CITED

Hunter v. Southam Inc., [1984] 2 S.C.R. 14.
R. v. Bartle, [1994] 3 S.C.R. 173.
R. v. Collins, [1987] 1 S.C.R 265.
R. v. D.B., [2008] 2 S.C.R. 3.
R. v. Grant, [2009] 2 S.C.R. 353.
R. v. Hebert, [1990] S.C.J. No. 64.
R. v. Levogiannis, [1993] 4 S.C.R. 475.
R. v. Mills, [1999] 3 S.C.R. 668.
R. v. Morgentaler, [1988] 1 S.C.R. 30.
R. v. Stinchcombe, [1991] 3 S.C.R. 325.
R. v. Suberu, [2009] 2 S.C.R. 460.

REPORTS

Nova Scotia, Royal Commission on the Donald Marshall, Jr., Prosecution, *Commissioners' Report, Findings and Recommendations 1989,* vols. 1–7 (Halifax: 1989) (Chair: Justice T. Alexander Hickman).
Ontario, Commission on Proceedings Involving Guy Paul Morin, *Report* (Toronto: Queen's Printer for Ontario, 1998) (Commissioner: Hon. Fred Kaufman).
Manitoba, *Report of the Commission of Inquiry into Certain Aspects of the Trial and Conviction of James Driskell* (Winnipeg: 2007) (Commissioner: Hon. Patrick J. LeSage, Q.C.)

CHAPTER 3
Criminal Justice in Canada: Exploring the Latest Trends

This chapter explains the major components of Canada's criminal justice system (policing, courts, and corrections) and provides some statistical context for the remainder of the volume. It also answers some of the most fundamental questions about the criminal justice system. For example, what is the nature and extent of crime in Canada? Which sentence is imposed most often by courts? How often do prisoners released on parole complete their sentences in the community successfully? These questions are best answered by reference to sound statistical information. The government agency responsible for the collection and dissemination of information about Canada's justice system is the Canadian Centre for Justice Statistics (CCJS), a division of Statistics Canada.

Mia Dauvergne and Anthony Matarazzo from the CCJS provide a comprehensive analysis of recent criminal justice trends (for further information, including data tables and the analytical publication *Juristat*, see the "crime and justice" portal of the Statistics Canada website (http://www.statcan.gc.ca); for earlier trends see Mihorean and Kong (2008)).

Anthony Matarazzo and Mia Dauvergne

The criminal justice system in Canada involves multiple levels of government and has three key sectors: police, courts, and corrections. Within each of these sectors, a number of decisions are made, ranging from determining whether a crime actually took place to imposing a sentence and deciding whether to release a prisoner on parole.

The first step for an alleged criminal act to enter the criminal justice system is for it to be perceived as criminal by either the victim or a witness, who in turn contacts the police (Figure 3.1). The police must then determine whether

Figure 3.1

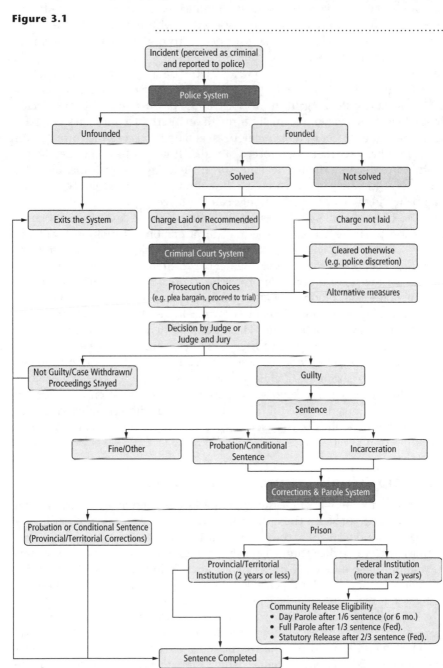

the incident is in fact a crime. In the absence of reasonable grounds to believe that a crime has taken place, the police record the incident as "unfounded" and no further official action is taken. If they believe a crime was attempted or committed they deem the incident "founded" and proceed to investigate. If an accused person is identified in connection with the incident, the police must decide whether to lay a charge or deal with the individual less formally by employing an alternative measure. For example, the police may resolve the matter by asking the individual to write a letter of apology to the victim.

If a charge is formally laid against the accused person, the case enters the criminal court system. Again, at this stage in the process the courts may decide to deal with the person informally through an alternative-measures program. If the case goes to court, a plea may be negotiated to avoid the formal court process; otherwise, that case proceeds to trial. If it goes to trial, a decision is made to proceed by the judge alone—or, if the option is available, by judge and jury. Ultimately, the accused can be found guilty or not guilty, the case can be withdrawn, or the proceedings can be stayed.[1]

Depending on the seriousness of the crime, if the accused is found guilty he or she can be sentenced to a term of incarceration, a conditional sentence of imprisonment, a period of probation, a fine, or some combination of these sentencing options. If the accused is sentenced to a term of incarceration, a conditional sentence, or a period of probation, he or she enters the correctional system. In the case of incarceration, depending on the length of the sentence, the offender will serve that time either in a provincial/territorial institution (for terms of less than two years) or in a federal institution (for terms of two years or more).

Prior to the termination of their sentence, inmates can be considered for some form of conditional release and serve part of their sentence in the community. For example, offenders serving a sentence of two to three years are eligible for day parole after serving six months of their sentence, for full parole after completing one-third of their sentence, and for statutory release after serving two-thirds of their sentence. The goal of these release options is to help prisoners reintegrate into society.

DIVERSION AND ALTERNATIVE MEASURES

Diversion and alternative-measures programs are alternatives to the formal criminal justice process. These programs can be invoked by criminal justice officials at various stages of the criminal justice system, from the point of first contact with the police through to sentencing by the courts. Such programs are administered differently from one jurisdiction to another. Differences can include variations in the types and number of programs available and the criteria that make an individual eligible for alternative measures.

Diversion programs exist for both youth and adults. The legislation governing the youth criminal justice system is the *Youth Criminal Justice Act* (YCJA). Under the YCJA, alternative measures have been incorporated under the extrajudicial measures scheme, which aims to provide greater guidance on the use, type, and objectives of diversion. Alternative measures for youth are currently known as extrajudicial sanctions. Other diversionary measures have been included in the legislation—namely, police warnings and referrals and Crown cautions. The proclamation of Bill C-41 in 1996 established an alternative-measures program for adults. Formal diversion programs for adults include apologies, community service, and personal service or financial compensation to the victim. Depending on the province or territory, the administration of formal diversion programs to adults or youth is carried out by three types of agencies: governmental agencies (e.g., probation services), nongovernmental organizations, and Youth Justice Committees.

POLICING

The primary mandate of the police is to serve and protect the public. As agents of the state, police officers are granted special powers to search, arrest, and detain individuals. Among their principal duties, police personnel are responsible for enforcing laws, maintaining the peace, preventing crime, responding to emergencies, and assisting victims of crime. The police are also involved in community support and outreach efforts (e.g., drug awareness programs and impaired driving campaigns). They are employed by municipal, provincial, and federal governments.

While the federal government is responsible for criminal law under the *Constitution Act*, each province and territory assumes responsibility for its own policing at the provincial, territorial, and municipal levels. Furthermore, many First Nations communities administer their own police services. The federal government, through the RCMP, is responsible for the enforcement of federal statutes in each province and territory as well as for providing services such as forensic laboratories, identification services, the Canadian Police Information Centre (CPIC), and the Canadian Police College.

Provincial policing involves enforcement of the *Criminal Code* and provincial statutes within areas of a province not served by a municipal police service (i.e., rural areas and small towns). In some cases, police boundaries may overlap. For example, in some areas the provincial police perform traffic duties on major provincial thoroughfares that pass through municipal jurisdictions. Newfoundland and Labrador, Yukon, the Northwest Territories, and Nunavut are the only areas in Canada without municipal police services.

The RCMP provides provincial/territorial policing and community policing services in all provinces and territories except Quebec and Ontario. These two provinces maintain their own provincial police services: the Sûreté du Québec and the Ontario Provincial Police. In Quebec and Ontario, the RCMP provides policing only with respect to federal matters. Where a provincial policing contract is granted to the RCMP, the RCMP automatically assumes provincial policing powers. In Newfoundland and Labrador, policing responsibility is shared between the RCMP and the Royal Newfoundland Constabulary (RNC).

Municipal policing consists of enforcement of the *Criminal Code*, provincial statutes, and municipal bylaws within the boundaries of a municipality or several adjoining municipalities that comprise a region (e.g., Durham Regional Police in Ontario) or a metropolitan area (e.g., Toronto Police Service). Municipalities have three options when providing municipal policing services: to form their own police service, to enter into a service-sharing agreement with an existing municipal police service, or to enter into an agreement with a provincial police service or the RCMP to have them assume policing responsibilities for the municipality.

In addition to federal, provincial/territorial, and municipal policing, various types of First Nations policing agreements are in place for Aboriginal communities across Canada.

Policing Costs Continue to Rise

Policing expenditures have been increasing consistently for more than a decade. In 2008, policing expenditures—including salaries, wages, benefits, and operating expenses (e.g., accommodation costs, fuel, and maintenance)—totalled $11.4 billion, or about $344 per Canadian. After controlling for inflation, this amount represented an increase of 6 percent over 2007 (Beattie 2009).

The Number of Police Officers Has Increased Since 1998

Police officer strength in Canada has been steadily increasing over the past decade, following a period of decline throughout the 1990s. In 2009 there were just over 67,000 police officers, representing 199 officers per 100,000 population. This 2009 figure was 9 percent higher than a decade earlier, though 4 percent less than at its peak in 1975. The number of female police officers has been gradually increasing. In 2009, women accounted for about one in five officers in Canada, compared to about one in eight a decade ago (ibid.).

Crime Rates in Canada Have Been Declining

The workload of the police is influenced largely by the volume and complexity of reported crime. While police work has evolved to include activities such as community policing and crime prevention, most police work can still be characterized as reactive. The police respond to public calls when a crime has occurred or is in the process of being committed. Even calls for service that are eventually deemed to be "unfounded" require police intervention. Also, the growing complexity of crime influences the amount and type of police intervention.

In 2009, police reported nearly 2.2 million *Criminal Code* incidents (excluding traffic incidents). Ten offences, most of them nonviolent, accounted for almost 90 percent of the total volume of police-reported crime in Canada: theft under $5,000 (25%), mischief (17%), break and enter (10%), common assault (8%), administration-of-justice offences (8%), disturb the

Figure 3.2 *Top-10 Most Common Police-Reported Offences, Canada, 2009*

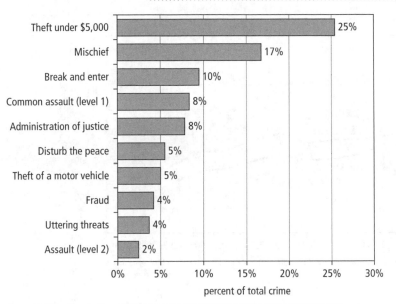

Source: Statistics Canada. Canadian Centre for Justice Statistics, *Uniform Crime Reporting Survey.*

peace (5%), motor vehicle theft (5%), fraud (4%), uttering threats (4%), and assault with a weapon or causing bodily harm (2%) (Dauvergne and Turner 2010; and see Figure 3.2).

In general, the volume *and* severity of police-reported crime in Canada have been decreasing over the past decade. Compared to the previous year, Canada's 2009 police-reported crime rate, which measures the overall volume of crime reported by police, dropped 3 percent, to its lowest level in over 30 years. The severity of crime, as measured by the police-reported Crime Severity Index, fell 4 percent in 2009—the sixth consecutive annual decrease (Figure 3.3).

About one in five crimes reported to police are violent. In general, the police-reported violent crime rate has been declining since 2000, due primarily to drops in high-volume crimes such as common assault and uttering threats. The severity of violent crime declined for the third consecutive year in 2009; that year, despite fluctuations, it was 6 percent lower than a decade earlier.

In general, the rates for most major police-reported crime categories have declined over the past decade. Between 1999 and 2009, the rates of each of the following crimes declined: break and enters (–42%), motor vehicle thefts (–40%), sexual assaults (–21%), robberies (–11%) and minor assaults (–10%). There are some exceptions to this trend, however. The rate of homicide, for

Figure 3.3 *Police-Reported Crime Severity Index and Crime Rate, Canada, 1999 to 2009*

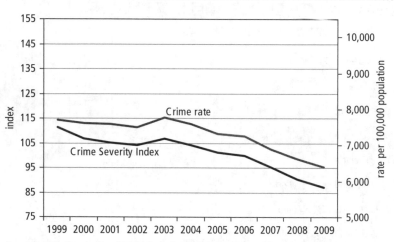

Source: Statistics Canada. Canadian Centre for Justice Statistics, *Uniform Crime Reporting Survey.*

example, has been relatively stable over this period, while the rates of serious assault and kidnapping / forcible confinement have increased (Dauvergne and Turner 2010).

About 4 in 10 Crimes Are Solved by Police

The extent to which police can clear or solve a case by laying a charge is an important measure of the effectiveness of the police in solving crime. In 2009 about 4 in 10 of the 2.2 million incidents reported by police were solved: 25 percent were cleared by charge and a further 16 percent were cleared otherwise.[2] Overall, police clearance rates have remained relatively stable over the past decade, with annual clearance rates for all *Criminal Code* incidents (excluding traffic violations) ranging from 35 percent to just over 40 percent.

Clearance rates vary, however, depending on the type of crime. For example, crimes that have direct victims and/or witnesses and that are reported in a relatively timely fashion tend to result more often in the police clearing the offence. For these reasons, violent crimes tend to have higher clearance rates than property crimes. In 2009, 71 percent of violent crimes were cleared compared to 33 percent of nonviolent crimes. Among several notable serious offences, clearance rates for 2009 were highest for assault (78%), followed by homicide (74%), sexual assault (65%), and robbery (39%). Clearance rates were lowest for motor vehicle theft (13%), theft over $5,000 (13%), and break and enter (16%).

Measuring Crime in Canada
....

There are three complementary ways to measure the nature and extent of crime in Canada: the police-reported crime rate, the police-reported Crime Severity Index, and the victimization rate.

The *police-reported crime rate* is the traditional measurement of crime in Canada. It measures the volume of crime and is calculated by dividing the total number of *Criminal Code* offences (excluding traffic offences) known to and substantiated by police into the total population of Canada and multiplying by 100,000. Each crime is counted equally, which means, for example, that one incident of bicycle theft is counted the same as one homicide. As a result, the police-reported crime rate is dominated by high-volume, less serious offences.

The *police-reported Crime Severity Index* takes into account not only the volume of crime but also the relative seriousness of different offences. Each type of offence is assigned a weight that is derived from court sentences. Offences having harsher sentences are assigned higher weights than those with less serious sentences. As a result, more serious offences have a greater impact on year-over-year changes in the Index (for further information on the Crime Severity Index, see Wallace et al. 2009).

As with the crime rate, the *victimization rate* measures the volume of crime in Canada. However, the number of offences is based on self-reported data from Canadians aged 15 years or older, for eight crime types: sexual assault, robbery, assault, break and enter, theft of personal property, theft of household property, motor vehicle/parts theft, and vandalism. Typically, the victimization rate is much higher than the police-reported crime rate since not all crimes are reported to police.

LEGAL AID

It is important that people charged with a crime receive legal assistance. Accused persons who appear in court without legal representation are at a great disadvantage. However, some people charged with a criminal offence lack the financial resources to pay for the services of a lawyer. Thus legal aid programs have been established in all provinces and territories to help low-income Canadians retain professional legal counsel. In most jurisdictions, legal aid coverage is available for those charged with serious criminal offences. The provision of legal aid services in Canada is a shared responsibility between the federal and provincial/territorial governments. Responsibility for the delivery of the legal aid services lies with each of the provincial/territorial governments; however, the federal government collaborates with each province and territory by providing contributions for both criminal and civil legal aid. Although the types of services and coverage vary from one province/territory to another (e.g., some jurisdictions offer minimal coverage for civil legal aid), most services across the country are delivered by a combination of staff and/or private lawyers.

Legal Aid Plans in Most Provinces Spend More on Criminal Matters Than Civil Matters

In 2008–9, legal aid plan expenditures in 11 provinces and territories amounted to nearly $730 million, or about $22 per Canadian (Statistics Canada 2010).[3] About 80 percent of the total legal aid plan budget, or $587 million, was spent on direct legal aid services such as the provision of legal advice, information, referrals to other agencies, representation, payments made to private lawyers, and service delivery by legal aid plan staff. The other 20 percent of expenses incurred by legal aid plans were for central administrative costs and other expenditures, which included external projects, legal research, public legal education, and grants to other agencies. After adjusting for inflation, legal aid plan expenditures have experienced both increases and decreases over the past decade, including a 6 percent increase in 2008–9 from the previous year.

Legal Aid Services Declining Since Mid-1990s

In the 11 reporting provinces and territories, approximately 10,000 lawyers from both the private sector and legal aid plans provided legal aid assistance in 2008–9. Almost 9 in 10 were private lawyers; the remainder were legal aid plan staff lawyers (ibid.). In general, the total number of lawyers providing legal aid services has been declining since the mid-1990s, including an 8 percent drop from 2007–8 to 2008–9. The decrease in legal aid services has coincided with a drop in the number of applications. Since peaking at about 1.2 million in 1992–93, applications for legal aid services have steadily fallen, reaching approximately 780,000 in 2008–9. Factors such as changes in pre-screening procedures, changes in legal aid coverage, and stricter eligibility criteria have likely contributed to this decrease.

COURTS

Essentially, there are four levels or tiers of courts in Canada, with responsibility shared among the federal, provincial, and territorial governments (Figure 3.4).

The Supreme Court of Canada holds the highest position in the Canadian court system and represents the final court of appeal from all other courts. It has jurisdiction over disputes in all areas of law, such as criminal, administrative, and constitutional law.

Figure 3.4 *Canada's Court System*

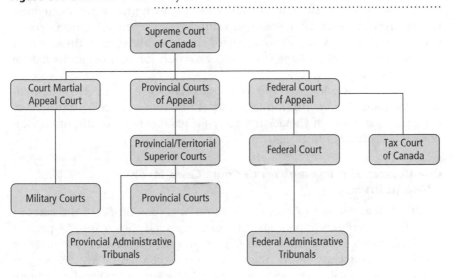

Note: The Military Courts, the Court Martial Appeal Court and the Tax Court of Canada are specialized courts that deal only with matters that fall within the jurisdiction given to them by statute.

The various provincial/territorial courts of appeal and the Federal Court of Appeal make up the next level of Canada's court system. Each province and territory has a court of appeal that hears appeals from decisions of the superior courts and provincial/territorial courts. As in the superior courts, judges are appointed and paid by the federal government. Court administration, however, is the responsibility of the provinces and territories.

At the third level of courts are the provincial and territorial superior courts, which deal with more serious crimes and which handle appeals from judgments rendered in the provincial/territorial courts. These courts also deal with civil law matters related to federal legislation—for example, the *Divorce Act*. While the judges for these courts are appointed and paid by the federal government, the courts are administered by the provinces and territories.

The final tier in Canada's court system is the provincial and territorial courts. These are found in all provinces and territories except Nunavut, and they hear the majority of cases that come into the system, which involve municipal bylaws as well as federal or provincial/territorial laws. These courts are administered exclusively by the provinces and territories. While the names and divisions of these courts may vary from one province/territory to another, their role is essentially the same. A number of courts at this level are "specialized" and deal exclusively with particular matters, offences, or offenders. For example, a number of cities across Canada have established Drug Treatment Courts, which handle cases involving nonviolent offenders whose criminal offences have been motivated by their addiction. Youth Courts are another example of specialized courts at this level; in these, young persons (12 to 17 years of age) are brought to court for offences under federal youth justice laws.

Figure 3.4 includes two types of administrative tribunals. Such tribunals resemble courts but are not formally part of the court system. They do, however, play a key role in Canadian society for various types of dispute resolutions (Department of Justice 2005).

One-Quarter of Adult and Youth Court Cases Involve a Violent Offence

Adult criminal courts in Canada completed or disposed of 392,907 cases in 2008–9 involving more than one million charges. Of these cases, 24 percent involved crimes against the person (e.g., homicide, robbery, assault, uttering threats, sexual assault) as the most serious offence in the case; 23 percent involved crimes against property (e.g., theft, break and enter, fraud, mischief); 21 percent were administration-of-justice offences (e.g., breach of probation and failure to comply with an order); and 14 percent were *Criminal Code* traffic offences, primarily impaired driving. The remainder of adult court cases were for other *Criminal Code* offences (e.g., weapons offences, prostitution, disturbing the peace; 5%) or for offences against other federal statutes (e.g., the *Controlled Drugs and Substances Act,* the *Income Tax Act,* the *Youth Criminal Justice Act*; 12%).

Youth courts in Canada dealt with 58,379 cases and just over 191,000 charges in 2008–9, the most frequent of which were cases involving crimes against property (38%), followed by crimes against the person (26%). While crimes against the administration of justice accounted for 11 percent of cases, other *Criminal Code* offences made up 5 percent. Not surprisingly, *Criminal Code* traffic offences were less common in youth court (2%) than adult court, whereas offences against other federal statutes were more common (18%), largely due to offences against the *Youth Criminal Justice Act.*

Number of Cases Appearing in Adult and Youth Courts Has Stabilized

Following a three-year downward trend in the number of cases disposed of beginning in 2004–5, the number of cases disposed increased by 3 percent in 2007–8 and then remained virtually unchanged in 2008–9, with only a slight decrease (–0.1%) from the previous year.[4] Overall, the number of cases disposed of in adult courts in 2008–9 was 2 percent higher than 5 years prior.

Overall, the number of cases heard in youth courts has followed a similar pattern as those heard in adult criminal courts. Youth courts in Canada disposed of 58,379 cases in 2008–9, which represents a slight decrease (–0.6%) from the overall caseload in 2007–8 but is 23 percent lower than in 2002–3, which was the year prior to the enactment of the YCJA (Milligan 2010). The largest decline in caseloads came in the first year of the new legislation, when youth courts disposed of 16 percent fewer cases. Since that time, the number of cases completed has remained relatively stable. Consistent with one of the key objectives of the YCJA, every province and territory has experienced drops in youth court caseloads since the introduction of this legislation, which in part aims to divert young persons who have committed less serious, nonviolent crimes away from formal processing within the youth justice system (see Chapter 25 of this volume).

Amount of Time to Dispose of Adult Criminal Court Cases Declining, While Youth Court Cases Taking Longer to Complete

Recently, the amount of time required to dispose of a case in adult criminal courts has declined slightly. In 2004–5 the median elapsed time for an adult court case to reach completion in the ten reporting jurisdictions was 128 days, and remained stable at 126 days for the three subsequent years. By 2008–9 the median had fallen slightly, to 124 days (Thomas 2010).

Unlike processing times in adult criminal courts, youth court cases are taking longer to complete. For youth court, the median elapsed time from first to last court appearance was 119 days in 2008–9. This is over one month longer (38 days) than in the year prior to the enactment of the YCJA in 2002–3, when it was 81 days. The largest jump in case processing time occurred in the first year of the YCJA, when the median elapsed time rose to 106 days (Milligan 2010). The peak in processing time of youth court cases in 2003–4 may be a result of increased handling of less serious cases by the police or Crown through extrajudicial and diversionary measures afforded by the youth justice legislation; this has left the courts with the most complex, serious cases. In 2008–9 about 60 percent of youth court cases involved multiple charges. In comparison, in 1991–92—the first year for which youth court data are available—multiple-charge cases represented about 45 percent of youth court caseload.

In Both Adult and Youth Court, About Six in Ten Cases Result in a Conviction

In 2008–9 the accused was found guilty in 66 percent of cases dealt with in adult criminal court; 3 percent ended in an acquittal (Thomas 2010). In a further 3 out of 10 cases (29%), the case was stayed, withdrawn, or dismissed, meaning that the court stopped or interrupted the proceedings against the accused. In the remaining 1 percent, a variety of other decisions were rendered, such as finding the accused not criminally responsible or deciding to waive the case in or out of the province or territory.

Overall, *Criminal Code* traffic offences (e.g., impaired driving) were those most likely to end in a finding of guilt (80% of cases). In comparison, guilty findings were recorded in 67 percent of offences against property (e.g., theft, break and enter, possession of stolen property) and 54 percent of crimes against the person, which encompass violent crimes such as assault, sexual assault, and robbery.

Trends in the type of decision are similar in youth court. In 2008–9, 59 percent of youth court cases ended in a finding of guilt and just over 1 percent in an acquittal. Compared to adult court, a higher proportion of youth court cases were stayed, withdrawn, or dismissed (39%); almost 1 percent ended for a variety of other reasons—for example, the case was transferred to another province or territory, the accused was unfit to stand trial, or the accused was found not guilty by reason of insanity. As in adult court, youth court cases involving *Criminal Code* traffic offences had the highest guilty rates (80%); 53 percent of property crimes and 58 percent of crimes against the person ended in a finding of guilt.

Custody Is the Most Serious Sentence Imposed in Adult Criminal Court While Probation Is the Most Serious in Youth Court[5]

At sentencing, the court will seek to impose a sentence that reflects the purpose, objectives, and guiding principles of the sentencing process, as outlined by the *Criminal Code* and the *Youth Criminal Justice Act*.

Custody was the most serious sentence handed down in adult court in 2008–9, imposed in 34 percent of all guilty cases. Probation was imposed as the most serious sentence in 29 percent of cases, and fines in 26 percent of all cases with a finding of guilt. A conditional sentence was the most serious sentence received in another 4 percent of the cases, while other sentences made up the remaining 7 percent (Figure 3.5).[6] Other sentences included restitution, absolute and conditional discharge, suspended sentence, payment of legal costs, and suspension of drivers licence.

Regarding the 34,434 youth court cases with a finding of guilt in 2008–9, probation was the most severe sentence imposed in half the cases. Custody, the most severe of the available sentencing sanctions, was meted out to youth in about one in seven (15%) guilty cases. Community service orders were given as the most severe sentence in 8 percent of guilty cases, while fines were imposed in another 5 percent. A further 4 percent of the guilty cases received-deferred custody or supervision as the most severe sentence, 2 percent ended with a reprimand, and 1 percent of guilty cases ended with the most serious sentence being intensive support or supervision or attending a nonresidential program. Intensive rehabilitation custody and supervision, compensation, pay purchaser, compensation in kind, restitution, prohibition, and seizure or forfeiture made up the remaining 15 percent of sentences in youth court cases with a finding of guilt in 2008–9.

Figure 3.5 *Sentencing Outcomes for Adults (18 years and older) Found Guilty of a Crime, Canada, 2008/2009*

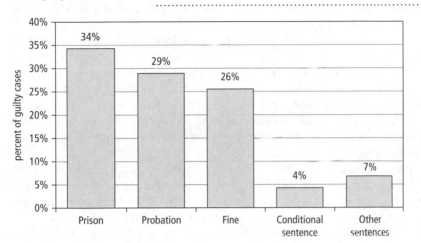

Source: Statistics Canada, Canadian Centre for Justice Statistics. *Adult Criminal Court Survey*. Vol. 30. No. 2.

CORRECTIONAL SERVICES

A number of responsibilities fall within the jurisdiction of adult and youth correctional services in Canada. Some of these responsibilities lie with the provincial or territorial governments, others with the federal government. Provinces and territories have exclusive responsibility for young offenders, meaning persons aged 12 to 17 at the time of the offence who are convicted in a youth court. Sanctions for youth are determined by both the *Criminal Code* and the *Youth Criminal Justice Act*. Correctional services are responsible for the custodial detention of youth as well as their supervision in the community. Examples of custodial programs for youth are remand (i.e., detention prior to or during court trial), secure and open custody, and the custody portion of an intensive rehabilitation custody and supervision order. Examples of supervision programs administered within the community are probation, intensive support and supervision orders, the community portion of a custody and supervision order, and deferred custody and supervision.

With respect to adult offenders, six primary responsibilities come under the umbrella of adult correctional services in Canada. These are custodial remands (i.e., detention prior to and during trial or sentencing); custodial sentences (i.e., imprisonment); conditional sentences; supervised probation; conditional release; and parole boards. Some of these responsibilities fall to the provinces and territories and some to the federal government.

Persons in custodial remand, offenders serving conditional sentences, and those on supervised probation are the responsibility of the provincial and territorial governments. Conditional sentences allow offenders sentenced to a term of custody to serve their time in the community under supervision. These offenders must comply with a number of conditions. If the offender violates the court-ordered conditions, he or she may be committed to custody for the time remaining on the sentence.

With respect to custodial sentences, the level of government that is responsible for the offender depends on the length of the sentence. Adult offenders who are sentenced to a term of imprisonment that is less than two years are the exclusive responsibility of provincial or territorial correctional services. The *Criminal Code* stipulates that all offenders sentenced to an aggregate custodial sentence of two years or more shall be imprisoned in a federal penitentiary. In Canada, all penitentiaries are the responsibility of the federal Correctional Service of Canada (CSC).

The responsibility of adult offenders on conditional release is shared between the jurisdictions and the federal government. Conditional release is the planned and gradual release of inmates back into the community through temporary absence passes, day parole, full parole, and statutory release.

Finally, Quebec and Ontario operate parole boards that have jurisdiction for all offenders in their provincial institutions, whereas the National Parole Board has jurisdiction over all adult offenders serving a sentence in a penitentiary and adult offenders in provincial/territorial correctional institutions where no parole board exists. Parole boards are administrative tribunals that have the authority to grant, deny, terminate, or revoke parole in their jurisdiction. The National Parole Board also has the authority to terminate or revoke offenders on statutory release, detain certain offenders, and grant unescorted temporary absences for some offenders in penitentiaries.

Federal System Costs More Than Provincial Correctional System

In 2007–8, correctional services in Canada cost $3.5 billion. Housing an inmate in the federal system is more expensive than housing someone in the provincial/territorial system. For example, in 2007–8 the average daily amount spent on keeping an inmate in a federal institution was $299 compared to $154 for housing a provincial/territorial inmate. A number of factors contribute to the difference in costs, including the higher levels of security required in the federal system and the greater number of treatment programs available to offenders serving longer sentences associated with federal custody.

Adults on Probation Account for the Majority of Offenders Under Correctional Supervision

In 2007–8 there were 184 correctional institutions for adult offenders in operation in Canada. Of these, 110 were provincial/territorial facilities (98 secure facilities and 12 open facilities such as halfway houses), and 74 were federal institutions. The federal institutions comprised 16 community correctional centres, 18 minimum-security institutions, 19 medium- and 8 maximum-security prisons, and 13 prisons with multilevel security. The total bed space capacity for provincial/territorial institutions was 22,973 individuals; federal prisons had bed space capacity for 14,693 offenders.

On any given day in 2008–9 there was an average of 37,234 adults in custody either serving a sentence, awaiting trial or sentencing (remand), or being held in another type of temporary detention (e.g., immigration hold). The number of adults in custody relative to the Canadian population aged 18 and older—also known as an "adult incarceration rate"—is one way of monitoring the use of imprisonment in Canada. In 2008–9 the adult incarceration rate was 141 adults per 100,000. The 2008–9 rate was 1 percent higher than the previous year, representing the fourth consecutive annual increase. Recent increases have been driven largely by increases in the number of adults held in remand (custody in provincial/territorial jails while awaiting trial or sentencing)—a number that has doubled over the past decade.

Few offenders receive a sentence of custody; most of the population supervised by correctional services is in the community. At the end of any given month in 2008–9 there were almost 120,000 adults in the community on probation, serving a conditional sentence or on conditional release. Of these, 8 in 10 were on probation.

Fewer Offenders in Sentenced Custody, but Numbers in Pre-Trial Detention Are Rising

Among the total number of adults in custody in 2008–9, about one-third (36%) were on remand. On average, there were 13,454 adults being held in remand each day in 2008–9, up 4 percent from the previous year. The 2008–9 increase in remand continued an upward trend that began in the mid-1990s. Over the past decade, the number of adults held in remand has doubled. For provincial and territorial correctional services, which are responsible for remanded adults and for those sentenced to less than two years, remanded adults accounted for almost 60 percent of their inmate population.

The reasons for the growing number of persons in remand include the following: 1997 amendments to the *Criminal Code* widened the grounds for justifying pre-trial detention; and longer court processing times led to increased durations in remand (Johnson 2004). Growth in the remand population, and the turnover within it, can affect the operations of correctional services. For example, it can lead to overcrowding, heightened danger for both staff and inmates, higher transportation costs as more prisoners make court appearances, and increased staff costs as more prisoners need to be supervised (ibid.). Accordingly, several jurisdictions have adjusted their operations to manage high remand populations; for example, some had made programming more readily available.

Most Offenders Complete Their Conditional Release Without Incident

In 2007–8, 9,218 people were conditionally released in Canada. Most of them (5,408) went to statutory release, 1,380 to provincial parole, and 2,430 to full or day parole by the National Parole Board. Most offenders complete their conditional release "successfully"—that is, they do not have their releases terminated because of a breach of conditions of their release or because of reoffending. Of the 10,205 federal offenders completing day parole, full parole, or statutory release in 2007–8, 68 percent completed their release successfully. Of those whose parole or statutory release was revoked, most often it was due to a breach of conditions (73%) rather than a new offence (27%). For provincial/territorial offenders completing day parole or full parole granted by the National Parole Board, 75 percent completed their parole successfully. Among those paroles that were revoked, 89 percent were for a breach of conditions rather than a new offence (11%) (Statistics Canada 2009).

Youth Corrections

The *Youth Criminal Justice Act*, which came into force April 1, 2003, emphasizes diverting youth from the criminal justice system and reserves sentences of custody for only the most serious offenders. The new law has had a dramatic effect on the number of youth in prison (see Chapter 25 of this volume). Declines in the number of youth formally charged with criminal offences have corresponded with declines in the number of youth entering the correctional system. In 2008–9 the overall number of youth aged 12 to 17 years admitted to correctional services dropped 3 percent compared to the previous year. This included a 2 percent decrease in the number admitted to sentenced custody and a 7 percent decline in youths in remand. Admissions to community supervision (–2%) and to probation (–3%) also fell. On an average day in 2008–9 there were 899 youth in sentenced custody and 981 in remand. For youth, probation is the most frequent sentence ordered by youth courts. At the end of any given month in 2008/2009 there were 18,012 youth serving this sentence in the community.

DISCUSSION QUESTIONS

1. *How does this overview of trends in criminal justice differ from your perceptions? That is, is there any specific finding that surprised you more than the others?*
2. *Alternative measures programs divert youth and adults from the formal criminal justice process. Do you agree with the use of such measures and, if so, in what circumstances is their use appropriate?*

REFERENCES

Beattie, Sara. 2009. *Police Resources in Canada, 2009*. Cat. no. 85-225-X.
    Ottawa: Statistics Canada.
Dauvergne, Mia, and John Turner. 2010. "Police-Reported Crime Statistics in
    Canada, 2009." *Juristat* 30, no. 2. Cat. no. 85-002-X. Ottawa: Statistics
    Canada.
Department of Justice Canada. 2005. *Canada's Court System*. Cat. no.
    J2-128/2005. Ottawa.

Gannon, Maire, Karen Mihorean, Karen Beattie, Andrea Taylor-Butts, and Rebecca Kong. 2005. *Criminal Justice Indicators, 2005.* Cat. no. 85-227-XIE. Ottawa: Statistics Canada.

Johnson, S. 2004. "Adult Correctional Services in Canada, 2002–3." *Juristat* 24. Cat. no. 85-002XIE. Ottawa: Statistics Canada.

Mihorean, Karen, and Rebecca Kong. 2008. "Criminal Justice Trends in Canada." In Julian V. Roberts and Michelle G. Grossman, eds., *Criminal Justice in Canada: A Reader.* 3rd edition. Toronto: Nelson.

Milligan, Shelley. 2010. "Youth Court Statistics, 2008–9." *Juristat* 30, no. 2. Cat. no. 85-002-X. Ottawa: Statistics Canada.

Statistics Canada. 2009. *Adult Correctional Services in Canada, 2007-2008, Reference Tables.* Ottawa.

——. 2010. *Legal Aid in Canada: Resource and Caseload Statistics, 2008–2009.* Cat. no. 85F0015X. Ottawa.

Thomas, Jennifer. 2010. "Adult Criminal Court Statistics, 2008–2009." *Juristat* 30, no. 2. Cat. no. 85-002-X. Ottawa: Statistics Canada.

Wallace, Marnie, John Turner, Anthony Matarazzo, and Colin Babyak. 2009. *Measuring Crime in Canada: Introducing the Crime Severity Index and Improvements to the Uniform Crime Reporting Survey.* Cat. no. 85-004X. Ottawa: Statistics Canada.

ENDNOTES

1. "Stay" or "withdrawal" refers to stays of proceedings, withdrawals, dismissals, and discharges at preliminary inquiry. These decisions all refer to the court stopping or interrupting criminal proceedings against the accused.

2. The category of "cleared otherwise" includes incidents where an accused is identified but not charged for reasons such as these: the complainant requests that charges not be laid, or the accused has died.

3. For the most part, the survey results exclude Newfoundland and Labrador and Prince Edward Island because legal aid plans in these provinces were unable to provide data for 2008–9. Any comparisons made to figures for previous years also exclude these jurisdictions.

4. Trend analysis of the adult criminal court data covers the five-year period 2004–5 to 2008–9 and is estimated to include 90 percent of the national adult criminal court caseload.

5. Court cases may have more than one type of sentence associated with the most serious offence in the case. As such, when cases involve more than one type of sentence (e.g., an individual receives a term of custody as well as a term of probation), they are categorized according to the "most serious sentence," meaning that cases are ranked from the most to least restrictive sanction.

6. Conditional sentencing data were not collected in Quebec for 2008–9, resulting in an undercount of conditional sentences.

CHAPTER 4
The Funhouse Mirror: Media Representations of Crime and Justice

Chapter 1 of this volume noted the existence of many public misperceptions about crime and criminal justice. These misperceptions exist in all Western nations. The public tends to perceive crime rates as constantly rising and to believe that the justice system is far more lenient than is in fact the case. The same public also has a very distorted view of important criminal justice trends such as imprisonment and parole rates. Where do these misperceptions come from? This chapter discusses the source of many public misperceptions about crime and justice: the news media.

Peter McKnight, a highly experienced journalist as well as a lawyer by training, discusses how the media represent crime and the justice system response to crime.

Peter McKnight, Vancouver Sun

Crime is epidemic and growing across the country. The overwhelming majority of crimes involve violence, and the most common form of violent crime is also the most serious: murder. Murderers, who are intelligent, otherwise upstanding members of the middle class, plan their crimes meticulously. Victims, who never know their killers, are typically young, affluent, Caucasian women. The murderers are usually caught, but justice is rarely done as offenders are either acquitted on a technicality or handed a slap on the wrist by lenient judges. And so the crime epidemic continues to grow and grow.

This scenario sounds like it was lifted from a dystopian science fiction novel. Yet to regular consumers of the newspapers or television or radio news the scenario will be instantly familiar: it is the world the news media have built. Even a brief review of the news media reveals that crime—and especially violent crime—is rampant and that we are all at great risk of becoming the next victims in an unstoppable crime wave. The picture is not entirely false. Rather, it is simply not the whole truth: violent crimes do occur, but not that often, especially relative to nonviolent property crimes. Some murders are carefully planned by high-status offenders, but most are the result of spontaneous acts committed by people under the influence of drugs, alcohol, or intense rage. White, affluent women are sometimes victims of murder, but most victims come from other demographic and socioeconomic groups. And while some people charged with murder are acquitted in court, most are convicted. Finally, all defendants convicted of murder in Canada receive a life sentence, and prisoners serving a life sentence for murder typically spend more time in prison than people convicted of murder in other Western nations.

The picture of crime painted by the media is therefore a distorted one. Or to use the metaphor most commonly applied to the media—they simply hold a mirror up to the world and reflect what is there—we must conclude that it is a *funhouse mirror*, one that accentuates certain aspects of the world, and of crime, at the expense of others. This distorted picture of crime takes on added importance in light of the exposure that crime receives in the media. In a study of American broadcast news, for example, Dorfman and Schiraldi (2001) found that throughout the 1990s, the national networks ABC, CBS, and NBC all devoted more time to crime than to any other type of story. Similar results were found for local U.S. television stations, with as much as 30 percent of news time devoted just to violent crime.

A series of studies (Ericson et al. 1987, 1989, 1991) of major news outlets in Toronto found even more striking results, with upwards of half of all stories dedicated to deviance. It should be noted, however, that in focusing on deviance, Ericson and his colleagues considered not merely stories involving crime, but also those covering departures from "organisational procedures and violations of common sense knowledge." We must be careful, then, not to infer too much about crime coverage in the media from Ericson and colleagues' studies (Reiner 2007). But the studies do show that deviance is "the defining characteristic of what journalists regard as newsworthy." And this leads us into a consideration of what journalists consider newsworthy, of how the media paint a distorted picture of crime through their selection of certain stories from the vast array that present themselves to journalists each day.

ELEMENTS OF NEWSWORTHINESS

Since Chibnall's classic *Law-and-Order News* (1977), many scholars have sought to identify the factors that lead the media to consider a story newsworthy. Chibnall identified five factors: novelty, immediacy, personalization, dramatization, and titillation. Since then, others have suggested at least a dozen more (Jewkes 2004). Let's consider some of the most often cited elements of newsworthiness.

Characteristics of the Offence

As noted above, deviance is itself newsworthy, but most forms of deviance or crime will not make it onto the evening news or the pages of a daily newspaper. To be worthy of coverage, a crime must meet a certain threshold of significance, and violent crimes are the most likely to meet that threshold. Marsh reviewed research on crime news in the United States and other countries between the 1960s and 1980s (Marsh 1991; Reiner 2007). All studies revealed that the media overemphasized violent offences and underemphasized property crimes. In the United States there were four times as many stories about violent crimes as property crimes, even though according to official statistics there were nine times as many property offences.

Violent crimes are, therefore, more likely to make it into the news; but not all violent crimes are equal. Murder, the most serious and one of the rarest of violent crimes, is most likely to attract coverage; one study revealed that murder accounted for between one-quarter and one-third of crime stories on American television news (Dorfman and Schiraldi 2001). Offences of a sexual nature also receive a disproportionate amount of press attention. In one month in Britain in 1981, crimes involving sex and violence accounted for nearly half of newspaper coverage, despite comprising little more than 2 percent of reported incidents (Ditton and Duffy 1983; Jewkes 2010).

Unlike Britain and the United States, media coverage of violent crime in Canada has not been the subject of exhaustive study. But crime reporting in Canada does appear similar, as murder stories are commonly seen on the front pages of newspapers and on evening newscasts, despite making up less than 1 percent of violent crime (Statistics Canada 2009b). Similarly, violent crime is more frequently covered than property crime, even though five times as many property crimes are reported to police and even this likely underestimates the problem, since many property crimes go unreported.

Finally, given their novelty, "new" crimes—behaviours that have only recently been conceptualized as crimes—also tend to preoccupy the press. The 1960s, 1970s, and 1980s witnessed increased reporting of what were then new crimes, including drug offences, child sexual offences, and domestic violence. Today, crimes such as road rage, carjacking and "grow rips"—breaking into a building in which marijuana is being grown—fill the pages of newspapers and the schedules of evening news broadcasts.

Characteristics of the Offender

Although official crime statistics suggest that the majority of offenders are young, low-income males, many studies have revealed that news reports overemphasize crimes committed by older, well-to-do men (Roshier 1973; Graber 1980). This suggests that sex is perhaps the only characteristic of offenders that the media reflect accurately. However, given the relative novelty of female offenders, crimes committed by women tend to receive a disproportionate amount of attention, particularly if the female offender is young and her crime involves violence. For example, in 1997, 14-year-old British Columbia resident Reena Virk was swarmed and killed by eight teenagers, all but one of whom were girls. Two of Virk's assailants were subsequently convicted of murder. The case received unprecedented press coverage from coast to coast, in large part because most of the assailants were girls. A national discussion on violence among teenage girls ensued, with sociologists suggesting that the event had prompted a "moral panic" over adolescent female violence (Barron and Lacombe 2005). The age of the offenders in the Virk case contributed to the media feeding frenzy, as the media typically overemphasize crimes involving child and youth offenders. Most infamously, news outlets around the world presented lengthy in-depth coverage of the James Bulger case, in which a two-year-old boy in England was abducted and murdered by two ten-year-old boys (Muncie 1999). Aside from age and sex, the offender's social status also plays a significant role. Almost any crime committed by a celebrity is deemed newsworthy, given that the public is already familiar with the offender (Greer 2003), and in the United States entire television shows are dedicated to the crimes of celebrities. The televised murder trial of O.J. Simpson was followed by huge numbers of viewers, and the announcement of the verdict in that case attracted millions of people to the screen.

While this trend toward celebrity crime is less common in Canada (given the limited number of bona fide celebrities), the news media do emphasize crimes committed by people who enjoy high social status, particularly politicians. In 2010, for example, Rahim Jaffer, a former Member of Parliament and husband of a sitting cabinet minister, was charged with possession of cocaine and driving with a blood alcohol level over the legal limit. Jaffer pleaded guilty to a lesser offence, which is not unusual; but given his position, the plea bargain received extensive press coverage. A year earlier, news media across the nation devoted great attention to the criminal charges laid against Michael Bryant, Ontario's former Attorney General. He had been charged with criminal negligence causing death and dangerous operation of a motor vehicle causing death (CBC News 2009).

Characteristics of the Victim

Although many violent crimes, and in particular homicides, involve offenders and victims who know each other, the media are much more likely to report stranger-on-stranger crimes (Reiner 2007). This serves to cast offenders as "predatory outsiders" rather than family members or friends (Beckett and Sasson 2004).

Consider the case of Wendy Ladner-Beaudry. In 2009, Ladner-Beaudry, the sister of a former Vancouver mayoral candidate, was found dead after jogging through a public park. Although her killer has not been apprehended, it has been assumed that she was killed by a stranger. Largely for that reason, the Vancouver media—and to a lesser extent, the national media—covered Ladner-Baudry's death extensively, with the case becoming the lead story on many nightly newscasts. The statistics reveal just how rare cases like Ladner-Beaudry's are. According to the latest Statistics Canada data, fewer than 10 percent of female homicide victims were killed by a stranger (Statistics Canada 2009a). In contrast, 92 percent of female homicide victims knew their killer, and in upwards of 60 percent of these cases the killer was a current or ex-spouse or a boyfriend of the victim. Yet homicides resulting from domestic violence receive scant attention in the press compared to those committed by an assailant unknown to the victim. Similarly, the media pay less attention to cases involving "innocent" victims. Gang violence in Toronto, Montreal, and Vancouver has received significant press coverage in recent years; yet it is not often noted that the majority of homicides in those cities have been committed by and against gang members. The media have therefore paid little attention to individual victims' stories, beyond noting their gang affiliations.

When an innocent bystander—particularly a child—gets caught in the crossfire, however, the case frequently becomes a *cause celebre* (Jenkins 1992). For example, a 1990s turf war between two Montreal motorcycle gangs caused the deaths of scores of people; but media coverage intensified considerably when 11-year-old Daniel Desrochers was killed by shrapnel from a car bomb in 1995. Similarly, after 15-year-old Jane Creba was killed by a stray bullet on Toronto's Yonge Street on Boxing Day 2005, unprecedented media coverage of the event led to intense discussions about gun crime, which likely had a significant effect on the 2006 federal election.

Even when victims are not affiliated with gangs, they may not be seen as innocent, and their deaths may therefore slip under the media radar. Between the early 1980s and 2002 more than 60 women went missing from Vancouver's impoverished Downtown Eastside, but those disappearances received relatively little attention, possibly because many of the women were Aboriginal sex workers battling mental health and substance abuse problems. To the media's credit, though, a series of articles in the *Vancouver Sun* did call attention to the disappearances. Robert Pickton was eventually convicted of six murders and stands charged with 20 more. The case led to widespread discussion about how the characteristics of the victims affected the amount of attention their disappearance attracted from the press, the police, and the public.

Characteristics of the Sentence

There has been extensive research on media coverage of crime, offenders, and victims; in contrast, relatively little research has been conducted on media reporting of sentencing decisions. But there is some evidence that just as the media tend to overemphasize rare and unusual crimes, they similarly select-ively report rare and unusual sentences—that is, sentences that appear to be unusually lenient. In response to public concerns that sentencing in British Columbia is unusually lenient, Doob and Webster (2008) compared sentencing patterns across Canada. While finding little reason to believe that B.C.'s sentencing practices are lenient compared to those of other provinces, they noted that popular belief "in sentence leniency is supported, if not strengthened" by the media. Several studies conducted in the 1980s bear this out (Doob and Roberts 1983; Roberts and Doob 1990). These studies revealed that people who read judges' reasons for sentences are much more likely to consider sentences appropriate than those who read newspaper reports about sentences. For example, in one study, half the participants read the court documents from a sentencing decision, while the other half read the newspaper story describing the sentencing hearing and the sentence. Afterwards both groups were asked what they thought about the sentence, the offender, and the judge. People who had read the newspaper account were significantly more likely to see the sentence as too lenient and to criticize the judge for not considering all the appropriate factors. This study suggests that just as the media selectively attend to certain sentences, they also tend to over- or under-emphasize certain facts about the law, the offence, and the offender. These facts are generally ones that lead people to believe that the sentence imposed was too lenient.

FACTORS AFFECTING DETERMINATIONS OF NEWSWORTHINESS

We have thus far considered various elements that the media believe make a crime story newsworthy. But we have yet to consider *why* the media value these elements. Many factors have been suggested to explain media determinations of newsworthiness. We will concentrate on two: news values, and the organizational structure of news organizations and news making (Reiner 2007).

News Values

Perhaps the single most important news value—and hence the most important factor in deciding on newsworthiness—relates to a common definition of news: news is that which is new, rare, and unusual (Hall 1979). By this definition, events that occur all day, every day, simply do not count as news. This is the case with property crime, except perhaps in small towns, where property crime may be rare enough to warrant press coverage. But in large cities and at the national level, commonplace events like property crimes are unlikely to receive coverage unless there is something unusual about them. For example, the theft of art from a museum might garner media attention, given its novelty. The theft of a number of famous paintings from a Paris art gallery in 2010 attracted widespread media coverage.

This emphasis on novelty also explains why the press focuses most intensely on the rarest of violent crimes. Similarly, female violent offenders are sufficiently rare to warrant inclusion, as are stranger-on-stranger crimes and ostensibly lenient sentences. Much of what the media consider newsworthy therefore arises directly out of the popular definition of news. This definition itself arises out of presumptions about what news consumers want to read and see. Few people are interested in hearing about things that happen all the time; consequently, news outlets strive to give them something different. And with profit margins dwindling, news organizations are ever mindful of the wishes of their readers and viewers. Every major news outlet conducts regular reader and viewer surveys, and these surveys typically reveal significant interest in crime, but also a great desire for personalization: readers and viewers want to know how the news, whether it concerns crime, health, or finance, affects them personally.

The overemphasis on violence is a form of personalization, since the average news consumer is much more concerned about becoming the victim of a violent crime than of having his or her wallet stolen. The media's emphasis on offenders who are reasonably well-to-do also stems from an attempt at personalization, since stories involving relatively high-status offenders are likely to resonate with many readers and viewers, given their similarities to such offenders. Similarly, the media's tendency to overemphasize crimes involving reasonably affluent, innocent victims also likely resonates with the audience members, most of whom are—or like to believe they are—affluent and innocent.

Organizational Structure

According to what is sometimes referred to as the "dominant ideology model," the media reinforce existing power structures; thus the emphasis on deviance is an inevitable consequence of the media's desire to maintain law and order (Hall 1979). While there is some truth to this model, much of the media's apparent law-and-order stance stems not from ideological commitments but rather from the organizational structure of news organizations and the pressures of news reporting.

The newsroom is governed by headlines and deadlines and is an intensely high-pressure environment. Reporters work under severe time constraints and typically have only a few hours to file their stories. On an average day, a reporter is assigned a story in the morning and must then familiarize him or herself with the issue, speak to the people involved, and by early afternoon produce a story that is accurate, fair to those involved, and accessible to the audience. The difficulty of this undertaking is compounded by the fact that many justice reporters have limited experience and knowledge of the justice system.

Consequently, reporters rely heavily on government officials and the police to provide them with information about crime. Besides the fact that such sources are often seen as trustworthy and authoritative, justice system officials hold scheduled press conferences, which allow journalists to schedule their day and which ensure that they have an opportunity to speak to interested parties. Also, courthouses function according to schedule and provide many interesting stories. Stationing reporters at courthouses therefore helps reporters manage their time, since they need not dig for stories or search for people to interview (Jewkes 2010).

These practices do, however, mean that reporters will receive the official version of events—typically from politicians and government officials, or from the police. And since these people are interested in defending their measures and actions, there is always the danger that they will shape their stories for the media in ways that reflect positively upon them (Schlesinger and Tumber 1992). Good reporters know to look skeptically upon the pronouncements of officials, but the serious time constraints under which they work sometimes result in a privileging of the officials' versions of events. Officials can there-fore play a significant role in determining what the media cover and the way they cover it. This is not necessarily the result of media and justice officials sharing an ideology; rather, it is the result of officials' awareness of the nature of journalism, and their willingness to work within that to get their word out.

Impact of the Media

The media's preoccupation with deviance and overemphasis on violent crime have led to concerns that media coverage can cause crime to rise. This long-standing debate is receiving renewed attention owing to concerns about the impact of violent video games on children and teenagers. Thus far the research on the "criminogenic" impact of crime news has been inconclusive (Livingstone 1996), in large part due to the difficulty of establishing real-world causal connections between news consumption and crime (Reiner 2007).

Given these difficulties, we might instead consider a more recently expressed fear: that media coverage of crime leads the public to support a more punitive approach to criminal justice (e.g., Roberts et al. 2003). Surveys suggest that that people who consume a lot of news tend to think that crime is much more prevalent than it is; that crime rates are rising even during periods when they are falling; and that "innocent" people—people not involved in criminal activity—are much more likely to be victims of crime that official statistics would suggest. Furthermore, there is some evidence that frequent consump-tion of television news is associated with higher degrees of fear (Chiricos, Eschholz, and Gertz 1997). It is not entirely clear, though, whether consuming television news causes fear or whether fearful people are more likely to watch the evening newscast.

In light of the media's emphasis on stranger-on-stranger crime and on offences that involve victims who share many characteristics with news con-sumers, it would not be surprising to find a causal connection between fre-quent consumption of news and fear. And when the media simultaneously highlight ostensibly lenient sentences, the public might easily conclude that there is a causal connection between high crime rates and lenient sentences. In this way the courts are portrayed as being responsible for stopping crime, then condemned for failing to do so. Needless to say, this can result in decreased public respect for the courts—and by extension, decreased respect for the Constitution, the rule of law, and the administration of justice. And it can lead to increased public support for more punitive measures, particularly those that limit judicial discretion in sentencing, such as mandatory minimum sen-tences, which serve to increase prison populations but which have not been shown to reduce crime rates.

CONCLUSION

We have seen that the media paint a distorted picture of crime thanks to their overemphasis on serious, violent crime, and that this can lead to increased and irrational fear as well as to support for counterproductive punitive measures. But seeing is the easy part; the difficult question is how to respond to this systematic distortion of reality. Changing news values won't be easy. It's unlikely that the media will cease publicizing novel events instead of common ones: serious, violent crimes will always receive more attention than trivial property crimes. But it is important that journalists understand the ways in which their business distorts reality, and to write and speak about it, or at least provide context for the stories they cover. The media will also always try to give the public what it wants, and this is where people can have a real and sustained impact on media coverage of crime. Journalism is not a monologue; it is a dialogue in which the press and the public speak to each other. For example, if the public object, loudly and vociferously, to sensational coverage of violent crime, the media will respond by at the very least toning things down. Similarly, if the public demands a broader range of stories, with a more penetrating analysis of crime, the media will comply. There is little that influences the media more than the desires of its consumers.

More than anyone else, courts and judges bear the brunt of the media's distorted picture of crime. This is not surprising, given that, in contrast to other justice system officials, judges typically avoid talking to the media and the public—as the saying goes, they "speak through their judgments." But if judges were to make themselves more available to the media, they could help shape the media's representations of their decisions. In short, we all have the ability to influence the media, to decide what is newsworthy, and to shape the stories the media tell. In this sense, we are all responsible for the distorted picture of crime we see, and we are all responsible for changing the picture. The media might always reflect reality like a funhouse mirror, but anyone can reshape its contours.

DISCUSSION QUESTIONS

1. *Do you think it would be possible or desirable to require the media to follow guidelines when reporting news about a very emotional subject such as crime?*
2. *How much variation do you see in the way that different news media (e.g., print versus electronic) cover crime stories?*

FURTHER READINGS

Mason, P. 2003. *Criminal Visions: Media Representations of Crime and Justice.* Cullompton: Willan.

Reiner, R. 2007. "Media-Made Criminality: The Representation of Crime in the Mass Media", in M. Maguire, R. Morgan, and R. Reiner, eds., *The Oxford Handbook of Criminology.* New York: Oxford University Press.

REFERENCES

Barron, C., and D. Lacombe. 2005. "Moral Panic and the Nasty Girl." *Canadian Review of Sociology and Anthropology* 42, no. 1.

Beckett, K., and T. Sasson. 2000. *The Politics of Injustice*. Thousand Oaks: Pine Forge.

CBC News. 2009. "Former Ontario AG Bryant Charged in Cyclist's Death." http://www.cbc.ca/canada/toronto/story/2009/09/01/toronto-cyclist-collision-death481.html#ixzz0nLeqlafr

Chibnall, S. 1977. *Law-and-Order News*. London: Tavistock.

Chiricos, T., S. Eschholz, and M. Gertz. 1997. "Crime, News, and Fear of Crime." *Social Problems* 44, no. 3: 342–57.

Ditton, J., and J. Duffy. 1983. "Bias in the Newspaper Reporting of Crime News." *British Journal of Criminology* 23, no. 2: 159–65.

Doob, A.N., and J.V. Roberts. 1983. *An Analysis of the Public's View of Sentencing*. Ottawa: Department of Justice.

Doob, A.N., and C.M. Webster. 2008. *Concern with Leniency: An Examination of Sentencing Patterns in British Columbia*. A Report to the Province of British Columbia. Vancouver: Attorney General's Office.

Dorfman, L., and V. Schiraldi. 2001. *Off Balance: Youth, Race, and Crime in the News*. Washington: Building Blocks for Youth.

Ericson, R., P. Baranek, and J. Chan. 1987. *Visualizing Deviance*. Milton Keynes: Open University Press.

——. 1989. *Negotiating Control*. Milton Keynes: Open University Press.

——. 1991. *Representing Order*. Milton Keynes: Open University Press.

Graber, D. 1980. *Crime News and the Public*. New York: Praeger.

Greer, C. 2003. *Sex, Crime, and the Media*. Cullompton: Willan.

Hall, S. 1979. *Drifting into a Law and Order Society*. London: Cobden Trust.

Jenkins, P. 1992. *Intimate Enemies: Moral Panics in Contemporary Great Britain*. Hawthorne: Aldine de Gruyter.

Jewkes, Y. 2004. *Media and Crime*. London: Sage.

——. 2010. *Media and Crime*. 2nd ed. London: Sage.

Livingstone, S. 1996. "On the Continuing Problem of Media Effects." In J. Curran and M. Gurevitch, eds., *Mass Media and Society*. London: Arnold.

Marsh, H.L. 1991. "A Comparative Analysis of Crime Coverage in Newspapers in the United States and Other Countries from 1960-1989: A Review of the Literature." *Journal of Criminal Justice* 19, no. 1: 67–80.

Muncie, J. 1999. *Youth and Crime*. London: Sage.

Reiner, R. 2007. "Media-Made Criminality: The Representation of Crime in the Mass Media." In M. Maguire, R. Morgan, and R. Reiner, eds., *The Oxford Handbook of Criminology*. New York: Oxford University Press.

Roberts, J.V., and A.N. Doob. 1990. "Media Influences on Public Views of Sentencing." *Law and Human Behaviour* 14, no. 5: 451–68.

Roberts, J.V., L.J. Stalans, D. Indermaur, and M. Hough. 2003. *Penal Populism and Public Opinion: Lessons from Five Countries*. New York: Oxford University Press.

Roshier, B. 1973. "The Selection of Crime News by the Press." In S. Cohen and J. Young, eds., *The Manufacture of News*. London: Constable.

Schlesinger, P., and H. Tumber. 1992. "Crime and Criminal Justice in Media." In D. Downes, ed., *Unravelling Criminal Justice*. London: Macmillan.

Statistics Canada. 2009a. *Family Violence in Canada: A Statistical Profile*. Cat. no. 85-224-X. Ottawa.

—— . 2009b. "Police-Reported Crime Statistics in Canada, 2008." *Juristat* 29, no. 3.

PART TWO
Voices of Actors in the Criminal Justice System

CHAPTER 5
Scenes from the Life of a Police Officer

As members of the public we often see police officers going about their business–in cruisers, or on the beat as it were. But these fleeting glimpses of the police tell us little about what it is like to be a police officer. The profession is a very demanding one that requires officers to act quickly in response to a wide variety of calls for service. In this chapter, Michael Waby, who served as a police officer in Canada and the United Kingdom, describes some of the challenges facing a police officer.

Michael Waby, Ministry of the Attorney General of Ontario

Police officers are the most readily identifiable professionals in the criminal justice system and for this reason alone they attract strong views from the public. While many people may have little if any contact with judges or lawyers throughout the course of their life, most people will have some personal contact with a police officer, be it as a motorist, a lost tourist, the victim of a crime, or a suspect or accused. The circumstances of this encounter as well as the conduct of the individual officer will determine the impression that a person takes away from the encounter and the judgments that they make of the police.

Impressions of the police may be held with genuine conviction, but they may not be entirely accurate or fair. Conversely, they may be entirely justified. Familiarity with something often tends to make us think we know more about it than we actually do. The aim of this chapter is to provide a window onto the realities of life as a police officer. While the duties and posts to which officers may be assigned are hugely varied, this chapter concentrates on the routine working life of a uniformed police officer—the kind of police officer most people are likely to meet on the street.

Not only is this the face of the police service with which most members of the public are most familiar, but before going on to wear a detective's badge, ride a police horse, or be promoted, all officers are required to begin their careers in this manner. The concept of beginning on the street as it were is at the heart of policing. We all begin by policing the streets. It is the common starting point for all police officers. Some officers happily spend their entire service as a uniformed officer patrolling the streets; others work as hard as they can to escape this particular role.

The uniformed patrol officer is typically the first to attend at the scene of an incident: the first to see the blood, hear the screams, offer comfort and help to victims, or start trying to pick up the pieces. It is this man or woman who will be racing to the scene of a "disturbance"—not always knowing where it lies on the continuum between a noisy but happy drunk making his way home or a violent street fight.

Unfortunately for the officer, it is surprising how often and how rapidly the feuding parties are prepared to set aside their respective differences in order to jointly turn on the person sent to help them. An aggrieved spouse will quickly leap to the defence of her partner when she sees him being handcuffed— despite the fact that, battered and bruised, it was she who called for help in the first place! Similarly, an angry crowd may quickly become hostile toward the uniformed authority figure who shows up to preserve the peace and to protect members of the public.

Police recruitment materials frequently emphasize the variety that police work can provide in the course of a working day. Since the role of uniformed police officers is largely reactive (as opposed to proactive), up to a point this is often true. Part of the enjoyment of the work lies in not knowing for sure precisely what the next radio call will bring when you arrive on the scene.

One winter's night I encountered a man who had apparently tried to kill himself by jumping off a six-storey building. As I launched into administering my finest police first aid skills, a neighbour approached and calmly told me that the man who had just thrown my attempted suicide off the sixth-floor balcony lived with the victim in flat 608. As an ambulance crew arrived, I ran up six flights of stairs to encounter a man wearing only a large pair of underpants, carrying an even larger kitchen knife. He did nothing to set me at my ease when he informed me that his name was "Peter the Apostle." Thankfully, no one else exited the building via the balcony and "Peter" found secure accommodation for some time thereafter. Needless to say, I had not anticipated this particular twist when I first arrived at the scene.

Although an ever-increasing amount of time is spent by officers on paperwork and red tape, much of their work still involves dealing with the people in the communities they serve. It is this element that provides the real variable in police work. Five different people may react in five entirely different ways to a similar set of circumstances, and it is part of a police officer's role to respond appropriately to each person, often with very little time to process what is happening. Not every victim of crime is hysterical or cooperative, and some people respond quite irrationally to police interventions.

It is inevitable that mistakes will be made, especially by those new to the often daunting role of police officer. Sometimes such mistakes are understandable; on other occasions they are unforgivable. Officers frequently discover that lessons are learned the hard way, often under harsh public scrutiny. Woe betide the officer who, to the great amusement of an assembled crowd, reverses his car into a stone pillar, or who forgets that when directing traffic that you don't suddenly stop the Mini directly in front of the large truck (the resulting collision acts as a firm reminder to the officer that the braking distances of these two vehicles are markedly different). These mistakes tend to be made only once.

Much of the role is about at least presenting a credible show of confidence to those with whom you are dealing. New officers, often younger in age, will have impressed upon them by their more experienced colleagues the fact that it doesn't matter how awful or chaotic the scene of an incident is, the one thing that has to remain constant in the eyes of the public is the apparently calm and authoritative figure of the attending police officer. Simply put, if you are busy vomiting or swooning at a gory or unpleasant sight, you are not doing your job.

Inevitably it is only with time and experience that officers are able to develop the necessary confidence and resistance to tackle some or the more unpleasant aspects of their work. If they are doing their job properly, no one should suspect that they may later be losing sleep over the unpleasant incident that they have just dealt with. Projecting this image of a calm individual in control is a skill that, like many others in life, takes time to acquire. Indeed, while to some officers it appears to come effortlessly, others never manage to acquire it.

Having joined the Metropolitan Police in London, England, at the tender age of nineteen, I can still vividly recall admiring myself in my new uniform in the reflection of a series of shop windows on my first few days out on patrol by myself. My belief in the invincible, professional image that I was sure I outwardly presented lasted until the first member of the public walked up to me to ask for directions—at which point a sense of panic gripped me and the limits of my knowledge seemed overwhelming. I have subsequently been informed by officers in both England and Canada that this pattern of dread alternating with bursts of self-confidence is common to most new officers. Thankfully, most live through it.

The learning curve of most officers is usually pretty steep. This means that in a fairly short space of time a great deal of knowledge is gained, and—especially in metropolitan areas—so too is a lot of hands-on experience. They will also be able to rely on the accumulated wisdom and experience of their longer serving colleagues. Advice is seldom far away if you have the sense to ask for it. Of course, part of the learning curve is to know who to listen to and, frankly, who to ignore. As societal attitudes have evolved, some officers have coped better with these changes than others. While the "common sense" advice of one long-serving officer may well sometimes be a quick route to discipline or disaster, most experienced officers are invaluable in terms of providing supervision, support, and essential advice to their younger colleagues. Their accumulated wisdom frequently disproves the maxim that you can only learn through your own mistakes, and it is often only more experienced colleagues to whom one can turn after a particularly bad day. Many young officers have been saved from themselves by their colleagues.

For the majority of police officers, the most enjoyable aspect of their work encompasses actually dealing with the wide variety of people and situations they encounter. Whether it is helping the vulnerable, bringing order from chaos, or arresting an apparently guilty party, it is this "hands on" activity that drew most to the job in the first place. Few relish the ever increasing burden of paperwork that now accompanies their role. It is the perennial complaint of officers that their time is increasingly occupied by filling in forms, many of which appear to duplicate their predecessor, rather than being out on the streets. It is a concern increasingly shared by many members of the public.

It is something of a paradox that the multifarious initiatives by various police services designed to address this concern seem to have had the opposite effect. Whether it is under the supposed rubric of the *Charter of Rights* or a product of a corporate police interpretation of our increasingly bureaucratic societies, the amount of paperwork that accompanies the most routine tasks that police officers now have to complete is remarkable. Notwithstanding the computer age that we now occupy, the time it takes to process a simple arrest today as opposed to 20 years ago is vastly longer.

As a case in point, in the early years of my police service, it was a matter of personal pride among officers that a simple arrest for an offence of theft or mischief, for example, would be properly processed from start to finish within an hour. The prisoner would be booked in, the officer would write his or her statement or notes surrounding the event and subsequent arrest, and then the officer would return to patrolling. A comparable event nowadays can easily see the officer completing paperwork for four of five hours.

Unfortunately, it does not take much for an officer to make an arrest at the start of the shift and not make it back out for the remainder of that shift. Some would contend that this increase in paperwork is necessary to better safeguard the rights of the accused and to provide valuable and useful statistics. These arguments frequently seem to overlook not only the sheer duplication of effort that is created, with its attendant implications for police resources, but also the fact that if an officer is inclined to be creative in his note writing or evidence of an arrest, then this theme will inevitably continue throughout all of the paperwork he completes. It is really only when and if his evidence is forensically examined in court that meaningful scrutiny may occur. A dishonest or sloppy officer will neither be discovered nor be reformed under reams of red tape.

THE NEED FOR A SENSE OF HUMOUR

While the job can often be emotionally demanding, officers frequently take refuge in the notoriously macabre sense of humour that many police officers share. Whether this is through habit or necessity, the ability of police officers to laugh at things that would make many people cry is an enduring aspect of police life. Police slang can also lend what can appear to outsiders as a flippant air to otherwise serious or sad situations. This coping mechanism can certainly be a double-edged sword. Among colleagues it can provide an essential release of tension, enabling them to perform delightful tasks such as collecting body parts at the scene of an accident or dealing with a failed suicide attempt. Unfortunately, to the uninitiated it can often appear cold and cruel.

I know of one former colleague who, to lighten the mood for a young officer dealing with his first dead body, placed his police hat on the head of the elderly gentleman who had quietly passed away in his pyjamas. This act certainly achieved its desired effect—until the deceased's son walked unannounced into the room and witnessed the spectacle. Similarly, attaching to photographs a *faux* judge's scorecard that marked the merits of the swallow dive of the poor unfortunate who leaped to his death from the end of a crane is an act that is legitimately open to mixed reviews.

DEALING WITH CRIME VICTIMS

Notwithstanding this tendency toward what might be termed "gallows humour," most police officers have a strong sense of propriety. This is particularly needed when dealing with the victims of crime in all its forms. At the more routine end of the scale is the patience that needs to be shown to those who have been the victim of a theft or a loss of some personal property. It is a depressing reality that many such offences are never likely to be solved; thus the reporting exercise is one conducted mainly for insurance purposes. However, it is never very politic to be as blunt as this to the person who has just had a wallet or purse stolen. The fact that it is the fourth such report that the officer has completed in as many hours is quite rightly of little consequence to the latest victim the officer encounters.

More tact and diplomacy is required when dealing with the victims, or relatives of victims, of violent criminal offences. Sometimes there will be a need to explain in detail what action the police are taking and why, or conversely what action they are *not* taking and why. Officers will encounter victims who are angry, afraid, or paralyzed by the experience of having been victimized. Frequently the victims of crime will not initially wish to provide a statement to police of what happened. Whether this is out of fear or indifference, it remains part of the officer's job to work with the victim as early as possible in order to obtain as much useful information as possible. The interests of the victim and the police will usually (but not always) coincide. Police officers should always remember that the impression that a victim of crime takes away from the encounter can have a significant impact on whether that person chooses to voluntarily get involved with the police in the future.

No matter how frustrated or busy the officer may be, leaving a victim of crime angry, upset, or confused is always counterproductive.

Sometimes there is no magic to the interaction between police officers and victims: it is simply a product of common humanity. Officers may simply do nothing more than hold a person while she cries. My father—who was a police officer some 50 years ago—was the first on the scene of a woman pedestrian who had been fatally struck by a car as she crossed the road. Knowing that she was dying, my father cradled her. She asked him to say a prayer for her. Not a particularly religious man, the only prayer my father knew was the Lord's Prayer. He recited this over the woman as she died in his arms.

THE CHALLENGES OF SHIFT WORK

Shift work is a necessary and established aspect of police work and frequently sets the rhythm for what officers encounter. Morning and afternoon shifts invariably bring with them different types of calls. This may be reflected in numerous calls from banks and other business premises as staff arrive for work and inadvertently trigger alarms, or in a wide range of property-related crimes from shoplifting to robberies. Many calls enable police officers to engage in an aspect of the job that always seems to retain its appeal, and that is the opportunity to race to the scene of a call with sirens blaring and lights flashing. Even the most jaded of officers seldom seem to tire of this act. The downside of course is the capacity to cause injury or damage on the way to dealing with the original incident. Regrettably, this does happen from time to time, and it is the perpetual nightmare of officers responding to an emergency call. Sometimes enthusiasm can outstrip an officer's driving ability.

Driving through a town or city during the daytime in order to respond to an urgent call—often in heavy traffic and sometimes in appalling weather—requires considerable skill and judgment. So too does the vehicular pursuit of people who have a very great incentive to flee and who often have no regard for those around them.

Typically, many more people are abroad during the working day than at night. This inevitably increases the number and variety of calls that day duty officers receive. A direct consequence of this is the element of havoc than can be created when large numbers of people are present, and unfortunately, few people and even fewer crowds are as patient as police officers would like them to be. In most instances, people's curiosity about what is going on soon gives way to impatience about getting on with their own business. Any police officer who has had to seal off a street or a building can attest to this impatience on the part of the public. It is sometimes quite remarkable how people react to even the most serious of situations. I have witnessed and even participated in arguments with people who have *insisted* that they are the exception to the rule and should be allowed to walk through a police cordon or enter a particular building even when they know that to do so would mean walking past the bomb disposal team working to defuse an explosive device.

That people are so willing to think that they are the exception to the rule is one of a number of truths that officers discover early in their career. It goes along with other golden rules, such as, "the rudeness of the driver is directly proportionate to the value of the car." That is, the more expensive it is, the ruder the driver will become. Similarly, as I can testify, it is a universal truth that if the location of a call is the upper floors of a building, the elevator will invariably be out of service.

COURT WORK

Another regular aspect of police work during the daytime is attending court. Officers often have to appear as witnesses, and sometimes as victims themselves. I know officers who would far sooner deal with an armed suspect than attend court to give evidence, as it can be one of the more nerve-racking aspects of an officer's job. Detached and insulated from the heat of the moment, judges and lawyers have the luxury of analyzing in detail—and at their comparative leisure—the actions of officers involved in incidents that may have lasted only a few seconds. The theatre of the courtroom and the sometimes intense—yet entirely proper—spotlight that it shines on the police can be a terrifying experience for some officers. I have witnessed police officers so unnerved by the prospect or experience of testifying in court that they have walked into the dock instead of the witness box, or have fainted while giving evidence. In one memorable incident, an officer even forgot his own name!

Before I practised as a barrister and became used to appearing in court, as a young police officer I once repeatedly forgot to advise the court of the fact that I had found a suicide note next to a body I had discovered. Slightly overawed by the occasion of giving evidence, I provided all the other information I could but neglected to mention this fairly useful detail. I was immune to the increasingly desperate attempts by counsel to elicit this from me, and it took an intercession by the coroner who had previously read my statement to confirm that we were probably not dealing with a homicide.

It is just as important for police officers not to seem too confident when giving their evidence. This seldom goes down well, although few go as far as one seasoned officer I encountered some years ago who, when asked which oath he wished to take prior to giving his evidence, produced, with a suitably theatrical flourish, his own copy of the Bible from his breast pocket. A copy of which, he informed an amused if disbelieving judge, he carried with him at all times. However traumatic the experience may be, most officers quickly learn the necessity to provide their evidence in a professional manner. As with all witnesses, and police officers are no different, a nervous disposition while testifying does not necessarily mean that they are being untruthful; nor is confidence always consistent with accuracy.

Of course the travails of giving evidence in court are only compounded when an officer does so following a 10- or 12-hour night shift and turns up at court bleary-eyed after, at best, a couple of hours' sleep. While potentially quite lucrative in terms of overtime payments for the officer, attending court "off nights" is an exhausting experience often undertaken after an extremely busy tour of duty and with the prospect of yet another night shift ahead.

POLICING AT NIGHT

There is something very particular about policing by night; perhaps unsurprisingly, it is the most unique of the shifts. If there is truth in the old adage that "bad weather is the best policeman," it is also the case that darkness can be the best friend of offenders. Most cities and towns assume a completely different identity by night, and you could often be forgiven for thinking that they are occupied by an entirely different population. Many officers experience a tension between the excitement that can accompany policing by night and the adverse effects on their body clock. As a general rule, younger officers tend to be far more enthusiastic about night duty work than their older colleagues, but many officers of any length of service will recognize that it usually becomes harder and harder to make the transition from days to nights and then back to days again.

By night, partygoers fill the bars and streets and inevitably problems occur through an excess of celebration. Without doubt a significant percentage of police work at night is linked to alcohol and/or drug use and abuse. Indeed, if alcohol was removed from the equation there would be a lot less work for all of the participants in the criminal justice system. The fights flare up more suddenly and, even if unintended, the injuries can be substantially worse.

Officers quickly learn to distinguish the happy but annoying drunk from the dangerous one. Breaking up incidents in pubs and bars can carry great risks for the police. The amount of glass that is ready to hand in a bar will make most officers nervous as they wade into a crowded space with a tense or hostile atmosphere. Fortunately, Canadians lack the apparent British compulsion to become as drunk as possible within the shortest possible time and then go on to wreak as much havoc as they can. Pub fights are a depressingly familiar aspect of policing in much of England, as are the marauding groups who frequently terrorize many town centres. A great many of the injuries sustained by officers are as a result of dealing with drunken, aggressive young males.

The different perspective that night work can bring can certainly be useful as it enables officers to appreciate and discover aspects of the communities they police that they would never otherwise come across. However, one of the greatest downsides of night work can arise when the bars have closed and the city finally begins to fall asleep. The absence of any apparent activity—or of any calls with which to deal—does nothing to help keep you awake, and at four o'clock in the morning it can be very difficult to stay motivated, let alone on your feet. The irony is that, half-asleep, an officer can suddenly be expected to respond to a serious incident, sometimes involving a life-or-death decision. Racing to the scene of a call in your scout car in this semicomatose state can be demanding enough. More especially, not many of us would wish to be placed in the situation of having to decide whether to shoot someone; unfortunately, this is not an infrequent occurrence for police officers. Trying to decide in a tense and fast-moving situation whether to pull the trigger is an incredibly difficult decision at the best of times. It is certainly not made any easier if the incident happens at night, with little or no warning and after exhaustion has begun to set in.

Along with many of our institutions, police services (they used to be called forces) have increasingly found that they are less able to rely on traditional respect or deference for the work they do. No doubt there are a number of complex explanations for this—some of them eminently reasonable—but the reality is that whatever reasons exist for this change, policing is neither a safer occupation nor an easier one to perform than it once was.

POLICE AND FIREARMS

In Canada, all police officers are armed. The United Kingdom remains perhaps the last major police service in the world that does not routinely provide firearms for its officers. In 1986 when I joined the Metropolitan Police, if an armed incident arose one of two things occurred. Along with many of my former colleagues, those nearest the scene typically chased after the armed individual, or ran into the bank that was apparently being held up, armed only with their wooden truncheon and a childlike faith in the fact that you probably wouldn't be shot. If this sounds particularly remarkable, it is not meant to. It was simply the typical response of most officers at that time. The alternative was, and I kid you not, to drive or run back to your police station and sign out one of the handful of aging revolvers that were kept under lock and key by the duty inspector. Having done this you then ran or drove back to the scene of the incident and hoped it wasn't already over.

Thankfully, things have improved somewhat since then, although most police officers in the United Kingdom are not trained in the use of firearms and do not carry one. This prevents many officers there from encountering some of the terrifying dilemmas experienced by their Canadian colleagues. Conversely, though, the two most pointless words to shout in the English language are "Stop! Police!" if you have neither a gun nor a police dog to hand.

That being said, police officers across the country experience situations on a daily basis that can be frankly terrifying. Moreover, they are not expected to turn tail and run but to deal with it. In the same way that we expect our firefighters to routinely run into blazing buildings, we legitimately expect our police officers to tackle dangerous situations and armed criminals. Coming out on top can be exhilarating, but as we all know, this is unfortunately not always the case. Often, pure blind luck may be the factor between triumph and disaster.

A very common theme that has developed for all police officers is the ever increasing amount of equipment they are now routinely expected to carry. Preparing to begin a shift takes longer than ever before; an officer has to ensure that he or she is properly, if exhaustingly, equipped for the tour of duty ahead. Armed or not, most officers now wear body armour (a welcome addition, but often heavy, hot, and uncomfortable) as well as a utility belt that would be the envy of your average superhero and that comprises pepper spray, handcuffs, surgical gloves, and a panoply of other items. The net result of this accumulation of kit is that police officers are certainly better equipped than ever before, even if they are thirty pounds heavier and far less likely to catch someone in a foot chase.

Thus prepared, officers then leave their respective stations or divisions for the day or night ahead. Unless assigned to the often mind-numbing tedium of a fixed-post duty, most uniformed police officers have little idea of what a "routine" shift holds in store for them. Within a few minutes of starting work they may find themselves completing routine but necessary paperwork in respect of a recent break-in or attempting to comfort a stranger to whom they have just delivered the devastating news that their child has been killed. They may find themselves running along dark alleys or rooftops while chasing a suspect who has great reluctance to be caught or providing first aid to someone knocked down by a streetcar. Their reality on any given day may prove to be exhilarating, or mundane in the extreme, or any combination of the two.

Their role is that of a veritable jack-of-all-trades. Police officers have to be prepared to be mediators, counsellors, peacekeepers, and enforcers. They are expected to perform any of their required roles at a moment's notice and will frequently be pilloried by at least one if not both of the parties involved. They will become depressingly familiar with people routinely lying to them, even when it makes no sense to do so, and they will see some of the very worst aspects of human nature. Yet we will still expect them to retain their humanity, good manners, and ideally a sense of humour.

The "Job" of serving as a police officer is unlike any other, yet it is mostly the same the world over.

DISCUSSION QUESTIONS

1. *To what extent does this account of the professional life of a police officer correspond to your perceptions of what a police officer does?*
2. *Do you think that all police officers should carry a firearm, or do you think the British model of having specialist armed officers is a better approach to policing?*

CHAPTER 6
The Role of the Prosecutor

Most people are familiar with the role and function of a defence lawyer: to argue the accused's side against the case of the State. This means rebutting evidence against the accused wherever possible and advancing the interests of the accused right through to the sentencing hearing (in the event of a conviction). At the sentencing hearing, the defence proposes a sentence that would be in the best interests of the accused, and his or her representation of the accused may not stop here if an appeal of the conviction or sentence is launched.

The role of the Crown is less well known. In this chapter, Brian Manarin, an experienced Crown attorney in the Province of Ontario, uses his experience to illustrate the role of the Crown or prosecutor. He discusses the various decisions that confront a Crown counsel, such as which charge should be laid (including whether it is in the public interest to proceed with a prosecution at all), whether the accused should be granted bail, and which evidence to submit on sentencing.

Brian Manarin, Crown Counsel[1]

The vast majority of criminal misconduct cases in Canada are prosecuted in the lower-level Provincial Division courts. If one pictures an inverted funnel, with the provincial courts representing the wide opening at the bottom and the Supreme Court of Canada representing the narrow spout at the top, one can better appreciate just how busy the provincial courts really are.

Crown attorneys (and any assistant Crown attorneys in their charge) are lawyers responsible for preparing and prosecuting cases for alleged criminal and quasi-criminal offences occurring within the province in which they are employed. Although countless statutes govern allegations of criminal conduct, the preeminent legislation that governs the prosecution of criminal offences in Canada is known simply as the *Criminal Code*.[2] Within this lengthy federal statute is a detailed sketch of what Parliament considers to be acceptable and unacceptable conduct in civilized Canadian society. Canada's *Criminal Code* can be considered the catalyst behind all criminal prosecutions that take place in the country.

The majority of prosecutors earn their living in the courtroom. Their role focuses on searching for the truth during the trial process. However, many issues that are integral to the administration of justice are dealt with far from the courtroom. Other prosecutorial responsibilities include drafting court documents and providing professional advice to the police, related agencies, and the general public on criminal matters. In addition, prosecutors must possess a thorough knowledge of criminal law and procedure and the rules of evidence, as well as a strong comprehension of the workings of the *Canadian Charter of Rights and Freedoms*,[3] which is the supreme law of Canada. Finally, prosecutors must bring superior judgment and a healthy degree of common sense to their workday duties.

What distinguishes prosecutors from any other type of lawyer is their role in the trial process. The parties to any criminal prosecution are Her Majesty the Queen on the one side and those accused of committing the offences on the other (Wijesinha and Young 1978, 1). The prosecution must ensure that the accused receives a fair trial. The end goal is not to register a finding of guilt, but rather to come to a just result born out of the evidence presented at trial. Without a doubt, the best definition of the role of the Crown can be found in the often quoted words of Mr. Justice Rand of the Supreme Court of Canada in the case of *Boucher v. R*[4]:

> It cannot be over-emphasized that the purpose of a criminal prosecution is not to obtain a conviction; it is to lay before a jury what the Crown considers to be credible evidence relevant to what is alleged to be a crime. Counsel have a duty to see that all available legal proof of the facts is presented: it should be done firmly and pressed to its legitimate strength, but it must also be done fairly. The role of the prosecutor excludes any notion of winning or losing; his function is a matter of public duty: in civil life there can be none charged with greater personal responsibility. It is to be efficiently performed with an ingrained sense of the dignity, the seriousness, and the justness of judicial proceedings.

The goal of every prosecutor is to meet the high standards that Justice Rand emphasized in his classic statement on the subject. However, prosecutors are human and thus subject to the same foibles and fallibility as any other person in any other walk of life. Putting aside one's passions to make way for moderation and impartiality requires constant effort.[5] Maintaining neutrality does not, however, translate into a lacklustre effort. To the contrary, the Crown counsel, like any other advocate, is entitled to advance his or her position forcefully and effectively.[6]

In contrast, the role of the defence counsel is to be openly partisan toward his or her client. The defence has a duty to protect the client from being found guilty of a criminal offence; and, to that end, the defence may use all the available evidence and defences as long as they are not false or fraudulent. Therefore, the defence is not obligated to assist the prosecution at trial. In fact, the defence is entitled to assume an entirely adversarial role toward the prosecution.[7] Whereas the prosecution must disclose the case in its entirety to the defence, the defence does not need to state in advance what specific defence will be made against the accusation, who the witnesses are, or what they will say on the witness stand. Distilled to its most fundamental, a person accused of committing a crime is presumed to be innocent until the prosecution proves his or her guilt beyond a reasonable doubt. As a result, an accused person has a right to remain silent to avoid the potential for self-incrimination. The burden of proving guilt always rests with the prosecution.

Thus, the prosecution and the defence each have different roles and responsibilities in the trial process. In order to illustrate the typical duties and obligations of a prosecutor practising in the provincial courts, the remainder of this chapter will describe three sets of tasks that a Crown attorney deals with during a normal week: (1) charge screening and disclosure; (2) bail hearings; and (3) sentencing. The trial process itself will not be dealt with in any direct way.

CHARGE SCREENING AND DISCLOSURE

Although there is always a need for policing in Canadian society, there is not a concurrent need to prosecute all alleged offenders. The decision to continue or terminate a prosecution is among the most difficult Crown counsel must make (*Crown Policy Manual* 1994, 1). At this early stage of the proceedings, prosecutors need to remember the true function of their job:

> A Crown attorney must be ever alert to prevent abuses of the criminal process. He [or she] must stand independent between the accused and overzealous police. He [or she] must recognize and prevent vexatious or multifarious charges being laid or prosecuted. He [or she] must recognize unworthy or vindictive complainants and not become wittingly or unwittingly an instrument of persecution. He [or she] must remain objective, exercising his own discretion and judgement, especially in cases that have caused public outrage or incensed his community. Cases that have political overtones, cases that have attained a great deal of publicity, or cases that appeal to prejudices, such as race or religion, must be dealt with in the same fashion (Bynoe 1968, 102).

Screening occurs when the prosecution receives a brief of the allegations from the agency responsible for laying the charge or charges—usually the police or an individual. Screening is an ongoing process and must be completed before a date can be set for a preliminary inquiry or trial. The Crown attorney screens each charge to decide (among other things) the following: (1) whether there is a reasonable prospect of conviction; (2) whether it is in the public interest to discontinue a prosecution even if there is a reasonable prospect of conviction; (3) whether the proper charge has been laid; (4) whether the investigation is complete; and (5) whether an offer of diversion should be made to the accused (*Crown Policy Manual* 1994, 2).[8]

If there is no reasonable prospect of conviction, then the Crown attorney must terminate the prosecution. The test objectively considers the availability and admissibility of evidence, the credibility of witnesses, and the viability of any apparent defences. After considering the issue of reasonable prospect of conviction, the prosecutor must then contemplate the public interest. Although deciding what is in the public interest can be a daunting task even for a seasoned prosecutor (or for the courts as well), the following questions guide the screening process:

- Is the incident in question grave or trivial?
- What are the victim's views?
- What is the age and health, both physical and mental, of an accused or witness?
- Would public confidence in the administration of justice be maintained by the screening decision?
- Are issues of national security or international relations involved?
- What is the degree of culpability for the accused in the grand scheme of the particular offence being alleged?
- Is there a prevalence of this type of offence being committed in the community?
- Would a conviction be unduly harsh or oppressive in relation to this particular accused person?
- Has the accused cooperated in the police investigation, or is he or she willing to do so now?
- How strong is the Crown's case?
- How old are the allegations?
- How long and costly will the prosecution be compared with the likely sentence for the crime?
- Are alternatives to prosecution available? (*Crown Policy Manual* 1994, 4–5)

Although police officers are required to have a sufficient working knowledge of criminal law to allow them to make arrests and lay charges, Crown counsel must ultimately decide at the screening stage whether the proper charge has in fact been laid or whether another charge should be substituted. Often a changing of charge can result in reducing duplicate charges, since one single action can result in the commission of many criminal offences. In other circumstances, substituting one charge for another can save valuable resources by keeping a case within the jurisdiction of a Provincial Division judge. Additionally, when prosecutors notice more subtle legal nuances, they can recommend that the police lay a more (or less) serious charge than they originally contemplated.

In addition, neither an accused person nor a prosecutor can truly assess the strengths or weaknesses of a particular case until the police investigation is complete. For this reason, the prosecutor must be satisfied that all avenues of a police investigation have been exhausted before completing the screening process. If not, then Crown counsel must direct the police to complete the areas of the investigation that are incomplete. At this point, the prosecution should invite the defence counsel to point out any other oversights by the police.

Finally, Crown counsel has the opportunity to divert a criminal charge away from the criminal justice system. This means that no prosecution will proceed, and the person accused of the offence will not acquire a criminal record. Historically, a prosecutor has always had the discretion to withdraw a charge or charges against an accused, as described in the *Criminal Code*. Today's prosecutors have the option to use diversion programs devised by the attorneys general, lieutenant-governors in council, or their respective designates in each province, collectively recognized as "alternative measures" by the *Criminal Code*.[9] Generally speaking, if an accused person admits to his or her involvement in the commission of an offence and does not wish a trial, the prosecutor may recommend alternative measures as long as they are not inconsistent with the protection of society. The interests of society and those of the victim are weighed against each other. Similarly, the prosecutor makes efforts to protect the interests of the accused in this process by (1) ensuring that he or she fully and freely consents to the alternative measures, and (2) ensuring that a trial is actually held if that is what the accused desires.

Alternative-measures programs may involve the diversion of charges for mentally disordered accused, prostitutes and their patrons, Aboriginal Canadians, young offenders,[10] and minor (and generally first-time) offenders. Each diversion requires the accused to complete a program or act of contrition that satisfies the prosecution's terms and conditions. By offering alternatives, the prosecutor discourages the offender from offending again and prevents a criminal record. Also, the state is spared the necessity of a costly trial.

BAIL HEARINGS

Bail, or "judicial interim release" as it is referred to in the *Criminal Code,* means the release from custody of accused persons so that they can maintain their liberty while awaiting trial. In certain circumstances, a police officer or a justice of the peace can arrange a person's release (Trotter 1992). However, this chapter will concentrate on bail hearings conducted in court where a prosecutor is called upon to make a decision whether an accused person should be detained in custody until trial.

The decision for or against bail is often difficult. Picture, if you will, bail court on a Monday morning where, in addition to the normal volume of weekend arrests, there have been raids on illegal establishments and final "take-downs" of various special police crime prevention projects, resulting in further large-scale arrests. The courtroom this morning is full. As you can imagine, to make intelligent, fair, and informed decisions about the release or detention of each detainee can be an overwhelming task. Digesting the allegations pertinent to each accused person, considering the positions of the police, defence, and complainants, and considering strategy for the bail hearings in such circumstances requires a cool head and a large measure of confidence.

The outcome of a bail hearing is often pivotal to the outcome of the case itself. Statistics show that over 80 percent of all charges dealt with in the Provincial Division courts result in guilty pleas (Martin 1993, 15). Moreover, experience has shown that persons detained without bail are much more likely to plead guilty so that they may start serving their sentence immediately. Justice through trial seems much less appealing when a person is waiting for his or her "day in court" without a release on bail. As such, it is perhaps at the bail hearing that the prosecutor is under the most intense pressure to be firm but fair.

What are the fundamental concerns at a bail hearing? The court will grant an accused person a form of bail unless the prosecution can show why the detention of the accused person is justified. In fact, the law requires that the least onerous form of release be granted to an accused person unless the prosecution can show why a more stringent form of release should be imposed.[11] However, six situations can shift the onus onto the accused to show why his or her detention is *not* justified. Five of these six situations are relevant to a Provincial Division bail hearing:

1. Has the accused person allegedly committed another indictable offence while on release?
2. Has the accused person allegedly committed an offence involving organized crime for which the maximum punishment is imprisonment for five years or more?
3. Has the accused person allegedly committed an indictable offence and is not ordinarily resident in Canada?
4. Has the accused person allegedly failed to attend court as required on a previous outstanding release or failed to otherwise live up to the terms of the previous release?
5. Has the accused person allegedly committed or conspired to commit an offence involving the production, trafficking, or importation of certain controlled drugs?[12]

Whether the burden is on the accused or the prosecution, bail hearings consistently address three different areas of concern: (1) Is the accused person's detention necessary to ensure his or her attendance in court in order to be dealt with according to law? (2) Is the accused person's detention necessary for the protection or safety of the public? (3) Is the detention necessary to maintain confidence in the administration of justice, having regard to all the circumstances, including the apparent strength of the prosecution's case, the gravity of the nature of the offence, the circumstances surrounding its commission, and the potential for a lengthy term of imprisonment?[13]

Although the *Criminal Code* clearly defines when a prosecutor may seek to detain a person in custody until trial, a prosecutor should not apply these criteria automatically. By rigidly following the rules, a Crown counsel can fall short of the standards of fairness that are expected from his or her office. The following three examples illustrate the point.

Example 1

A refugee claimant from Cuba has come to Canada to escape the repressive Castro regime, where he had been a vocal opponent. He has left family and friends behind. Six months into his stay in Canada, he is charged with a street robbery that occurred in an area of Toronto plagued by this type of offence. The identity of the perpetrator of this crime is clearly an issue at trial. No significant injuries were suffered by the victim. Although the accused person has no real roots in the community, he has no criminal record and has two sureties who will guarantee his release on bail and who will, in addition, offer a cash deposit.

Although protection of the public is important, as well as the fact that this type of offence generally commands a lengthy term of imprisonment upon conviction, the foremost concern in this situation tends to be whether the accused will flee if granted bail. Since this accused has no ties to the community, it would appear that flight from prosecution should be a concern. Should Crown counsel simply point out that because the accused is not normally resident in Canada, he should be detained, and that it is up to the accused to show why he should be released? Or do the facts require more detailed consideration?

Although the accused has not yet established himself in Toronto, the prosecution clearly is aware that he has come to Canada to escape his homeland. Why would a person flee to a country where he knows he faces likely persecution? Moreover, there are weaknesses in the Crown's case, because the accused has not been clearly identified as the culprit. The fact that the accused has no criminal record bodes well for his release. For these reasons, the Crown could suggest a form of release without abdicating its duties as a minister of justice.

Example 2

The police are called to a residential dwelling, the scene of an earlier domestic assault by a husband on his wife. The accused had been drinking heavily at the time of the incident but is now sober and remorseful. The accused has no criminal record, and the police discover from family sources that his behaviour was an aberration likely stemming from the loss of his job. Although there are no apparent injuries, the victim is concerned that her husband broke a sacred trust between them, and she fears that he may repeat this conduct if he is granted bail. The victim is financially dependent on her spouse and has two small children to care for. The accused has a surety who will allow him to live at his home, far away from the family abode, while awaiting trial. He will also get the accused some treatment for what appears to be an alcohol problem.

Society's general abhorrence for spousal assault cannot be overstated. What was once considered a problem to be worked out within the family is now understood to be a serious criminal offence that brings with it significant criminal sanctions. Both police and prosecutors realize that an inordinate number of homicides result from domestic violence. However, the truly objective prosecutor must not be influenced by his or her disgust for certain alleged conduct. Although it is understandable that the spouse may fear a repetition of the abuse, all indications reveal that this assault was an isolated incident.

The fact that a strong surety has come forward who can put some physical distance between the abuser and the victim should also alleviate certain concerns. Despite the seriousness of this kind of violence, the Crown counsel really has no choice but to immediately concede that this accused person is a candidate for bail. Although complete protection of the victim can only be achieved in certain situations by denying the abuser any form of release, in this case, a carefully crafted bail order would meet the ends of justice.

Example 3

The accused person is on a police release for communicating for the purpose of engaging in prostitution. One of the terms of his release is that he abide by a curfew that requires him to be in his place of residence between 11:00 p.m. and 6:00 a.m. every day. He is seen by the police staggering down the road at 3:00 a.m. on the day in question, and, upon investigation, it is discovered that he is in violation of his curfew. The accused is clearly guilty of failing to comply with a fundamental condition of his release. Although this is a reverse-onus situation, the accused seeks another bail and can produce a substantial surety to the court. At the time, the accused has no criminal record.

Prosecutors can fall into the habit of rationalizing that since an accused will likely be found guilty at trial, the notion of release pending that foregone conclusion is inappropriate. Certainly, the strength of the prosecution's case is an important consideration when deciding whether bail is a viable option; but in a situation like this one, other factors must be considered. Except for his curfew violation, this accused would be a candidate for the alternative-measures program for his prostitution-related offence. As for the curfew violation itself, despite the fact that violating a release condition is a serious offence, it is highly unlikely that the accused would be sentenced to a period of custody. As such, a detention order at the accused's bail hearing would be overly harsh given what he could expect as a just punishment for either or both offences. Sound judgment dictates a further release for this accused person, but with more restrictive conditions.

SENTENCING

Arguably nothing is more vexing for a prosecutor than making submissions on sentence. By definition, the accused now stands guilty as charged as a result of a guilty plea or after being found guilty at trial. In either situation, the accused is at his or her most vulnerable, and so is the Crown counsel. The former is vulnerable because the passing of sentence can result in the loss of liberty as well as the stigmatization of the offender for several years. The latter is vulnerable since the quality of justice is often measured by the submissions of the prosecution on sentence. A lack of impartiality at this most emotional stage of the proceedings can tarnish the entire office of the Crown attorney, not just the reputation of the individual prosecutor. For this reason alone, the role of Crown counsel has been measured on the strength of the following statement: "With the result, as with the verdict at the trial, he is enormously unconcerned" (Humphreys 1955, 748). In other words, prosecutors must remain unemotional in their role, without any appearance of desiring a particular outcome.

However, being unconcerned about the outcome of a prosecution is not the same as being apathetic, such as in a situation where the Crown counsel had relinquished his or her responsibility to strive for a just sentence. Thus, historically, the prosecution is expected to display a lack of concern at the end as well as the beginning of the trial process, to acquit itself without feeling in order to dispassionately reach a just conclusion.

The purpose and principles of sentencing are now largely incorporated into Canada's *Criminal Code*.[14] Entire texts have been written on the subject of sentencing, which makes the topic too complex to discuss in a single chapter. However, hearings are governed almost entirely by the facts presented, rather than by laws or theories. Therefore, no two proceedings are ever exactly the same, despite efforts to treat like offenders in similar fashions.

One area of sentencing worthy of special comment pertains to the *conditional sentence*.[15] Amendments to the *Criminal Code* in 1996 created a new type of sentence in Canada. When a person is convicted of an offence that does not have a minimum term of imprisonment spelled out in the *Criminal Code*, the court may order that the offender serve the sentence in the community. The sentence must be less than two years of imprisonment, and the court must be satisfied that the offender will not be a danger to the community. In addition, the court must be satisfied that serving the sentence in the community would be consistent with the fundamental purpose and principles of sentencing as set out in the *Criminal Code*.

The advent of the conditional sentence means that offenders who traditionally went to jail are now increasingly serving their sentences in the community subject to conditions. But so far, many prosecutors have had difficulty accepting the conditional sentence as a reasonable alternative to traditional incarceration, for these two reasons: (1) it is hard to appreciate how the value systems in Canadian society have shifted so dramatically in recent times that Parliament has allowed offenders who would have been jailed before to serve their sentences in the same community whose trust they violated; and (2) due to scarce resources, the administration of criminal justice is ill equipped to monitor or prosecute those offenders who do not live up to the conditions of their sentences in the community. A shortcoming of the conditional sentence is that many judges, defence counsel, and prosecutors view it as a second-class form of punishment. It is bandied about more as a tool for plea-bargaining purposes than as a legitimate form of sentence. Anecdotal evidence suggests that conditional sentences are more often imposed for a guilty plea than they are for a guilty verdict.

How should Crown counsel remedy the misuse of the conditional sentence? The answer is obvious. The prosecution has a positive duty to apply the law as expressed by Parliament and to actively urge conditional sentences upon the court whenever the circumstances dictate. This would be in keeping with the highest traditions of the Crown and entirely consistent with the expected objectivity that goes with the office. To lead by example is to conscientiously discharge the duties of the prosecution.

CONCLUSION

The Provincial Division courts are the cornerstone of the Canadian criminal justice system. They have been variously described as ungovernable battlefields and as arenas of remarkable cohesion. Regardless, the prosecution plays an essential role in making the busiest of all Canadian courts a functional role model for the administration of justice. By maintaining an objective frame of mind, Crown counsel ensures that the adversarial process works. It is not always an easy task.

DISCUSSION QUESTIONS

1. *As noted in the introduction to this reading, the criminal justice system is attempting to become more sensitive to the needs of crime victims. Some people have suggested that prior to making a plea bargain with an accused, the Crown should seek and obtain the approval of the victim. Do you think this is a good idea?*

2. *As Mr. Manarin notes, the accused in a criminal trial is not obligated to take the stand to testify. But in some cases, it would make the Crown's task easier if the accused were compelled to testify. What is your reaction to changing the rules of evidence to compel the accused to testify if the Crown so desires?*

FURTHER READINGS

Brockman, J., and G. Rose. 1996. *An Introduction to Canadian Criminal Procedure and Evidence.* Toronto: Nelson Canada.

Stenning, P.C. 1994. "Current Issues Concerning the Court Process." In C.T. Griffiths and S.N. Verdun-Jones, eds., *Canadian Criminal Justice*, 2nd ed. Toronto: Harcourt Brace Canada.

REFERENCES

Bynoe, B. 1968. "The Role and Function of Crown Counsel." 3 C.R.N.S. 90.
   Crown Policy Manual. 1994. Policy # C.S.-1, Charge Screening, January 15.
Humphreys, C. 1955. "The Duties and Responsibilities of Prosecuting
   Counsel." *Criminal Law Review* 739: 748.
Martin, G. 1993. *Report of the Attorney General's Advisory Committee on Charge
   Screening, Disclosure, and Resolution Discussions.* Toronto: Queen's Printer.
Trotter, G. 1992. *The Law of Bail in Canada.* Toronto: Carswell.
Wijesinha K., and B.J. Young. 1978. *Aids to Criminal Investigation.*
   Scarborough: Panju Canada.

ENDNOTES

1. The comments found herein are solely those of the author, made in his personal capacity.
2. R.S.C. 1985, c. C-46, as amended.
3. S. 33, Part I of the *Constitution Act*, 1982, being Schedule B to the *Canada Act* 1982 (U.K.), 1982, c. 11.
4. *Boucher v. R.* (1955), 110 C.C.C. 263 at 270.
5. *R. v. Bain* (1992), 10 C.R. (4th) 257 at 264 (S.C.C.), wherein Mr. Justice Cory recognizes that passions are not easily stilled, even when considering counsel for the Crown: "[T]hey, like all of us, are subject to human frailties and occasional lapses ... I do not make these observations in order to be critical of Crown Attorneys. Rather they are made to emphasize the very human frailties that are common to all, no matter what the office held."
6. *R. v. Daly* (1992), 57 O.A.C. 70 at 76, para. 32 (C.A.).
7. *R. v. Stinchcombe* (1991), 68 C.C.C. (3d) 1 at 7 (S.C.C.).
8. Contained therein is a more exhaustive list of considerations that must be addressed by the Crown attorney's office.
9. *Supra* note 2, ss. 716, 717.
10. *Young Offenders Act*, R.S.C. 1985, c. Y-1, s. 4, as amended.
11. *Supra* note 2, s. 515(1).
12. Ibid., s 515(6).
13. Ibid., s. 515(10).
14. Ibid., ss. 718–718.2.
15. Ibid., ss. 742–742.7.

CHAPTER 7
The Role of a Defence Counsel

One of the most important professions in the criminal justice system, and the one with which people may be most familiar from court shows on television, is the defence counsel. Although people know what defence lawyers are, they don't necessarily have a good understanding of their role in the criminal justice system. Moreover, when asked to rate the performance of different criminal justice professionals, Canadians assign relatively poor ratings to members of the defence bar. People appear to overlook the vital role that defence lawyers play in the adversarial system of justice.

In this chapter, Paul Burstein, an experienced criminal defence lawyer practising in Toronto, discusses the professional life of a defence counsel and addresses a question he is frequently posed.

Paul Burstein

As a criminal defence lawyer, I am often asked by friends and family whether it bothers me to work so hard in the defence of someone whom I know is guilty. For reasons that I hope to make clear a little further on, I have never found this to be a very difficult question to answer. However, the other day, my seven-year-old daughter asked me a slightly different question, one that I found myself struggling to answer.[1] She asked me how I could defend bad people. My daughter's question led me to rethink the soundness of the explanations that I had long offered to critics of criminal defence lawyers. Fortunately, after some long periods of thought, I have managed to once again come to terms with this skepticism with respect to the importance of criminal defence work for our society.

In order to emphasize the importance of what criminal defence lawyers do, I think it is necessary to first explain what it is that we do. Simply put, criminal defence lawyers represent people who find themselves accused of crimes. As a result of the proliferation of television legal dramas, most people mistakenly perceive a defence lawyer's job to begin and end with the trial. In fact, most of a criminal defence lawyer's time is spent helping clients long before their cases actually get to trial. Indeed, the vast majority of criminal cases do not ever go to trial. Although the numbers have varied over the past couple of decades, no more than 5 to 10 percent of criminal charges are resolved through trials. If so few criminal cases result in trials, what are all those criminal defence lawyers doing hanging around the courthouses? It may sound trite, but they are trying to help their clients stay out or get out of jail.

THE CLIENT AT THE POLICE STATION

Typically, a criminal defence lawyer's "job" begins long before the client's case even gets to trial. In fact, a criminal defence lawyer often becomes involved in a case even before the client goes to court. In Canada, s. 10(b) of the *Canadian Charter of Rights and Freedoms* provides that:

10.   Everyone has the right on arrest or detention …
 (b)   to retain and instruct counsel without delay and to be informed
        of that right …

Canadian courts have interpreted this constitutional right to mean that the police must tell someone who has been arrested that he or she can immediately contact a lawyer for free legal advice.[2] Where a "detainee" (i.e., a person who has been detained) requests to speak to a lawyer, our courts have also held that the police are obliged to help that detainee get in touch with a lawyer right away, such as by providing him or her with a phone and a phone book.[3] For those detainees who call a lawyer from the police station (not all of them do), the defence lawyer will almost always urge the detainee to assert his or her right to remain silent.

Contrary to a popular misconception, even detainees who are not guilty can end up "confessing" to the police while being held in detention. In effect, these "innocent"[4] people provide the police with a false confession. In addition, detainees who are not guilty of the charge sometimes end up providing the police with an account of the events that is confused or mistaken. After all, these people are being held in custody and are being interrogated by very skilled and experienced questioners. More often than not, those police interrogators confront the detainee with overblown claims of a case against the person in the hope of stimulating some sort of incriminating statement. These overblown accusations can frighten an accused into agreeing to a lesser accusation, even if it is untrue. Thus, to prevent the creation of unreliable "confessions," the law guarantees a detainee the right to remain silent upon arrest. The defence lawyer must not only remind the detainee of this right during that first phone call but also help the detainee build the courage to maintain that silence in the face of any subtle or confrontational police questioning. In my experience, the vast majority of police officers, when told by the criminal defence lawyer of the detainee's desire to remain silent, will do the honourable thing and refrain from questioning that detainee any further. To the chagrin of many defence lawyers, certain clients, no matter how many times they come in contact with the criminal justice system, never seem to be able to learn what it means to "shut up"![5]

RELEASE OF THE CLIENT ON BAIL

The other task of a criminal defence lawyer during that first phone call from the police station is to attempt to persuade the police to allow the client-detainee to be released on bail. While the police usually have already made a decision about bail, a defence lawyer's input can help satisfy the arresting officer that it is appropriate to release the detainee directly from the police station. If not, then the defence lawyer will ask where and when the client-detainee will be brought to court for a hearing before a justice of the peace to determine whether or not the client should be released on bail. The *Criminal Code* requires that a person who has been arrested and who has not been released at the scene or at the police station be brought before a justice of the peace within a day or two of the arrest for a bail hearing. Many lawyers believe that the bail issue is the most important one in the criminal process. Given the long delays that occur between the time of the arrest and the time of trial, some people will have a strong incentive to plead guilty to their charge(s), even when they are not in fact guilty, simply to avoid a lengthy wait in a pre-trial remand facility for their trial date.

In preparation for a bail hearing, a defence lawyer will need to help his or her client find a *surety*—someone who is willing to pledge a sum of money as a guarantee of that person's ability to supervise the detainee if released. In many cases, defence lawyers also must function as social workers or counsellors and help arrange for their clients to obtain treatment, secure employment, or re-enroll in school, since the justice of the peace will want to know that the client isn't sitting at home watching television until the trial date arrives. I cannot tell you how many times I have been in bail court and have heard the expression "the devil finds work for idle hands."

DEFENCES

Win or lose, the bail hearing does not end the case for a person who has been charged with a criminal offence. The next stage in the process involves trying to determine whether the client has a defence to the charge(s) he or she faces. At the risk of grossly oversimplifying what I do, criminal defences can generally be divided into two categories: *factual defences* and *legal defences.* The factual type of defence involves a challenge to the evidence that the police have gathered in the course of the investigation that resulted in the charge(s) against the client. Perhaps the witness is lying. Maybe he or she implicated the accused in order to benefit himself or herself, such as through a lesser sentence for his or her own charges or for a monetary reward. Maybe the eyewitness is mistaken. As noted elsewhere in this book (see Chapter by Campbell and Denov), eyewitness identification is notoriously unreliable.

The other type of defence, the legal kind, focuses on whether or not what the person is accused of doing should be considered "criminal." For example, there may be no dispute that my client shot her husband, but it may have been in self-defence and, thus, is legally justified. In trying to determine what (if any) defence a client has to a criminal charge, the defence lawyer needs to gather information relevant to the case. That information comes from the police reports and witness statements, which the prosecutor is legally obliged to disclose to the defence in advance of the trial,[6] as well as any information the client and other potential witnesses provide. (This practice is known as the Crown providing "disclosure" to the defence.) In addition, the defence lawyer may have to do some research into the law that governs the features of the client's case—for example, whether the police have engaged in an illegal search, whether self-defence includes the defence of one's property, or whether two lovers in a parked car are in a "public place." Once the defence lawyer has determined the nature and extent of the available defences, the lawyer is ready to advise the client how next to proceed.

At this juncture, the defence lawyer presents the client with two options: plead guilty in the hope of obtaining a more lenient sentence from the court as a reward for sparing everyone the time and expense of a trial, or schedule a date for a trial, at which time the client can plead not guilty and contest the prosecutor's case. As noted above, in the vast majority of cases, persons charged with criminal offences opt to have their lawyer try to negotiate a plea bargain with the prosecutor (see Chapter by Verdun-Jones).

The term *plea bargain* connotes exactly what it means: in exchange for giving up the right to a full trial, the accused receives the prosecutor's recommendation for a more lenient sentence than would normally be sought in a trial sentencing. This bargaining is often done at the prosecutor's office and is sometimes mediated by a judge. Upon learning the bottom-line offer of the prosecutor, a defence lawyer must always seek the input of the client before accepting or rejecting it. When asked by clients whether I would take the plea bargain if I were in their shoes, I am always left to explain that my risk–benefit analysis of trial versus guilty plea will, by definition, be different from theirs. As I tell them, given the nature of my work, I am quite used to spending my days in jail and am quite comfortable hanging around with criminals. If, on the other hand, the client is one of the minority who decide to reject the plea bargain in favour of a trial, the court will schedule a trial for some time down the road.[7]

PREPARING FOR TRIAL

Preparing a case for trial is very much like producing a film or a play. First, you have to develop the story on which the play will be based. By this, I certainly do not mean that lawyers help clients fabricate stories in order to avoid conviction. I am simply referring to the development of the narrative that takes into account the evidence that the defence lawyer believes will be accepted by the jury (or judge) at the end of the case *and* that is consistent with innocence. That is what a criminal defence lawyer does in representing a client at a trial: develop an "innocence" narrative to compete with the "guilty" narrative constructed by the police. For instance, the police may not have interviewed all of the potential witnesses, some of whom may not only cast doubt on the claim by others that a client is the guilty party but also shed light on the true identity of the perpetrator.

However, to develop a competing narrative is no easy task. By the time a defence lawyer becomes involved in a case, the prosecution narrative has already been constructed. The raw material (i.e., the evidence) is rarely still sitting at the scene waiting to be collected and examined. Nevertheless, a defence lawyer must visit the scene of the crime to discover the competing innocence narrative. Perhaps the one feature of criminal defence work that is fairly reflected on television is the sleuthing that criminal defence lawyers do in the preparation of their clients' cases.

I recall once going to a seedy hotel in downtown Toronto in preparation for a murder case where my client, a young female prostitute, had been charged with stabbing her customer to death. The case was about whether she had acted in self-defence. Thus, her opportunities to escape would play a critically important role in the jury's decision. After waiting for the elevator for 10 minutes down the hall from the room where the stabbing had occurred, I decided to take the stairs back down to the lobby. It was only then, when I saw that the staircase had been locked (apparently to prevent prostitutes from servicing clients in the stairwell and thereby avoiding the $50 room charge) that I better understood why my client would have felt that there was no means of escaping her attacker. This visit provided me with evidence to present at trial.

The next element of the trial drama is the cast of characters, and some are indeed characters. Who are the people who will tell the story to the jury? What is their background? Are they neutral and impartial, or are they motivated by revenge against the client? Do these people have a criminal record or a history of substance abuse? Usually, as part of the disclosure, the defence lawyer receives this sort of information about the proposed witnesses. However, in some cases, a defence lawyer must hire a private investigator to gather information about the witnesses. Unfortunately, even with the assistance of a private investigator, a criminal defence lawyer will never have the investigative resources that were (and are) available to the police and prosecutor. This is one of the principal justifications for insisting that the prosecutor bear the burden of proving guilt beyond a reasonable doubt, rather than asking the accused to prove that he or she is innocent.

With the storyline developed and the cast of characters defined, the defence lawyer must then turn to "directing" the play. In stark contrast to television legal dramas, most criminal defence lawyers do not simply stand up after the prosecutor finishes questioning a witness and begin cross-examination of that witness. Cross-examination must be carefully thought out and planned so that it does not do more harm than good. Moreover, a criminal defence lawyer must also maintain the jury's interest in the case: important points that arise in the middle of a long and meandering cross-examination of a witness will be lost if the jury are daydreaming. In an effort to maintain the jury's interest, lawyers also use visual aids to illustrate the testimony of the witnesses, such as by diagrams, photographs, or computer simulations. The ultimate efficacy of the "production" in the courtroom depends on the time invested in its planning.

CONSTITUTIONAL ISSUES

While the outcome of the majority of trials depends on the narrative created by the witnesses and the evidence, some trials are not about who did what, where, why, and to whom. Occasionally, a trial focuses instead on the law itself.

One of the most famous Canadian examples is the trial of Dr. Henry Morgentaler. Most Canadians recall that in 1988, the Supreme Court of Canada declared that anti-abortion laws violated Section 7 of the *Canadian Charter of Rights and Freedoms*. What most laypeople do not appreciate, however, is that this ruling was made in the context of Dr. Morgentaler's trial on criminal charges for performing abortions. Dr. Morgentaler never denied that he had performed the abortions on the women in contravention of Section 251 of the *Criminal Code*. Instead, his defence focused on the constitutional validity of the law itself. In other words, Dr. Morgentaler's lawyer argued that it did not matter whether or not his client had done what the prosecutor was alleging because even if he had done those things, the *Charter* prohibited the Government of Canada from making it a crime to do those things.

Section 52 of the *Constitution Act, 1982,* known by lawyers as the "supremacy clause" states:

> 52(1) The Constitution of Canada is the supreme law of Canada, and any law that is inconsistent with the provisions of the Constitution is, to the extent of the inconsistency, of no force or effect.

In plain English, this means that the Canadian government is not entitled to make laws that violate the rights that are set out in the *Canadian Charter of Rights and Freedoms*. Accordingly, a trial judge has the power to strike down a provision of the *Criminal Code* that is inconsistent with the *Charter*, just as the Supreme Court of Canada did when it struck down Section 251 of the *Code* in Dr. Morgentaler's case. This means that a lone criminal defence lawyer, armed with nothing more than a solid legal argument, can make (or rather, unmake) law, a feat not possible even for the prime minister.

It was not long into my career as a criminal defence lawyer before I started to raise "Section 52" challenges to criminal laws that I (and my clients) felt were oppressive and unfair. In 1993, about a year-and-a-half after being called to the bar, I launched a challenge to Canada's criminal prohibition on marijuana on behalf of a client who was charged with growing some plants in his house for his own personal use. As a result of a very good plea bargain that quickly followed that challenge, the court was never given the opportunity to decide the issue. However, less than two years later, along with my friend and mentor Professor Alan Young, I became involved in another challenge to Canada's criminal prohibition on marijuana that has since wound its way to the Supreme Court of Canada. If the Supreme Court of Canada agrees with our reasoning that the law violates the rights enshrined in Section 7 of the *Charter*, it will declare the law to be "of no force or effect" pursuant to the supremacy clause in Section 52 of the Constitution. This will mean that our client has been acquitted of the marijuana offences with which he was charged back in 1995. More important, though, it will also mean that no other Canadian can henceforth be convicted of breaking this law because the law itself has been effectively erased from the books.

In some instances, criminal defence lawyers instead challenge only the *scope* of a particular criminal law, as opposed to the law itself. For example, in the marijuana case, one alternative argument is that the criminal prohibition on cannabis, as it is referred to in the legislation, should be limited to the type of cannabis that people can use to get high. While it may sound silly to think that people could be convicted of possessing hemp, the non-intoxicating form of cannabis, the law is unfortunately not so clear. Indeed, the drug analyst who testified at the trial admitted that based on the testing protocol, he would willingly certify a piece of hemp clothing as cannabis, since the clothing would contain all of the elements that the law required for something to be certified as cannabis. Rather than compelling the court to strike down the law, this argument would simply require the court to redefine the law in a way that would produce a more appropriate definition of the "crime."

In a similar vein, I was also involved with Alan Young in a challenge to the breadth of the criminal law that prohibited the "Thornhill Dominatrix" from offering her clients sadomasochistic services for hire. She had been charged with operating a common bawdyhouse on the basis that the sadomasochistic services were the equivalent of criminally proscribed sex-for-hire. On the strength of expert evidence concerning its sociological, psychological, and cultural dimensions, we argued that the nature and purpose of S&M activities is not sexual but rather psychological stimulation—namely, the thrill associated with the anticipation and experience of pain (and/or humiliation).[8] Therefore, we argued, the criminal prohibition should not apply as it was properly limited to activities that were specifically aimed at providing sexual stimulation in exchange for money. But despite the inferential support to the argument provided by prior case decisions, the courts reaffirmed their monopoly on being paid to administer punishment and rejected these arguments.

My involvement in these constitutional challenges highlights another important feature of being a criminal defence lawyer: the need (or opportunity) to study new disciplines beyond the confines of law. For the constitutional challenge concerning marijuana, I had to educate myself on the psychopharmacological, sociological, criminological, botanical, and historical perspectives on the criminal prohibition of marijuana. For the Dominatrix case, I had to become versed in the culture of S&M in order to be able to explain it to the court and, more important, to be able to demonstrate why the stereotypical perception of this practice is misguided.

For other cases, I have had to learn about psychiatry, literature, chemistry, toxicology, biology, and even entomology (i.e., the study of bugs). This pursuit of knowledge can be a burden of the criminal defence lawyer's job. Indeed, I recall having to spend all of my Friday evenings, for weeks on end, sitting on a stool in the cramped office of our engineering expert in the "Just Desserts" murder case, in order to learn all about digital image processing in preparation for the case. Then again, this is probably one of the great benefits of being a criminal defence lawyer: the opportunity to learn about things in the world to which I might never otherwise have been exposed.

DEFENDING PEOPLE WHO MAY BE GUILTY

Despite the very long hours, the limited financial rewards, and the general lack of respect from the public, most of the time I love my job. I meet interesting people, learn fascinating new things, and visit places I would otherwise likely never have gone. In many ways, the job of a criminal defence lawyer is exotic and exciting.

Having explained why someone might want to be a criminal defence lawyer and what it is that criminal defence lawyers do, I am left to answer the question as to how I could defend someone whom I "know" is guilty. To begin with, it is important to remember that the Canadian criminal justice system, while good, is far from perfect. One need only pay heed to the increasing number of wrongful convictions that are emerging in Canada (and in the United States as well). Indeed, look back to the media coverage of the arrest of Guy Paul Morin, a man now proved innocent of the murder with which he was charged. But back in 1985, the public "knew" he was guilty. It was not until almost a decade later that the public realized its mistake. Perception is not reality.

The only way to reduce the number of wrongful convictions is to ensure that the system never cuts corners, no matter how heinous the crime. If someone truly is guilty, the system should be able to arrive at that determination in a fair and just manner—that is, by following the usual rules. Everyone must be subject to the same set of rules, no matter who he or she is or what he or she has been accused of doing. Unfortunately, there are many countries where that is not the case. In those places, the rules depend upon who you are or whom you know. These are governments that exist in part because there are no defence lawyers to challenge the arbitrary detention and imprisonment of people these governments label as "criminals." While Canada is a long way off from that paradigm,

Canadians must never take for granted their rights and freedoms nor those whose job it is to defend those rights and freedoms. Defending the "guilty" is a necessary part of ensuring that Canadians all continue to enjoy their rights and freedoms. In short, defence lawyers keep the criminal justice system honest.

That still leaves me with my daughter's question of how I can defend "bad" people, as opposed to people who have been accused of doing a bad thing. Why is it that "bad" people should benefit from all of my hard work as a criminal defence lawyer? Why should someone who has a long history of violating other people's rights be entitled to the same rights and freedoms as everyone else? The answer is that for better or for worse, the Canadian criminal justice system is one that seeks only to punish people for what they have done, not for who they are. It has to be that way.

Consider what it would mean to base punishment decisions on whether a person was "good" or "bad." Even in that sort of system, it would be unfair to punish those who were bad through no fault of their own—for example, those who suffered from fetal alcohol syndrome or those who had grown up being physically abused in group homes after being abandoned by their families. Instead, we would have to punish bad people only after having a trial to determine if they were bad by choice or by circumstances. If we did not care to make that distinction, we would have to be prepared to charge all those who may have contributed to the person's crime of being bad, such as parents, schools, peers, and government. Of course, when I explained all of this to my daughter, she was quick to agree and reminded me that by that logic, I should therefore be the one serving her detention at school, because it is my fault, not hers, that she was bad.

Spoken like the daughter of a criminal defence lawyer.

DISCUSSION QUESTIONS

1. *Consider this chapter in light of the preceding chapter written by a prosecutor. How does the role of a defence counsel differ from that of a prosecutor?*
2. *Some people think that the system is too protective of the rights of the accused. Others believe the opposite, that the state has too much power in prosecuting accused persons. What is your opinion?*

FURTHER READING

Greenspan, E. 1980. "The Role of the Defence Counsel in Sentencing."
    In B. Grosman, ed., *New Directions in Sentencing*. Toronto: Butterworths.

ENDNOTES

1. Being the father of Courtney, age 7, and Nikki, age 4, has taught me more about how to ask and how to answer more "tough" questions than my many other experiences in the criminal law sphere.
2. *R. v. Bartle* (1994), 92 C.C.C.(3d) 289 (S.C.C.).

3. You would be amazed at how many first-time detainees go about choosing the defence lawyer who will represent them by simply going to the section in the Yellow Pages that lists "criminal lawyers" and starting at the A's. You would, no doubt, be equally amazed at how many criminal defence lawyers were named "AAAAAAAAAASmith" at birth!

4. Whether they are "factually" innocent (i.e., did not do what the police have alleged) or "legally" innocent (i.e., have not done something that actually amounts to a crime).

5. For example, in *R. v. Manninen* (1987) 34 C.C.C.(3d) 385 (S.C.C.), one of the seminal cases on the "right to counsel" in Canada, the accused, a "rounder," is savvy enough to assert his right to speak to a lawyer when arrested on a robbery charge. However, he then proceeds to engage in the following dialogue with the arresting officer:

   Q. Where is the knife that you had along with this [showing the accused the CO2 gun found in the car] when you ripped off the Mac's Milk on Wilson Avenue?

   A. He's lying. When I was in the store I only had the gun. The knife was in the tool box in the car.

   Q. What are these for?

   A. What the fuck do you think they are for? Are you fucking stupid?

   Q. You tell me what they are for, and is this yours? [showing the grey sweatshirt]

   A. Of course it's mine. You fuckers are really stupid. Don't bother me anymore. I'm not saying anything until I see my lawyer. Just fuck off. You fuckers have to prove it.

6. See *R. v. Stinchcombe* (1991), 68 C.C.C.(3d) 1 (S.C.C.).

7. The lag between the "set date" and the trial can range up to a few years. The length of the delay is dependent upon the jurisdiction and upon the nature of the case; more complicated cases require more court time and, thus, are harder to slot into already very busy schedules.

8. Apparently, much like bungee jumping, skydiving, or white-water rafting.

9. Throughout history, criminal defence lawyers have been accused of being unpatriotic. In one of the most eloquent descriptions of the importance of defence lawyers, Henry Brougham, defending Queen Caroline on charges of adultery before the English House of Lords many centuries ago, said: "An advocate, in the discharge of his duty, knows but one person in all the world, and that person is his client. To save that client by all means and expedients, and at all hazards and costs to other persons, and, among them, to himself, is his first and only duty; and in performing this duty he must not regard the alarm, the torments, the destruction which he may bring upon others. Separating the duty of a patriot from that of an advocate, he must go on reckless of consequences, though it should be his unhappy fate to involve his country in confusion" (*Trial of Queen Caroline*, by J. Nightingale, vol. II, The Defence, Part I (1821), at p. 8).

CHAPTER 8
A Day in the Life of a Judge

Many people think that judges simply supervise trials and sentence convicted offenders; but judges have a great deal more to do than that. Judges are required to perform many judicial functions over the course of a typical day. In addition to their in-court activities, they also supervise pretrial conferences, meet with lawyers, see police officers about search and other kinds of warrants, write judgments (quite lengthy at times), and stay current with a large number of areas of the law. The professional life of a judge is not helped by the backlog of cases.

In this reading, a very experienced provincial court judge in one of Ontario's busiest courts describes a typical day in his professional life.

Judge David P. Cole, Ontario Court of Justice, Toronto

I became a lawyer in 1975, practising exclusively as criminal defence counsel until my appointment as a judge of the Ontario Court of Justice (Provincial Division)[1] in 1991. What follows is a narrative of a typical day in one court at the Metro East (Scarborough) court facility in Toronto, including its major phases and players, and the latter's communications with one another and before the bench. In order to better present what happens in a judge's life, the following explains—from one judge's perspective—daily life in court as court personnel and I go about our duties in dealing with the accused.

When I arrive at the court building each morning, I find on my desk in my office the list of the cases scheduled to be heard that day (the "docket"). On the day that I shall describe (September 1, 1998), I had to deal with the following charges: failing to appear (Mr. Ashbury); impaired driving (Ms. Andrus); breach of probation (Mr. Burns); assault (Mr. Fisher); mischief to private property / prowl by night (Mr. Goode); and two young offenders, K.B. and R.S.[2] On this particular day, Ms. Crisante[3] was the Crown assigned responsibility for prosecuting all the new cases on the trial list. Normally—though, regrettably, by no means always—the trial Crown is given the Crown files ("briefs") for preparation the afternoon before the court hearing.

The paperwork for even the simplest cases is often voluminous. For example, the charge of failing to appear against Mr. Ashbury was legally quite simple: Could the Crown establish to my satisfaction that Mr. Ashbury had an obligation to appear in court and that he had failed to do so? Once the Crown could prove these things, the *Criminal Code* directed that Mr. Ashbury would be found guilty of this offence unless he could establish that he had a lawful excuse for not appearing. However, there is considerable paperwork necessary to prove such a charge; at a minimum, the Crown would need certified copies of the form of the accused's release on bail, a certified copy of the charge that he failed to appear, and a certificate of the court clerk indicating that he had not appeared on the scheduled date. The trial Crown would then have the responsibility for checking to see that the investigating police officer (or, in this case, the accused's probation officer) had included all the necessary documents in the brief. Failure to do so would likely result in an aborted prosecution.

The Crown brief for the impaired driving charges against Ms. Andrus might be several centimetres thick, depending on the facts and issues raised. It would usually contain the statements of police officers and civilian witnesses, a computer printout of the accused's breath readings, reports from a toxicologist explaining the significance of those readings, and a videotape of some of the time she was in the police station. Also likely to be included would be photocopies of precedents from other cases that Crown counsel thinks the defendant might submit in arguing her case.

Unlike some European systems in which the presiding judge is deeply involved in investigating every detail of cases from their outset, the Canadian justice system is designed in such a way that the judge is supposed to know as little as possible about the cases he or she is assigned. Thus, I would not usually see much, if any, of this paperwork prior to the trial. Similarly, fairly elaborate steps are taken to ensure that I am not assigned to try cases of which I have any previous knowledge.

Before going into court, I normally do not look at the docket of the new cases I am about to try. On this day, the only cases with which I was familiar ahead of time were those concerning the two young offenders, K.B. and R.S. I had already started these cases on prior occasions, and these were the only cases to which Mr. Kerr, the other Crown listed on the court docket, had been assigned. As the day developed, he dealt with some of Ms. Crisante's cases in order to maximize efficient use of court time. She prepared herself to respond to last-minute arguments that defence counsel in Ms. Andrus's impaired driving case (driving with over .80 milligrams of alcohol per millilitre of blood) had announced he was going to raise.

As the first item of business, the Crown usually calls up the cases that defence counsel or the investigating police officer has not spoken to her about in order to determine the status of the cases. When Mr. Burns's case was called, he told me that he had not been able to arrange for a lawyer to represent him on the charge of breaching a probation order because he could not afford the $25 fee to process his application for legal aid. He asked to have his case adjourned. I examined the paperwork, which disclosed that Mr. Burns was charged with not paying the restitution that was part of a previous probation order. It also revealed that he had agreed several months earlier that he would proceed to trial on September 1 regardless of whether he had counsel. If I were to find Mr. Burns guilty, he faced the possibility of going to jail (depending on the circumstances of the breach and his previous record). Nevertheless, given his previous indication that he was prepared to proceed to trial without counsel, I ruled that unless there was some extraordinary reason for him to have another chance to get a lawyer, I would not grant a further adjournment.

Mr. Burns then told me that since the charge had been laid, he had paid off the outstanding order for restitution. At this point, Crown counsel intervened, saying that her brief indicated that while partial restitution had been made, a balance of $200 remained outstanding at the time the brief had been prepared, and that unless she received further information, she was not prepared to withdraw the charge. Mr. Burns said, "My old lady took a hundred dollar money order down to my PO [probation officer] last week."

I told the accused that while, in his mind, it might be true that he had "fixed it ... with his PO," could he please explain how he could have done this while $100 apparently remained outstanding? In response, Mr. Burns simply stared at the floor. The Crown explained to the accused that the probation officer had caused the accused to be charged because, in the probation officer's opinion, Mr. Burns had willfully declined to complete paying restitution when he was in a position to do so. I told Mr. Burns that it was up to the Crown, not his probation officer, to decide whether the charge would proceed, but that we should wait for the probation officer to arrive at court (due to pressure of work, they are almost always late) to further update the Crown.

Mr. Burns then told me that he could not wait because he had to go to work and asked what he "would get ... if I cop [plead guilty] to the charge." Such an inquiry by an accused is quite common and raises several difficult issues for the court system. First, while I told Mr. Burns that I would not and could not tell him in advance what I might do if he were to plead guilty, strictly speaking, this was not true. There are many cases in which I am consulted in advance if a plea bargain is contemplated. I did not feel comfortable doing so in this case because Mr. Burns had neither his own counsel nor duty counsel to advise him. For this reason, I sent him off to the duty counsel office in the hope that the standby duty counsel might be able to advise him. Unfortunately, he returned to court a few minutes later, saying that he had been told that the standby duty counsel was busy and would not be available for some time, if at all.

Surprising as it may sound, many accused enter pleas of guilty despite the fact that they may have legal or factual defences to the charge. They decide for their own reasons, which often seem very sensible to them, that they are not interested in presenting a defence. As a judge, I cannot accept a plea unless the accused makes an informed waiver of his or her rights and is prepared to admit to all the elements necessary to support the Crown's case. In this case, had Mr. Burns insisted on pleading guilty, because he was not represented by counsel, I would have conducted what is termed a "plea comprehension inquiry," reviewing with him his understanding of his right to contest the allegations and his willingness to admit to each element of the Crown's case. If he had balked at any stage, I would likely have struck the plea and remanded the case to another trial date. The practical difficulty that arises is that on the next date, the accused may go through the same process, this time pretending that he is making an informed waiver and conceding the elements of the case just so he can get it over with.

Luckily, by this time, Mr. Burns's probation officer had arrived. Crown counsel suggested that the case be "held down" to allow the parties the opportunity for some brief discussion. Although I was not privy to discussions among the accused, the probation officer, and Crown counsel, they eventually presented me with a compromise. Mr. Burns's case would be adjourned for 30 days. The parties agreed that if he voluntarily performed 25 hours of community service prior to the return date by way of extra punishment for not having done what he was supposed to do, the criminal charge would be withdrawn on the next appearance.

This case neatly illustrates several of the time allocation dilemmas regularly faced by the criminal justice system (and the extent to which the professionals are driven by the need to use court time as efficiently as possible). Given the relative unimportance of this case compared with the others on the list, the Crown likely had very little interest in prosecuting Mr. Burns that day, particularly since, being unrepresented, his case would probably have taken about 90 minutes to try. According to the Ministry of the Attorney General's current guidelines, a court day is supposed to consist of eight hours of trial time.[4] After extensive discussion in our court's delay reduction committee, our trial coordinator has been instructed to "load" 14 hours of trial time per day into a court such as this one. This is based on assumptions—well understood by court professionals though not by some accused and the general public—that a substantial number of cases will not proceed to trial despite having been scheduled as if they would be. As will be learned from what follows, Mr. Burns's case was the first of several that day to be diverted away from a trial.

Moreover, by the time the trial date comes up, Mr. Burns's probation term will have expired, thus making the agreement negotiated on the court date virtually unenforceable. When Mr. Burns's case next comes before the court (on September 30), if he has not performed the agreed-upon community service, all that can be done is to process the original charge of breaching his probation by failing to make restitution. Once again, Crown counsel assigned to this court on that date, facing another list containing at least 14 hours of cases, will not likely have much interest in prosecuting the charge.

Did Mr. Burns know or guess some or all of this? Did he put off the day of reckoning by luck or by design? I do not know for sure. Ironically, in our adversarial system, the judge in the courtroom is usually the person who least knows the accused. Apart from the brief series of questions I asked in response to his request for an adjournment, I am not supposed to engage in much dialogue with an accused. (And if Mr. Burns had had counsel there to represent him, he would likely have stood mute, leaving it up to his lawyer to speak on his behalf.) Because of this, over the years, I have learned to try as hard as I can to resist the human temptation to speculate and judge without sufficient evidence.

Although this example illustrates an acceptable way of proceeding, problems can and do occur when cases are not completed the same day that they start. This is particularly the case when the evidentiary portion of a trial has to be remanded to another day, as in the case of Ms. Andrus. The accused's lawyer brought a pretrial motion to dismiss the charges on the basis that she had not been given her constitutionally guaranteed right to counsel.[5] Because of the time needed to deal with the cases ahead of hers, her case could not be started until the afternoon (this is quite typical). The defence counsel's evidence on the motion to stop the proceedings (on the basis that her *Charter* rights had been violated) was already completed. In reply, the police testifying had given most of their evidence. Unfortunately, because of insufficient time, I had to defer the remainder of their testimony (including cross-examination by the defence) to March 4, 1999. After taking ten minutes of court time to deal with the trial coordinator's concerns and those of the lawyers, I determined that this was the earliest date that the time required could be matched with the schedules of the witnesses, the lawyers, and me.[6]

In such cases, in addition to taking what I hope are accurate notes of what is said by each witness as he or she gives his or her evidence, as soon as I leave court at the end of the day, I try to make notes immediately of how I am responding to the evidence as it is unfolding (recognizing, of course, that my preliminary impressions may change during the case). This includes such things as whether I think there is an adequate connection between Fact A and Fact B, why certain questions have not been asked (or properly answered), and, most importantly, what I think of the witnesses' credibility. While I try not to make up my mind until I have heard all the evidence and the lawyers' submissions, the reality of the situation is that given these lengthy delays and the danger of wrongly convicting an innocent person, most judges in this position would be more likely to acquit when the case is resumed six months later. This kind of ongoing resource problem is something that all court professionals are well aware of, and that is likely why the Crown seems resigned or disappointed while the defence seems quietly elated when the conclusion of the case is put off like this.

Why were more consecutive days not scheduled to avoid such unreasonable delays? This is a constant systemic problem that can be solved if more resources are available. As a result of aggressively pre-trying cases, Scarborough's courts have made significant efforts toward reducing the backlog of case.[7] However, despite repeated requests, no more resources are likely to be made available in the near future. As a result, cases such as this one tend to "slip through" the system.

What happened in Ms. Andrus's case was this: as soon as defence counsel decided that he wished to launch a "right to counsel" constitutional challenge, the court rules required him to serve a formal "Notice of a Constitutional Question" on the Crown and with the court. This notice must be filed at least 15 days prior to the trial date in order to give Crown counsel an opportunity to prepare to respond to the motion. He did not do so, asking that I permit him to proceed with his motion despite his failure to file it on time (which I have the power to do). He claimed that the reason he did not do so was simple inadvertence on his part. Crown counsel responded by saying that this was "too bad. The rules are there for a purpose. I am sick and tired of defence counsel going about their business as if the rules don't exist."

While I appreciated the defence counsel's apparent candour, how did this help me in deciding whether to allow him to argue the motion? Although I have not seen him for many years, the defence counsel was known to me as someone whose word could be accepted. Was he subtly reminding me, as an ex-defence counsel, that I, too, might have made such a slip and that I should not show him up in front of his client? Was he signalling to me that he wasn't really serious about the motion and was just going through the motions of presenting a defence? (After all, "right to counsel" issues are probably the most frequently argued motions under the *Charter*. A counsel as experienced as he surely would have noticed the issue earlier. From what I know of the case to date, that should have been easy.) Or was he signalling perhaps that his client was not paying him as quickly as he would have liked and that he was "playing hardball" with her, refusing to file the motion until she had completed paying his retainer?

And how should I have responded to the Crown's position? Should she, as soon as she realized that the defence had filed a motion, have filed a written application to dismiss it as being beyond the time frame allotted by the rules of procedure? That is doubtful unless this was an extremely serious case; and apart from the clerk in the office making sure that the motion was put in the Crown brief, no one in the Crown's office would have looked at the motion until late on August 31. What if the motion ultimately turned out to be valid, and the charges were dismissed for a breach of the accused's constitutional rights? Should I have refused to hear it simply because it was not filed on time?

What have I learned about this for the future? Should I be more careful with this particular lawyer if I see him in the future? Should I modify my practice in such cases to penalize counsel for sloppy conduct by saying that I will hear only out-of-time motions if they agree to pay for a complete transcript if the case has to be remanded to another date? Or might that only penalize the poor? Should I have ordered a transcript so that I am not forced to rely on my substantive notes of the evidence when the case is resumed?

The court clerk occupies a very important position. In addition to ensuring that all the various court documents are located and brought to court each day by the scheduled start time, he or she ensures that each time I make an order, it is accurately reflected in the court records. This may be as simple as ordering that a case be remanded to another date, or it may be very complicated, such as ensuring that varying terms of imprisonment or probation are properly apportioned to each charge. As I write this, the newspapers have reported an apparently appalling case in which an accused wrongly spent a week in jail. This took place despite several supposedly fail-safe procedures designed to protect against this very kind of miscarriage of justice. Apparently, someone had ticked off the wrong box on a court form designed to record judicial orders. Instead of recording that the accused had been given a year to pay his fine of $1,000, it was recorded that the accused had been sentenced to jail for a year. No one, including the justice of the peace who made the order, noticed the mistake.

In order to protect against this very type of error, many of the orders that I make—particularly penalties of various forms—are presented to me at least twice for signature: once when the court clerk writes up what I have said, and again when the formal order has been typed. On a very busy day, I might be asked to sign upward of 50 orders. Although I suppose I could refuse to sign them until I have had an opportunity to check them against my notes, the reality is that if I do that, everything will be delayed. If I delay signing remand papers for incarcerated accused, the jail will refuse to accept them, which means that the backlog of incoming prisoners to the jail at the end of the day will be extensive. If I decline to sign probation orders immediately, those placed on probation may tire of waiting and leave the court, not knowing when and where they are supposed to report next. Because I have realized that it causes all kinds of problems if I stop to read each paper in detail, like many other judges I have tacitly condoned the practice of agreeing to sign them as they are prepared. The result is that I am constantly having such papers thrust at me throughout the day, even when I am on the bench trying to concentrate on the proceedings. In practice, this means that the judge relies heavily on the court clerk and the support staff who type the orders to ensure their accuracy.

The problem does not end there. Despite the best efforts of the court personnel, errors occur because the staff are simply not trained to pick up some types of errors. This week, our court probation officer saw me about a case from some months ago. She pointed out that I had clearly made an error by imposing a period of probation in circumstances in which I had no power to do so. I did not spot the error at any stage (the day had been a particularly busy one), nor did the lawyers (who had urged this disposition on me). What is even sadder is that the accused, a man of limited intelligence, was clearly in no position to realize that he had been improperly dealt with.

According to ministry statistics, in 1997 I dealt (however briefly) with some 2,400 cases. Like other judges, I often worry about cases in which I may have made mechanical errors (such as errors writing the warrant), which may have resulted in an improper process being applied (or not applied[8]) against an accused.

As I have previously mentioned, the trial coordinator has been instructed to put more cases onto a trial list than can actually be dealt with. What happened with the rest of the cases is a good illustration of how this kind of daily gamble works.[9]

While Ms. Crisante was outside the courtroom "brokering" Mr. Burns's case, as usually occurs, she was also able to plea-bargain or divert all but Ms. Andrus's case. Some of the cases were relatively simple for her to deal with. In Mr. Fisher's case, the alleged assault victim (complainant) did not turn up at court, which happens in about 40 percent of cases. There may be many reasons for this: the complainant may have moved since the charge was laid on December 30, 1997, and may not have received the mailed subpoena; or the complainant may simply have decided that, having called in the police to intervene, he or she is not interested in proceeding with the charge.[10]

Even when complainants do come to court, as occurred in Mr. Goode's case, they may tell the Crown that they would be satisfied with a reduced charge. In that case, Mr. Goode, the accused, while drunk[11] and despondent about breaking up with his girlfriend, had hung around her townhouse one night intending to persuade her to resume their relationship. When she spurned his advances, he smashed the windshield of what he assumed was her new lover's car. In fact, the vehicle belonged to, as I was told, "her religious advisor."[12] What the ex-girlfriend wanted was an order for the accused to stay away from her. What the male complainant wanted was the cost of repairing his car. After verifying that the accused had lived up to the term of his bail order that required him not to communicate with his ex-girlfriend, Crown and defence counsel jointly proposed that I order the accused to post a "peace bond." In exchange for having the charge withdrawn, the accused would promise to keep the peace and be on good behaviour for one year. If he did not live up to the conditions of the order (staying away from the two complainants and making restitution for the windshield), he stood to lose $500 (the amount of the peace bond) and to be liable to be prosecuted for being in breach of the bond. All parties left the courtroom content.

Mr. Ashbury's case raised different issues. Given the carnage on our roads, police forces tend to be very intolerant of suspected drunk drivers. Even where there are few signs of impairment and the accused's breath reading is just over the limit (as happened here), police are under instructions to lay charges rather than sending the accused home in a cab. Because of aggressive lobbying by groups such as MADD (Mothers Against Drunk Driving), Crown counsel for many years have been under a directive to prosecute vigorously all drinking and driving charges. In part because of their lobbying, the severity of the mandatory minimum penalties has been increased considerably.

Unlike most other criminal charges, large numbers of middle-class people are charged with drinking and driving offences. As they wish neither the inconvenience of being without a licence (up to a year for a first offender) nor the stigma of a criminal record, they are often prepared to invest considerable resources in defending themselves against these charges. Thus, in most cities there are specialist defence counsel who devote much of their practices to defending impaired drivers.[13] They frequently employ expert toxicologists whose role is to uncover technical flaws in the Crown's case.

Once again, Crown counsel was faced with a dilemma that day. As only one other court had offered help (by now it was about noon), she could not send out Mr. Ashbury's case (or that of Ms. Andrus) to another court. Thus, she was virtually forced to enter into a plea bargain with Mr. Ashbury's very skilled defence counsel. Although I was not present during the plea bargaining (which all happened in Crown counsel's office), having done it myself for some 16 years, I can imagine that the conversation went something like this (salty language deleted):

Crown: If I agree to drop the charge of failing to appear, will your client plead to the over .80?

Defence: Forget it, I've got my tox [expert toxicologist] on standby, and he'll be able to provide "evidence to the contrary."

Crown: Well, in that case, I'll proceed on both, one at a time. Even if I lose one, if we don't finish today, you'll just have to come back. I've got to get something out of this.

Defence: You might lose both. You know these charges have been going since '92, and they might get thrown out for undue delay.

Crown: Yeah, but that's only because your client disappeared and wasn't rearrested until '97. Besides, you haven't filed a motion under the new rules, so you can't argue it anyway.

Defence: Judge Cole will let me abridge the time. You know these ex-defence counsel ...

Investigating Officer: Look, I've got better things to do than watch you two try to out-macho each other. I've been talking to the accused outside. He isn't a bad guy. He's got no other driving record that I know of and the [breath] readings were pretty low. I'm not interested in blood. I'll be content as long as he gets a big fine.

Crown: All right, with this reading, the new directive allows me to let him plead to careless driving under the provincial *Highway Traffic Act*. But he'll have to plead to the fail to appear.

Defence: Sounds good to me. At least, this way, he'll keep his licence. Give me ten minutes to talk to him.[14]

The bargain ultimately proposed was as follows: the Crown would allow the accused to plead guilty to the lesser charge of careless driving. Both parties would agree that the accused should be fined $1,000. The accused would plead guilty to failing to appear; in exchange, Crown counsel would agree not to ask for jail but would join in asking for a fine of $300. The accused would be given six months to pay.

According to the rules that are expected to guide me, I may depart from plea bargains if I find them offensive; but in order for all parties to know what to expect, I normally go along with them. I was entirely content to do so in this case. On the basis of what I was told (unlike some other cases, the first I heard of the contents of the plea bargain was in open court), the proposed disposition seemed entirely sensible, having been made by experienced counsel well aware of the strengths and weaknesses of the case.

During the time that Ms. Crisante had been negotiating outside court, Crown counsel Mr. Kerr was speaking to the continuing cases of the two young offenders (R.S. and K.B.) assigned to me. I describe these two cases in some detail not because young offenders are generally more violent (that is a myth unfortunately perpetuated by those who seek to make political hay through scaremongering), but because they illustrate the range of cases with which I deal on a daily basis.

In February 1997, I found R.S. guilty of armed robbery and aggravated assault. The accused had begun to demonstrate a variety of disturbed behaviours from about age ten. He was hospitalized from time to time, complaining that he had visual hallucinations and that demons were controlling him. He identified his parents as persecutors and from time to time had little to do with them, withdrawing to his room for days on end. One night in June 1996, just after his fourteenth birthday, he told his father he was going to the neighbourhood convenience store. He concealed a knife in his jacket, which he brandished at the proprietor. The accused fled the store, having taken 50 cents that happened to be sitting on the countertop. He was pursued by a friend of the proprietor. As they reached the other side of the road, R.S. was tackled to the ground. He stabbed his pursuer several times, necessitating some 40 stitches. Some of the victim's scarring was permanent.

The accused was arrested a few minutes later. When he was taken to the police station, he gave some coherent responses to questions asked by the officers. Sometimes, however, he spontaneously broke into monologues, claiming, "Kurt Cobain told me that the guy in the store was the Devil, and that I had to kill him or I would go to hell forever."

At first, there were questions about whether the accused was fit to stand trial. After some period of assessment in a psychiatric facility, during which he was assessed as suffering from a severe form of schizophrenic disorder, he was stabilized on medication so that he was deemed fit to stand trial. As the doctors who assessed him considered that he had been insane at the time he committed the offences, he raised the defence of insanity at his trial. I rejected that defence[15] and sentenced him to two-and-a-half years.

The *Young Offenders Act*[16] provides that an accused in these circumstances has the right to have his status reviewed every six months. R.S. insisted on availing himself of that right (I suspect because it gave him a day out of the facility he was being held in) despite the fact that, for many months, he had refused to take the medication that he so obviously needed. In his untreated state, he was prone to assaulting other prisoners and staff, which of course meant that he could not put together any release plan that had any hope of success. According to a report that had been forwarded to me as part of his review, progress seemed to have been made. He was now taking a medication that agreed with him (many schizophrenia medications have unpleasant side effects), and the social workers reported that he had become much easier to manage. Through his counsel, he agreed that his case should be remanded for another six months. I assumed that if his counsel felt that R.S.'s progress was sufficient, he would request a substantial hearing, at which time I could be asked to release him on probation.

The second young offender I dealt with that day was K.B. She was born in another country, and her father died in an accident when she was a few months old. Because her mother objected to that society's deeply rooted custom that women should not remarry, she elected to come to Canada, leaving the six-month-old K.B. in her grandparents' care. Although K.B. saw her mother every year for a few weeks, she did not live with her until she was six years old. Both agreed that, as unfortunately happens so frequently in these situations, mother and daughter did not bond well. This was compounded by the fact that soon after they began to live together, the mother became involved with a man whom she ultimately married.

Sometime after K.B. started high school, she began to go through teenage rebellion, albeit in a very moderate form. Her parents objected to the fact that she began to go out with J.C., a boy from a different culture. They told her that she could not continue the relationship. There were fights, often of a physical nature, between mother, stepfather, and daughter.

In April 1998, the parents told K.B. that she would be grounded until she stopped seeing J.C. The young couple met secretly and persuaded each other that the only way out was for them to murder her parents and get their money so that they could flee to the United States, where they "could live happily ever after."[17] After discussing this for a few days, K.B. let J.C. into her house in the middle of the night. By prearrangement, he had a mask and was armed with a large knife that he had taken from home. He crept into the parents' bedroom and started to slash at them while they were sleeping. He nearly severed the mother's thumb and stabbed both parents numerous times, fortunately not fatally. All the while, K.B. remained outside the room, listening to what was going on. After J.C. escaped, the police were called.

Since the parents were initially unclear as to whom their assailant was, K.B. was asked by the police to provide a description of the intruder. She told them that it was a "black youth with a Jamaican accent."[18] On the basis of her description, the police conducted an investigation. As the case had attracted some public attention, they issued a public warning containing this description and handed out fliers to neighbours warning them to be vigilant. Two days later, K.B. was questioned again, and this time she admitted that she had lied. J.C. was arrested and charged with attempted murder. (Ironically, he had confessed to his parents, who had assisted him in disposing of the knife and mask. They, too, were arrested and charged with obstructing justice.)

As this was an important case, one Crown counsel was immediately assigned to all three cases. The Crown applied to have J.C. transferred to be tried as an adult (he was fifteen); that hearing would take place before another judge at Scarborough court.[19]

Crown counsel Mr. Kerr realized from the outset that he had considerable legal hurdles in the prosecution of K.B. The only evidence against her on potential charges related to the attempted murder of her parents was her own confession to the police. Because the officers dealing with the case had not been fully trained in taking statements from young offenders, they had taken the incriminating statement from her as though she had been an adult. Unbeknown to these officers, the Supreme Court of Canada had recently insisted on very high standards of informed waiver before a statement taken from a young person could be admitted into evidence. It did not take long for Mr. Kerr to realize that he could not use K.B.'s statement to convict her.

The only other way the Crown could hope to convict K.B. would be to call J.C. as a witness against her. This could be very risky for the Crown. If J.C. was called without the Crown's knowing what he might say on the stand (he would likely refuse to cooperate with the Crown unless he got some benefit from it), he could say anything, some of which might hurt the Crown's case against K.B. If he was to be a cooperative witness, the Crown would likely secure his cooperation only by agreeing to some reduced charge against him, which it was not prepared to do, given the circumstances and the severity of the injuries caused. For these reasons, Crown counsel proposed (and defence counsel was only too happy to accept) to proceed only on a charge of public mischief (lying to the police) against K.B.

Although I was not the scheduled pretrial judge on the day the parties came to their proposed plea bargain, they asked to see me in chambers. This happens regularly at the Scarborough court. The lawyers "judge shop" as part of their plea bargain, seeking to find a judge who will agree in advance to commit him- or herself to a range of sentence.[20] They told me that the Crown would ask for a sentence of 12 to 18 months, but that I should make some allowance for the amount of pretrial custody that the accused would have served by the time I ultimately sentenced her. The defence would ask for probation, arguing that the amount of pretrial custody was equivalent to some ten months,[21] and that was sufficient given her age and Parliament's view of the seriousness of the offence, as expressed by the maximum possible penalty of two years. I agreed that counsel's suggestions were in the range, and that so long as mental health assessments (which I would order as soon as she pleaded guilty) were not devastating, I would not exceed the sentence sought by the Crown.

The accused entered her plea of guilty that same day, and the case was remanded so that mental health assessments and a predisposition report (a social history of the accused prepared by a youth probation officer) could be obtained. On September 1, the parties made their formal submissions based on the facts and what was disclosed in the various reports. Having heard what they said, I told the lawyers that I needed time to think about what they had said and put the case over until after my next chambers day on September 4.[22]

During the sentencing hearing, a joint victim impact statement was filed on behalf of both parents. I accepted it because both parties agreed that it should be filed. As I thought more about the case, I wondered if I should have done so. The report documented the devastating impact their daughter's behaviour had had on the parents' lives. They were both physically and mentally unable to work; it appeared that because they could not pay their mortgage, they would lose their home, their only form of substantial saving. However, because of the accused's guilty plea, I was not, strictly speaking, sentencing her for her part in causing harm to her parents. I concluded that what had happened on that awful night only provided the backdrop for the lies that she told the police. As a result, I decided that I should factor in the victim impact statements only to the extent that they would give me some sort of clue to the accused's likelihood of reoffending (the psychiatric report concluded that it was low), and only because they told me that her parents were not prepared to offer her any support at this time.

On September 10, I gave oral reasons, sentencing the accused to 10 months of open custody, followed by 12 months' probation. The lengths of the various terms were tailored around the accused's schooling (school is a real strength for her). Like R.S., she could come back to ask me to review her status after six months of open custody.

This, then, is part of a day in the life of a busy court. It is usually intense, sometimes tragic, always human, and endlessly fascinating. It may even be socially useful.

DISCUSSION QUESTIONS

1. *In this chapter, Judge Cole discusses the issue of plea bargaining, a common practice in the Canadian criminal justice system. Some people argue that this practice should be abolished since it undermines public confidence in the justice system. What is your opinion?*

2. *Judge Cole notes that the law generally prohibits the publication of the name of a young person facing a charge in youth court. The news media often argue that they should be free to routinely publish the names of young persons appearing youth court. Do you agree or disagree with their position?*

ENDNOTES

1. At the time of writing, the Provincial Division of the Ontario Court of Justice comprises about 260 judges, about 180 of whom preside over 95 percent of the criminal cases in the province.
2. Initials are used because the *Young Offenders Act* provides that no young offender's name may be published.

3. As of the date of writing, this particular Crown's office employs almost 50 percent women, up from about 30 percent when I started as a judge in Scarborough in 1991. This reflects the general trend in the Ontario bar, where now over 50 percent of recent graduates are women. Currently in Ontario, the percentage of Provincial Division women judges is still less than one-third, and even fewer in the Superior Court.

4. I have no idea where the bureaucrats come up with this notional figure. To allow for the movement of prisoners from remand centres to the court (some may be transported as much as 40 km through rush-hour traffic), experience demonstrates that it is almost impossible to start a trial court before 10:00 a.m. Because it is very difficult for court reporters to concentrate for longer than about 90 minutes at a time, on the best of days, morning court goes from 10:00 a.m. to 1:00 p.m. with a 15- to 20-minute break. Court normally resumes at 2:00 p.m., again with an afternoon break. Court usually recesses at 4:30 p.m. to allow court staff to finish their paperwork and prisoners to be returned to their remand centres.

5. Section 10(b) of the *Canadian Charter of Rights and Freedoms* provides: "Everyone has the right on arrest or detention to retain and instruct counsel without delay and to be informed of that right." The Supreme Court of Canada has generally interpreted this to mean that an accused should have the right to telephone a lawyer as soon as practicable following arrest or detention. Police forces have responded to this by providing private access to duty counsel or a private lawyer by telephone from the police station.

6. The reason that this cumbersome process took place on the record in open court was that, in fact, there were some earlier dates available. Knowing that the case was already on the verge of being dismissed for taking too long to come to trial, everyone (including myself in an oblique way) felt the need to protect his or her position by saying that, while he or she could be available, it was the other party's "fault" that they could not take advantage of those dates. Some of the final compromises were interesting. The police officer had to telephone his staff sergeant to get approval to come to court on a date he was scheduled to be away, thereby being eligible to "pick up a court card," entitling him to be paid at double the normal shift rate. He was obviously delighted. Defence counsel and the accused were also content because they could defer the potential day of reckoning by another six months (if convicted, Ms. Andrus stood, at the very least, to lose her licence for a year). Crown counsel, who is currently working part-time, seemed mostly concerned about adjourning this to a date when her child care needs could be accommodated (so that another Crown attorney would not be forced to take over the case). For myself, March 4 was a scheduled "chambers day," a regularly scheduled time during which I am supposed to read the approximately 500 pages of case law, legislative updates, and other items of interest that cross my desk each week, or to write judgments or articles (such as this one).

One of my concerns was whether the trial coordinator could find me another chambers day.

7. Since January 1996, as a result of the police, the Crowns, the Legal Aid Plan, and the judges finding new resources or diverting existing staff, we have cut our backlog by 32.5 percent. However, because we have done so well, the bureaucrats have deemed that we are no longer on the chronic list of courts experiencing extreme delays, and it has been difficult for us to argue that our Crown and judicial complement should be maintained. As a result, both complements have been somewhat cut back, and we are beginning to slip again, as this delay signifies.

8. An example of this arose here. As I was typing this article, I realized that in the case of Mr. Ashbury's charge of failing to appear, I should have at least considered whether to impose a 15 percent victim surcharge to his $300 fine under the *Criminal Code*. These surcharges are to be applied to raise money for various forms of victim support services. Neither the Crown nor the clerk drew this to my attention, and I simply neglected to raise the issue.

9. I leave it to the reader to consider whether this fits the definition of a "working" criminal justice system. Some observers have questioned whether it is "a system" at all.

10. This seems particularly to be the case in charges of wife assault. Consistent with data from other jurisdictions, recent Toronto figures suggest that about 40 percent of complainants do not appear for trial. (Anecdotal evidence from Crowns who prosecute such cases puts the figure even higher.) This is the case despite police and prosecutorial directives mandating "no tolerance" responses to such incidents.

11. There is some consensus among criminal justice professionals that alcohol or drugs figure in about 75 percent of criminal offences.

12. What he was doing there at 11:00 p.m. on a Saturday night was not made clear to me. Sometimes criminal court offers wonderful opportunities for creating fantastic fiction à la Marquez or for reciting Shakespearian verse à la Rumpole!

13. The going rate in Toronto for some of the top counsel at the time of writing is about $5,000 per case, not including the costs of various experts. It may even be higher in areas of the country where there is no public transit. Accused people willingly pay this fee because of the economic and social costs of doing without a licence.

14. Variants of this type of conversation occur every day. Depending on the exhaustion level of the lawyers, more bargaining (some would call it haggling) can take place over the amount of the proposed fine. Interestingly, the lawyers would be unlikely to bargain about the length of time the accused should have to pay the fine. For his part, the accused might be less concerned about the amount of the fine; he would likely be more concerned about how long he would have to pay it. This illustrates one of the fundamental differences between lawyers and accused.

The former tend to be more concerned about form, while the latter tend to be more concerned with substance.

15. Insanity pleas are quite rare. This is the only one I have had since my appointment. On the other hand, dispositions of "not criminally responsible" (another type of mental impairment defence) are relatively frequent. I probably hear one (usually on consent of both parties) about once every two months.

16. On April 1, 2003, the *Young Offenders Act* was replaced by the *Youth Criminal Justice Act*. The processes here remain the same under the new law.

17. K.B. later told the police that one of her other motivations for the offence was that her stepfather had sexually assaulted her on several occasions. She refused to provide the police with any further information and indicated that she did not wish to have her stepfather charged.

18. The racial stereotyping is particularly troubling.

19. Obviously, that judge and I refrain from talking with each other about our respective cases. Given the seriousness of the matters, each of us might have to solicit the advice of our colleagues, who, as always, are generous with their advice. We have agreed to handle this by leaving the lunchroom whenever the other wishes to discuss the case with another colleague.

20. Appellate courts across the country have been very clear that, because plea bargains so obviously give the impression that what happens in open court merely rubber-stamps what has been worked out in advance (the very term "plea bargain" is frowned on by the appellate courts, and judges usually prefer to use such neutral phrases as "pretrial discussions"), the judge should decline to agree to any particular sentence and agree only, if at all, to a particular range or type of sentence. Frankly, this is observed daily in the breach in busy provincial courts. Many of us consider that if we do not agree to precise plea bargains, our lists will likely be even more backlogged. Luckily, in this case, the parties came to me with a range of sentence rather than a precise sentence proposal.

21. Although, as a matter of law, I do not have to make any allowance for pretrial custody in the sentence ultimately imposed, the Supreme Court of Canada has ruled that an allowance should normally be made, usually on a "two-for-one basis." In other words, for each day spent in pretrial custody, two days should be taken off the normally appropriate sentence.

22. In fact, in addition to my chambers day, I spent a lot of time reading and thinking about this case throughout the Labour Day weekend. The judicial life may seem "cushy" to outsiders (our salaries are good, our pensions are excellent, we get 8 weeks of holidays and up to 36 chamber days per year, and we cannot be fired except in the most extreme circumstances). However, most judges I know spend much of their weekends and some of their holidays preparing for upcoming cases.

CHAPTER 9
The Probation Officer's Report

When most members of the public think about the criminal justice professionals who run the justice system, lawyers, judges, and police officers come most readily to mind. Probation officers have a lower public profile than these other professions; yet in many respects, their role in the criminal justice system is critical because most offenders are sentenced to community-based sanctions. As Karen Middlecoat, an experienced probation officer in Ontario, describes in this chapter, members of the probation service supervise offenders on probation, offenders serving conditional sentences of imprisonment in the community, and provincial parolees.

Supervising offenders is a challenging task. Although the probation officer must ensure that the court-ordered conditions of the probation order or conditional sentence order are observed, offenders also need assistance in taking steps toward rehabilitation. When a condition of a probation order or conditional sentence order appears to have been violated, the probation officer must decide whether to return the offender to court. This is a difficult decision, since it may well result (particularly if the offender is serving a conditional sentence) in the imprisonment of the offender.

Karen Middlecoat, Probation Officers' Association of Ontario

Several years ago, a distinguished justice at the Superior Court of Ontario was invited to be a guest speaker at a professional development day for probation and parole officers. He praised us for helping troubled individuals in times of dwindling social resources and expressed almost bewildered admiration for us. In fact, he confessed, "To be honest with you, when judges don't know what to do with someone, we put them on probation." The feelings of relief and validation in the room were practically palpable: finally, a judge was acknowledging what we had known all our professional lives.

CASELOAD OF A PROBATION OFFICER

In Ontario, approximately 1,000 probation officers supervise approximately 75,000 individuals, comprising about 20,000 young persons and 55,000 adults. Young persons (aged 12 to 17) are actively supervised as alternative-measures cases, probation cases, and open custody residents. Adults (aged 18 and older) are probationers, conditional sentence cases, and provincial parolees. Probation officer caseloads vary significantly from small towns to major cities, and the duties of probation officers vary widely across the province. In parts of northern Ontario, probation officers have smaller caseloads but are required to fly into remote areas to see clients. In Toronto, probation officers have adult caseloads that average approximately 120 clients. Young person probation officers may have fewer clients, but their responsibilities are more extensive, since they must maintain ongoing contact with parents, schools, and counselling agencies.

Generally, most probation officers supervise adult offenders, who are defined as persons 18 years of age or over on the date of their offence. Adults report to probation officers for several reasons, but most are supervised on a *probation order*. A probation order is a legal document requiring the offender to comply with certain probation conditions for a specific period of time. An adult probation order cannot exceed three years, although some offenders can be on probation continuously for several years, if judges continue to place them on probation each time they are sentenced. Probation orders have four standard conditions:

1. The offender shall keep the peace and be of good behaviour;
2. The offender shall appear before the court when required to do so by the court;
3. The offender shall notify the probation officer before any change of name or address; *and*
4. The offender shall notify the probation officer before any change of education or employment.

In addition, judges can impose other conditions designed to respond to the specific needs of the particular offender. For example, a court can order an offender to reimburse the victim or perform unpaid work for the community. Probationers may also be ordered not to go to certain locations. An example of this type of condition would be one prohibiting the offender from entering certain premises where the offence occurred. Someone found guilty of shoplifting could be forbidden from entering the store where the offence was committed; a man convicted of assaulting his wife could be prohibited from returning to the marital home; or a woman convicted of communicating for the purpose of prostitution could be barred from entering a part of the city after the judge has specified the perimeter of the prohibited area.

ENSURING THAT THE CONDITIONS OF PROBATION ARE OBSERVED

Despite the obvious intent of the probation conditions to assist offenders while deterring them from committing further offences, these same conditions are fraught with enforcement difficulties. The enforcement of probation conditions is an important part of a probation officer's job. According to Canada's *Criminal Code*, an adult has breached probation when he or she has failed or refused to comply with a probation condition "without reasonable excuse." Therefore, not every violation of probation results in the offender's return to court; and probation officers must make the final decision whether or not to charge an individual with breaching a probation order.

Discretion is often exercised regarding the reporting condition (the obligation to report to a probation officer) of a probation order, as it is the most common optional condition and therefore the most often violated. Probation officers will rarely charge a client who has missed one or two appointments, even if the reason is one of simple forgetfulness. However, if the offender establishes a pattern of missing scheduled appointments after having repeatedly been cautioned, a probation officer will pursue a charge, since this is clearly unreasonable. In the case of high-risk offenders, the probation officer would not wait for a pattern to be established because the safety of a victim or the general public would be of paramount concern. Conversely, if there are extenuating circumstances, a probation officer may choose not to charge an individual even if the reporting condition has been violated.

Difficulties can arise in some circumstances when the offender has mental health problems and doesn't understand the importance of keeping appointments. In these cases, a "reasonable excuse" is somewhat evident, but the probation officer will not take the risk of leaving such an individual in the community without some sort of ongoing supervision. Instead, the probation officer will override the reasonable excuse rule, err on the side of caution, and lay a breach of probation charge in order to protect the individual and the community, especially if medication or the lack thereof was of particular concern.

The case of Benjamin illustrates this issue. Benjamin was a 30-year-old who suffered from a bipolar affective disorder and refused to take medication. He was also in a wheelchair due to the amputation of both his legs following a suicide attempt at a subway station. He was on a two-year probation order for fraud accommodation and assault, resulting from a hotel stay for which he refused to pay and spat on one of the employees. Benjamin was ordered to report to a probation officer as often as directed, but he had no fixed address and could not be contacted. The probation officer made contact with Benjamin's parents and left messages for Benjamin, since he would phone his parents occasionally to ask for money. Benjamin called his probation officer twice and flatly stated that he had no intention of reporting. The probation officer decided to charge him for not reporting and issued a warrant for his arrest.

Approximately three months after the warrant was issued, Benjamin was arrested again in a hotel room for damaging furniture and smashing mirrors. He was sentenced in court several months later and received more probation with a condition to attend for psychiatric counselling. Unfortunately, he never reported and within two months had committed suicide. In this case, the probation officer had realized that Benjamin, given his medical condition, would probably never report or attend psychiatric counselling, regardless of how many probation orders he was given or how many times he was charged with breaching probation. Yet the probation officer still charged him in an attempt to protect Benjamin from himself and to fulfill probation services' responsibility to the community and to the justice system. Unfortunately, doing all the right things did not ultimately help Benjamin.

Community service work, which requires the offender to perform volunteer work, can cause problems if the offender has full-time employment as well as other responsibilities that limit his or her ability to complete the hours ordered. Occasionally, community service work has been ordered on offenders who are long-distance truck drivers, construction workers who work twelve-hour shifts, single mothers with full-time jobs, and young offenders in school with homework and part-time jobs. Individuals in these categories have difficulty performing the work ordered by the court.

Even more problematic is community service work that is imposed on individuals, such as sex offenders and persons with disabilities, who are difficult to place in a community service work agency. Community service is equally imposed on individuals who are capable of performing the hours but who choose not to perform the prescribed hours. When community service becomes problematic, the probation officer must consider all the facts and decide whether or not to charge the offender, keeping in mind that the *Criminal Code* states that a breach of probation has been committed when the offender has failed or refused to comply with probation "without reasonable excuse."

The different situations of Charlene and David illustrate the discretion that a probation officer must exercise regarding community service work enforcement. Charlene was a 36-year-old single mother of a 6-year-old girl. She had been convicted of shoplifting and ordered to perform 100 hours of community service work at a rate of 10 hours per month during a one-year probation order. However, because she had a full-time job, Charlene had only limited time on weekends to perform community service at the food bank to which she had been assigned. She managed to perform community service every month but never completed the prescribed monthly rate of 10 hours. At the expiration of her probation, Charlene had completed only 68 of the 100 hours ordered; yet her probation officer decided to exercise her discretion not to return her to court. Given Charlene's circumstances, she had made a reasonable effort toward completing her community service work.

In contrast, David was a 20-year-old, convicted of possession of stolen property. He lived with his parents, who were aware of his offence and his probation term with its requirement to perform 100 hours of community service work at a rate of 10 hours per month during a one-year probation order. For the community service, David was placed at a church that provided hot meals and beds to homeless people. David was not in school and worked sporadically for a friend's roofing business when work was available. David failed to perform any hours for the first three months, citing forgetfulness, work opportunities, and vague references to insufficient time. He was cautioned that if he failed to begin his hours he would be returned to court and charged with failing to perform community service work at the monthly rate.

During the third quarter of probation, David performed a total of 22 hours; and in the final three months, he completed another 15 hours, for a total of 37 hours. He was returned to court, found guilty of not completing community service work, and given another year's probation with a condition to perform a fresh set of 100 hours of community service work. One may assume that the judge's intention was to let David know that he could not avoid the imposition of community service work; certainly, David knew now that he had a second conviction on his criminal record. During his second probation order, David performed 53 hours, but his employment situation had not changed and his reasons for incompletion remained vague and unsubstantiated. He was again returned to court and fined $400 with no more probation or community service work.

RESTITUTION

The court's intention when imposing a restitution condition is more straightforward; yet the "reasonable excuse" clause raises much more complex issues. When the amount of money is relatively small and the offender's ability to make restitution is established, then restitution is usually paid and no enforcement is necessary. However, if the amount is considerable and the offender is unable to pay the entire amount, then he or she is practically set up for failure and subsequent enforcement.

Although the probation officer could exercise discretion and not breach the individual if the "reasonable excuse" clause is applicable, all restitution cases have victims, unlike community service work, and the recipients are persons who have no recourse to reclaim their money except via the courts. In these cases, probation officers are very reluctant to deny the victims their entitlement to see the offender held accountable for nonpayment. For this reason the offender will be brought back to court and a judge will decide what the appropriate response to nonpayment should be.

The case of Edward is a good example of the way in which a court's best intentions can miscarry, creating a dilemma for the probation officer. Edward was a 46-year-old man convicted of defrauding his landlord of approximately $30,000. Edward was sentenced to the maximum of three years' probation to allow him as much time as possible to repay the victim. However, the court's restitution condition read as follows:

> ... to pay restitution at a monthly rate until the restitution is paid in full. A monthly amount will not be specified but a payment must be made each and every month until probation expires.

Unfortunately, the order did not stipulate that the full amount of restitution was to be paid by the end of the probation period; and as no monthly rate was given, the offender made a monthly payment, by money order, of one cent. In an attached letter that accompanied his first payment, the offender made it clear that he was not breaching the restitution condition in any way and even acknowledged that, although he had to pay four dollars every month to purchase a money order, he would still pay only one cent monthly to the victim.

Although the probation officer had the option to return the case to the original judge and request a variation in the payment schedule, the effort may not have gained the desired result; and the offender, or his attorney, could express an objection to a more onerous payment system. Nevertheless, the probation officer was able to advise the victim that financial recovery was available to him through a civil court action. The victim agreed to pursue this remedy but expressed great frustration at the expense of time and money to regain his own money.

Another example of an unsuccessful restitution case is that of Frank, a 33-year-old convicted of mischief to private property. Following an argument in a bar, Frank left the establishment and vandalized his opponent's truck. He was convicted and ordered to pay $1,800 restitution over a two-year probation period. Frank lived in the basement apartment of his parents' home but had very little interaction with them, since his parents were aware that Frank sold drugs while receiving disability income. However, they felt somewhat protective of Frank as he had developed some brain damage from years of drug use and could not maintain regular employment. Over the two years of probation, Frank reported regularly but insisted that the victim would just keep the $1,800, as his insurance company would cover the cost of the repairs. Frank was advised repeatedly that he had still been held responsible by the court for damages and had a legal requirement to compensate the victim.

While on probation for mischief, Frank was arrested and convicted of cocaine possession and sentenced to two weeks' imprisonment and one year's probation. Upon expiration of his first probation order, Frank had paid only $350 of the total restitution and was returned to court for breaching probation. At the time of his trial Frank stated that he could not afford to pay the stipulated amount due to his limited income on disability, but had done the best he could. He was acquitted of the charge of breach of probation.

Cases such as Edward's and Frank's reinforce probation services' ongoing desire not to be utilized as collection agencies by the courts; however, when restitution is successful, it communicates a worthwhile lesson for the offender and provides the victim with a sense of closure rarely experienced by other victims in the justice system.

ENFORCING CONDITIONS THAT RESTRICT AN OFFENDER'S LIFESTYLE

Ironically, the easiest violations of probation to prove are also the most difficult on which to obtain convictions; these are the "lifestyle" conditions. Such conditions include requiring the offender to abstain from alcohol or drugs, or to see a mental health professional on a regular basis. Violations of these abstinence- or treatment-related conditions are often discovered by the police, who apprehend the individual in an intoxicated state, or by the probation officer, who can determine a client's compliance with psychiatric treatment though a phone call to the relevant mental health professional.

Although the offender's noncompliance can be clearly established, determining that the offender breached the condition "without reasonable excuse" is very difficult, as some judges may consider substance abuse and mental illness medical conditions over which an individual has little control. As a result, a court that imposes a probation condition prohibiting the offender from consuming alcohol or nonprescription drugs can unintentionally bring the offender back into the system. Furthermore, requiring the offender to seek treatment for substance abuse, psychological difficulties, or even spousal abuse does not guarantee that the offender will comply with the condition, and a return to court for a breach of the treatment condition may hold the offender accountable without addressing the underlying problem that gave rise to the offending.

The most common cases are those like George's, involving substance abuse. George was a 48-year-old convicted of assault. After consuming alcohol, George slapped and pushed his wife, who called police. He was found guilty and placed on probation for 18 months with a condition to attend counselling for partner assault. However, the court acknowledged that alcohol was a factor in the assault and added a condition on the probation order that instructed the offender "to consume alcohol moderately." Unfortunately, no one advised the court that George was in fact an alcoholic, and that by his standards, moderation in alcohol consumption was not in all likelihood the standard that the court intended. The probation officer could not send George to alcohol counselling as only partner abuse counselling had been ordered, and George expressed no interest in going voluntarily. Therefore, although the probation officer arranged partner abuse counselling and cautioned George that failure to complete the program would result in a breach, his inherent problem of alcohol abuse remained untreated.

Probation orders that require the offender to "abstain absolutely from the purchase, possession, or consumption of alcohol" also cause enforcement difficulties for probation officers. Monitoring these conditions is simply not possible, and violations are rarely discovered unless the offender is in public and arrested by police. Interesting exceptions, however, are cases like Harry, an admitted alcoholic, who was found guilty of impaired driving. He was fined $1,200, placed on probation for one year, required to attend a program, and prohibited from drinking for one year. Harry was self-employed in his own well-established renovations company and stated that he could not attend any residential program but agreed to attend weekly AA meetings held at the probation office.

Within a few months, Harry's wife notified the probation officer that Harry had been violating his abstinence condition. As she was the only person who could testify that Harry had been drinking, she was advised that she would be required to attend court as the sole witness. Immediately she stated that she would not go to court to testify against her husband. When the probation officer indicated that the incidents would be discussed with Harry at his next appointment, she begged the officer not to say anything to Harry as he would know she had informed the probation officer of his violations. In such cases, probation officers are placed in a difficult position: between confronting the offender on the one hand, and violating the wife's request for secrecy on the other. Here, if the probation officer returned Harry to court to hold him accountable for violating his abstinence condition, the case risked a withdrawal if Harry's wife, who was the sole witness, failed to testify. Furthermore, once Harry's probation order expired, he would be able to resume drinking and cease attending AA meetings, and one could only hope that the program would have had a sufficiently positive effect on him to encourage him to seek out meetings in the community voluntarily.

Treatment and counselling conditions raise similar concerns, and no offence is a better example than domestic assault. Ian was a 32-year-old convicted of assaulting his wife. He was prohibited from returning home until he had completed a program for partner assault and had obtained written permission from his wife allowing him to return home. Ian attended two sessions of the 16-week program and then stopped, stating that he had no time to go. He was charged by the probation officer, returned to court, found guilty, and ordered to attend the program again. Again he failed to complete the sessions; he also began harassing his wife with phone calls and unscheduled visits. She called the police, and again, Ian was returned to court. He was sentenced to 30 days in jail and probation for one year, with a condition, for the third time, to attend counselling. He failed to attend the program and within weeks had seriously assaulted his wife, breaking her arm and nose. He was incarcerated for eight months; but despite three probation orders, counselling conditions, and custodial sentences, Ian believed that his right to see his wife superseded any legal authority that stipulated otherwise. Cases like Ian's are common in the justice system, and despite the thorough work of police, probation officers, and the courts, Ian's wife and women like her continue to live in fear.

Indeed, all cases that involve high-risk offenders, high-need offenders, or persons with serious charges require more intensive supervision from the probation officer. Within the past five years, procedures regarding the supervision of sex offenders, domestic assault offenders, and mental health and substance abuse cases have become more complex and stringent, stressing ongoing contact with the offenders, victims, and treatment agencies. Although probation officers recognize the necessity of these standards, the resulting escalation in workload has detracted from their time spent with lower-risk clients, some of whom form a bond with their probation officers and grow to rely on them for support and guidance. Many probation officers choose their profession because they enjoy human interaction and genuinely want to "help people." Ironically, the ones they may be able to help the most are the ones with whom they can't spend enough time, due to ever-increasing workloads and the court's reliance on community supervision as the most frequently used sentencing option.

CONDITIONAL SENTENCE OFFENDERS

Probation officers also supervise offenders serving conditional sentences of imprisonment. Conditional sentences were introduced in 1996 as an additional sentencing option to fill the void between probation and incarceration. Conditional sentence offenders have committed a crime that warrants imprisonment, but because the court does not consider them a threat to the community, they are allowed to serve the sentence at home. Some examples are offenders who have committed serious frauds or violent offences, but who may have full-time jobs and families to support.

The conditions of probation orders are also standard on conditional sentences, but the reporting condition that is optional on a probation order becomes a mandatory condition for a conditional sentence. Notably, the only additional mandatory condition on conditional sentences prohibits the offender from leaving the province without written permission from the probation officer. One major difference between probation orders and conditional sentence orders is that the latter will often include a condition of house arrest that confines the offender to his or her home, except for court-authorized exceptions. Unfortunately, when judges list exceptions beyond work, religious services, and medical emergencies, house arrest loses much of its perceived effectiveness. The recent case of John illustrates this problem.

John was given a one-year conditional sentence for aggravated assault and assault causing bodily harm against an ex-girlfriend and her new boyfriend. He was placed under house arrest, but among the exceptions to confinement was permission to shop for groceries. This exception gave John free rein to be in the community, since he would have a ready explanation for any absence from home. Conditions with exceptions of this kind create problems for the probation officer and do not enforce the intended restrictions.

Theoretically, the enforcement of conditional sentences is intended to be a much swifter process than probation enforcement; but in practice this is generally not the case. Unlike an alleged breach of probation, which is an entirely new criminal charge, an alleged breach of a conditional sentence simply results in a court hearing, during which the onus is upon the offender to prove that he or she did not violate the conditional sentence. If a breach is deemed to have occurred, the presiding justice has four options:

1. Take no action;
2. Change the optional conditions;
3. Suspend the conditional sentence and direct that the offender serve a portion of the unexpired sentence in custody with the balance to resume upon release; *or*
4. Terminate the conditional sentence and direct that the offender serve the full balance of the conditional sentence in custody.

Unfortunately, the conditional sentencing process is in its legal infancy, and the implications of conditional sentence conditions are still being discovered. An example is the case of Lloyd, who received a one-year conditional sentence for assaulting his wife for the second time in three years. Lloyd was ordered to attend partner abuse counselling and to complete it by the end of his conditional sentence. Due to an extensive waiting list and some delays on Lloyd's part, he began the program nine months after the conditional sentence started. Lloyd attended every session until his conditional sentence expired, at which point four sessions remained outstanding. Lloyd refused to complete the program but could not be breached by the probation officer because no balance remained on the order that could be converted to custody.

YOUNG PERSONS

Probation for young persons offers many of the options available to adults; however, the maximum period for young person probation is two years, rather than the three years for adults. The same issues exist for monitoring and enforcing young person orders; however, a notable distinction relates to the influence of peer groups—an effect seen regularly among young persons whose offences involve co-accused who occasionally are fellow gang members.

Mark was a 17-year-old found guilty of theft over $5,000 and possession over $5,000. He had stolen his parents' car; and when police found him in a parking lot with two friends hours after the car had been reported stolen, all three were charged, although Mark's two co-accused eventually had their charges dropped. One of Mark's conditions prohibited him from having any contact with his two friends; however, information from the police indicated that Mark had stolen the car as part of his initiation into a gang and had met his friends to show successful completion of his task. Mark denied any connection to a gang during interviews with his probation officer, and the requisite loyalty to his group overrode any court-imposed nonassociation condition or any threat of enforcement that his probation officer could make.

Generally, the courts impose as few conditions as possible on young persons, favouring the restorative and rehabilitative aspects of probation as they relate to the offence. However, some conditions become onerous and present the probation officer with clear challenges.

Nagenthan was a 17-year-old found guilty of theft under $5,000 after he shoplifted a portable CD player from an electronics store. He was placed on probation for one year and prohibited from entering the electronics store. Nagenthan was also ordered to take classes in English as a Second Language. Although he was 17 at the time of the offence, he had turned 18 by the time of sentencing and had already graduated from grade 12, with plans to attend college the coming September. Because the ESL condition had no relevance to his offence and conflicted with his college schedule and part-time job at a local restaurant, the probation officer exercised his discretion and advised Nagenthan that the ESL condition would be set aside providing that the youth continue his education and employment.

Another notable difference between adult and young person supervision is the involvement of parents. The probation officer must establish contact with the parents or guardians to ensure that information is being exchanged regularly. However, some parents have the misplaced belief that once their child has been through the justice system and now has a probation officer to whom he or she must report and legal requirements with which to comply, discipline issues and behavioural problems at home will be corrected. Sadly, this is not the case. Probation officers explain to parents that, as agents of the court, they can only enforce the conditions of probation and offer the youth some guidance, not guarantee improvements in the youth's behaviour. Probation officers often receive calls from parents complaining that their child is out late, not doing house chores, or not telling them where he is going or with whom he is socializing. Indeed, a parent once called her son's probation officer and complained that he was still leaving dirty dishes in the kitchen sink and not cleaning his room, despite being on probation!

Obviously, the probation officer has no authority over the young person in these circumstances, although some parents believe that probation officers could fix problems in one year that had developed over the previous sixteen. Conversely, some probation orders will require the youth to "be amenable to the routine and discipline of the family home," and in many cases this stipulation will bring some sort of clear expectations into the household, especially if the probation officer meets with the youth and his parents and writes a contract that all parties sign.

Regrettably, this well-intentioned condition may not achieve its desired results, as in the case of Paula, a 16-year-old found guilty of assaulting her mother for refusing to give her money. Paula was placed on probation for 18 months and required to report to a probation officer, write a letter of apology to her mother, reside at home, and be amenable to the routine and discipline of the home. The probation officer met with Paula and her mother and wrote out a contract with four rules regarding curfew, chores, phone privileges, and respectful behaviour.

Approximately five months later, Paula's mother advised the probation officer that the home situation was deteriorating and that rules were not being followed. At the next probation appointment, Paula admitted that she was breaking rules but that her mother was becoming too unreasonable. The probation officer suggested family counselling but Paula refused. The probation officer then arranged for Paula and her mother to attend the next appointment together; however, Paula's mother called the officer within a few weeks and advised that money and jewellery were missing and that Paula's whereabouts were unknown.

Clearly, the probation officer had a difficult decision to make: either wait and hope that Paula would resurface, thus avoiding reinvolvement in the court system with more criminal charges; *or,* issue a warrant for her arrest and have the police actively look for her so as to forestall any harm she might encounter on the city streets. By the next week, Paula's mother called the officer. She'd heard from friends of her daughter that Paula was staying with various acquaintances and had no intention of returning home. Paula's mother was becoming extremely anxious about her daughter's safety and questionable companions, and the officer decided to issue the warrant. Paula's mother was advised and encouraged to tell Paula's friends of the warrant in the hope that Paula would contact the probation officer. Soon enough, Paula called her officer to question the existence of the warrant, but she refused to go to the local police station to address the outstanding charge and stated unequivocally that she had no intention of returning home.

Months later, Paula was arrested for shoplifting and the outstanding warrant came to light. Paula was found guilty of both offences and despite her mother's statement that she would accept Paula back home, Paula told the court she did not plan to return home. She was given another year's probation, and was instructed to report as required and to live at a residence approved by her probation officer. Since Paula had had no approved residence since her mother's, any friend's house or city shelter became an approved residence because the alternative was the street. Paula continued to report satisfactorily and was advised that the probation officer would be calling the residences she provided to confirm her housing. However, by the expiration of probation, Paula was 18 with no fixed address, no employment, and no family support, despite the best intentions and efforts of probation services.

SUCCESSES

Fortunately, not all cases end as bleakly as Paula's; and when an individual does appear to have benefited from probation supervision, the officer feels a rare sense of success, as in the case of Rick. Rick was a 25-year-old factory worker convicted of assault, arising from a fight outside a bar. He was placed on probation for one year, with conditions to report as directed, to maintain employment, and not to be on the premises where the offence had been committed. Rick reported regularly and complied with conditions, but the probation officer suspected that Rick had an alcohol problem, among other issues. However, she could not engage him in meaningful conversation. At the third appointment, the probation officer asked Rick about his activities and interests, and he expressed surprise that the probation officer would care about subjects that did not relate to probation supervision. She responded that he seemed somewhat troubled and unhappy and that she was willing to listen if he felt like talking. He again expressed surprise but offered little response. However, over the next few appointments, he spoke about his estrangement from his family, with the exception of his only sister, who lived in British Columbia; he even spoke fondly about his cat, Sully. He mentioned AA meetings that he'd attended in the past but had not found helpful and that he wasn't interested in resuming them.

The probation officer's next contact with Rick was a phone call. He was in a phone booth and admitted he'd been drinking. He planned to withdraw all his money from his bank account, buy alcohol, rent a motel room, and commit suicide. The probation officer asked what had happened, but Rick simply stated that he was fed up with life. As the probation officer continued to talk to him, she waved down a colleague passing in the hallway and wrote a note explaining the ongoing emergency. Rick's probation officer managed to learn that Rick was in a phone booth near his bank, as well as the bank's location and even what he was wearing. At one point, Rick stated, "I know what you're trying to do, but it won't work." The probation officer reminded him that his life mattered, to his family, his sister, and even his cat, which would be abandoned and neglected without him.

In the meantime, the probation officer's colleague had relayed Rick's description and whereabouts to police, and eventually, officers located Rick in the phone booth and transported him to hospital. Rick remained there for a few days and, upon his release, reported to his probation officer. He could not verbalize any event that had led to his suicidal thoughts—only that he had felt a general depression that became exacerbated by his alcohol consumption. Nevertheless, he thanked his probation officer for helping him that day and revealed that, after he returned home from hospital, he had phoned his sister in British Columbia and resumed contact. As Rick's probation came to an end, he decided that he was going to use his banked savings to move to British Columbia to be near his sister, who was happily expecting him. A few months after Rick's probation terminated, his probation officer received a postcard. Rick was living with his sister temporarily and working at a landscaping company, and he had attended two AA meetings. He ended the note by thanking the probation officer again for caring. She heard from him only one more time: he sent her a Christmas card that year, enclosing a photograph of him and Sully.

Although cases like Rick's are somewhat outnumbered by less successful ones, these are the cases that make the probation profession worthwhile; and the opportunities to make a difference, and the challenges therein, never cease. Many cases are never resolved the way the courts intend and probation officers wish, but the desire to help individuals who've made mistakes to move beyond them and get their lives back in order remains. Like the judge at the professional development day, probation officers may not always initially know what to do with their offenders either, considering the challenges of each case and the complexities of the probation officer's role. We are responsible for ensuring that the offenders comply with their conditions; for returning them to court when those conditions are violated; for providing support, counselling, and direction to assist in rehabilitation, thereby reducing recidivism; and for keeping the victims and general public protected at all times to the best of our abilities. As long as probation officers continue to accomplish these goals, they continue to derive satisfaction from knowing they are doing the right thing.

DISCUSSION QUESTIONS

1. *After reading this chapter, what in your view is the hardest part of the job of being a probation officer?*
2. *In your opinion, do probation officers have too much discretion, not enough discretion, or about the right amount of discretion in terms of dealing with offenders?*

FURTHER READINGS

Abadinsky, H. 1997. *Probation and Parole: Theory and Practice*. Upper Saddle River, NJ: Prentice Hall.

Bottomley, K. 1990. "Parole in Transition: A Comparative Study of Origins, Developments, and Prospects for the 1990s." In M. Tonry and N. Morris, eds., *Crime and Justice: A Review of Research*, 12. Chicago, IL: University of Chicago Press.

Petersilia, J. 1998. "Probation and Parole." In M. Tonry, ed., *Oxford Handbook on Crime and Punishment*. Oxford: Oxford University Press.

CHAPTER 10
The Professional Life of a Federal Parole Officer

Most prisoners serving time in Canada's prisons leave prison before their sentence has expired to spend the rest of the sentence in the community under supervision. The most well-known form of "early release" is *parole*. Most inmates can apply for release on full parole after having served one-third of their sentence in prison. Once in the community, these individuals are supervised by parole officers. But the professional activities of a parole officer are probably less well-known to the general public than are those of other professionals involved in the criminal justice system, such as defence lawyers. In this chapter, a federal parole officer with over a decade of professional experience describes his role in the criminal justice system.

Sheldon Schwartz, Correctional Service of Canada

Few Canadians understand the roles and duties of a parole officer (PO). The average person seems to know that a PO deals with offenders and monitors their behaviour. This is true and represents a good start. However, it is also very general. I have been a federal parole officer with the Correctional Service of Canada (CSC) for ten years. The federal correctional system deals mainly with individuals who are serving sentences of two years or more. Offenders serving sentences of less than two years fall under the jurisdiction of the provinces. There is one exception: in parts of Canada where there is no provincial correctional system in place, all offenders sentenced to a term of incarceration end up in the federal system.

In dealing with offenders serving two years or more, federal POs work with every type of offender up to and including those serving sentences of life imprisonment. I should also mention that I am a community-based PO. Whereas some parole officers are assigned to prisons, I supervise only prisoners who have been released to the community. For example, a significant number of offenders who are serving life sentences have now been paroled. Assuming that they remain in the community (they may be returned to prison for a violation of their release conditions), POs will supervise them until their death.

Parole officer is a universal term in Western societies. In Canada, however, it may be somewhat misleading. The Canadian correctional system has both *day parole* and *full parole* releases of federal offenders. An individual released on day parole is required to reside in a community residential centre or a community correctional centre (better known as a *halfway house*). A full parole release is a conditional release to the community, with the offender residing in a location he or she has chosen and that the National Parole Board has approved.

In Canada, there is also a form of release referred to as *statutory release* (SR). Where an offender has not applied for or been denied release on day parole or full parole, he or she will usually be released on SR at the two-thirds mark of his or her sentence. The release is also a conditional release to the community. It is a legislative right of an offender and only rarely is it denied. If a prisoner is believed to represent a risk to the community, he or she may be detained[1] in prison until the end of the sentence. My experience has been that few people know about SR and assume that any prisoner serving a portion of his or her custodial sentence in the community must have earned release on parole. However, for several reasons,[2] many offenders do not even apply for parole. Instead, they wait for their SR date. Generally speaking, offenders released on SR pose more of a risk than the average offender released on parole because the higher risk inmates are either denied parole or don't bother applying for parole.

I work with the Team Supervision Unit (TSU) in Toronto. This unit deals only with the highest risk offenders. Almost all the individuals whom we supervise left prison on SR. As a result of the recommendations of a number of inquests in the early 1990s, the TSU was developed to focus on the higher risk offenders and to provide more intensive supervision of these individuals. While a stable federal offender who is supervised by a regular parole unit may be required to meet with his or her PO only once a month (or even once every three months in some cases), offenders in the TSU program are seen by their POs at least twice a week. In addition, the POs conduct unannounced curfew checks at night, showing up at the individual's residence to verify that he or she is in fact at home as required by the conditions of the release.

Another public misconception is that the CSC and the National Parole Board (NPB) are the same organization. In fact, these agencies are separate. The NPB is composed of appointed members who decide which inmates are to be granted release on parole and who determine the conditions of parole. In contrast, the CSC provides an assessment report about each prisoner applying for parole. Such reports usually contain recommendations regarding whether or not the prisoner should be granted parole. However, the NPB is not bound by CSC recommendations. While usually agreeing with those recommendations, the NPB may vote against a CSC-recommended course of action. The CSC also has the power to temporarily reincarcerate a released offender (i.e., suspend a release). However, the NPB has the final say on the suspension.

The CSC is the agency responsible for managing and enforcing an offender's sentence of imprisonment. In the community, the PO enforces the conditions of release and the offender's adherence to a correctional plan. The development of the offender's correctional plan commences soon after the offender has been sentenced. By the time the offender is released, the plan represents a finely tuned blueprint of what is required for an offender's risk to be considered manageable in the community and what he or she needs to do to reintegrate successfully both during the sentence and in the long term. The principal duties of a PO include monitoring an offender's behaviour, performing ongoing risk assessments, and taking timely and effective action when necessary.

The CSC in the Toronto community is multidimensional. Front-line POs managing and working with released offenders also work with a Programs Department, a Psychology Department, a contracted psychiatrist, and a Chaplaincy Section. Additionally, the CSC works closely with the main mental health and substance abuse agency in Toronto, other contracted psychologists, a contracted employment service, and various social services and agencies. It also works in partnership with local, provincial, and federal police services and other law enforcement agencies such as the immigration service. In particular, there is an ongoing dialogue (including meetings and training) between POs and specialized police units, such as the Robbery Squad, the Sex Crimes Unit, the Gangs and Guns Unit, and the Outlaw Biker Unit.

The cases of offenders on PO caseloads, all of whom are serving sentences of two years or more, are multifaceted. While we do categorize offenders (sex offenders, organized criminals, street gang members, property offenders, and so forth), within each category no two cases are alike. I have supervised every type of offender, from one who had consumed a human body part, to those who had sexually abused their own children, to property offenders who could not walk a city block without being tempted to steal something. Many offenders fall into more than one category.

POs must get to know the individuals they supervise by being aware of all significant areas of an offender's life. People may wonder what a property offender's relationship with his girlfriend has to do with his risk of reoffending. However, there is considerable evidence that risk is affected by interpersonal relationships. Individuals in stable relationships are less likely to relapse into the kinds of habits that give rise to offending. In addition, offenders who are in meaningful relationships have more to lose if their parole status is cancelled and they are recalled to prison. I have rarely had a problem overcoming the objections of an offender about needing to know about significant areas of his or her life, once I explain the relevant rationale.

What does a PO do? To supervise a caseload effectively, a PO must consider many issues—for example, medications and their effects, medical diagnoses, physical and mental diseases and disorders, legal requirements and legislation (corporate, offender, family, etc.), law enforcement, psychology, and financial accounting. Legally, POs are peace officers who enforce the conditions of an offender's release. To a large degree, the PO is also a broker who refers the offender to relevant resources in the community and who engages other professionals to assist with case management. Whether these other professionals realize it or not, they become extensions of the case management team. For instance, if an offender is on a program of methadone (a legal medication that helps an offender overcome heroin addiction), the relevant methadone doctor is an essential resource not only for the offender but also as a consultant for the PO. In many instances, that doctor will learn before the PO does that an offender has breached his drug abstinence condition.

Parole officers meet with offenders both at and away from the office. While it is easiest to meet with offenders in the office, it is also important to observe the offender in other environments, particularly at home and at his or her place of employment. It is also useful to communicate with *collateral contacts* in the community in order to get other perspectives on an offender's performance. Examples of these collateral contacts include police officers, employers, family members, friends and acquaintances, program delivery officers, psychologists, and landlords. Collateral contacts have varying degrees of reliability when it comes to gathering accurate information on the offender and his other activities; that said, the greater the range of collateral contacts, the more accurate the overall picture will be. Of course, contradictory information will lead the PO to further investigate the relevant matter for clarification.

The main objective of a parole officer is to protect the community. Ideally, this is achieved through the successful reintegration of offenders back into the community. In such cases, everyone is a winner, and this is the best long-term investment for society. However, sometimes protecting the community is achieved by taking measures of varying degrees of severity, up to and including removal of an offender from the community. Partnerships with other law enforcement agencies, such as the police and immigration authorities, are ever evolving and being improved. All of these professionals ultimately have the same objective; thus timely sharing of information, improved communication mechanisms, and awareness of all our roles in the justice system help make everyone's work more successful.

To meet the objective of protecting the community and to perform his or her duties, a PO must meet standard operating practices (SOPs). These formally documented SOPs have been developed over the years and are continually being refined and amended, based on experiences with cases and "best practices" models.

Most POs would agree that one of the main challenges of the job is to balance time management with meeting professional standards. If a PO ever says, "I'm all caught up," there is a problem. I can honestly say that I have never been "all caught up." While a PO may have reached certain standards for that week and may have met relevant deadlines, I can guarantee that there are more file reviews, collateral contacts, and case conferences that need to be done. So time management is a key skill, as is prioritization of job-related duties; both of these come with experience on the job. The Government of Canada screens applicants for time-management skills using the "in-basket" test. This test gives applicants a list of outstanding matters that need to be resolved. Applicants must prioritize these matters and indicate the actions they would take as well as how much time they would spend on each. Such screening helps ensure that new POs have good time-management skills.

As with any other job, a PO has a daily/weekly/monthly agenda. However, each day can be full of surprises—in this environment, not generally positive ones. Learning that the offender has failed a drug test, receiving a phone call from a spouse claiming she has been assaulted by an offender, being contacted by the police who are investigating an offender for new charges, and not being able to locate an offender are just some examples of typical surprises. Depending on the type of new information, an entire day or more may end up being dedicated to one situation, and the original agenda goes out the window.

A PAROLE OFFICER'S CASELOAD

In a regular supervision unit, a PO supervises caseloads averaging 20 to 25 cases. These offenders are required to report to their PO anywhere from eight times per month to once every three months. This frequency of contact is determined in a structured manner and depends on the rating of a case, the level of risk, and the needs of the offender. However, in the high-risk offender TSU where I work, each PO has a maximum of ten cases. Each PO has two or three face-to-face interviews per week with each offender. Additionally, the POs must make numerous collateral contacts in order to gain accurate perspective and observation on the offender's community functioning.

Safety and Security Concerns

I am regularly asked about the dangers of the job and whether I carry a gun. (I do not.) It would be naive to not recognize that the job of a PO involves potential danger and risk. The safety and security of POs is always under discussion and examination. Within a prison, security systems and safety processes have greater structure and foundation; in the community, such systems are still evolving. For example, in my TSU, curfew checks are performed by POs in partnered pairs. Indeed, where there is concern about risk, community-based contacts with an offender are usually conducted by POs in pairs, and in some cases, this pairing is mandatory. At the office, POs must follow safety policies and know how to use emergency equipment, such as personal alarms.

On October 6, 2004, PO Louise Pargeter became the first federal parole officer to be murdered in the community by an offender under supervision. The offender had previously been convicted of manslaughter. Since Pargeter's murder, safety and security systems and policies have been further amended and refined. This process continues to evolve. A PO should be extremely prudent, not only while on duty but when off duty as well. POs deal with individuals whose behaviour cannot always be predicted. For example, I go out of my way to protect my personal information. As well, even when walking through a mall on my own time, I try to be aware of what's going on around me at all times.

Dangerous situations sometimes stem from the most unlikely sources. For example, one evening during June 2004, my partner and I had just completed a curfew check on an offender in a high-rise apartment building. We left the apartment unit, and while we were waiting for the elevator, doors at both ends of the hallway simultaneously burst open and two police officers from each end ran toward us with guns drawn, screaming "Get down, face down!" I thought this was some kind of joke, but it didn't take long to realize that the officers were deadly serious. We hit the floor. They seemed somewhat nervous themselves. Within seconds, my partner and I had four semiautomatics pointed at our heads at close range. On the way down to the floor, my partner was able to get out the words: "We're parole officers."

Once we were lying flat, one officer asked for ID. I said that I had this in my pocket. He told me to get it. As I placed my hand in my pocket, I was praying that the officers on the other side of the hallway had heard their colleague tell me to reach into my pocket. I took out my badge and slid it to the officer as instructed. They immediately apologized, there was some chuckling by all, and the officers were quickly on their way. My partner and I then had to descend 18 stories on foot, since the elevators had been shut down. We later learned that there had been a report of an individual pointing a gun at others in the building.

Professional Instincts

Instincts play a large role in supervising offenders. Parole supervision is a "people" business; thus, individuals who are interested in working as a PO are "people persons" and have good instincts. Good instincts help a PO anticipate an offender's behaviour. Effective supervision often involves staying one step ahead of the offender. This trait can help a PO gather, process, and assess information and can possibly help predict what is about to happen, thereby preventing further crime. It is one thing to take action after a crime has occurred or when an event is known to have happened; it is better to prevent such an event. A PO's action (such as reincarcerating the offender) is often taken based upon an assessment of the offender's deteriorating behaviour before an actual negative event has occurred. In such cases, the PO may never know what actions he or she prevented. The probability, though, is that it was something undesirable.

However, instincts cannot be defined easily and certainly cannot form the basis of an action taken or a recommendation on a case. A PO's actions and recommendations must be based on facts and credible information. In some cases, the action/recommendation is glaringly obvious; in other less obvious circumstances, the PO must make a case to support an opinion. The case management team forms opinions and recommendations that represent several perspectives. Where there is dissenting opinion, the PO and his or her supervisor have the final recommendation, since the supervisors are accountable for the enforcement of the release conditions and for the management of risk. When the PO and parole supervisor (PS) disagree, the PS has the final say.

Supervising offenders also involves managing some basic instincts. A PO may want to believe what an offender is saying; however, experience dictates that much of what offenders say must be verified. Years ago, I worked in public auditing. There was an audit principle employed that was referred to as *reasonable skepticism*—that is, you should always exercise a reasonable degree of skepticism in the workplace. I still apply this principle in my work as a PO. Most offenders sit in front of me, especially at the commencement of their release, and tell me about all the plans they have for life after release from prison. In the TSU where I work, many of these plans fail to materialize. I often tell the offender: "Every offender sitting across from my desk tells me the same thing. Why should I believe you?" This will also set the ground for an offender understanding why a PO has to keep on verifying information the offender is providing. In time, an offender's word becomes credible after a pattern of honesty and openness has been established. However, this level of trust takes time.

The Balancing Act

Parole officers have numerous roles to perform, although some are more significant than others. The role a PO plays in supervising and managing a case is to a large degree determined by the offender. Part of my initial interview with a newly released offender is to convey this message to him. I tell the offender that my role and style of interaction depend on his or her performance and response to supervision. I explain that his or her case presents positive signals or negative ones. An experienced PO learns to balance the good with the bad and knows what role to play and when. Supervising a case without the right balance can upset the case and raise the risk to the community. Thus, the PO must learn about the offender and become aware of his or her reactions to certain structures, interventions, and communication styles. In the end, the offender is responsible for his or her own behaviour. However, case management can help create a positive outcome when the PO's style and interventions complement an offender's positive behaviours and when that PO is able to monitor and take timely action in response to an offender's negative behaviours.

In addition, decision making in a case can be quite complex. The complexity of decision making explains why there is a case management team. Here is an example of a very common situation that can present a difficult decision-making process:

> A parole officer is supervising an offender, 25 years of age, who is serving time for multiple robberies. The offender has no drug addiction history, and the robberies were committed strictly for financial gain. Correctional planning has identified that the offender's attitude is a matter of consider-able concern because he tends to make impulsive and antisocial decisions when he is under financial pressure. Another area of considerable concern is employment. The offender has never held a job for any significant period and has very few marketable skills. During his community release, he has secured employment as a landscaper. An employer has taken him under his wing and is teaching the offender landscaping skills and the skills of oper-ating a small business. The landscaping job requires workers to work long hours in the spring, summer, and fall. The workday often extends well into the evenings. The employer has made it clear that he requires the offender for all of these hours, as his right-hand man.

The strategy for returning this offender to the community includes placing him on a waiting list for a CSC program that teaches offenders about changing their values to more prosocial ones by thinking about and avoiding situations that can lead to undesirable consequences. Several weeks into the offender's employment (which has been going very well), the PO receives a call from CSC programming saying that the program the offender is wait-listed for is about to commence. The program will run 3 evenings per week for 12 weeks beginning at 6:00 p.m. The offender will have to leave work by 4:00 p.m. on these days in order to get to the program on time. However, the employer cannot accept this schedule; thus, the offender would have to quit his job to participate in this program. What should the PO do?

Should the PO have the offender terminate his employment for the sake of the program, or should the PO endorse the employment contrary to a com-ponent of the offender's correctional plan? Obviously, there is a choice to be made, since the offender cannot do both. Which plan stands to benefit society more in the long run? Quitting work to attend the program will likely cause a great deal of frustration for the offender. However, a decision by the PO to maintain the employment and not force the offender to participate in the program may become be a source of disagreement among the PO, the programs department, and management. What should the PO do? If it were me, I would stress that the development of work ethic, marketable skills, and business acumen would form a more solid foundation and a better long-term investment than a program would. However, this assessment is subjective.

Another complex task for a PO arises when disclosure about the nature of an offender's offences needs to be made in order to protect the community.

The criterion used here is *foreseeability of risk*. When a team assesses an offender and determines that his or her release meets this criterion, disclosure regarding the nature of the relevant offences needs to be made. Disclosure may need to be made to a potential girlfriend, an employer, a relative, or a landlord. When it has been determined that disclosure needs to be made in order for risk to be managed, I usually allow offenders a short period of time to make the disclosure themselves. However, I tell them that I will be confirming what they told the relevant party and that I will fill in any gaps if I need to, in order to ensure that the individual has an adequate level of awareness to make an informed decision. Here is a practical example of such a situation.

An offender with an extensive history of property theft lands a job with a computer business that carries an extensive inventory of computer products. This situation presents a foreseeable risk, and the employer will have to be informed accordingly. However, there is also a significant chance that the employer will not want to hire the offender after being notified of his situation. There is the duty to notify the employer, but is there a way to do so that would be less likely to jeopardize the offender's employment? In this scenario, the PO may offer to meet the employer together with the offender so that, in addition to notifying the employer about the offender's history, the employer can be reassured that the offender is under supervision. Plenty of employers are willing to give a known offender a chance—as long as he or she is reassured that community supervision is in place.

In some such situations, the employer may decide to terminate the offender's employment. Obviously, this can have a very negative effect on the offender's confidence and attitude. However, the bottom line is that the community must be protected. There are many other situations where difficult decisions have to be made. Allowing an offender to leave his jurisdiction for a family event, waiving a curfew for employment purposes, and allowing an offender with a history of domestic violence to date a woman (a degree of disclosure would have to be made to the woman) all represent situations where there may be a perceived conflict between flexibility in allowing an offender the opportunity to reintegrate successfully into the community on the one hand, and potential risk to the community on the other.

DOCUMENTATION AND REPORT WRITING

In addition to travelling, meeting with offenders and collateral contacts, attending staff and professional meetings, investigating incidents, and receiving training, a significant amount of time must be spent on documentation and report writing. Each relevant contact (including telephone contacts) and/or meaningful discussion about a case must be recorded. Additionally, at regular intervals POs have to complete reports and applications for the NPB regarding the offender's progress or regarding other significant developments. There are time frames and deadlines for all of these, everyday case notes included (there is a five-day deadline for a case note to be documented from the time an event has occurred). The PO's job and the correctional environment in general are very documentation oriented. The premise is that any event could become relevant in a future court case or other legal proceeding. Thus, documentation must be accurate and precise and include all dates and times.

Consider the following scenario. A PO has a scheduled appointment for an offender to report to him at the PO's office. The offender phones him in advance of the appointment time and complains that the transit system is currently slow and that he may be a few minutes late. In the background, the PO can hear the sound of subway trains. However, the PO doesn't write down the phone call and therefore doesn't record its time. The offender shows up at the PO's office on time. The PO records the details regarding the meeting. The next day, the Hold-Up Squad contacts the PO and reports that the offender is a suspect in a bank robbery that occurred the previous day during a period just prior to the offender's meeting with the PO. The PO has the precise time of his meeting with the offender. He also recalls the phone call before the meeting, but he does not have the precise time. Obviously, this time could be critical information to the police investigation. Could the robbery have occurred between the offender's phone call to the PO and the meeting? Maybe the phone call was planned this way to provide an alibi for the offender. How should the PO respond to questioning by the police regarding the time of the phone call?

In my opinion, the worst thing the PO could do in this scenario is guess about the time of the phone call and provide it as fact. This could actually provide an alibi for the offender based on the PO's estimate. In responding to the police investigation, any estimate of time should be qualified as such. It is better to say, "I don't know for sure, I inadvertently forgot to record it," than to state something as factual when it is not.

POs render opinions and are sometimes called upon to predict future behaviour. That said, if an element of current and past dynamics has not been verified as factual, it cannot be recorded as a fact. Words such as "apparently" and "seemingly" are very important to use when conveying unverifiable opinion. An offender's self-disclosure is not always taken at face value, for obvious reasons. It is a good idea to complete documentation with the attitude that it could make its way to court. While this may seem overly cautious on the surface, it is prudent conduct for a PO. There is a healthy concept that I refer to as "reasonable paranoia" : a PO ought to function, not with undue fear, but prudently enough to cover his or her backside when documenting.

WORKING WITH VICTIMS OF CRIME

In recent years the CSC and the NPB have been placing a greater emphasis on communicating with victims, providing relevant information about offenders, and listening to victims' concerns. Victims may formally register as victims so that they can receive information about offenders and their locations and supervision and ensure their own safety. Victims or potential victims who are not formally registered can contact relevant POs to express concerns and ask questions. While respecting the privacy rights of the offender, the PO can discuss what he or she is allowed to discuss and can take effective and timely action when necessary. The main objective is to protect the community. Parole officers are trained to be mindful of victims, both past and future.

CONCLUSION

The job of a federal parole officer is challenging, stressful, and at times thankless. However, it is also rewarding and fulfilling. Most POs would say that there are no two days alike in this job. My colleagues would also tell you that they are clock watchers; but unlike the clock watchers who want time to go more quickly, the POs I know want it to slow down. When they see it is 2 p.m., they wish it was still noon. It sounds strange, but I believe it speaks to the challenge of time management, always being busy, and finding the job challenging and interesting.

DISCUSSION QUESTIONS

1. *The author describes two release programs: parole and statutory release. Prisoners have to apply for the first, but the second is granted almost as a right. Do you think all prisoners should have to apply for release from prison?*
2. *Having read this chapter, you now have a much clearer idea of the job done by federal parole officers. What in your view is the most challenging task that they face?*

FURTHER READING

The Correctional Service of Canada website at http://www.csc-scc.gc.ca is comprehensive and includes relevant legislation, policies, standards, and a list of publications.

ENDNOTES

1. In order detain an offender to the end of his or her sentence, correctional authorities must have reasonable grounds to believe that the offender is likely to commit one of the following crimes before the expiration of their sentence: a sexual offence involving a child, an offence causing death or serious harm to another person, or a serious drug offence.
2. Some prisoners may not wish to go through the steps to apply for parole or may believe their chances of getting released on parole are slim. Instead, they will just wait until the two-thirds mark, and then leave prison on statutory release, as they are entitled to by law (unless correctional authorities deem and can establish that the prisoner represents a danger to the community if released).

CHAPTER 11
A Life Prisoner's Story

In a snapshot profile of the federal prison population, lifers accounted for almost one out of every five inmates. This chapter tells the story of one female life prisoner in her own words. Gayle was 43 when she was sentenced to life imprisonment with no possibility of parole until she had served 10 years. The chapter contains extracts from two interviews with Gayle. The first was conducted while she was still in prison (in 1990); the second was conducted in the community after she had been released on parole (in 2001). A life sentence never ends; although most prisoners sentenced to life will eventually be released on parole, they will be on parole for the rest of their natural lives.

Gayle

Life sentences are cruel. I mean, they give you a sort of mandatory [sentence of life imprisonment]. You serve a certain amount of time, but that doesn't mean anything. The hoops you have to jump through ... Even a National Parole Board member told me, "If you ask me to tell you what I did ten years ago, I wouldn't be able to tell you, so I find it hard to ask somebody if they have remorse over something they did ten years ago." And that's ten years. Can you imagine what the life–25 guys [life imprisonment with no parole until 25 years have been served in prison] are like? It's beyond reality. Before the death penalty was abolished, second degree was seven years instead of ten, so after five years you were eligible for day parole; three years, you're out on passes. Now that is fairly logical—a reasonable amount of time. Before the death penalty was abolished, the number of first degree and second degree convictions, as a percentage of all homicides, was only in the twenties—27 percent or something. The rest were manslaughter convictions. And right after the death penalty was abolished, the total numbers turned around. As a matter of fact, manslaughter convictions were only 19 percent of all homicide convictions; the rest were first and second degree.

I think every case has to be taken individually. In my case, I don't see how putting me in prison is justified at all. I have to say that, honestly, because I'm not a threat to society, number one. I'm a totally productive person, and, I mean, you could force me to work for the government for 20 years. That would be penalty enough. You know, I mean, I could be productive. You could say to me, "Okay, for 10 years 50 percent of your salary has to be donated to this family you offended." I could be productive. Why lock me up and tell me to behave like a seven-year-old kid and take away every kind of value that I have? Or try and take it away? All it does is make me bitter. I have no respect for any authority in this system.

What society has to understand is that people don't go out and say, "I'm going to go out and kill somebody tonight." That is not the reality. Four out of five murders are murders that are committed on people they know—family or close friends. All the research has been done. They already know all that. And the murder during the commission of a crime, say an armed robbery or something, well, I really don't know—I don't know if prison is really the answer there either. Because why does that person want to take money and stick a gun in somebody's face? But nobody cares about why. Putting people in prison isn't going to change that kind of attitude, especially because they are desensitized persons in the first place. They don't give a fuck. They go out and they couldn't care less how you're feeling at all about what they're going to do. So putting them in prison and not caring about them is not going to teach them how to care. It doesn't make sense.

The only people who should be in prison in my estimation are people who cannot control themselves from one moment to the next and sexual offenders who need intensive therapy. And an institutionalized environment is the only place they're going to actually be able to get it, where you can control them and make sure they're going to do it. What's wrong is wrong—but how can I compensate? I cannot bring the person back, so the only thing I can do is try and be as productive a person as I can.

[This second interview with Gayle took place at her home in the Lower Mainland in the spring of 2001.]

To help prepare for my parole application, I knew I needed to do a couple of things. The authorities agreed to call in a woman psychologist, and I saw her for three years, so that was great. The other thing is I knew I needed to have some kind of pass experience behind me before I could go up for day parole. I finally got a pass to go to Simon Fraser University to pick up my certificate in liberal arts. That was my first pass. Other than that, there was not a lot done that I did: it was my sisters who campaigned feverishly among friends and family to get letters written. I had about 65 letters to the parole board. I had a tremendous amount of support. Plus, I had to find a halfway house. Since I was federal, that was the big dilemma. I didn't want to go to the only one available for women, because it was under provincial jurisdiction. When different halfway house people would come in, I would talk to them to see if they would accept a woman. Seven Steps was the only one. I knew some people that were there and they had lifers there. They were willing to take me for a three-year duration, so everything was sort of set for me to be successful at my first parole hearing. What happened was they granted me an unescorted temporary absence for 30 days. During that time, I applied for parole right from Seven Steps, and I was granted day parole based on the 30-day performance.

A friend of mine went with me to be there as support at the parole board hearing. Des Turner is a retired gentleman who became interested in prison and parole issues after my sister had spoken to him about my case. Because you're a lifer, you have to have three board members there. Naturally, they ask you questions about whether or not you have remorse and what your feelings are about everything, and so on and so on. They felt that I was quite aggressive at the time. I tried to be as calm as I could, but of course I was quite anxious. That hearing versus the hearing later on when I went to get my full parole after I had served three years on day parole—I went to the board then and they commented on how calm I was and what a change had come over me and they felt that I was really showing signs of being rehabilitated. I basically said, "Well, I'm not inside, that's why I'm calm." It's so simple and it's so obvious, but it's not obvious to people who don't know what it's like to serve time.

I had to see a parole officer, originally once a week and then once every two weeks, and then once a month for two years. In the third, year it was every second month. Now I see her every three months. I've been very fortunate. I had an excellent parole officer the first time around, and I had him for two years. He was really good, very supportive, and didn't seem to be overly suspicious—he took me at my word. Then I had another gal and she was pretty good. I have another woman now, and she's very good. As far as making suggestions, they really didn't have to make a lot of suggestions with me because I already had my family support and jobs lined up. I was already working towards things. I basically reported to them on what I was doing. Things were still there for me. I had my family and friends there. Everybody sort of welcomed me back. I had a car. I got a job within four months. I wanted to finish my degree so I did that first at SFU.

But I didn't feel like I was back. I didn't feel like I belonged. I thought that … it was amazing to me that if I felt like that after having a full life, a full career, a family, and everything before, what would happen with people that have nothing? I always said it was a little bit harder for me in some respects to go inside because I was leaving so much behind, whereas other people were leaving very little. But returning after a certain period of time (for me it was seven years), I found myself quite paranoid, which is something that most lifers talk about. I didn't feel that I belonged. My son had to remind me to buy new clothes, to change, to get in step with things. I couldn't have cared less because I got used to wearing the same thing every day. As long as it was clean, I didn't care. I'm still like that. Basically, my family is still saying, "Why don't you get dressed up?" So that's something that I lost that was actually, in my opinion, a good thing to lose because it was so superficial. In effect, the real world is like that. The real world wants to see you keep up with the fashion and look a certain way.

Then driving, I found it very strange because the things that I had left behind weren't there. A lot of the buildings were gone and the streets had changed. Some were one way. There were new highways, new bridges. I had a difficult time in the beginning to find my way around—I'd get turned around very easily. If there was an accident or if I saw a policeman pull somebody over, I would just start shaking. I was terrified of being pulled over and sent back, even though I had no reason, I wasn't doing anything, but I had that great fear. So that part of me, it took me about two years before I felt that I belonged here. Up until then, I didn't feel I belonged. It's a hard thing to describe what I mean by that. I don't really know how to describe it other than I didn't feel safe; I didn't feel a part of this world anymore; I was still inside. In some respects, part of me always will be inside.

There's a saying: "You may be out of prison but the prison is never out of you." What happened was I just sort of went back to being who I was in a way: getting into business, getting back into the industry that I was in before, rushing around, having family dinners, shopping—a regular sort of life. But part of me still was involved with what was going on because I felt so indebted, and I still feel indebted, to people inside who helped me through that time. We shared an existence that was akin to what people share in the trenches during wartime.

One of the things that is vitally important for me occurred when I was in Kingston at the Prison for Women (P4W). Prior to going inside, I worked in an industry that was male-dominated. I had male children, was married, had a lot of friends who were men—I wasn't really trustful of women. I realized, through speaking with the psychologist and so on, that I had quite a bit of suspicion and resentment towards women. One of the reasons was being part of one race and part of another, I was rejected quite a bit. I only had certain friends who accepted me at that time. This is a historical thing; things aren't like that any longer, but they were like that then. If I'd be called names, racial slurs, it would be mainly by other girls, because that's who your peer group is. When I went to Kingston, I learned very quickly—it was like a thunderbolt that struck me—how women were so wonderful to one another. All of these women who had come from terribly abusive homes and conditions of extreme poverty, who were illiterate, a lot of them, who didn't have families who were supportive of them, who really had nothing and no chances, were like sisters to one another, were like mothers to one another, took care of each other, found time to do the most incredible, creative things and give everything they had to each other. When somebody was in trouble, for instance, this one young woman, Corine, who is dead now, when she slashed we would hide her so she wouldn't be taken to the hole. We'd try and bandage her up and keep her quiet. The one time this same young woman, when the guards came to take her to the hole, everybody in the top tier came out. That's 25 women who came out and stood outside their cells and said, "No, you're not taking her." That kind of solidarity, that kind of concern, willing to stick your neck out, literally, because they could bring in the storm troopers, was such an example of love for one another. I gained so much respect for women that I never had before I went inside. They cared a great deal for me and so fasted when I was fasting, alongside me, to support my efforts to get back to B.C.

When I went to Matsqui institution, we still wrote to one another. I still contributed articles to the *Tight Wire,* the prison newspaper there, and the articles, as I read them now, were full of a huge amount of rage and anger. Then when I got to Matsqui, there were a few guys who weren't happy to have a woman there. Part of them was threatened, I guess, part of them thought that I had privileges because I could wear my own clothes, even though I didn't have access to a lot of the things that they had access to, but they didn't see it like that. The majority of guys were extremely good to me, treated me like a sister, very protective. I was probably the safest woman in Canada at the time. There were a lot of fellows who needed someone to talk to and they couldn't talk to a guy about problems they were having with their wife or girlfriend because they'd be considered wimps and cry-babies, but they'd talk to me. We'd talk for long periods of time about what was going on, so I got very close. When things were happening to me, when they tried to ship me out and served me with an involuntary notice, the lifers group signed a petition to try to keep me there.

They tried to ship me to Burnaby Correctional Centre when they just opened it. I didn't want to go to the provincial prison because, number one, the conditions were terrible there compared to what I had. I had open visiting privileges, all the programs, the hobby shop. I would have had nothing. Also, I knew that my chances of parole and getting in a halfway house were a lot better if I stayed in the federal system versus going to provincial. So, I certainly didn't want to go. They served me with an involuntary transfer notice to say, "No, you're going, whether you want to or not." The lifers group signed a petition, the student union guys signed petitions to show their support for me at Matsqui. That was amazing. They didn't have to do that. It wasn't my suggestion—they just did it on their own. I was part of the student council at that time and part of the lifers group. I was on the board of the lifers group. I had been nominated for the prisoners' committee as hospital rep even though I was denied the opportunity to run by the warden. The guys showed me a tremendous amount of respect. We had a lot of solidarity between us. Their issues I understood very well, particularly the lifers. Because there were so many of them, we could really do a lot of things and share opinions about things. It broadened my view on the whole prison system. I saw the differences in the men's systems versus the women's. I saw the differences in the way the staff treated men versus the way the staff treated women. I was quite amazed that guys could basically swear a lot of times and not get charged, whereas a woman, all she had to do was give somebody a dirty look and she could be charged with threatening.

I was in the hospital unit at Matsqui, so I saw a lot of the prisoners being brought in for medical treatment. They came in from all the different prisons in the region. In particular, there was one fellow who had a tremendous number of headaches. He was an Aboriginal fellow, one of their best carvers. What happened was he was diagnosed with an inoperable brain tumour. He was in a tremendous amount of pain. Before that, he was only getting Tylenol. If you were not a prisoner, you would have gone to a regular doctor, probably had a CAT scan. After a certain period of time, they would have discovered that and you would certainly have been relieved of your pain. So he suffered a tremendous amount until they finally agreed, and this was after two or three tests, that he did have a brain tumour. I was with him right until he died. I'd go into his room, which was next to mine, and clean his room for him just because he couldn't stand to have guards around. Seeing the differences between what happened to him and what would happen to other people outside, it was so obvious that it wasn't right.

There was Craig Hill, who was in a wheelchair. Claire Culhane [a prisoners' rights advocate] was instrumental in finally getting him out on Royal Prerogative of Mercy. He was a young man who couldn't do much for himself since he was very debilitated, dependent on his wheelchair, and couldn't stand alone without leaning against the wheelchair; nevertheless, the parole board said that since he could still stand he was still a danger to society and had denied him again. I was charged with disobeying a direct order because I had gone into a prisoner's bedroom when I heard him fall, to pick him up. That was another thing, in a regular situation you would naturally go to help your neighbour who had fallen, and you knew they were very sick. I think there were four or five fellows who died during the time I lived in the hospital. So, as soon as you are a prisoner, you're treated differently. I was amazed that it went right through the so-called health care as well. I saw the same thing with the women in Kingston; if they slashed, they went to the hole first, not to the hospital to get fixed.

Do I see the prison system as having improved over the years? One step forward, two steps back. If I look at myself, I was so naive that I thought as soon as you walked inside the door the most important thing would be to be productive, to work on everything you could do to make yourself a better person so that when your time came to walk out the door you would be better prepared, whether it was addressing some physical problem you had, or an emotional or a mental instability, or ... gaining training or going to school, or learning something concrete that you could use in the outside world. But no. As a matter of fact, anybody who achieves anything inside does it despite the system, not because of the system. Especially now, they have all these programs that are six weeks long, and they shuffle people through. They are just numbers to prove that they are taking all these so-called programs. Cognitive skills, how to think properly, anger management.

To give you an idea, I remember in Kingston they brought this anger management course in. They decided that I was one of the people that needed to take this. There were seven of us in the class. After the first class of anger management, because you're naturally bringing up a lot of issues that make you angry, you've got nobody to deal with the issues, so within 24 hours, I was the only one who wasn't charged with having a fit of temper or whatever.

Along with anger management, there should be assertiveness training. There are two sides of the coin. How do you deal with issues that are beyond your control? How do you sort out which are beyond your control and which you can do something about, maybe not immediately but step by step, and then you can achieve some kind of relief from the frustrations that you're feeling? The way that it's taught was basically point the finger: it's all your fault, so you're the one who needs to control things and realize that you're wrong. I used to tell women: "You have a right to be angry, you have a reason to be angry." There are times when anger is a totally normal human response. I guess this is the problem with the prison system. Once you're a prisoner, you're a prisoner. You're not a person anymore.

When Lucie McClung [the commissioner of Correctional Service Canada at the time] says the Canadian prison system is the best system in the world, it means, obviously, that the prison systems around the world are really brutal and terrible. We already know that. To say that the Canadian system is best in the world is a crock. They may have one part of it that may be a good idea but they don't expand it enough. In other words, in the women's system, they decide to build all these regional facilities, and they were going to have all these beds for women to have children with them. Well, they now have more segregation beds than they have ever had; in fact, they have about ten times more beds in maximum security than they do for women with children. So they've downplayed, cut back that whole program in favour of having more and more maximum-security beds. They're continually going towards a more controlled model. Even the healing lodge, which was originally a great concept—it was supposed to be an Aboriginal healing lodge with Aboriginal staff, and everything went around treatment or healing concepts—now it's moved towards a control model. The staff is gradually being replaced with CSC staff.

There's one healing lodge: Maple Creek, Saskatchewan—the Okimaw Ohci Healing Lodge. That's right, that was where Yvonne Johnson was and where Rudy Wiebe went to visit her when they were working on her book *Stolen Life: The Journey of a Cree Woman*. To give you an idea, she was doing quite well there. I have a lot of respect for Yvonne, she's been through a lot. She wanted to address some of the problems about being abused as a child. She went through tremendous abuse. The elders there now didn't feel that the healing lodge was the appropriate place to deal with it. Well, where else for God's sake if not the healing lodge? It's supposed to be a place for healing. So what do they do? She agreed to go to Sask Pen, to the women's unit to deal with some issues. She gets there ... I got a letter from her a couple of weeks ago. She gets there, no programs, she's now being warehoused. She can't get back to the healing house so she's in a men's penitentiary right now.

I wasn't invited to the closing of P4W [Prison for Women, which housed federal female offenders]. Correctional Service Canada (CSC) wouldn't pay for any travel expenses to the people who were invited. They were supposed to invite all the original task force members to be there but they weren't going to pay for their travel, which I thought was interesting. So it ended up being mostly CSC people with the big celebration for closing P4W. Meanwhile, now the women actually have it worse in some respects. They're separated into small groups in four different regions, and there are so many staff there, and there is a coercive kind of tactics going on. Women are afraid to speak out. They tell me that they can't even write a letter without a guard over their shoulder saying, "Well, I don't think you should write that." They don't know what their rights are; they don't know how to access them. Right now, they are always threatened that they'll be sent to a men's SHU [Special Handling Unit] if they step out of line. Unfortunately, I think there are 13 women in the SHU in Prince Albert, and they call it a women's unit. I think, out of the 13, 11 are Aboriginal women. All the women from P4W should have gone to the regional facilities. Number one, there's no reason for any of the women to be in maximum security in men's facilities. They have enough beds in the regional facilities. What they need to do is move the minimum-security women out of the regional facilities and into the community.

There's a huge amount of money being spent in corrections, as everybody knows, over one-and-a-half billion dollars a year now. Most of it is in salaries. If you look at the people that are doing the so-called programs, they're all guards, basically. Not many of them have any real qualifications. I know that they say they like to have somebody with a year's university, but that really doesn't say anything about training, does it? So there are no programs going on inside except for the ones CSC calls programs. Unfortunately, the people who are taking those so-called courses aren't learning anything that they can use in the outside world. In other words, their certificate in living skills or anger management doesn't help them get a job, it doesn't train you to get a job. It gives you no education. The university program was really the only thing that people serving long sentences could do and continue on and increase their learning and their knowledge versus other programs. If you're finished in six weeks and you're doing a life sentence, what good is a six-week program? By the time you're ready to move along, you'd have to retake the program.

Meanwhile, you have to take all of these things; otherwise, they won't recommend you to parole. People are forced into taking things that they know aren't helping them a damn bit and there's no continuity to anything on the outside, so it's a dead end. They go to the board, and they've got all these tick marks opposite their name, but it hasn't increased their ability to function in the outside world in the slightest. There are some parts of the programs, I'm sure, that are good; but overall they're costly and don't really help the person to reintegrate and become a better member of society.

What they need is real training for people. If they have a vocational program, such as the machine shop, it should be identical to the one outside. So when people go through the program, they have an actual certificate that is equivalent to something they would achieve outside. So they can go out and get a job and make enough money to keep their families relatively well or at least get some place. At this point in time, it is very difficult to get a job. It was even difficult for me. The only reason I was able to was because I had some friends who were able to get me on. It was not an easy thing—and I had a lot of training. If I had been able to get new training, I would have gone into a new area, but I wasn't able to get anything like that.

People coming out of prison can totally appreciate how scary it must be for people who've never been to a prison, never talked to anybody who has been in prison. They think that all prisoners are dangerous or all former prisoners are dangerous. Prisoners need to come out into the community and speak at community centres and volunteer their time and have some kind of normalization period so that both the public and the prisoner can get used to one another again. The fact is that everybody's going to get out of prison—we all know that. You need to have halfway houses because they have structure there. They have hours that you have to be in and hours that you can be out. There need to be more services, though, transportation and so on for people coming out so they know how to get along and get around. People who live in communities that don't want prisoners as a group might consider having transition houses where they have a mix of people. There are lots of street people and battered wives, for instance, who have a lot in common with women coming out of prison. They've all had a lot of the same experiences. Transition houses could accommodate some, but there needs to be more safe housing, period. You want the neighbourhood to be safe, too. It's a matter of screening the people that come into the halfway house. That's very important. I can appreciate people not wanting to have a serial criminal in their midst; I can totally appreciate that. But people who have been incarcerated one time in their life, there's no reason to think that they can't make it on the outside and can't contribute to a better society again. It's an irrational fear that the public has about what a criminal is.

I had never been to prison before; I didn't know anybody in prison. I was busy with my life, working and raising my family, and I thought that anybody who is in prison must have done something wrong and that's why they were there, and assuredly they'd be there learning some kind of a trade or getting more education, and learning how to become better people and when they got out they would be able to get jobs and get on with their lives. If they didn't want to work and they wanted to have it easy, which is my idea of what people were trying to do that ended up in prison, then they'd go back and that's what they deserved. That's how naive I was. I honestly thought that people went inside and learned how to become better people. I thought that's what they were doing in there. In fact, that's so far from the truth that it's very, very sad and depressing. All that money is wasted. Instead of somebody going inside to try and increase his or her knowledge, go to school, do a trade, all that happens is you learn how to exist and survive in prison. That means you learn how to cope with the constant pressure to put on a face that is acceptable to the administration and to get along with other people that you might have never met in your whole life but who are also in prison.

You're caught up with trying to stay in touch with the real world outside, which is your family and friends and community, and living in the world of prisons that is a totally unreal world. Nobody in the outside world could imagine what it is like never to feel safe in your own shower, never to feel safe or be able to sleep through a night. A lot of the people who are inside are there because they have never been able to communicate or build relationships. One of the reasons is because they're illiterate. They are full of fear all the time, they're fearful of not being able to do something correctly, they never build any confidence and just do what they need to do to survive. The money that is being spent—you could hire teachers to go in and teach. Never mind guards to teach. Guards should just be doing what they're trained to do and that's guarding. All the rest of the people inside could be going to classes, could be researching, and going back to when they were kids and trying to figure out what it is that they wanted to do with their lives.

I'm a lot calmer now, mainly because I don't have the stressors any more. I don't have to worry about the door slamming in my face. I feel very sad about what's happened to people who I know inside, people who are still there. It forces me to maintain contact because I feel that a lot of those people helped me to get through the time. I want to try and be there for them, even in a limited way. I belong to a group called Strength in Sisterhood Society. It's a group of former prisoners and prison advocates and supporters that try to provide a voice for women. We attend different conferences and we do a lot of speaking engagements, write letters to Parliament. We network with other women's organizations and justice groups across the country. I still go to West Coast Prison Justice Society, which is another nonprofit society that was formed while I was still inside at Matsqui. They provide legal information to prisoners and produce a newsletter that talks about current cases. I've done radio shows; for example, we did the Prison Justice Day special on August 10th on CBC. I've also done quite a few newspaper interviews and comments, things like that.

The other side concerns my own family and what their needs are, and trying to be there for them as well. Without a doubt, I'm a better person because of the prison experience. I'm a lot more compassionate and understanding, less judgmental. I think with 16 percent of the female federal prison population serving sentences for life and 15 percent of the men, you've got a population that is growing, aging, and that could be contributing in so many ways; but instead they're being used primarily to keep the prisons calm. I think it's so necessary for lifers to keep in touch with one another, to see what's going on in each region, to see what's available when they do get out, just to find out what everybody's doing.

Lifers are a very close-knit group of people. As soon as you meet somebody else who is doing life, you know what it means, and you want to know that they're safe and hopefully that they are doing okay. I know that the women I've gone in to see when I was in Kingston were so happy that I'm doing well. It gives them a great incentive to know that they can get out and they can do it.

DISCUSSION QUESTIONS

1. *Does anything in this chapter change the perceptions that you have of offenders sentenced to prison for life?*
2. *In your view, is there enough emphasis on rehabilitation in Canada's prisons?*

FURTHER READINGS

Melnitzer, J. 1995. *Maximum, Medium, Minimum*. Toronto: Key Porter.

Murphy, P. and L. Johnsen. 1997. *Life-25: Interviews with Prisoners Serving Life Sentences*. Vancouver: New Star.

Murphy, P., L. Johnsen, and J. Murphy. 2002. *Paroled for Life: Interviews with Parolees Serving Life Sentences*. Vancouver: New Star.

PART THREE
Current Issues in Criminal Justice

CHAPTER **12**

Community Policing in Canada: The Broad Blue Line

Community policing represents one of the most important developments in policing in Canada and elsewhere. The community policing approach ree-merged in the 1980s in response to a certain degree of disenchantment with traditional policing. At the heart of the community policing movement is a desire to produce a closer connection between the police and the commun-ities they serve. However, the so-called community policing revolution may now have run its course, perhaps returning to more traditional policing fol-lowing the 9/11 terrorism events. In this article, policing expert Barry Leighton explores the nature and function of community policing.

Barry N. Leighton, Carleton University

The idea of community and police working together to solve local crime and disorder problems is an old idea: public policing in uniform was originally conceived by Sir Robert Peel in 1829, when he established modern public policing in London, England. When working in partnership with the com-munity they serve, police can form a "broad blue line" to solve local crime and disorder problems.

This metaphor of the "broad blue line" is an adaptation of the "thin red line" imagery used to describe the defeat of a Russian cavalry charge on British forces during the 1854 Battle of Balaklava in the Crimean peninsula. When there were too few troops available to cover the line against the Russian cavalry, British troops were commanded to stand fast in ranks two-deep rather than the customary four. This "thin red line" strategy succeeded, thereby dispelling the military wisdom of the day that infantry could not withstand a mounted horse charge. Since then, the romantic picture of a beleaguered few, defying the odds and overcoming them, has often been used in descriptions of military confrontations. This same "us against them" strategy using a small number of uniformed police, all spread thinly against much larger opposing numbers, has also worked well for the traditional approach to policing. However, community policing turns this on its head by placing the local police on the same side as society. Such an alliance between police and the community they serve transforms the thin blue line of uniformed police into a "broad blue line."

To better explain the police-community alliance, this chapter discusses the following questions: How can we define "community policing"? What are its main strategies and tactics? What is the broader context of community policing? How does community policing contrast with traditional policing? What theories support this approach? How is community policing practiced in Canada? What is the empirical evidence showing that community policing works? Finally, what is the future of community policing?

DEFINITION AND CORE STRATEGIES

The term *community policing* has also been labeled *community-oriented policing*, *community-based policing*, and *problem-oriented policing*, although any differences between these terms is marginal. Further, while the meaning of *community policing* may be in the eye of the beholder, the broad concept is so compelling that it has become the most widely-recognized approach to public policing in western industrialized countries. Community policing may be defined as "a philosophical, organizational, and operational approach to urban policing which emphasizes a police-community partnership to solve local crime and disorder problems" (Leighton, 1991). Consequently, the two core strategies of community policing are problem solving and community partnerships.

Problem solving means addressing identified local crime and disorder problems by finding patterns among similar incidents (Goldstein, 1979). Rather than responding to each call from the public as a separate case, the police take appropriate crime reduction and prevention steps to solve the common, underlying causes. For example, these actions may involve "target hardening" (e.g., installing better locks and lighting) and other prevention tactics prescribed by the *environmental design approach*, whose main strategy is to reduce opportunities for crime. Reducing crime opportunities may also include arranging for more intensive policing around crime locations at higher risk of hosting criminal events. In these crime *hot spots*, or *hot places* at *hot times*, police routinely play the lead role in reducing opportunities for crime.

The second core strategy of community policing is a broad *community partnership* between the police and the community they serve. This partnership usually takes the form of public participation and consultation. Partnership activities provide the focal point for identifying local crime and disorder problems, setting priorities for the problems, and developing solutions. Problems are viewed as shared problems with shared solutions which are provided by the police and other criminal justice agencies in partnership with social service agencies and other resources in the community. This partnership in identifying and ameliorating local crime and disorder problems makes them "co-producers" of order and civility (Wilson and Kelling, 1982; Murphy and Muir, 1984) and "co-reproducers of order" (Ericson, 1982). As suggested at the outset, the police and their community become allies as a "broad blue line" to reduce crime at the local level.

These two strategies of problem solving and community partnerships also have a number of organizational prerequisites (Leighton, 1991). In particular, decentralized police management and resource deployment empower police officers to work with their community to use whatever tactics are appropriate to the neighbourhood and its specific crime problems. Other innovations include a proactive approach to delivering services rather than knee-jerk responses to emergency calls or aimlessly cruising the streets in patrol cars.

In addition, community policing uses a variety of *tactics* within the context of the two core strategies. For a particular crime problem in a particular community, tactics may include the following: police ministations or storefronts; neighbourhood patrol by car, foot, bicycle, or even by boat or horseback; dedicated beats or zones; "differential" or specialized response; interagency partnerships; and consultative committees. Not all are appropriate for all communities; for example, foot patrol may not be very effective in low-density, spread-out suburbs. But because the objective of these tactics is to facilitate greater police-citizen contact, the right tactics must be chosen to reduce particular crime problems, and they must be appropriate for the community's circumstances.

The specific tactics and police services delivered by the police depend on the needs of a particular neighbourhood, on the local crime and disorder problem being addressed, and on the solutions jointly developed by the police and the community. While there is no standard template or model, the appeal of community policing lies is its flexibility to deliver its two core strategies through a variety of tactics that differ from community to community and from problem to problem. In other words, "designer policing" tailors its tactics and services to each community.

When talking about community policing, we should also clarify two key terms. Widespread confusion over the meaning of *community* can render the notion of *community policing* almost meaningless. This is because most traditional definitions of *community* focus on geographical space, such as neighbourhoods. But in a highly mobile society that is increasingly more connected electronically than it is geographically, this idea is outmoded. Adopting a traditional definition transforms community policing into a romantic fiction of old-fashioned self-policed communities with little crime. Modern definitions of *community* replace geography with *social networks*. These new definitions allow community policing to embrace both local (homes) and non-local (professional, business, and recreational) types of communities (Leighton, 1988).

We can then apply "community as network" to a whole range of different community types other than neighbourhoods, including the electronic "global village" connected by social networking tools such as the Internet, blogging, Facebook, YouTube, and Twitter. The notion of the networked community is also helpful in understanding how different types of non-local crime problems operate, such as transnational organized crime and terrorism.

COMMUNITY POLICING IN CONTEXT

Community policing can also contrasted with other policing approaches. All approaches to policing belong within the broader social science concept of *social control*. During the last century, sociologists theorized that, when the informal mechanisms of family, religion, school, and community failed to adequately socialize people with the appropriate norms and values of the dominant society to create internalized control, then "leakage" would occur and formal controls would take over. In one sense, potential criminal tendencies would move from being controlled by a "policeman in our heads" to having a "policeman at our elbows." Because of the weakening of traditional societal institutions, the maintenance of order in society now relies more on formal social control mechanisms, including the police at our elbows and in the streets.

At one end of this spectrum of social control, *private police* or *para-police* serve the security needs of individuals and corporations, largely for the protection of property, although high-profile politicians, business leaders, and celebrities also employ security guards for their physical safety. Next on the spectrum are the public police. In Canada, they are organized along jurisdictional grounds that reflect constitutional responsibilities as applied geographical or jurisdictional responsibilities: at the local level, public police serve a municipal function; regionally they may have a provincial function; and nationally, they serve a federal function where Canada's national police force, the RCMP, are joined by other federal agencies such as Canada Border Services Agency, to combat major crime. However, while these three levels are distinctive, their operations are often closely linked, such as when the federal police combat organized crime where it has roots in local communities.

The national end of the policing spectrum, with a mandate to tackle terrorism, transnational organized crime, and other threats to national security, more clearly shows that the police act as agents of the state. This "higher" level of protecting Canada's national security has been called *high policing*, in contrast to *low policing* (Brodeur, 1983). However, these terms are confusing, because those dedicated to community policing consider the pursuit of community safety to be the more noble and "higher" form of policing, whereas agencies combating terrorism often get into serious skullduggery under the guise of national security.

Public policing has many of its roots in the history of technological innovations. The technology of order maintenance has changed dramatically since the days when troops were called out to re-establish order in communities. For example, the Twenty-sixth Cameronian Rifles quelled the "Gavazzi Riots" in Montreal during the summer of 1853 (Atherton, 1914). Between community-based watch systems and formal troops with fixed bayonets, there were few options available to civil powers. But calling in the army was a very costly exercise, both in terms of expense and lives lost.

The subsequent development in Canada of public policing solved this problem, as well as helping to reduce the cost of private policing. Foot patrol of neighbourhoods quickly became the core strategy, eventually aided by the technological advance of police telephones on street corners so they could ask for help when needed. With the advent of police patrol cars, a rapid response to crimes in progress became the watchword for motorized patrol. The downside of this invention was that it distanced police from the communities they served. Wireless two-way radios fostered more rapid response, while on-board computers allowed police to check information on suspects. But it took the invention of global positioning systems (GPS) and personal digital assistants, such as the Blackberry, to really free police from the patrol car, allowing them to keep in touch electronically while patrolling neighborhoods on foot or bicycle. On the other hand, some critics suggest that these same technologies also served to enable supervisors back at the station to keep track of and control the otherwise footloose policemen on patrol.

Meanwhile, other technologies may contradict this renewed image of the friendly community police officer, particularly the bulky bullet-proof vest and other pieces of equipment previously used only by tactical or emergency response units. Moreover, in addition to carrying a firearm, police officers on foot now carry a variety of other weighty tools on their belts, all of which project quite a different image from what Peel had originally envisioned: that of a member of the community who just happened to be in a simple blue uniform with a distinctive helmet. The combination of these two contrasting images—the community police officer and the tactical squad member in full battle dress—invites further exploration.

TWO MODELS OF POLICING

Community policing differs from other approaches to public policing, especially from the professional (or bureaucratic or traditional) model of policing. Under the professional policing model, crime is the exclusive "property" of the police, who use a technology-driven, rapid-response strategy combined with random motorized patrol, assuming all of this has a deterrent effect on potential criminal events (Kelling and Moore, 1988). Usually associated with the crime control approach under which the police "own" crime problems and exercise a monopoly on the response to it, the professional police are seen as forming a "thin blue line" against crime. However, with crime as their exclusive professional domain, these police unfortunately may also end up forming a thin blue line against the community. In contrast, community policing forms a "broad blue line" or coalition against local crime and disorder problems, because the police-community partnership unleashes new or underutilized community resources.

The difference between the community policing model and the professional model can be illustrated with a health-care analogy. Professional policing corresponds to a police force that works like a hospital operating exclusively as an emergency ward. Most of the time the staff would be patiently waiting for a 911 call for an ambulance to make a rapid response to a life-threatening incident, even though these incidents are relatively few in number compared with most hospital visits. Doctors would randomly cruise the streets in ambulances as a deterrent for accident-prone, high-risk people who are driving unsafely or under the influence of alcohol or illegal drugs. On vary rare occasions, perhaps when cruising accident *hot spots*, they might come across an accident in progress and then be readily available for assistance. Consequently, most patients would arrive only by an emergency-response ambulance, regular wards would be used only for follow-up care, and the underlying causes of health problems would remain unaddressed.

In contrast, community policing is closer to preventive medicine, with an ambulance making an emergency response in only a small proportion of calls for health care. The focus of treatment and response (or the *unit of analysis*) is the individual, rather then the event or incident. This holistic approach to health care promotes and maintains good health through exercise and a balanced diet in much the same way that building a healthy community results in a safer community with a lower risk of crime and disorder problems. As a result, the police business costs less, is more affordable for communities, and is less of a burden on society in the long run. In short, community policing is sustainable policing.

But are these two, apparently conflicting models incompatible for police on the beat? First, much of the glamour of policing, and what may attract most recruits, is "extreme policing." That is, the para-military tactical units in combat gear who respond to terrorist or hostage incidents. By contrast, much of routine policing is just boring, such as directing traffic, handing out parking tickets, checking false alarms, and driving around on patrol, all the while waiting for the "big call." Yet much of routine policing is related to the tactics of community policing. Guth (1994) calls these two models the "brown" (for para-military policing) and the "blue" (for community policing). The first reflects police organizations with "force" in their name whereas the second reflects those which changed their name to "police service." As well, the first model focuses on enforcing the law through "law enforcement" officers whereas the second favours "peace officers" (i.e., the legal status of police in Canada) who facilitate peace in the streets by using tactics of which only one is enforcing the law. But some uncharitable critics have called these two models "real policing" and "social work." So can police perform both roles at the same time, perhaps in a mutually dependent way? In practice, however, our police are asked to fulfill both of these apparently conflicting roles, thereby placing a great deal of pressure on their daily lives on the job.

COMMUNITY POLICING IN THEORY

While a comprehensive theory of community policing has yet to be developed, the *broken windows* argument advanced by Wilson and Kelling (1982) has academic credibility (Sparrow, Moore and Kennedy, 1990; Kelling and Coles, 1996) and widespread appeal. The broken windows argument mirrors the notion of the self-fulfilling prophecy, as developed in 1929 by sociologist W.I. Thomas: if people define a situation as real, then it will be real in its consequences.

The broken windows theory proposes that, when potential offenders perceive neighbourhood decay and deterioration (such as broken windows, derelict cars, or graffiti), then they will likely conclude that the neighbourhood has few defences against crime and is "ripe for the picking." However, when the visible signs of crime and urban decay are removed, then the neighbourhood is more likely to be perceived as being low in crime because it is well defended, resulting in an actual reduction in crime. That is, when changes in perceptions and attitudes result in changes in reality, then crime is actually reduced, thereby making streets and homes safer.

But the idea that a neighbourhood in decay will inevitably lead to disorder and then to crime has been challenged (Greene and Mastrofski, 1988). Critics argue that it "explains too much" and might better serve as simply an explanation for neighbourhood disorder and order maintenance, rather than overextending itself to cover crime as well. On the other hand, compelling research (Skogan and Hartnett, 1997) demonstrates an empirical link between disorder and crime, thereby providing strong support for this theory.

One idea supporting community policing is that its effectiveness is directly related to the degree of community involvement in solving crime and disorder problems with the local police—and vice versa. However, this notion has been criticized by those who are suspicious of police being involved in the community beyond what is necessary to respond directly to crime. Under the *minimalist policing, fire-hall,* or *"brown" model*, police are trusted only enough to wait in the police station until called out in emergencies. Under a *maximalist, "community penetration" or "blue" model*, the police are seen as the Big Brother who exploits the community policing ruse to spy on and place tighter handcuffs on the community (Gordon, 1987). Yet if we look at police involvement with the community through a more positive lens, we can recognize that the old professional model of policing reflects a minimalist policing approach, while community policing reflects a maximalist approach.

COMMUNITY POLICING IN PRACTICE

Despite much rhetoric in the media, the reality of community policing practices in the closing decades of the 20th century did not live up to its own advertising. Indeed, community policing was originally introduced as an add-on program, a sideline on the organization chart along with public relations, victim services, and crime prevention units. The impact of this approach was to marginalize and render it ineffective. For example, the first police mini-stations and storefront offices in Victoria, B.C., were not authorized to take calls for service from the public or do problem-solving projects (Walker and Walker, 1989). Instead, they ended up being no more than stationary "grin and wave squads" or public relations outposts handing out crime prevention brochures, making school visits, or sending police out on foot patrol and bicycle patrols. It is not surprising, therefore, that community policing was mistakenly identified with highly visible but marginal add-on programs to "real policing."

A quick assessment of the state of community policing in Canada at the turn of this century suggest that it was well supported—at least officially. For exaple, it reflected the rhetoric and official positions of the majority of Canadian police chiefs and police boards. Second, it was officially endorsed by Public Safety Canada (the federal department known then as Solicitor General Canada) as the preferred approach to modern urban policing (Normandeau and Leighton, 1990). Third, several provincial governments made it their official policy and the Ontario government formalized it in legislation (the *Ontario Police Services Act*). Fourth, Canada's national police service, the RCMP formally adopted community policing.

As well, anecdotal evidence suggests that the core strategy of problem solving was working well in many cities and the partnership strategy was evident through the widespread use of community consultative committees. Some of the successes were published through police- or government-sponsored reports, such as about policing in Edmonton (Koller, 1990) and in Montreal (Laudrum, 1998). However, beyond this meager evidence, the lack of empirical research on policing in Canada continues to be lamentable (Leighton, 1994). Indeed, there are far more commentaries on this subject than there are evaluations and research studies.

By 2000, the available evidence suggests that: (1) community policing was the "official" approach to policing in most Canadian police services; (2) it went beyond the stage of experimentation and demonstration; and (3) it became integrated into the daily operations of policing. On the other hand, there were still many police services where (1) community policing remained marooned as an add-on program with highly visible tactics; (2) the two core strategies of community policing were disconnected; (3) the tailoring of a specific package of tactics to specific community needs was not widespread; (4) there was little support for community policing at the working level in police forces; (5) too few resources were invested in implementing and maintaining this model of policing; and (6) the so-called integration of community policing into routine police operations is likely more rhetoric than reality. However, far more independently conducted research studies or evaluations are required before we can confirm these initial conclusions about the state of community policing at the end of the 20th Century.

DOES COMMUNITY POLICING WORK?

Whether or not community policing is effective in reducing and preventing crime is a key question (Rosenbaum, 1994). Some critics claim there is very little proof that community policing works. But even if there is such proof, they say that instead of reducing or preventing actual crime, community policing just makes people "feel good" by simply changing their perceptions of crime and level of fear of being personally victimized.

An experiment by the New York Police Department during the 1990s provides some insight into whether community policing works. Police Commissioner William Bratton claimed that reductions in crime during were due to the effectiveness of community policing. He had just taken over the NYPD after significantly reducing crime on the New York subway by applying the broken windows strategy of cleaning up the signs of crime, especially graffiti. Beginning in 1983, the NYPD produced daily crime statistics for each precinct and then compared them in weekly meetings (called "compstats") in order to provide feedback to precinct commanders on the relative success or failure of their problem solving and other community policing exercises. These statistics helped the commanders make decisions about reallocating resources to new crime hot spots at different times and places once previous ones were successfully handled (Silverman, 1999).

However, critics have suggested that the NYPD emphasis on comparing statistics merely encouraged precinct commanders to reduce at almost any cost the number of crime incidents reported to the police by the public. Hence, the celebrated *compstat factor* may reflect the manipulation of crime and clearance rates as much as it does the success of problem solving and related tactics. To further muddy the waters, official rates for serious and violent crime declined for five years in a row across the United States during this same period, not just in New York City. Consequently, it is difficult to untangle all the factors that contributed to a decline in crime. Some of the other factors include more affluent economic conditions, which reduce the motivations for engaging in criminality, as well as an aging society in which there are fewer young, at-risk males. There were also tougher laws, more aggressive law enforcement, and more severe sentences. So the jury is still out as to how much the decline in crime in New York City can be credited to community policing and how much can be attributed to broad social trends.

By contrast, rather than focusing mainly on reducing official crime rates, Canadian police sought a balance between crime reduction and crime prevention through the police-community partnership. Four evaluations of the effectiveness of community policing programs could inform the "does it work" question. One study of the Metro Toronto Police mini-stations found them to be "well received" by local residents (Murphy and de Verteuil, 1986; Murphy, 1988). Another evaluated community police stations in Victoria, finding that a significant proportion of the residents contacted their local community station (Walker and Walker, 1989). A series of five studies of the Windsor Police Service's use of evaluation evidence found that community policing did have an impact on crime trends, despite little support by its member officers and an attitude spilt among management (Schneider, Pilon, Horrobin and Sideris, 2000). Perhaps one of the most rigorous evaluations of a community policing program conducted anywhere is that of the Edmonton Police Service's Neighbourhood Foot Patrol Project, where 21 constables on foot were based in mini-stations strategically located in selected neighbour-hoods (Hornick et al., 1991). This evaluation reported that the project (1) significantly reduced the number of repeat calls for service in the beat neigh-bourhoods with foot patrol; (2) improved user satisfaction with police services; (3) improved constables' job satisfaction; and (4) increased constables' know-ledge of the neighbourhoods and their problems. This pilot project led to the department-wide implementation of community policing.

CONCLUSION: THE FUTURE OF COMMUNITY POLICING

In light of government and police focus on terrorist events during the first decade of the 21st century, it is reasonable to ask whether community policing has any future at all. It appears that community policing was its height in the 1980s when many police forces had, to varying degrees, integrated the two core strategies and multiple tactics of community policing into what came to be called "integrated policing." However, during the 1990s, com-munity policing shifted toward the priority of policing the more serious or "hard crimes," such as organized crime, serial murders, and mass murders involving automatic weapons. Because much of this approach requires hard evidence or "criminal intelligence" from a variety of sources, it is often called "intelligence-led policing" (see Deukmedjian and de Lint, 2007). But it is interesting to note that this reliance on timely, accurate information to set policing priorities and allocate resources uses the same logic as community policing which uses empirical evidence such as local crime statistics to solve local crime problems, namely, the problem solving strategy. Moreover, com-munity policing tactics once again became "add-on" programs, sitting on the sideline of "real policing."

Then, in the first decade of the 21st century in the wake of 9/11 terrorist incidents in 2001, public policing retrenched into the professional model. North America "circled the wagons" by hardening the borders to forestall potential terrorists. As Murphy (2005) notes, Canadian police rapidly became "securitized." We might call this defence-driven style of policing the "Fortress America" approach, characterized by the "brown" policing model. So there are clear signs that professional or traditional policing is once again the dom-inant model for policing in Canada. Yet by placing policing in the context of broader developments in "late-modern times (de Lint, 1999), contemporary public policing in Canada may be swept away by societal and global forces, along with our romantic notions of community policing, in favour of new, per-haps hybrid policing forms (Murphy, 1998; de Lint, 2005). In the shorter-term, however, it remains to be seen whether community policing survives the recent trend back to old-style policing once the panic over terrorism diminishes.

DISCUSSION QUESTIONS

1. *How would you characterize the nature of police presence in your community? Does it correspond to the community policing model, or does it more resemble the old-style kind of professional policing?*
2. *Would you say that in your community, a good relationship exists between the police and the public that they are supposed to serve and protect?*

FURTHER READINGS

Kelling, G. and Coles, C. 1996. *Fixing Broken Windows*. New York: Free Press.
Rosenbaum, R. (Ed.). 1994. *The Challenge of Community Policing: Testing the Promises*. Thousand Oaks, CA: Sage Publications.

REFERENCES

Atherton, W. 1914. Montreal, 1534–1914. *Under British Rule, 1760–1914*, Vol. II. Montreal, QC: S. J. Clarke.
Brodeur, J.P. 1983. High policing and low policing: Remarks about the policing of political activities. *Social Problems*, 30: 507–520.
de Lint, W. 1999. A post-modern turn in policing: Policing as pastiche? *International Journal of the Sociology of Law*, 27(2): 127–152.
—— . 2005. Policing public order: A tough act to follow? *International Journal of the Sociology of Law*, 33: 179–199.
Deukmedjian, J.E. and de Lint, W. 2007. Community into intelligence: Resolving information uptake in the RCMP. *Policing and Society*, 17(3): 239–256.
Ericson, R. 1982. *Reproducing Order*. Toronto: University of Toronto Press.
Goldstein, H. 1979. Improving policing: A problem-oriented approach. *Crime and Delinquency*, 25: 236–258.
Gordon, P. 1987. Community policing: Towards the local police state. In Scraton, P. (Ed.), *Law, Order and the Authoritarian State*, (pp. 121–144). Milton Keynes: Open University Press.
Greene, J.R. and Mastrofski, S. (Eds.), 1988. *Community Policing: Rhetoric or Reality*. New York: Praeger.
Guth, DeLloyd J. 1994. "The traditional Common-Law constable: form Bracton to the Fieldings to Canada" in R. Macleod and D. Scheiderman (Eds), *Police Powers in Canada*. Toronto: University of Toronto Press.
Hornick, J., Burrows, B., Phillips, D., and Leighton, B. 1991. An impact evaluation of the Edmonton neighbourhood foot patrol program. *Canadian Journal of Program Evaluation*, 6: 47–70.
Kelling, G. and Coles, C. 1996. *Fixing Broken Windows*. New York: Free Press.

Kelling, G. and Moore, M. 1988. "From political to reform to community: The evolving strategy of police" in J.R. Greene and S.D. Mastrofski (Eds.), *Community Policing: Rhetoric or Reality. New York: Praeger.*

Koller, K. 1990. *Working the Beat: The Edmonton Neighborhood Foot Patrol.* Edmonton: Edmonton Police Service.

Laudrum, K. 1998. Measuring the results of community policing. *Canadian Police Chief Magazine,* July, 10–20.

Leighton, B. 1988. The concept of community in Criminology: Toward a social network approach. *Journal of Research in Crime and Delinquency,* 25: 351–374.

——— . 1991. Visions of community policing: Rhetoric and reality in Canada. *Canadian Journal of Criminology,* 33: 485–522.

——— . 1994. Community policing in Canada: An overview of experience and evaluations. In D. Rosenbaum (Ed.), *The Challenge of Community Policing.* Thousand Oaks, CA: Sage Publications.

Murphy, C. 1988. Community problems, problem communities and community policing in Toronto. *Journal of Research in Crime and Delinquency,* 25: 392–410.

——— . 1998. Policing Postmodern Canada. *Canadian Journal of Law and Society,* 13 (2).

——— . 2005. "Securitizing" community policing: Towards an alternative Canadian public policing model. *Canadian Review of Policing Research,* 1.

Murphy, C. and de Verteuil, J. 1986. *Metropolitan Toronto Community Policing Survey.* Ottawa: Ministry of the Solicitor General of Canada.

Murphy, C. and Muir, G. 1984. *Community-Based Policing: A Review of the Critical Issues.* Ottawa: Ministry of the Solicitor General of Canada.

Normandeau, A. and Leighton, B. 1990. *The Future of Policing in Canada.* Ottawa: Solicitor General Canada.

Rosenbaum, R. (Ed.). 1994. *The Challenge of Community Policing: Testing the Promises.* Thousand Oaks, CA: Sage Publications.

Schneider, F., Pilon, P., Horrobin, B., and Sideris, M. 2000. Contributions of evaluation research to the development of community policing in a Canadian city. *Canadian Journal of Program Evaluation,* 15: 101–129.

Silverman, E. 1999. *NYPD Battles Crime.* Boston, MA: Northeastern University Press.

Skogan, W. 1990. *Disorder and Decline.* New York: Free Press.

Skogan, W. and Hartnett, S. 1997. *Community Policing Chicago Style.* New York: Oxford University Press.

Sparrow, M., Moore, M., and Kennedy, D. 1990. *Beyond 911.* New York: Basic Books.

Walker, C. and Walker, G. 1989. *The Victoria Community Police Stations.* Ottawa: Canadian Police College.

Wilson, J. and Kelling, G. 1982. Broken windows. *Atlantic Monthly,* March: 29–38.

CHAPTER 13
The Decision to Detain or Release: The Nuts and Bolts of Bail

When the State lays a criminal charge against an accused person, there may be reasons to detain that person in custody until the case comes to trial. For example, the individual may be considered a risk to the public, or there may be fears that the accused may not appear for trial. In these cases the accused will be held in custody. The decision to detain or release an individual pre-trial is not taken lightly, however. After all, people are considered innocent until and unless the State proves the offence in court of law and beyond a reasonable doubt.

In this chapter, Judge Renaud, a very experienced judge who has written a great deal on the criminal justice system in Canada, describes the law and procedures followed in the determination of whether to grant bail. He notes that the reality of bail decision-making is very different from the image most people have of courts.

Gilles Renaud, Ontario Court of Justice

Once they have been charged, most accused persons may safely be allowed to remain in the community until their first appearance in court to face the charge against them. These people are released on bail. For a small minority of people, however, the State may be justified in ordering their detention. The law of bail guides courts in determining whether an accused should be released on bail or detained.

To the public at large, the decision whether an accused who is presumed innocent should be jailed pending trial is made in a matter of seconds without input from the lawyers. At least this is how it appears in each episode of television shows such as *Law and Order*. In accordance with the nature of the criminal charge or the specific province involved, bail decisions are made by a justice of the peace, Provincial Court judge or Superior Court judge. Some people believe that the court looks at the criminal charge, then the accused, and simply states "bail denied" or "bail granted: one million dollars," and with the bang of the gavel, the matter has ended. Nothing could be further from the reality of bail law in Canada.

In Canada, individual liberty is at the heart of a free and democratic society. Particularly in criminal law, the importance of this fundamental freedom is embodied in the presumption of innocence and more specifically in the notion of bail. Bail is a form of guarantee—usually an amount of money—undertaken by the accused or a surety to guarantee that the person in custody will appear for trial if he or she is released. Accordingly, bail must be set by the court at an amount within reach of the accused or the surety. A *surety* is a person who agrees to provide the guarantee for the accused and who is liable for the determined amount. If the accused fails to appear for trial, the money will be forfeit to the State.

When a person is arrested for a criminal offence and taken into custody, the police must bring the person before court for a bail hearing, normally within 24 hours or as soon as possible thereafter. Since liberty plays a vital role in Canadian society, bail is usually a way to grant freedom to the accused, who, in exchange, agrees to respect certain conditions while awaiting trial. These conditions aim to ensure that the accused appears in court to face the charge.

To illustrate the importance that liberty plays in this context, Justice Iacobucci of the Supreme Court of Canada, in a famous and controversial case, stated:

> [47] At the heart of a free and democratic society is the liberty of its subjects. *Liberty lost is never regained and can never be fully compensated for;* [Emphasis added] therefore, where the potential exists for the loss of freedom for even a day, we, as a free and democratic society, must place the highest emphasis on ensuring that our system of justice minimizes the chances of an unwarranted denial of liberty. [Emphasis added]

> [48] *In the context of the criminal law, this fundamental freedom is embodied generally in the right to be presumed innocent until proven guilty, and further in the specific right to bail.* [Emphasis added] When bail is denied to an individual who is merely *accused* of a criminal offence, the presumption of innocence is necessarily infringed. This is the context of this appeal, one in which the "golden thread" that runs through our system of criminal law is placed in jeopardy. And this is the context in which laws authorizing pre-trial detention must be scrutinized.

In light of Section 11(e) of the *Canadian Charter of Rights and Freedoms,* the Court reminds us that judges, as guardians of liberty, must ensure "that pre-trial release remains the norm rather than the exception to the norm, and to restrict pre-trial detention to only those circumstances where the fundamental rights and freedoms of the accused must be overridden in order to preserve some demonstrably pressing societal interest" (*R. v. Hall).* In other words, courts must make every effort—consistent with a concern for public safety—to allow the accused to remain in the community until he or she is required to answer the charge.

Thus the accused should normally be granted bail, unless detention can be justified by one or more of the following three reasons found in the *Criminal Code:*

Three Grounds for Detention According to the Bail Reform Act

To ensure that the accused attends court (detention is more likely to be ordered in cases where the accused has a history of failing to attend court or to respect other court orders);

To protect the public (detention is more likely to be ordered if the accused has a criminal record for similar offences, a history of violence, or poses a risk to the community);

To maintain confidence in the administration of justice (detention is more likely to be ordered in cases of serious offences, the potential of a lengthy jail term, or when it is justified by the circumstances surrounding the commission of the offence).

These legislative criteria must be taken in context and considered on a case-by-case basis when determining whether to grant or deny bail. Judges therefore have to be vigilant to ensure that a serious charge in and of itself, or a bad record of prior crimes, does not automatically lead to the detention of the accused before a trial is held. In this chapter these elements will be explored in greater detail.

As suggested in these preliminary remarks, the law of bail is of fundamental importance to all Canadians. It is also a controversial concept entrenched in our Constitution. My purpose in this chapter is twofold: to pull back the metaphorical veil that too often appears to shroud the pre-trial proceedings devoted to the fundamental question whether an accused person should be at liberty awaiting his criminal trial, and to explain in clear language what takes places in the thousands of bail courts operating each day across this country. Indeed, I aim to identify the "nuts and bolts" of the decision-making process at all levels, including the formal public hearing if one is held. As will be seen, the "law of bail" should be understood to be "the law of discretion" as to the conditions governing the behaviour of persons charged with a criminal act pending their trial.

DISCRETION: A LOOK BACK TO ASSIST IN UNDERSTANDING CONTEMPORARY EVENTS

Since the introduction of bail, legal discretion—instead of the strict words of the law—has been at the heart of much of the decision-making process in bail courts. In *Crankshaw's Magistrates' Manual being a Practical Guide to Police Magistrates and Justices of the Peace* (3rd ed.), by James Crankshaw, K.C., the author devotes most pages to the "discretion" that judges have regarding bail and states that magistrates—today's justices of the peace and judges—are asked to safeguard the public interest and the reputation of the administration of justice by locking up, until the day of their trial, individuals charged with crimes in situations where their release is thought to be contrary to the common good. Those who can be trusted should be released on conditions. This should be a well-grounded decision based largely on discretion. Despite the strict legislative criteria previously mentioned, judges today continue to rely on discretion when deciding whether to grant bail.

THE PIONEERING WORK OF PROFESSOR FRIEDLAND

Parliament brought numerous changes to the law of bail in 1972, chiefly as a result of the work of Professor Martin L. Friedland (1972), whose study, "Detention Before Trial," made it clear that detention prior to a quick guilty plea was the option chosen by many detainees in order to avoid prolonged pre-trial detention. The legislation inspired by this study aimed to change certain practices by adopting measures that are still in place today. These measures relate to granting the police powers to avoid arrest or detention after initiating a legal accusation; the identification of clear legislative reasons establishing when detention is justified; and the onus that usually rests on the Crown to prove that bail should be denied.

1. The Primary Ground for Denying Bail: The Risk of Flight (s. 515(10)(a))

Having introduced the general lines for the exercise of discretion, it will be of assistance to draw direct attention to the legislative rules that are said to guide and control the exercise of that discretion. Parliament has directed that persons accused of crimes be detained pursuant to Section 515(10)(a) of the *Criminal Code* if they are not likely to be present at trial. In other words, the primary justification for refusing to grant bail rests on the common belief that judging from the person's record, past, contemporary actions, and possible lengthy jail period, the accused is at risk of fleeing the country or town.

Based on the severity of the offence and the limited spaces for detention, an accused with no prior record who faces a modest fine for a minor theft will not be detained no matter how likely it is that he will be convicted; on the other hand, a person accused of terrorism whose lifetime record displays an unrelenting crusade against State authorities, who has no ties to Canada, and who faces a lifetime jail sentence, is unlikely to wish to attend a trial that will likely result in a finding of guilt. In fact, the courts will primarily examine elements such as the nature of the allegation; the record (if any), with particular attention to the accused's history of compliance with court orders; the strength of the accusation; the ties to the community; the likely sentence; and other factors, such as the possibility of living outside Canada. All these factors will be taken into account by the court when determining whether to detain or release the accused.

2. The Second Ground: The Risk of Further Crimes (s. 515(10)(b))

Parliament has ordered for reasons of public safety that all offenders ought to be granted bail, assuming they are not shown to be undue flight risks, unless "the detention is necessary for the protection or safety of the public, including any victim of or witness to the offence, having regard to all of the circumstances including any substantial likelihood that the accused will, if released from custody, commit a criminal offence or interfere with the administration of justice ..."

In other words, courts are tasked with the unenviable duty of weighing the likelihood of further misconduct and assessing the risk that further crimes will be committed based on previous criminal charges or the accused's history. Once again, the risk analysis must take into account the legislative criteria but also the contextual background, including the limited number of "remand" places, the jail beds for those not yet convicted, and the constitutional limits briefly pointed out in the opening paragraphs and to be discussed below.

By contextual background I refer to the obvious fact that many offenders may breach their bail conditions because they are fighting addictions, mental illness, inadequate socialization in childhood, extreme poverty, racism, and a host of other "sad life" deficits. These problems make it harder for individuals to comply with bail conditions such as a curfew. Furthermore, many of the anticipated breaches may be of a minor nature—petty mischief, causing a disturbance, and so on.

Quite often, the fact of the matter is that an offender is granted two chances—two "strikes," if you will—prior to having the bail revoked, unless the matter is quite serious. In most of these instances, the prosecution bears the practical (if not the legal) onus of satisfying the justice of the peace or the judge that "old Charlie" or "poor Mary" should be "jugged" (i.e., detained in custody) until the trial, especially if the likely remand period will far exceed the anticipated sentence.

The best judicial example of the discretion conferred upon judicial officers tasked with deciding whether to grant bail under this provision is found in *R. v. Morales*, [1992] 3 S.C.R. 711. Former Chief Justice Lamer of the Supreme Court of Canada stated at page 737:

> ... Bail is not denied for all individuals who pose a risk of committing an offence or interfering with the administration of justice while on bail. Bail is denied only for those who pose a "substantial likelihood" of committing an offence or interfering with the administration of justice, and only where this "substantial likelihood" endangers "the protection or safety of the public". Moreover, detention is justified only when it is "necessary" for public safety. It is not justified where detention would merely be convenient or advantageous. Such grounds are sufficiently narrow to fulfil the first requirement of just cause under s. 11(e).

However, despite this position, the legislation requires for certain more severe allegations—namely, violent offences involving firearms, murder, or drug trafficking—that the accused demonstrate that his freedom is justified pending trial. This is known as a "reverse onus." This means that although the onus is usually upon the State to justify the detention of the accused, for certain cases the obligation is upon the accused to justify his release on bail.

In discharging this legislative function, Parliament is merely seeking to protect the public by supporting the common belief that the more serious the accusation is, the greater are the chances of achieving public protection by detaining the accused. Stated otherwise, the lawmakers have chosen to place upon the accused, and not the State, the burden of demonstrating that detention is not required in the circumstances. This "reversal of onus" is in keeping with the traditional view that serious allegations of misconduct be treated with great concern for the public interest and also with the commonsense view that the accused is better placed to explain how his or her interim liberty is consonant with public safety. The reality is that most offenders are released pending trial, notwithstanding the serious allegations they face, as that is clearly Parliament's intention and consistent with the *Charter*, as will be discussed presently.

3. The Third Ground: Public Confidence in Justice (s. 515(10)(c))

As discussed at length in *Hall*, Parliament intended that a limited number of situations should result in the accused's detention even though the two first criteria that justify detention—namely, the risk of flight (515 (10)(a)) and the risk of further crimes (515(10)(b))—have not been met. The remaining criteria that justify detention read as follows:

> (c) if the detention is necessary to maintain confidence in the administration of justice, having regard to all the circumstances, including
> (i) the apparent strength of the prosecution's case, (ii) the gravity of the offence, (iii) the circumstances surrounding the commission of the offence,

including whether a firearm was used, and (iv) the fact that the accused is liable, on conviction, for a potentially lengthy term of imprisonment or, in the case of an offence that involves, or whose subject-matter is, a firearm, a minimum punishment of imprisonment for a term of three years or more.

Not unlike the comments consigned earlier in discussing the question of the reverse onus, this exceptional provision reverses the traditional exercise of discretion and appears to reflect a legislative design consonant with the view that certain alleged offences or offenders should be detained with a view to fostering public confidence in the administration of justice.

SECTION 518: EVIDENCE AT A HEARING INCLUDING HEARSAY

According to Section 518 of the *Criminal Code*, the justice who presides over the hearing may receive and base his or her decision on evidence considered credible or trustworthy. This allows the parties to introduce hearsay evidence. Hearsay evidence is defined as information that is not witnessed directly by the person testifying. For example, police officer A may testify that civilian B told her that her husband slashed her repeatedly in the torso area with a Rambo-style knife. The police officer did not actually see the assault—he is simply testifying about what the civilian told him regarding the knife attack.

Crown practices can vary considerably in each case and in practice must deal with the fact that most witnesses are not available to testify since hearings are often delayed or adjourned and at times are suspended after having started (see discussion in Weinper and Sandler 2003).

On the ground, technology is influencing the way information is received by courts. As a matter of practicality, many Crown and defence witnesses, particularly experts, testify using new forms of technology, thereby considerably reducing costs and delays. In addition, delays between the hearing of the original bail application and the appeal from the denial or refusal of bail are being reduced now that transcripts are being produced more quickly electronically. For example, a CD recording of earlier proceedings can be presented on the day the request is made (see *R. v. Pennell.*).

THE THREE DAY RULE AND OTHER CAUSES OF DELAY, S. 516

The long delay the accused often faces in custody before having a bail hearing is a problem the criminal justice system must address. Hamlet spoke of the "the law's delays," and this aptly summarizes the plight of accused persons awaiting trial. Indeed, in more and more cases the accused is requesting that proceedings be ended (a judicial stay of proceedings) because of unreasonable delay before a bail hearing. In *R. v. Zarinchang,* a trial judge granted an order under the *Canadian Charter of Rights and Freedoms* staying the proceedings against Mr. Zarinchang on the ground that the judicial system had failed to provide him with a bail hearing for some 24 days from the time of his arrest. The trial judge further ordered the Crown to pay the court costs of the respondent. The Ontario Court of Appeal reviewed the decision and noted that stays may be granted in exceptional cases for such difficulties. The law is still evolving.

LEGAL MANOEUVRING AS A SUBSTITUTE FOR LEGAL COMPLIANCE WITH RULES

Another cause of delay relates to the tactics used by the two parties—the accused and the State. Each side seeks to gain a tactical advantage for the forthcoming trial as a result of, first, the emphasis placed on discretion in the legislation, and second, the existence of the legal factor often referred to as "the strength of the Crown's case," by which the ultimate justice of pre-trial detention is often justified. In most hearings that deal with serious accusations and grave circumstances, such as allegations of sexual violence, murder, or large-scale drug trafficking, lawyers wish to position themselves well to confront the other side's case and obtain the detention or release of the person in question. In most hearings, though, the result can be described as follows: the accused will be detained due to his or her record of previous breaches, *or* will be released based on the absence of a serious record or the presence of a sound plan of supervision reducing to an acceptable level the risk of further offending conduct.

A recent example of interest in the nuts-and-bolts element of tactical advantage in bail hearings can be found in *R. v. Badgerow*, in which the accused was charged with first degree murder. One legal question that the court had to decide was whether the Crown attorney would be allowed to stop the investigating officer from being closely interrogated by counsel for the defence. As noted earlier, the *Criminal Code* allows the parties to lead hearsay testimony—that is to say, information that the witness did not perceive directly. The Crown often prefers to do so, for it is not realistic to have police officers or civilian witnesses appear in the bail court due to time constraints and scheduling concerns (a further topic of discussion). In *Badgerow*, the Crown did not wish the chief investigator to testify; but it was not because of these concerns, but rather to impede the defence counsel's ability to probe for weak points.

The judge referred to *R. v. John*, in which the defence argued that the Crown should be required to bring the officer in charge of the case to give evidence at the bail hearing. The Crown stated that a police officer without direct involvement in the investigation could present evidence at the bail hearing by reading aloud from the witness stand a statement or synopsis prepared by one or more of the officers directly involved in the investigation. In rejecting the Crown's position, Justice Casey Hill stated that according to paragraph 64:

Where oral evidence is required, according to the submissions of certain Crown counsel in the history of this case, everything should be done by the government to avoid calling a witness with any direct or personal knowledge of the investigation in order to prevent the defence from having the opportunity to cross-examine an individual who is likely to be a witness at trial. *While this "free crack at the witness" philosophy has meritorious attraction in the case of victims or complainants, beyond this it has little to recommend it.* Indeed, given the contribution of meaningful cross-examination to the truth-seeking process, the policy approach of conscripting an uninformed reader ("any" officer or a "court officer" or "court security officer") apart from serving convenience, can, in certain circumstances, amount to a deliberate artifice designed to frustrate the court's pursuit of the truth. The Court has the authority to control questioning within relevant limits. [Emphasis added]

As a general rule, most practices during bail hearings serve tactical purposes instead of addressing whether the person accused should be detained or not. This development is a direct result of the highly discretionary nature of interpretations of the rules governing bail—notably, the importance given to the strength of the Crown's case, which is a highly illusory element. Parliament might be well served to consider removing this element from consideration in order to reduce the length of these hearings.

BAIL DECISIONS ON REVIEW: FURTHER EXERCISE OF DISCRETION

I turn now to the subject of appeals or reviews of bail decisions. Parliament has enacted an elaborate set of rules for reviewing the merits of earlier decisions, and it will suffice for present purposes to note that the reviewing court is granted a great deal of discretion. Guidelines on the review of bail orders are provided in *R. v. Moss* and suggest that a judge who reviews the bail decision must take a new look at the evidence submitted before the original judge and take into account any additional evidence offered by the parties. Once again, the judge may exercise discretion in deciding whether the accused has demonstrated that the previous decision should be overruled. The discretion, however, must be reasonable and fair to both parties.

BAIL DOES NOT AMOUNT TO FREEDOM: LIMITED LIBERTY IS THE NORM

Space constraints limit the discussion of this subject, but it must be understood that a decision to liberate an accused from custody pending trial (or appeal) does not result in the granting of freedom. On the contrary, most detainees who are released on bail are bound by stringent rules and often guarantee their pledge of good behaviour by means of monetary deposits and charges against real property. Unfortunately, most court dockets are replete with accusations of breaching these varied obligations. The public is regularly informed by the media about the electronic surveillance—including in-house cameras and electronic tagging—that many individuals under security certificates face. This practice may one day become the norm in bail decisions due to the lower costs entailed.

CONCLUSION

When a lawyer or a judge refers to "the law of bail," it sometimes puts a smile on justice officials' faces. Some are of the view that there is very little law involved around bail: at best, the legal requirements of the *Criminal Code* are viewed as providing the formal context to the proceedings, but local practices and experiences dominate the actual decision making. Indeed, most decisions affecting the potential release of a detained individual are made by police officers and not by lawyers or members of the judiciary. Also, when matters of release are debated, this tends to be on a case-by-case basis, leaving aside the legal jargon, to ensure that proceedings can be followed by lay witnesses, notably the families of the accused and victims.

Bail law should be a priority, given the fundamental issues of personal liberty and public safety. The law in this area should undergo an important reform, and the first element to be considered might well be the discretionary nature of decisions made whether to free (or not) a detained person accused of a crime.

DISCUSSION QUESTIONS

1. *Do you agree that certain accused persons should be required to justify their release on bail or do you believe that the onus should always be on the State to justify the detention of the person charged with a crime?*
2. *Some people argue that the decision to grant or release an accused should not include consideration of the effect on public confidence. Where do you stand on this question?*

FURTHER READINGS

Coughlan, S. 2009. *Criminal Procedure*. Toronto: Irwin Law.
Roach, K. *Criminal Law*. Toronto: Irwin Law.
Salhany, R. 2009. *Canadian Criminal Procedure*. 6th ed. Aurora: Canada Law Book.
Trotter, G. 1999. *The Law of Bail in Canada*. 2nd ed. Toronto: Carswell.

REFERENCES

Crankshaw, J. 1921. *Crankshaw's Magistrates' Manual*. 3rd ed. Toronto: Canada Law Book.
Friedland, M. 1972. *Detention Before Trial*. Toronto: University of Toronto Press.

Trotter, G. 1999. *The Law of Bail in Canada*. 2nd ed. Toronto: Carswell.

Weinper, F. and M. Sandler. 2003. *Criminal Procedure Cases, Notes, and Materials*. 2nd ed. Toronto: Butterworths.

CASES

R. v. Badgerow, 2010 ONSC 932

R. v. Hall, [2002] 3 S.C.R. 309

R. v. John, [2001] O. J. No. 3396

R. v. Morales, [1992] 3 S.C.R. 711

R. v. Moss (2003), 229 Nfld. & P.E.I.R. 67

R. v. Pennell, [2006] N.J. No. 321, 2006 NLTD 185, 261 Nfld. & P.E.I.R. 339

R. Stephenson, [2006] O. J. No. 5033

R. v. Zarinchang, 2010 ONCA 286

CHAPTER 14
Plea Bargaining

Judges are often criticized for imposing lenient sentences, especially for crimes of violence (although the news media do not always give the full story). Another important source of public dissatisfaction concerns the practice known as *plea bargaining*. Many people were outraged when Karla Homolka was sentenced to only 12 years in prison for her role in the Bernardo murders. That sentence, which was universally denounced as too lenient, came about as a result of a plea bargain. Polls have shown that people have a very negative perception of plea bargaining (Cohen and Doob 1989). As with sentencing, however, public perceptions of this phenomenon may well be at odds with reality. We should not let individual examples of plea bargaining that led to unpalatable consequences determine our reaction to all instances in which discussions take place between the Crown and the counsel for the accused.

As the following reading makes clear, plea bargaining involves more than a simple exchange in which the offender receives a lenient sentence for having agreed to plead guilty. The public has the perception that plea bargaining always works to the offender's advantage and at a cost to the State or the victim. Systematic research into plea bargaining suggests that this perception is not necessarily accurate.

Simon Verdun-Jones, Simon Fraser University

In countries such as Canada, Australia, and the United States, up to 90 percent of criminal cases are resolved through the entry of a guilty plea (Canadian Sentencing Commission 1987; Seifman and Freidberg 2001; Verdun-Jones and Tijerino 2005). Although it is not possible to be precise, a significant percentage of these guilty pleas are entered following a so-called *plea bargain* between the prosecuting and defence lawyers.

For many years, plea bargaining has been one of the most controversial—and, perhaps, least understood—practices in the Canadian criminal justice system (Griffiths and Verdun-Jones 1994, 317). For criminal justice researchers, plea bargaining is a compendious term that describes a broad range of behaviours that may occur among actors in the criminal court system (Verdun-Jones and Hatch 1988, 1). The police, Crown counsel, and defence counsel may engage in conduct that ranges from simple *discussions* through to *negotiations* and on to concrete *agreements*, all of which are perceived to be binding on the parties. Of course, discussions and negotiations may not ultimately lead to any form of agreement between the parties; nevertheless, these activities have generally been considered by researchers to constitute components of the practice of plea bargaining (Griffiths and Verdun-Jones 1994, 318). In order to provide a clear focus for discussion, this chapter focuses on the concept of a *plea agreement*, which constitutes the outcome of a successful process of negotiation between the Crown and the defence counsel.

One of the most useful definitions of *plea agreement* was furnished by the Law Reform Commission of Canada (1989, 3–4), which stated that a plea agreement is "an agreement by the accused to plead guilty in return for the prosecutor's agreeing to take or refrain from taking a particular course of action" (see also Cohen and Doob 1990, 85). The term *plea agreement* is more appropriate than *plea bargain* because, in Canada, there is no guarantee that any agreement will ultimately be carried into effect by the sentencing judge, who is not bound by any promises made by the Crown to the defence.[1]

Furthermore, some researchers have questioned whether the term *plea negotiations* is appropriate, given the realities of the criminal justice process. For example, Ericson and Baranek (1982) asserted that the word *negotiate* is not meaningful in light of the stark imbalance of power between the police and the Crown on the one hand and the defendant on the other. These researchers argued that it is more realistic to view the accused's decisions within the criminal justice system as "coerced" or "manipulated" and that, therefore, the accused will scarcely perceive any accommodation with the Crown as constituting a genuine "bargain" (see also McCoy 2005).

However, assuming that it is feasible for the Crown and the defence counsel to enter into a *plea agreement*, what may the Crown offer in order to persuade the defendant to plead guilty? Broadly speaking, the promises that may be made by Crown counsel fall into three overlapping categories: (1) promises relating to the nature of the charges to be laid (*charge bargaining*); (2) those relating to the ultimate sentence that may be meted out by the court (*sentence bargaining*); and (3) those relating to the facts that the Crown may bring to the attention of the trial judge (*fact bargaining*).

These three categories of plea bargaining encompass a considerable variety of promises that the Crown may offer the accused. For example, Verdun-Jones and Hatch (1985, pp. 74–75) set out the following list of possible promises and agreements:

1. Charge bargaining
   (a) Reduction of the charge to a lesser included offence;
   (b) Withdrawal or stay of other charges, or the promise not to proceed with other charges;
   (c) Promise not to charge friends or family of the defendant; *or*
   (d) Promise to withdraw a charge in return for the defendant's undertaking to enter into a peace bond.[2]

2. Sentence bargaining
   (a) Promise to proceed summarily rather than by way of indictment;
   (b) Promise to make a specific sentence recommendation;
   (c) Promise not to oppose defence counsel's sentence recommendation;
   (d) Promise to submit a joint sentencing submission;
   (e) Promise not to appeal against sentence imposed at trial;
   (f) Promise not to apply for a more severe penalty (e.g., by not giving notice to seek a higher range of sentence based on the accused's previous conviction based on s. 727 of the *Criminal Code*);
   (g) Promise not to apply to the trial court for a finding that the accused is a dangerous offender (s. 753 of the *Criminal Code*) or a long-term offender (s. 753.1 of the *Criminal Code*);
   (h) Promise to make a representation as to the place of imprisonment, type of treatment, etc.; *or*
   (i) Promise to arrange the sentence hearing before a particular judge.

3. Fact bargaining
   (a) Promise not to "volunteer" information detrimental to the accused during the sentencing hearing;
   (b) Promise not to mention a circumstance of the offence that may be interpreted by the judge as an aggravating factor (see, e.g., the aggravating factors listed in s. 718.2(a) of the *Criminal Code*).

THE RESPONSE OF CANADIAN JUDGES TO PLEA NEGOTIATIONS

Over the past 30 years, the extent to which the courts have been willing to accept plea bargaining as a legitimate component of the system of criminal justice in Canada has changed tremendously (Griffiths and Verdun-Jones 1994, 319–22; Verdun-Jones and Tijerino 2001, 2004, 2005). Until the final quarter of the 20th century, plea bargaining was routinely "frowned upon" and most criminal justice personnel were loath to admit that it took place at all (Cousineau and Verdun-Jones 1979). As recently as 1975, the Law Reform Commission of Canada (1975, 14) scornfully proclaimed that plea bargaining was "something for which a decent criminal justice system has no place." Significantly, this derisive attitude toward the practice was subsequently echoed by Chief Justice Brian Dickson of the Supreme Court of Canada in his judgment in *Lyons* (1987), where he quoted from the very same Law Reform Commission Working Paper: "justice should not be, and should not be seen to be, something that can be purchased at the bargaining table" (para. 103). However, by 1989, the Law Reform Commission had undergone a remarkable change: after boldly asserting that "plea negotiation is not an inherently shameful practice," it even recommended that the practice become more open and accountable (Law Reform Commission of Canada 1989, 8). Around the same time, the Canadian Sentencing Commission (1987, 428) recommended that plea bargaining be recognized as a legitimate practice subject to judicial scrutiny and control.

Most significantly, in 1995, the Supreme Court of Canada roundly endorsed the view that plea bargaining was indispensable to the functioning of the Canadian criminal justice system. Indeed, in *R. v. Burlingham* (1995, 400), Justice Iacobbucci stated:

> To the extent that the plea bargain is an integral element of the Canadian criminal process, the Crown and its officers engaged in the plea bargaining process must act honourably and forthrightly.

There is little doubt that the tolerant stance adopted by the Supreme Court of Canada toward the practice of plea negotiations has been firmly embraced by the appellate and trial courts of the various Canadian provinces and territories. For example, in 2001, the B.C. Court of Appeal placed its seal of approval on plea negotiations and sent a clear signal to the trial courts that, since plea bargaining is vital to the efficient operations of criminal justice, trial courts should generally endorse the contents of plea agreements entered into by Crown and defence counsel. Indeed, in *R. v. Bezdan* (2001, para. 15), Madam Justice Prowse stated:

> It is apparent that the administration of criminal justice requires coopera-tion between counsel and that the court should not be too quick to look behind a plea bargain struck between competent counsel unless there is good reason to do so. In those instances in which the sentencing judge is not prepared to give effect to the proposal, I also agree that it would be appropriate for that judge to give his or her reasons for departing from the "bargain."

Why have the courts been willing in more recent years to accept the legitimacy of so-called plea bargaining in spite of its somewhat tarnished public image? The major reason seems to be pragmatic: namely, there is a perception among many judges and prosecutors that without a steady stream of guilty pleas, the criminal court system would collapse under the weight of a massive backlog of delayed trials (Di Luca 2005; Lafontaine and Rondinelli, 2005).

The perception that plea negotiations are necessary was strongly reinforced by the report of the Martin Task Force (Ontario Attorney General 1993), which was established to devise remedies for what was considered to be a serious crisis in the Ontario court system in the early 1990s. The Task Force recommended that, where appropriate, defendants should be routinely encouraged to plead guilty through the offer of sentence discounts (Roach 1999, 98–99). To this end, trial judges were exhorted to participate in pre-trial conferences that would facilitate plea bargaining—primarily by giving an indication of the perceived appropriateness of any recommended sentence. Roach (1999, 99) concluded that the report of the Martin Task Force constituted powerful evidence that plea bargaining in Ontario "was no longer a 'dirty secret' hidden in the corridors of the courtroom but was now openly facilitated in the judge's office."

It is significant that in the same year as the Martin Report, the Crown in Ontario made a plea bargain that attracted a considerable degree of public criticism (McGillivray 1998). In the notorious case of Karla Homolka (1993), the Crown accepted a plea from Homolka to a charge of manslaughter and advanced a joint sentencing submission to the effect that the accused should be sentenced to a term of imprisonment of 12 years. The Crown took the view that it was necessary to offer this plea bargain to Homolka, who was considered a willing accomplice to the killings of Kristen French and Leslie Mahaffy by her husband, Paul Bernardo. At the time the bargain was made, Crown counsel was apparently convinced that without Homolka's testimony against her husband, it would not be possible to convict Bernardo of the murders. In response to the public expressions of anger at the perceived lenience of Homolka's sentence, an independent inquiry was established to investigate the circumstances underlying the Homolka plea bargain. Ultimately, the inquiry found that given its knowledge of the circumstances at the time, the Crown had absolutely no choice but to enter into the plea agreement with Homolka's counsel if it wished to ensure the conviction of Paul Bernardo (Galligan 1996, 215–18).[3] There was widespread criticism of the sentence that was jointly recommended by the Crown and the defence; nevertheless, the *Homolka* case shows the extent to which plea bargaining has become accepted as a necessary—albeit somewhat unattractive—element in the administration of justice in Canada. The growing acceptance of plea bargaining in Ontario is best demonstrated by *Boudreau v. Benaiah* (2000). In this case, the Ontario Court of Appeal upheld a trial court's ruling that an accused person was entitled to receive substantial damages from his counsel because the latter failed to properly communicate with him the contents of a proposed plea agreement with the Crown.

The extent to which Canadian courts have accepted the reality of plea negotiations is also demonstrated by their willingness to accept joint sentencing submissions advanced by both the Crown and the defence counsel (Manson 2001, 204–5). It is significant that joint sentencing submissions are generally predicated on the acceptance of a plea agreement by the accused.

In *R. v. G.W.C.* (2000), the Alberta Court of Appeal forcefully articulated the view that trial courts should be reluctant to undermine plea negotiations by rejecting a joint sentencing submission that has been agreed upon by both Crown and defence counsel. Indeed, Justice Berger stated (para. 17):

> The obligation of a trial judge to give serious consideration to a joint sentencing submission stems from an attempt to maintain a proper balance between respect for the plea bargain and the sentencing court's role in the administration of justice. The certainty that is required to induce accused persons to waive their rights to a trial can only be achieved in an atmosphere where the courts do not lightly interfere with a negotiated disposition that falls within or is very close to the appropriate range for a given offence.

THE LACK OF A FORMAL PROCESS FOR REGULATING PLEA NEGOTIATIONS IN CANADA

The Canadian judiciary has accepted that plea negotiations play a significant role in the efficient administration of justice and has embraced sentencing policies that largely give effect to agreements negotiated by Crown and defence counsel. Yet despite the recommendations of the Canadian Sentencing Commission (1987) and the Law Reform Commission of Canada (1989), there is still no formal process that requires Canadian courts to scrutinize the contents of a plea bargain and to ensure that there is adequate protection for the rights and interests of all the affected parties—the Crown, the accused, the victim(s), and society in general (Verdun-Jones and Tijerino 2005).

In contrast, in the federal and state courts of the United States, trial judges are required to scrutinize plea agreements between the prosecuting and defence attorneys and have the power to accept or reject them (Pan and Kaiser 2001; Herman 2004). Judges are expected to examine the basic facts surrounding the charges laid against the accused and to consider the interests of all the affected parties, including society in general, the justice system, the accused, and the victim(s) of the offences (Verdun-Jones and Tijerino 2001, 2004). In many American jurisdictions, the victim of an offence is entitled to provide input to the court during a plea agreement hearing, although in no jurisdiction is the victim given a right of veto over a proposed agreement (U.S. Department of Justice 2002). Judges do not involve themselves in the negotiation process; their power is limited to accepting or rejecting the proposed plea agreement. The major advantage of this procedure is its transparency, since the existence of the plea agreement is openly acknowledged and is usually examined in open court. Furthermore, plea agreements are, by law, regulated by the judiciary.

Canada's *Criminal Code* does provide for formal pretrial hearings before a judge in order "to consider the matters that, to promote a fair and expeditious hearing, would be better decided before the start of the proceedings, and other similar matters, and to make arrangements for decisions on those matters" (s. 625.1). However, these pre-trial hearings are not held for the specific purpose of examining a proposed plea agreement. Indeed, the *Criminal Code* does not require that the existence of a plea agreement be made known to the court in the course of such hearings; nor does the *Code* impose a duty on trial judges to investigate the circumstances underlying a plea agreement, if it comes to their attention that an agreement has, in fact, been reached between Crown and defence counsel.

Since 1992, the *Criminal Code* has required that a trial judge take steps to ensure that an accused person who pleads guilty is doing so voluntarily. More specifically, Section 606(1.1) requires that before accepting a plea of guilty, the trial judge must first be satisfied that the accused person is pleading guilty voluntarily and that he or she "understands that the plea is an admission of the essential elements of the offence, the nature, and consequences of the plea, and that the court is not bound by any agreement made between the accused and the prosecutor." Clearly, Section 606(1.1) only provides protection for the rights of the accused person. Unlike American judges, a Canadian trial judge is under no duty to scrutinize the facts underlying a plea agreement and is not required to hear evidence as to whether it serves the best interests of the various stakeholders concerned (including the victim(s) and the community at large).

THE ROLE OF VICTIMS IN RELATION TO THE PLEA NEGOTIATIONS PROCESS

Since there is no formal judicial procedure for scrutinizing plea agreements in Canada, there is no opportunity for the victims of crime to express their views to a trial judge concerning the contents of a proposed plea agreement. However, victims may have a role to play at an earlier stage of the pre-trial process.

Most Canadian provinces and territories have enacted legislation that entitles victims of crime to receive information concerning the status of the investigation and the prosecution of "their" cases (Roach 1999; Verdun-Jones and Tijerino 2001, 2004, 2005). However, at present, the only Canadian jurisdictions that have enacted legislation that explicitly deals with the role of victims in the plea negotiation process are Manitoba and Ontario. The Ontario legislation merely requires that victims "should have access to information" about "any pretrial arrangements that relate to a plea that may be entered by the accused at trial" (*Victims' Bill of Rights*, S.O. 1995, c. 6, s.2(x)). It is significant that the Martin Report (Ontario Attorney General 1993), which was published two years before the enactment of the Ontario *Victims' Bill of Rights,* had recognized that victims should be consulted about plea bargains "where appropriate and feasible." However, as Roach (1999, 99) points out, the recommendations of the Martin Task Force were not designed to enhance the level of direct victim participation in the criminal justice process in Ontario, making it clear that victims should not be given the right to veto an agreement of which they disapproved. According to Roach, the report assumed that the exercise of power in plea bargaining should remain squarely in the hands of criminal justice professionals; the primary goal of the Task Force in recommending more widespread acceptance of plea bargaining was not that of victim empowerment but rather that of enhancing the efficiency of a court system that would collapse if most defendants decided to exercise their right to a full trial (ibid., 99).

Moreover, in 2000, the Province of Manitoba implemented part of a new *Victims' Bill of Rights* (C.C.S.M. c. V55), which created a right for victims to be *consulted* (as opposed to merely *informed*) about various aspects of the prosecution of "their" cases. Unfortunately, even when provincial legislation grants rights to victims in relation to proposed plea agreements, these rights may not be enforceable in the courts. For example, in *Vanscoy v. Ontario* (1999), a judge of the Ontario Superior Court of Justice held that Ontario's *Victims' Bill of Rights* did not create any substantive rights. In this case, the complainants asserted that their right to be informed about plea negotiations had been violated when the Crown failed to inform them that a plea agreement had been reached with defence counsel. Justice Day ruled (para. 22) that the Ontario legislation did not create enforceable *rights;* rather, it articulated certain *principles*:

> I conclude that the legislature did not intend for s. 2(1) of the *Victims Bill of Rights* to provide rights to the victims of crime. The Act is a statement of principle and social policy, beguilingly clothed in the language of legislation. It does not establish any statutory rights for the victims of crime.

It is noteworthy that Manitoba's *Victims' Bill of Rights* is a trailblazing statute insofar as it creates an administrative mechanism designed to hold criminal justice officials to account if they fail to perform their statutory duties to provide information to—and consult with—victims of crime. Disgruntled victims may take their complaints to the Director of Victims' Support Services and may also seek the assistance of the provincial Ombudsperson, who must appoint a Crime Victim Investigator to deal with such complaints (Verdun-Jones and Tijerino 2005, 196).

RESEARCH INTO PLEA NEGOTIATIONS IN CANADA

Although plea negotiations constitute a significant element in the criminal justice system in Canada, there is a surprising paucity of empirical research into the phenomenon. Some evidence suggests that police officers and prosecutors are willing to admit that plea negotiations occur with frequency. For example, a study by Jonah and colleagues (1999) examined the practices, perceptions, and attitudes of 1,545 police officers across Canada in relation to the enforcement of impaired driving laws. About two-thirds of the police officers surveyed indicated that plea bargaining had occurred in impaired driving cases in which they were concerned (28.2 percent indicated it occurred in at least some cases; 36.7 percent responded that it occurred frequently). The major reason cited for plea bargaining was to "speed up the court process" (59.2 percent). Similarly, in a study of decision making by Crown counsel in relation to dangerous offender applications in British Columbia and Ontario, Bonta and colleagues (1996, 39) found that 71 percent of Crown counsel indicated that "they would consider plea bargaining as a viable option if evidentiary problems existed."

The most comprehensive Canadian study of plea negotiations was conducted some 25 years ago. A group of researchers at the University of Toronto's Centre of Criminology conducted a major study of discretionary decision making in the criminal justice process. The study employed several research methods, including direct observation of the plea bargaining process. In all, 101 accused persons were tracked through the criminal justice system from arrest to sentence. The data from this study were reported in several sources, the most comprehensive of which was a book by Ericson and Baranek (1982).

To create a detailed picture of plea negotiation processes in one county in Ontario, this study kept verbatim transcripts of interviews with the accused and interviews with lawyers. It also recorded conversations in the Crown attorney's office. Researchers also observed the court appearances of the defendants in the sample. The result was the first Canadian study in which researchers were able to document the complex dynamics involved in plea bargaining.

Ericson and Baranek (1982, 117) employed the term *plea discussions* rather than *plea bargaining*, because the former expression makes clear that discussions may be entered into without an agreement ever being reached. They concluded that "plea discussions were a widespread and integral part of the order out of court" (121). In this respect, they found that lawyers for as many as 57 of the 80 accused said that they had entered into plea discussions (117–18). Furthermore, they discovered that participation in plea discussions was not confined to Crown and defence counsel; indeed, the police were frequently involved at various stages in the plea discussion process (121).

Ericson and Baranek suggested that the existence of multiple charges appears to constitute a major element in the circumstances that lead to plea discussions taking place. Of the 23 accused whose lawyers did *not* engage in such discussions, 17 had only one charge laid against them (compared with only 9 of the 57 accused whose lawyers were involved in plea discussions). The authors believed that multiple charging is a vital component of the plea discussion process in Canada; and that without the existence of multiple charges, the defence would not be able to negotiate for the withdrawal of some charge(s) in return for the entry of a guilty plea to others. Lawyers who engaged in discussions with the Crown reported that withdrawal of charges was the major topic of conversation in plea discussions (ibid., 119).

Given the finding that there was widespread involvement of lawyers in plea discussions, what was the most likely outcome of these encounters? Ericson and Baranek discovered that although many of the lawyers engaged in plea discussions, only about one-quarter of them stated that they had reached an agreement that could be considered a bargain (143). For this group of lawyers, the most frequently mentioned agreement was one that included a sentence concession. Of the remaining lawyers who entered plea discussions, 12 percent stated that they had not reached an agreement, while lawyers for the remaining 88 percent claimed that the agreement reached brought no real advantage for the accused. More than half the lawyers (representing 23 accused) thought that an agreement had brought no tangible benefit because the charges that were withdrawn or reduced in their cases did not represent a genuine concession, but were merely the result of overcharging by the police in the first place (145).

Solomon (1983) also analyzed the data from this study and concluded that plea negotiations "did not result in important concessions for the accused." In the Provincial Court, almost 80 percent of the criminal cases that were not withdrawn by the Crown terminated with guilty pleas, and 60 percent of these cases involved plea discussions. It appears that the discussions between defence counsel and the Crown and/or police usually focused on the charges to which the accused would plead guilty, rather than on the sentence (although there was some discussion of the approach that the Crown would adopt at the sentencing stage).

Plea agreements resulted in the dropping of charges (which were often not justified in the first place) and at least a tacit agreement as to the Crown's recommendation for a sentence. However, Solomon pointed out that there was no clear relationship between the charges to which the accused ultimately pleaded guilty and the sentence handed down by the court (37). Furthermore, the sentencing recommendations made by the Crown had no direct impact on the sentence actually handed down by the court. In these circumstances, an accused person who entered into a plea arrangement with the Crown had no guarantee that his or her guilty plea would make any difference whatsoever to the ultimate outcome of the case.

This pioneering study by the University of Toronto criminologists provides a valuable snapshot of plea negotiations as they took place almost a quarter-century ago. Circumstances have undoubtedly changed considerably since then, and as noted above, the courts are now considerably more willing to accept joint sentencing submissions from Crown and defence counsel. So it would be unwise to assume that the findings by Ericson and Baranek and the analysis by Solomon reflect the nature and scope of contemporary plea negotiations either in Ontario or in other parts of Canada. Clearly, there a similar type of study needs to be conducted in contemporary circumstances.

More recent research has identified a powerful reason for accused persons to seek a plea agreement with the Crown. Indeed, a recent study by Kellough and Wortley (2002) concludes that the detention of an accused person in custody prior to trial is a significant factor in persuading him or her to enter into plea negotiations with the Crown. In a study of more than 1,800 criminal court cases that came before two Toronto bail courts in a six-month period (October 1993 to April 1994), Kellough and Wortley found that accused persons who had been held in custody were more likely to plead guilty than their out-of-custody counterparts. When an accused person had been held in custody, the Crown usually refused to drop any of the original charges until he or she pleaded guilty to other charges. However, if an accused person had been released on bail into the community, he or she was less willing to plead guilty to any of the charges, thereby making the Crown's task of obtaining a conviction more difficult. In this respect, Kellough and Wortley (2002, 204) concluded:

> An out-of-custody accused is more likely to have all of the charges dropped but a detained accused who resists pleading guilty is more likely to spend more time in custody. In the majority of cases, being in custody prior to trial eventually means being persuaded of the wisdom of entering into plea negotiations with the Crown.

A study by Simon Fraser University researchers, Viljoen, Klaver, and Roesch (2005) indicates that another reason that may influence accused persons to enter into plea negotiations with prosecutors is their perception of the strength of the case against them. A study of legal decision making by youths detained in a Washington State pre-trial facility found that adolescents (aged 15 to 17) were more likely to plead guilty and enter into a plea agreement if they perceived that the evidence against them was strong.

CONCLUSIONS

Plea negotiations are a well-established feature of contemporary criminal justice in Canada. The courts have accepted the legitimacy of this practice and have encouraged it by demonstrating their willingness to accept joint sentencing submissions by Crown and defence counsel. Plea negotiations are accepted as a necessary evil in a criminal justice system in which the Crown has finite resources with which to prosecute cases. Since the Crown does not have the ability to take the majority of criminal cases to a full trial, it needs to provide an incentive to criminal defendants to plead guilty to at least some criminal charges (Roberts 2000; Bjerk 2005). The strongest incentive for a guilty plea is the offer of a less severe sentence. There is no doubt that defence counsel enter into negotiations with Crown counsel in the belief that a plea agreement will make provision for a sentence that is more lenient than the sentence that is likely to be imposed should the accused person be convicted of the original charges following a full trial (Ericson and Baranek 1982; Solomon 1983, 41).

While plea negotiations have acquired a certain degree of acceptance and grudging respectability, they are still not subject to a formal process of regulation by the judiciary, as is the case in American criminal courts. As McGillivray (1997–98) has aptly commented: "plea bargaining is a closed-door and often hasty process, unmediated by the judiciary" (para. 20). If plea negotiations are indeed an "integral element of the Canadian criminal process" (to quote the Supreme Court of Canada), it would surely constitute sound public policy for the Parliament of Canada to amend the *Criminal Code* with a view to establishing the necessary machinery for their regulation by the courts. Furthermore, there is a need to open the process of plea negotiations to public scrutiny and to create an opportunity for victims to have their views heard concerning proposed plea agreements. Finally, the other Canadian provinces and territories should follow the lead of Manitoba and require prosecutors to consult with victims before entering into plea agreements with defence counsel.

Plea negotiations have certainly come of age in the 21st century. However, the criminal justice system has been excruciatingly slow in developing mechanisms to regulate plea negotiations and has failed to ensure that plea agreements serve not only the traditional interests of prosecutors, offenders, and the court bureaucracies, but also the compelling interests of the victims of crime and of Canadian society as a whole.

DISCUSSION QUESTIONS

1. *The large volume of criminal cases being processed by the system and the high percentage (approximately 90 percent) of accuseds who plead guilty means that abolishing plea bargaining would swamp the courts with additional trials. Abolition of this practice is therefore unlikely. Even if it were possible, however, would it necessarily be a good thing?*
2. *Victims are sometimes shocked to learn that the Crown has accepted a plea to a lesser, included offence rather than proceed to trial on a more serious charge, with the accused pleading not guilty. Victims are seldom consulted or kept apprised of developments in negotiations with the accused. Should individual victims have a greater say in plea negotiations? Should they be given the power to overrule any plea arrangement?*

FURTHER READINGS

Ericson, R. and P. Baranek. 1982. *The Ordering of Justice: A Study of Accused Persons as Dependants in the Criminal Process.* Toronto: University of Toronto Press.

Law Reform Commission of Canada. 1989. *Plea Discussions and Agreements.* Working Paper no. 60. Ottawa: Law Reform Commission of Canada.

Verdun-Jones, S. and A. Hatch. 1985. *Plea Bargaining and Sentencing Guidelines.* Ottawa: Department of Justice.

REFERENCES

Bjerk, D. 2005. *On the Role of Plea Bargaining and the Distribution of Sentences in the Absence of Judicial System Frictions*. Hamilton: McMaster University, Department of Economics. http://socserv.mcmaster.ca/bjerk/pleabargain1.pdf

Bonta, J., A. Harris, I. Zinger, and D. Carriere. 1996. *The Crown Files Research Project: A Study of Dangerous Offenders*. Ottawa: Public Safety and Emergency Preparedness Canada. http://ww2.psepc-sppcc.gc.ca/publications/corrections/pdf/199601_e.pdf

Canadian Sentencing Commission. 1987. *Report of the Canadian Sentencing Commission*. Ottawa: Supply and Services Canada.

Cohen, S. and A. Doob. 1989. "Public Attitudes Towards Plea Bargaining." *Criminal Law Quarterly* 32: 85–109.

Cousineau, D. and S. Verdun-Jones. 1979. "Evaluating Research into Plea Bargaining in Canada and the United States: Pitfalls Facing the Policy-Makers." *Canadian Journal of Criminology* 21: 293–309.

Di Luca, J. 2005. "Expedient McJustice or Principled Alternative Dispute Resolution? A Review of Plea Bargaining in Canada." *Criminal Law Quarterly* 50: 14–66.

Ericson, R.V. and P. Baranek. 1982. *The Ordering of Justice: A Study of Accused Persons as Dependants in the Criminal Process*. Toronto: University of Toronto Press.

Galligan, P.T. 1996. *Report to the Attorney General of Ontario on Certain Matters Relating to Karla Homolka*. Toronto: ADR Chambers.

Gillis, C. 2005. "Karla Homolka: Girl Next Door." *Macleans*, March 15, 2005. http://www.macleans.ca/topstories/justice/article.jsp?content=20050321_102168_102168

Griffiths, C.T. and S. Verdun-Jones. 1994. *Canadian Criminal Justice*. 2nd ed. Toronto: Harcourt Brace Jovanovich Canada.

Herman, G.N. 2004. *Plea Bargaining*. 2nd ed. Charlottesville: LexisNexis.

Jonah, B. et al. 1999. "Front-Line Police Officers' Practices, Perceptions, and Attitudes About the Enforcement of Impaired Driving Laws in Canada." *Accident Analysis and Prevention* 31: 421–43.

Kellough, G. and S. Wortley. 2002. "Remand for Plea: Bail Decisions and Plea Bargaining as Commensurate Decisions." *British Journal of Criminology* 42: 186–210.

Lafontaine, G. and V. Rondinelli. 2005. "Plea Bargaining and the Modern Criminal Defence Lawyer: Negotiating Guilt and the Economics of the 21st Century Criminal Justice." *Criminal Law Quarterly* 50: 108–27.

Law Reform Commission of Canada. 1989. *Plea Discussions and Agreements*. Working Paper no. 60. Ottawa.

——. 1984. *Disclosure by the Prosecution*. Report no. 22. Ottawa: Ministry of Supply and Services.

——. 1975. *Criminal Procedure: Control of the Process*. Working Paper no. 15. Ottawa: Information Canada.

Manson, A. 2001. *The Law of Sentencing*. Toronto: Irwin Law.

McCoy, C. 2005. "Plea Bargaining as Coercion: The Trial Penalty and Plea Bargaining Reform." *Criminal Law Quarterly* 50: 67–107.

McGillivray, A. 1998. "'A Moral Vacuity in Her Which Is Difficult if Not Impossible to Explain': Law, Psychiatry, and the Remaking of Karla Homolka." *International Journal of the Legal Profession* 5: 255–88.

——. 1997–98. "*R. v. Bauder*: Seductive Children, Safe Rapists, and Other Justice Tales." *Manitoba Law Journal* 25: 359–83.

Ontario, Attorney General. 1993. *Report of the Attorney General's Advisory Committee on Charge Screening, Disclosure, and Resolutions Discussions*. Toronto: Queen's Printer.

Pan, J. and M.G. Kaiser. 2001. "Thirtieth Annual Review of Criminal Procedure: Guilty Pleas." *Georgetown Law Journal* 89: 384–437.

Roach, K. 1999. *Due Process and Victims' Rights: The New Law and Politics of Criminal Justice*. Toronto: University of Toronto Press.

Roberts, J. 2000. *Plea Bargaining with Budgetary Constraints and Deterrence*. Working Papers from University of Toronto, Department of Economics. Toronto: University of Toronto. http://www.chass.utoronto.ca/ecipa/archive/UT-ECIPA-JOROB-00-01.pdf

Seifman, R.D. and A. Freidberg. 2001. "Plea Bargaining in Victoria: The Role of Counsel." *Criminal Law Journal* 2: 64–74.

Solomon, P. 1983. *Criminal Justice Policy, From Research to Reform*. Toronto: Butterworths.

U.S. Department of Justice. 2002. *Office for Victims of Crime, Legal Series Bulletin # 7: Victim Input into Plea Agreements*. Washington: Office for Victims of Crime. http://www.ojp.usdoj.gov/ovc/publications/bulletins/legalseries/bulletin7/welcome.html

Verdun-Jones, S.N. and A. Hatch. 1985. *Plea Bargaining and Sentencing Guidelines*. Ottawa: Department of Justice Canada.

Verdun-Jones, S.N. and A.A. Tijerino. 2001. *Victim Participation in the Plea Negotiation Process in Canada: A Review of the Literature and Four Models of Law Reform*. Ottawa: Department of Justice Canada.

——. 2004. "Four Models of Victim Involvement During Plea Negotiations: Bridging the Gap Between Legal Reforms and Current Legal Practice." *Canadian Journal of Criminology and Criminal Justice* 46: 471–500.

——. 2005. "Victim Participation in the Plea Negotiation Process: An Idea Whose Time Has Come?" *Criminal Law Quarterly* 50: 190–212.

Viljoen J.L., J. Klaver, and R. Roesch. 2005. "Legal Decisions of Preadolescent and Adolescent Defendants: Predictors of Confessions, Pleas, Communication with Attorneys, and Appeals." *Law and Human Behavior* 29: 253–77.

CASES CITED

Boudreau v. Benaiah (2000), 142 C.C.C. (3rd) 97 (Ont. C.A.).

R. v. Bezdan, [2001] B.C.J. No. 808 (C.A.)(QL).

R. v. Burlingham, [1995] 2 S.C.R. 206.

R. v. G.W.C., (2000) 150 C.C.C. (3d) 513 (Alta. C.A.), Supplementary Reasons, [2001] 5 W.W.R. 240 (Alta. C.A.).

R. v. Lyons, [1987] 2 S.C.R. 309.

R. v. Neale, [2000] B.C.J. No. 668 (C.A.)(QL).

Vanscoy v. Ontario, [1999] O.J. No. 1661 (Ont. S.C.)(QL).

ENDNOTES

1. The principle that courts are in no way bound by a plea agreement is illustrated by the most unfortunate case of *R. v. Neale* (2000). Neale had agreed to plead guilty to a charge of robbery in exchange for the Crown's undertaking to make a submission in support of a five-year sentence, less the time already spent in custody. Unfortunately, counsel neglected to inform the trial judge that this plea agreement had been reached. Subsequently, the trial judge sentenced Neale to seven years in prison. Even though Neale did not receive the sentence recommended by the Crown (and even though the trial judge was never informed that a plea bargain had been struck), the Court of Appeal dismissed the appeal against the sentence. Justice Lambert noted (para. 14) that, in his opinion, "no injustice is being done to the appellant in this particular case through the processes before the sentencing judge." He stated that "the sentence is a fit one with the appropriate range and the circumstances of the sentencing were not such as to create any injustice."

2. Peace bonds may be imposed under Sections 810, 810.01, 810.1, and 810.2 of the *Criminal Code*. Under a peace bond, an accused person enters into a "recognizance" (a binding promise) to be of "good conduct" for a period up to 12 months. Breach of this recognizance is a criminal offence (s. 811 of the *Criminal Code*). This procedure is followed where there is a reasonable fear that the accused person will commit a serious offence— for example, a sexual assault against a child or a crime of domestic violence (see Bala 1999).

3. Homolka eventually served the entire 12 years of her sentence in prison. She was not granted parole or statutory release (see Gillis 2005).

CHAPTER 15
Serving Time at Home: The Conditional Sentence of Imprisonment

The term "sentenced to custody" usually means being ordered to spend time in a prison. However, some forms of custody involve placing restrictions on an offender's liberty but without requiring him to enter an institution. Most criminal justice systems allow certain offenders to serve their sentences of imprisonment at home, provided they comply with a number of conditions. If these conditions are violated, the offender is required to appear in court and may be ordered to serve the remainder of the sentence in prison. The *conditional sentence* of imprisonment in Canada is an example of a sentence of custody that is served at home. One of the most often discussed conditions imposed on offenders serving a conditional sentence of imprisonment is the curfew or house arrest.

What is it like to live under house arrest? This chapter reports findings from interviews with offenders who are serving a sentence of imprisonment—at home. This research also explores the experiences and perceptions of people who live with offenders serving these sentences. Their views are important for two reasons: first, because they share many of the restrictions imposed on offenders; and second, because they play an important role in ensuring that the offender complies with the conditions imposed by the court.

Julian V. Roberts, University of Oxford

In 1996, Canada's Parliament added a new sentence to the range of options available to the courts. The phrase *conditional sentence of imprisonment* is in a sense a paradox: it is a term of custody that the offender serves at home. If a judge believes that no sentence other than imprisonment is appropriate, he or she must then decide whether the offender will serve the sentence at home or be committed to a prison. Certain criteria must be met before the offender is allowed to serve the sentence at home. For example, if the offence carries a mandatory term of imprisonment, the offender is not eligible. If the offender is ordered to serve his or her sentence at home, the court imposes a number of conditions. The offender may have to obey a curfew or strict house arrest. This means being confined to home except for court-authorized absences—for example, to go to work or attend school. In addition, the court may order the offender to follow a treatment program and perform service for the community. The offender will also be supervised by a probation officer. In the event that the offender violates the court-imposed conditions without a reasonable excuse, the offender will be brought back to court and may be ordered to serve the remainder of the sentence in an institution.

PUBLIC STEREOTYPES OF SENTENCING

Misperceptions about prison life can lead people to dismiss a sentence of years in prison as "a slap on the wrist," one that the offender can do "standing on his head." For this reason, it's not surprising that there are misperceptions about home confinement. One public stereotype of the conditional sentence of imprisonment is that offenders serving sentences at home enjoy all the benefits of home life, and that the conditions they must obey (such as going to work or school and attending medical appointments) are simply those duties that any law-abiding citizen must do on a daily basis This somewhat naive (and cynical) view of a conditional sentence accounts in part for the widespread public opposition to the use of home confinement for offenders convicted of crimes of violence. For violent crimes, the public expects a severe response from the courts. To most of the public, being confined to one's home is not severe enough to represent an adequate response to violent crime.

At one time, this perception may have been fairly accurate. In the early days of the conditional sentence regime, offenders on whom this sentence was imposed had few conditions to follow. House arrest, for example, was practically unheard of (Roberts, Antonowicz, and Sanders 2000). Curfews were rare and many were very flexible (e.g., requiring the offender to be home only after 10:00 p.m. and until 7:00 a.m.). In some respects, the sanction was little different from a term of probation. Since then, however, conditional sentence orders have become tougher: house arrest is more frequent, and curfews tend to be more restrictive, beginning shortly after the offender has finished work for the day (Roberts 2002). An accurate picture of the true impact of any sanction can only be gained from understanding the perspective of the people who experience it. What do offenders think about a sentence of imprisonment served at home?

OFFENDER ATTITUDES ABOUT SERVING TIME AT HOME

> "It is like being with the people that I love, and doing my time with them, but it's not easy. Actually, I think it's tougher than being in jail."[1]

Institutional versus Community Imprisonment

Many people may be surprised to learn that some offenders prefer to go to prison rather than serve a tough community-based sanction. This reaction reflects the perception that prison is always more punitive than its alternatives. In addition, research examining the impact of conditions such as electronic monitoring and home confinement reveals that there are important parallels between prison and home confinement: many (but by no means all) of the "pains of imprisonment" can be reproduced in the home. Payne and Gainey (1998) compare the experience of prison to life on electronic monitoring. They point out that many of the aversive features of imprisonment, including loss of personal autonomy and deprivation of liberty, are endured by people on electronic monitoring.

Several individuals serving sentences at home have commented that while community imprisonment was clearly preferable to prison, it was not necessarily easier; living on a conditional sentence created challenges and difficulties not encountered in prison. In one sense, prison was the easier sanction, because offenders simply had to "wait out" the sentence: "I didn't like being behind bars, but being out is harder than being in jail." Another offender described life on a conditional sentence in the following words: "You have to think about what you are doing." Some individuals expressed pride at having lived through house arrest. One said: "It's been a long haul but I'm proud of what I've done." Such statements are seldom heard from people leaving prison or from those ending a period on parole.

Perceptions of Active versus Passive Sentencing

> "In jail, you know what you got. What you're doing. You may as well sit there for six months."

Prison creates a passive environment: prisoners react and respond to instructions from the institutional authority. In contrast, a conditional sentence is a far more active disposition: the offender can (and should) take steps toward rehabilitation and restoration. Some judges impose obligations on offenders to actively change their lives. This contrast between the two forms of imprisonment was brought home by one offender who said: "I've been in jail and there's nothing to do, you just eat. If you don't want to eat, you sleep. You stay the whole day sitting down. Being outside is preferable because I can prove to myself that I'm not that kind of person. I can prove to [other] people that I'm not that kind of person." This illustrates the positive potential of serving a sentence at home rather than in prison.

Daily Life in the Virtual Prison

"I was working in the kitchen while in remand, that was the only thing worthwhile in prison ... The community is the better way to go. It's also a lot harder, it teaches you [to make] a lot of sacrifices.

I have a bit of a problem sitting at home on a beautiful day when the 7-Eleven is five steps away.

The hardest part would be dealing with your friends and family, explaining why you couldn't go out.

The hardest for me was absolute house arrest, it's hard when ... you've gotta do something, and you can't. For example, our lease is up ... and I got to go find another place, and I can't do it"

What is it like to live under a tight set of court-ordered conditions, including house arrest or a strict curfew? Many offenders in Canada and elsewhere report that living under home confinement conditions was harder and the conditions more intrusive than they had anticipated (see Church and Dunstan 1997). The conditions that are hardest to respect are likely to account for the most breaches. The one issue on which all the Canadian offenders agreed was that the most difficult part of serving a conditional sentence was complying with house arrest or a very restrictive curfew. This result is consistent with Petersilia and Deschenes's (1994) research, wherein offenders were asked to rate the perceived difficulty of a number of community correctional conditions. House arrest with electronic monitoring was rated as the most difficult condition imposed on them.

Many of the offenders interviewed had been sentenced to absolute (i.e., 24-hour) house arrest. The consequences of this condition included these: it prevented offenders from participating in social activities; it interfered with family outings and special occasions; and it created a stigma when other people realized that the offender was serving a sentence. For one offender, the hardest condition was performing community service on top of his job. Nevertheless, he found it a rewarding experience: "When you're working 50 hours a week, it makes for some very long days. But it wasn't just a punishing experience, it was a rewarding experience."

IMPACT OF CONDITIONAL SENTENCE ON CHILDREN OF THE OFFENDER

An important consideration in imposing a community sentence rather than prison is the presence of a family. There is an additional incentive for courts to avoid incarcerating the offender if he or she has dependents, and many of the offenders who spoke to us about the experience of home confinement often had families and young children. The most punitive element for these offenders was the impact that the sentence had on their children, whose daily lives and interactions with their parents were affected for the duration of the sentence. One offender noted that the sentence was "especially hard on the kids ... because we used to go out, especially in the summer. Every time they ask me, I say I can't."

A female offender discussed the house arrest condition in the context of other conditions imposed: "The absolute curfew is the hardest thing. I can't go anywhere without telling my PO [probation officer]. Absolute curfew is like house arrest. My daughter wants to go the park, but I can't take her." She added that it put a lot of strain on her when she had to try and explain why they couldn't go to the park: "Sometimes I'd say, 'Oh, I'm tired,' or 'We just can't do that today.' It's hard because I don't know what to say. [pause] I have to make excuses." However, she added that staying home was easier than going to jail. She preferred staying home with her children and believed that if not for the children, she would have been sent to jail.

EFFECT ON INTERPERSONAL RELATIONSHIPS

One must be wary of generalizations about the effect of home detention on issues such as relationships. Close confinement for long periods has different effects depending on the personalities of the individuals involved, the nature of the relationship, and the home environment. Although not yet formally tested, an *intensification* effect may exist: home environments characterized by conflict and tension are likely to become worse as a result of the enforced confinement of the offender. Walters (2002) found that offenders on curfew orders in England and Wales reported that the curfew placed a strain on their relationships because it was hard to "walk away from arguments" (32). It is worth noting that these offenders were on curfew orders for a relatively short period: fully 70 percent of those interviewed in that study were serving curfew orders of less than four months. Facing a curfew order of two years—as is possible in Canada—would be a far more daunting proposition, one that might place even more stress on relationships.

Partners are also affected by the sentence. One offender said:

> [It has] been very hard on my girlfriend. She felt strapped down. She couldn't go nowhere, I couldn't drive her anywhere ... It was also hard for her because she didn't want to tell her friends that I was on a conditional sentence ... My girlfriend often tells me how it affects [their relationship]. All we can do is cook some supper if I get groceries on Sunday. All we can do is watch movies if she goes and gets them. I don't have a problem with [the other conditions imposed] but the 24 hours at home are too much.

On the other hand, home detention in generally positive environments may enhance human relationships. There is certainly evidence from the Canadian research that young adult offenders confined to homes with loving parents reported that the sentence had been a positive experience. The restrictions on the offender's movements can help rupture antisocial contacts and prevent individuals from being drawn into life patterns that can lead to further offending.

Feeling Pressure to Lie to Others about the Sentence

Few members of the public stop to think about the impact of a conditional sentence on the ways people react to an offender. These reactions can amplify the stigma associated with the sentence. Offenders talked about the stigma they felt when they told their coworkers about the court order and its associated restrictions.[2] Some individuals expressed concern about potential "whistle-blowers," people who might call the police if they believed that the offender was violating some condition of his or her order. This reaction underlines the important reality that surveillance is not the exclusive domain of probation officers. If it were, ensuring compliance would be impossible, since probation officers simply have too many clients to adequately monitor their behaviour. The negative reaction of friends and coworkers appears to create pressure on conditional sentence offenders to passively hide their status or actively deceive other people.

Offenders sentenced to a conditional sentence and obliged to wear an electronic monitor often have to explain their status to people with whom they have some kind of relationship. In Canada, few offenders are subject to electronic monitoring, since the equipment is not currently available in most provincial correctional systems. However, the restrictions on their movements mean that most offenders have to confront the question of how much to disclose to other people. Fearful of the consequences, many offenders elected to hide their status, particularly with respect to the workplace. In the case of employers, some offenders said nothing rather than explain the true state of affairs. As one individual noted: "I think I'll get fired if I tell my employer." In some cases, however, it was impossible to hide the fact of the sentence, since there were occasions when they were expected to stay after work.

Having to explain the court order to other people, particularly to children, was a source of considerable anxiety for many offenders. In the case of relatively young children, some offenders resorted to deception or simply said (in response to requests to go out) that they "couldn't go out right now." Other offenders explained matters more fully: "My son is fourteen. I sat down with him this summer and I told him what I did and what had happened. The main reason I told him is because he's approaching that age. I told him I don't want him to follow in my footsteps."

Loss of Spontaneity

Serving a term of imprisonment at home means that daily life has to be planned far more carefully. Offenders have to consider whether particular acts will constitute a breach of the court order, and they have to contact their sentence supervisors in order to apply for permission to attend particular events.

For older offenders, making an application to a younger probation officer was a "humbling" experience, as one such individual remarked. In order to join people for coffee after one of his group therapy meetings, he had to obtain the permission of his probation officer; otherwise, he would have been in breach, as the order required him to return directly home once the meeting had ended.

Most (but by no means all) offenders seemed concerned about the consequences of breaching the order by returning home late. One individual noted: "I never actually ran out of time [returning home after a court-authorized shopping trip], but I was always worried about running out of time." Time pressures were a source of considerable stress for these offenders. For the general public, the worst consequence of dawdling while shopping is missing the bus home; for conditional sentence offenders, being late home may result in arrest and, ultimately, committal to custody (for breaching the conditions of the sentence).

CONCLUSION

The portrait of community custody that emerges from this research is quite different from the image projected by the news media. Offenders serving their prison sentences at home are subject to numerous constraints that change their life in a dramatic manner. As well, there is little discussion in the media about the impact on third parties, or the role that family members play in helping "administer" the sentence of the court. One of the strengths of this sanction is that it draws upon the resources of the community—the social networks of the offender—to achieve some of its objectives. This strategy, however, comes at a cost: the effect of the sentence is amplified through these networks, and other people's lives are affected in significant ways. Of course, this is true of imprisonment as well. When an offender is committed to custody, his partner and his family suffer the loss of their loved one and have to accustom themselves to the inconveniences of visiting hours. The isolation of a prison sentence, however, has a destructive effect on social relations; this is why such a high percentage of relationships fail to survive a lengthy term of incarceration. A conditional sentence may actually strengthen the links between people.

Families and partners of offenders sentenced to conditional sentence have an onerous task thrust upon them, and in most jurisdictions they have no institutional support or backup. Yet despite the negatives, there is ample evidence in the research that offenders and their families see a positive element to conditional sentences, and not simply because the sanction spares them the experience of prison. Although on occasion home detention may cause or heighten tensions among family members or between partners, for most offenders the increased time at home appears to have a positive effect on relationships. Many offenders recognize that serving a conditional sentence creates opportunities to change their lifestyle and to preserve social relations that otherwise would be threatened or ruptured by incarceration. In this sense, offenders perceive the sanction as a novel form of custody. Whatever other people may feel about this new form of custody, offenders seem well aware of the potential of the sanction.

DISCUSSION QUESTIONS

1. *Some people argue that serving time at home is never going to be as harsh as spending the same amount of time in prison. What is your view?*
2. *Should the other people sharing the offender's home have to agree before a sentence of home custody is imposed?*

FURTHER READINGS

Gibbs, A., and D. King. 2003. "Home Detention with Electronic Monitoring: The New Zealand Experience." *Criminal Justice* 3: 199–211.

Roberts, J.V. 2004. *The Virtual Prison*. Cambridge: Cambridge University Press.

Roberts, J.V., L. Maloney, and R. Vallis, R. 2003. *Coming Home to Prison: A Study of Offender Experiences of Conditional Sentencing*. Ottawa: Department of Justice Canada.

REFERENCES

Church, A., and S. Dunstan. 1997. *Home Detention: The Evaluation of the Home Detention Pilot Programme 1995–1997*. Wellington: New Zealand Ministry of Justice. http://www.justice.govt.nz/pubs/reports/1997/ homedetention/ Default.htm

Payne, B., and R. Gainey. 1998. "A Qualitative Assessment of the Pains Experienced on Electronic Monitoring." *International Journal of Offender Therapy and Comparative Criminology* 42: 149–63.

Petersilia, J., and E. Piper Deschenes. 1994. "Perceptions of Punishment: Inmates and Staff Rank the Severity of Prison versus Intermediate Sanctions." *Prison Journal* 74: 306–28.

Roberts, J.V. 2002. "The Evolution of Conditional Sentencing in Canada." *Criminal Reports* 3 (6th Series): 268–82.

Roberts, J.V., D. Antonowicz, and T. Sanders. 2000. "Conditional Sentences of Imprisonment: An Empirical Analysis of Conditions." *Criminal Reports* 30: 113–25.

Walters, I. 2002. *Evaluation of the National Roll-Out of Curfew Orders*. Home Office Online Report 15/02. London: Home Office: Research, Development and Statistics Directorate.

ENDNOTES

1. Unless otherwise indicated, all offender quotes in this chapter come from focus groups and interviews with conditional sentence offenders and their co-residents, conducted in Canada (see Roberts, Maloney, and Vallis 2003).

2. Of course, being sent to prison carries a great deal of stigma too; but an offender who spends three months inside can easily explain his absence from the community by saying that he was away. In this sense, imprisonment at home is a more *public* punishment and may carry even more stigma than imprisonment. This is especially true in small communities.

CHAPTER 16
Do Police Discriminate Against Minority Youth in Canada?[1]

The most important quality of any criminal justice system is fairness. If justice is administered unfairly, without respect for the rule of law, the system will lose its legitimacy in the eyes of the community. Once perceived legitimacy is lost, the system will fail, as members of the public find other ways of redressing wrongs. Criminologists around the world have for many years conducted research into the possibility of discrimination. A considerable body of research has now demonstrated that in all Western countries one minority or another is treated more harshly. In Canada, research has been accumulating for years on the treatment of visible minorities by the criminal justice system. In this chapter the authors review the evidence relating to the treatment of visible minority youth by the police. They explore the overrepresentation of minority youth in crime and criminal justice statistics and then discuss potential explanations for these disturbing trends.

Peter J. Carrington, University of Waterloo, and
Robin T. Fitzgerald, Griffith University

Youth belonging to certain racial and ethnic minority groups are overrepresented as offenders in the criminal justice system. This problem has been documented at different stages of the criminal justice system, in many countries, and at different points in time (e.g., Australian Bureau of Statistics 2008; Commission on Systemic Racism 1995; Engen, Steen, and Bridges 2002; Fergusson, Horwood, and Swain-Campbell 2003; Wortley and McCalla 2003). Disproportionate minority contact with the police, the subject of this chapter, refers to the overrepresentation of certain minority groups among the people who are stopped, searched, questioned, arrested, or charged by police. It is a problem that brings into question the principles of justice and fairness that underpin the criminal justice system.

Not surprisingly for an issue that has such important political and human rights implications, disproportionate minority contact has been the subject of heated debate among social scientists. In Canada there is general agreement among researchers about the overrepresentation of some minority groups in incarcerated populations (La Prairie 1992; Roberts and Melchers 2003; Wortley 1999). There is also partial agreement about the extent to which this overrepresentation occurs at the earliest stages of the criminal justice process—police stops, searches, and arrests. However, there is also disagreement on this subject—see, for example, the debate in *Canadian Journal of Criminology and Criminal Justice* (Gabor 2004; Gold 2003; Melchers 2003; Wortley and Tanner 2003, 2005), which has been precipitated by allegations of racial profiling by the Toronto Police Service, made in the *Toronto Star* (Rankin et al. 2002a, 2002b, 2002c). What is much more difficult to establish, and more hotly contested, is the explanation for any observed minority overrepresentation in contact with the police.

EXPLAINING OVERREPRESENTATION: MORE CRIME OR MORE POLICE ATTENTION?

There are two commonly proposed explanations for disproportionate minority youth contact with the police. Proponents of the first explanation—termed "differential involvement"—argue that such contact results from minority youths' greater involvement in delinquent behaviour. Since (according to this argument) minority youth commit more crime, they are naturally, and justly, more likely to come into contact with the police—and also more likely to be arrested, charged, found guilty, and incarcerated.

Proponents of the second explanation—"differential treatment"—argue that disproportionate contact results from differences in the ways minority youth are treated by the police and other stages of the criminal justice system. These two explanations are not mutually exclusive: differential involvement in crime and differential treatment by police could both contribute to differential minority contact. This chapter evaluates these two explanations for overrepresentation, drawing on recent research on racial disparities in youth contact with the police in Canada.

Adolescence is a critical period to consider with respect to minority overrepresentation in the justice system. While almost all teenage boys, and a majority of teenage girls, indulge in some illegal behaviour, it is the ones who come into contact with the police, and may be arrested, charged, and found guilty, who are most at risk of becoming repeat offenders and of continuing to commit crimes as adults. Looking more closely at youth contact with the police therefore provides an opportunity to understand the influence of the first exposure to the criminal justice system on racial disparities.

IS THERE RACIAL DISPARITY IN YOUTH CONTACT WITH THE POLICE?

Research in Canada demonstrates that minority youth are more likely to be stopped, searched, and arrested by the police. Importantly, the research also suggests that racial and ethnic groups—and in particular visible minority groups—cannot be treated as monolithic with respect to their contact with the police; rather, some groups are at higher risk for police contact than others. For example, in a survey of Toronto high school students, Wortley and Tanner (2005) found that, as a group, visible minority students were *not* more likely to be stopped and/or searched by the police than white students. However, when they looked more closely at individual race and ethnicity categories, they found that the proportion of black students who reported that they had been stopped and searched by the police in the two years preceding the survey was 1.5 to 2.5 times greater than the proportions of youth from other racial groups. Similarly, Fitzgerald and Carrington (2009) examined data from a nationally representative survey of youth aged 12 to 17 years and found that as a group, black, Aboriginal, and Arab and West Asian youth were nearly three times more likely than others to have had contact with the police for something the police thought they had done. Table 16.1 shows the overrepresentation of these high-risk minority groups among Canadian youth aged 12 to 17 who reported a police contact in the past year—35 percent of high-risk minority youth reported a police contact, compared with only 13 percent of other visible minority youth and 16 percent of White youth.

Similar patterns of overrepresentation have been reported in Canadian research assessing official police data directly, though these studies have not distinguished between adult and youth populations. In a study of police stops in Kingston, Ontario, Wortley and Marshall (2005) found that over a

Table 16.1 *Percent of Canadian Youth Aged 12 to 17 Who Reported a Police Contact in the Past Year*

	Police contact in past year?		
	Yes	No	Weighted
Racial/ethnic group	%	%	N
Black, Aboriginal, Arab, and West Asian	34.9	65.1	189
Other visible minority	13.0	87.0	366
White	15.7	84.3	3,609
Weighted N	678	3,486	4,164

Note: *"Police contact" was determined by this question: "How many times in the past 12 months were you questioned by the police about anything they thought you did?" The analysis compares youth who had any contact with the police to those who had no contact.*

Source: Statistics Canada. *National Longitudinal Study of Children and Youth, Cycle 4, 2000-2001.*

one-year period, black residents were three times more likely than their white counterparts to be stopped by the police. They also found that black overrepresentation was greatest at the earliest stages of police interaction—the race differential was greater for police stops than for actual arrests.

LaPrairie (1992) has demonstrated that overrepresentation of Aboriginal people as offenders in the criminal justice system is highest in the Prairie provinces, where their representation in the general population is also greater. A study of police-reported incidents in Winnipeg, Manitoba, supports this view, showing that over the one-year period for which the data were collected, Aboriginal youths and adults were about seven times more likely than all others to be identified by the police as offenders (Fitzgerald and Carrington 2008).

More recent research in the aftermath of the 9/11 terrorist attacks on the United States indicates that in Canada and other Western countries, Arab and West Asian people have been attracting greater security/criminal justice attention—from police, intelligence, and border security agencies—than they did in the past. Members of the Arab-Canadian community have claimed that they are increasingly the targets of police racial profiling and have raised concerns about laws (such as Bills C-11 and C-36) that provide law enforcement agencies such as the RCMP with the opportunity to use excessive power to place citizens under surveillance (Khalema and Wannas-Jones 2003).

EXPLANATIONS OF DISPROPORTIONATE MINORITY CONTACT

As noted, the two dominant explanations for the observed racial disparity in contact with the police are "disproportionate minority involvement" in crime and "disproportionate minority treatment" at various stages of criminal justice processing (Piquero 2008). Those who support the "differential involvement" explanation argue that minority youth are more likely to have contact with the police because they are more likely to commit crime, and/or to commit the type of crime that comes to the attention of the police—for example, serious violent crime (Tonry 1997). The implication here is that the police treat youth equally, regardless of their race or ethnicity. Thus, proponents of this view would argue that if minority youth had the same level and type of criminal behaviour as white youth, there would be no disproportionate minority contact with police.

This suggests a means of testing the differential involvement explanation. If minority youth are found not to have higher levels of crime, or of certain kinds of crime, this explanation must be rejected. However, even if minority youth do have higher levels of crime or of certain kinds of crime, the researcher can statistically "control for" the higher level or type of minority crime. By statistically controlling for or "holding constant" the level and type of crime, the researcher creates a situation where there are no differences in criminal behaviour between minority and nonminority youth. If the racial/ethnic differences in police contact disappear as a result of this statistical manipulation, then the differential involvement hypothesis is supported. However, if racial/ethnic differences in police contacts persist even after controlling for differences in involvement in crime, then differential involvement is not the explanation for those differences. In performing such a test, the usual official data on criminal involvement cannot be used, as this information comes from police records and therefore reflects any existing racialized police practices. Rather, some independent source of data must be used; normally this is "self-report" data on involvement in crime that comes from the youths themselves.

The "differential treatment" explanation says that disproportionate minority contact results from decision-making processes that operate differently for members of different races and ethnicities at various stages of the criminal justice system. At the initial stage of police contact, this means that minority youth are more likely to be selected by the police for stops, searches, arrests, and/or formal charges, regardless of their actual involvement in crime.

There are at least three versions of the differential treatment explanation where police contact is concerned. In the first version, researchers have argued that police—as organizations and individuals—tend to pay more attention to certain kinds of youths (regardless of their race)—for example, those who are older, male, unsupervised by parents or other caregivers, and of lower socioeconomic status—and that some of these social characteristics are more prevalent in some racial and ethnic groups than in others (Engen, Steen, and Bridges 2002, 196). In a second version of the differential treatment explanation, police tend to pay more attention to certain places—for example, areas with higher socioeconomic disadvantage, higher perceived social disorder, or crime "hotspots"—and members of some minority groups tend disproportionately to be found in these places (see, e.g., Sampson and Wilson 1995). In a third version of the differential treatment explanation, police are directly influenced by race/ethnicity itself in their decision making. The first two versions do not concern police racial bias *per se*; rather, they suggest that members of certain minority groups are more likely to have some personal, family, and neighbourhood characteristics that are risk factors for police contact; in other words, disproportionate minority contact is due not to police bias, but to systemic social discrimination that results in certain racial/ethnic minority groups being disproportionately represented in social and geographic locations at greater risk of police attention (Wilson 2009).

IS THERE EVIDENCE TO SUPPORT THE DIFFERENTIAL INVOLVEMENT EXPLANATION?

There is evidence that youth belonging to particular racial and ethnic minority groups commit more crime than others, and particularly more of the type of crime that is likely to be reported to the police. More serious crimes, such as violent offences, are more likely to come to the attention of the police and are also more likely to result in police action than other types of crimes (Blumstein et al. 1983; see also Kennedy and Veitch 1997). Based on self-reports of delinquency by a nationally representative sample of Canadian youth, Fitzgerald and Carrington (2009) found that black, Aboriginal, and Arab and West Asian youths reported higher levels of contact with the police *and* higher involvement in violent delinquency than other youth, but this was not the case for other categories of delinquency relating to property and/ or drugs. Similarly, in their survey of Toronto schools, Wortley and Tanner (2005) found that black students reported higher levels of deviance—based on a scale measuring involvement in illegal activities—but lower levels of drug and alcohol use than white students.

Despite the association between race and violent offending observed in these studies—and consistently in American studies (Morenoff 2005)—there is no evidence that disproportionate minority contact with the police is *explained* by the disproportionate offending behaviour. Specifically, when the level of self-reported violent delinquency was statistically controlled, neither study found that the observed disproportionate minority contact disappeared or was even reduced.

In other words, even though there was evidence of differential minority involvement in violent crime, this differential involvement did not explain differential police contact: the influence of race on the chances of police contact continued to be an important factor, over and above the youths' criminal behaviour.

IS THERE EVIDENCE TO SUPPORT THE DIFFERENTIAL TREATMENT EXPLANATION?

We now turn to the three versions of the differential treatment explanation of disproportionate minority police contact. As noted, the first two versions of this theory claim that racial/ethnic minority groups have higher levels of certain personal, family, and neighbourhood characteristics that are also associated with greater chances of police contact. It is the greater exposure to these risk factors among certain groups and not any police racial bias that explains their disproportionate police contact. It is well established in the literature that police—for discretionary, operational, or larger policy or legislative reasons—direct their attention toward certain kinds of individuals and locations.

WHAT KINDS OF YOUTH, IN WHAT PLACES, ARE MORE LIKELY TO RECEIVE POLICE ATTENTION?

Research has found that youth are at higher risk for police contact if they are older, male, unsupervised or undersupervised by parents or other caregivers, have delinquent friends, and come from families of low socioeconomic status or single-parent families. The likelihood of police contact may also be affected by the nature of the neighbourhood and the city or town in which the juvenile lives or "hangs out." Disadvantaged and "socially disorganized" neighbourhoods believed by police to have high levels of crime tend to be overpoliced and to be disproportionately the object of more formal and coercive methods of policing (Klinger 1997).

TESTING THE "RISK FACTORS" VERSION OF THE DIFFERENTIAL TREATMENT EXPLANATION

In Canada, there is evidence that Aboriginal youth have higher levels of at least some of the risk factors for greater police attention described above—for example, family socioeconomic disadvantage, low adult supervision (Trocmé, Knoke, and Blackstock 2004), and living in socioeconomically disadvantaged neighbourhoods (Fitzgerald and Carrington 2008; LaPrairie 1995). In addition, there is evidence that Canadian black and other visible minority groups, including Arab and West Asian populations, may have lower levels of socioeconomic status and higher levels of some of the other risks for police contact (Hajnal 1995; Kazemipur and Halli 1997). Thus, the first part of the "risk factors" version of the differential treatment explanation is supported: members of certain Canadian minority groups do have higher levels of risk factors, apart from their race, for police contact.

Many American studies have found that racial disparity in police contacts is explained by the social and economic conditions in the neighbourhoods in which the contacts take place (e.g., Sampson and Wilson 1995; Smith and Visher 1981); however, there have been fewer direct tests of this proposition in Canada. Nonetheless, Fitzgerald and Carrington (2009) found that high-risk visible minority youth were more likely to live in large cities and neighbourhoods characterized as unsafe; however, these factors were not found to be associated with police contact. Fitzgerald and Carrington's (2008) study of police-reported crime in Winnipeg showed that the neighbourhood explained a large part of the higher likelihood that Aboriginal offenders would be apprehended by the police. That study concluded that a substantial part of the over-representation of Aboriginal people in police-reported crime incidents could be explained by the structural characteristics of the neighbourhoods in which Aboriginal people lived.

Testing the second part of the risk factor version of the differential treatment explanation requires that the level of risk factors (including neighbourhood) be statistically controlled to see if this causes the racial disparity in police contacts to disappear. A few studies have done this (Fergusson, Horwood, and Swain-Campbell 2003 in New Zealand; Huizinga et al. 2007 in the United States; Wortley and Tanner 2005 and Fitzgerald and Carrington 2009 in Canada). These studies have found no evidence to support the proposition. While members of high-risk minority groups in these studies were more likely to have individual characteristics that were also associated with police contact—for example, low household income and lower levels of parental supervision—statistically controlling these factors did not reduce the racial disparity in police contacts. The higher levels of risk factors among certain minority youth do not explain their higher likelihood of police contact.

IS THERE EVIDENCE THAT POLICE USE RACE AS A FACTOR IN DECISION MAKING?

The fact that racial differences in contact with the police remain after controlling for differences in delinquent behaviour (differential involvement), and for differences in other risk factors for police contact (differential treatment), suggests that race itself may be a factor in police decision making. To further explore this possibility, some studies have compared racial disparities in police contact among nondelinquent and delinquent youth.

Recent Canadian research shows that race differentials in police contact are most evident among the youth who should be least likely to attract police attention—those who engage in nonviolent delinquent behaviour or in no delinquent behaviour at all (Table 16.2; see also Wortley and Tanner 2005; Fitzgerald and Carrington 2009). Moreover, the higher level of risk factors among these nondelinquent minority youth does not explain why they report that they are subjected to more police attention than their non-delinquent white counterparts (Fitzgerald and Carrington 2009). Wortley and Tanner (2005, 596) have argued that one interpretation of this type of finding is that "good behaviour does not protect Black youth from police suspicion to the same extent that it protects White youth. Regardless of how well Black students behave, the data suggest that there is a high probability that their skin colour alone will invite suspicion and ultimately result in police stops."

Table 16.2 *Percent of Canadian Youth Aged 12 to 17 Who Reported a Police Contact in the Past Year, by Self-Reported Violent Delinquency*

	Violent delinquency in past year?		
	Yes	No	Weighted
Racial/ethnic group	%	%	N
Black, Aboriginal, Arab, and West Asian	49.9	28.5	189
All other youth	39.0	10.1	3,975
Weighted N	789	3,375	4,164

Notes: Cell entries are the percentage of youth in this category who reported a police contact in the past year. "Violent delinquency" includes using a weapon and/or causing injury while fighting, carrying a knife or gun, using threats to rob someone, and sexual assault.

Source: Statistics Canada. *National Longitudinal Study of Children and Youth, Cycle 4, 2000-2001.*

CONCLUSION

The possibility of racial disparity in contact with the police has significant implications for individual youth and indeed for society as a whole. Despite the importance of the issue, there has been little agreement among researchers on possible explanations for any racial disparities that may exist. In this chapter we have presented current Canadian research testing the two dominant explanations of the problem of disproportionate minority youth contact with the police. Although the number of studies directly testing these propositions is limited, some conclusions can be drawn.

First, youth belonging to some racial minority groups—for example, Aboriginal, black, Arab, and West Asian groups in Canada—are more likely than others to be stopped, searched, or arrested by the police. Second, there is no empirical support for the proposition that differential involvement in crime explains race differences in youths' contact with the police. There is some evidence that youth belonging to particular racial minority groups are more likely to be involved in the most serious forms of delinquency, which are most likely to receive police attention. However, this higher level of offending does not explain their overrepresentation in various forms of police contact.

Third, there is also no evidence to support the "risk factor" versions of the differential treatment explanation. Although high-risk visible minority youth are more likely to have individual characteristics that are also associated with police contact—for example, low household income, reduced parental supervision, or residing in a disadvantaged neighbourhood—accounting for these factors does not explain away the racial disparity in police contacts. Finally, some evidence suggests that disproportionate minority contact may be most likely to affect minority youth who are least deserving of police attention: nondelinquent youth.

The research evidence reviewed in this chapter *suggests* that disproportionate minority youth contact with the police in Canada is at least partly a result of racially discriminatory policing practices. Does it prove it? No. The factors involved in police decision making are complex, and research to date has been unable to control for many competing explanations of disproportionate minority police contact. Future Canadian research needs to consider a broader range of possible intervening factors that may partly or fully explain any racial disparity in police contacts. In addition, more Canadian research is needed that studies police practices directly (e.g., Wortley and Marshall 2005) and that considers the contexts in which police make their day-to-day decisions—including local police policies and practices and larger crime policies and legislation.

DISCUSSION QUESTIONS

1. *If there is evidence that police officers discriminate against some minority youth, what in your view can be done to remedy this problem? Is it a question of better recruitment and training or is a more radical solution necessary?*

2. *The research reviewed here "suggests" that disproportionate minority youth contact with the police in Canada is at least partly a result of racially discriminatory policing practices. What would you consider to be definitive proof of discrimination? Can you think of a research study that might generate a more definitive answer to the question posed in the title of this chapter?*

FURTHER READINGS

La Prairie, C. 1995. *Seen But Not Heard: Native People in the Inner City*. Ottawa: Department of Justice Canada.

Piquero, A.R. 2008. "Disproportionate Minority Contact." *The Future of Children* 18: 59–79.

Wortley, S., and J. Tanner. 2005. "Inflammatory Rhetoric or Baseless Accusations? A Response to Gabor's Critique of Racial Profiling Research in Canada." *Canadian Journal of Criminology and Criminal Justice* 47: 581–609.

REFERENCES

Australian Bureau of Statistics. 2008. *Prisoners in Australia 2008*. Canberra: ABS.

Blumstein, A., J. Cohen, S. Martin, and M. Tonry, eds. 1983. "Research on Sentencing: The Search for Reform." *Report of the NAS Panel on Research and Sentencing*. Washington: National Academy Press.

Commission on Systemic Racism. 1995. *Report of the Commission on Systemic Racism in the Ontario Criminal Justice System*. Toronto: Queen's Printer.

Engen, R., S. Steen, and G. Bridges. 2002. "Racial Disparities in the Punishment of Youth: A Theoretical and Empirical Assessment of the Literature." *Social Problems* 49: 194–220.

Fergusson, D, L.J. Horwood, and N. Swain-Campbell. 2003. "Ethnicity and Criminal Convictions: Results of a 21-Year Longitudinal Study." *Australian and New Zealand Journal of Criminology* 36: 354–67.

Fitzgerald, R.T., and P.J. Carrington. 2008. "The Neighbourhood Context of Urban Aboriginal Crime." *Canadian Journal of Criminology and Criminal Justice* 50: 523–57.

——. 2009. "Disproportionate Minority Youth Contact with the Justice system: Testing the Differential Involvement Hypothesis." Paper presented at the Annual Meetings of the American Society of Criminology, Philadelphia, PA, USA.

Gabor, T. 2004. "Inflammatory Rhetoric on Racial Profiling Can Undermine Police Services." *Canadian Journal of Criminology and Criminal Justice* 46: 457–66.

Gold, A. 2003. "Media Hype, Racial Profiling, and Good Science." *Canadian Journal of Criminology and Criminal Justice* 45: 391–99.

Hajnal, Z. 1995. "The Nature of Concentrated Urban Poverty in Canada and the United States." *Canadian Journal of Sociology* 20: 497–528.

Huizinga, D., T.P. Thornberry, K.E. Knight, P.J. Lovegrove, R. Loeber, R., K. Hill, and D.P. Farrington. 2007. *Disproportionate Minority Contact in the Juvenile Justice System: A Study of Differential Minority Arrest/ Referral to Court in Three Cities*. Report to the Office of Juvenile Justice and Delinquency Prevention. http://www.ncjrs.gov/pdffiles1/ojjdp/grants/219743.pdf

Kazemipur, A., and S. Halli. 1997. "Plight of Immigrants: The Spatial Concentration of Poverty in Canada." *Canadian Journal of Regional Science* 20: 11–28.

Kennedy, L., and D. Veitch. 1997. "Why Are Crime Rates Going Down? A Case Study in Edmonton." *Canadian Journal of Criminology* 39: 51–69.

Khalema, N., and J. Wannas-Jones. 2003. "Under the Prism of Suspicion: Minority Voices in Canada Post-September 11." *Journal of Muslim Minority Affairs* 23: 25–39.

Klinger, D.A. 1997. "Negotiating Order in Patrol Work: An Ecological Theory of Police Response to Deviance." *Criminology* 35: 277–306.

La Prairie, C. 1992. *Dimensions of Aboriginal Over-Representation in Correctional Institutions and Implications for Crime Prevention.* Ottawa: Solicitor General of Canada.

—— .1995. *Seen But Not Heard: Native People in the Inner City.* Ottawa: Department of Justice Canada.

Melchers, R. 2003. "Do Toronto Police Engage in Racial Profiling?" *Canadian Journal of Criminology and Criminal Justice* 45: 347–66.

Morenoff, J.D. 2005. "Racial and Ethnic Disparities in Crime and Delinquency in the United States." In M. Rutter and M. Tienda, eds., *Ethnicity and Causal Mechanisms.* Cambridge: Cambridge University Press.

Piquero, A.R. 2008. "Disproportionate Minority Contact." *The Future of Children* 18: 59–79.

Rankin, J., J. Quinn, M. Shepard, S. Simmie, and J. Duncanson. 2002a. "Singled Out: An Investigation into Race and Crime." *Toronto Star,* October 19, A1.

—— . 2002b. "Police Target Black Drivers." *Toronto Star,* October 20, A1.

—— . 2002c. "Black Crime Rates Highest." *Toronto Star,* October 26, A1.

Roberts, J.V., and R. Melchers. 2003. "The Incarceration of Aboriginal Offenders: Trends from 1978 to 2001." *Canadian Journal of Criminology and Criminal Justice* 45: 211–42.

Sampson, R.J., and W.J. Wilson. 1995. "Toward a Theory of Race, Crime, and Urban Inequality." In J. Hagan and R. Peterson, eds., *Crime and Inequality.* Stanford: Stanford University Press. 37–54.

Smith, D.A, and A. Visher. 1981. "Street-Level Justice: Situational Determinants of Police Arrest Decisions." *Social Problems* 29: 167–77.

Tonry, M. 1997. "Ethnicity, Crime, and Immigration." In M. Tonry, ed., *Ethnicity, Crime, and Immigration: Comparative and Cross-National Perspectives. Crime and Justice: A Review of Research* 21. Chicago: University of Chicago Press.

Trocmé, N., D. Knoke, and C. Blackstock. 2004. "Pathways to the Overrepresentation of Aboriginal Children in Canada's Child Welfare System." *Social Service Review* 78: 577–600.

Wilson, W.J. 2009. *More Than Just Race: Being Black and Poor in the Inner City.* New York: Norton.

Wortley, S. 1999. "A Northern Taboo: Research on Race, Crime, and Criminal Justice in Canada." *Canadian Journal of Criminology* 41: 261–74.

Wortley, S., and L. Marshall. 2005. *Police Stop Search Activities in Kingston, Ontario*. Kingston: Kingston Police Services Board.

Wortley, S., and A. McCalla. 2003. "Racial Discrimination in the Ontario Criminal Justice System." In J.V. Roberts and M.G. Grossman, eds., *Criminal Justice in Canada*. 3rd ed. Toronto: Thomson Nelson.

Wortley, S., and J. Tanner. 2003. "Data, Denials, and Confusion: The Racial Profiling Debate in Toronto." *Canadian Journal of Criminology and Criminal Justice* 45: 367–89.

—— . 2005. "Inflammatory Rhetoric or Baseless Accusations? A Response to Gabor's Critique of Racial Profiling Research in Canada." *Canadian Journal of Criminology and Criminal Justice* 47: 581–609.

ENDNOTES

1. The authors thank Statistics Canada and the South Western Ontario Research Data Centre for access to confidential micro-data used in this chapter. The views expressed in this paper are solely those of the authors and do not necessarily reflect the views of Statistics Canada.

CHAPTER 17
Inhuman Rights in Prison

Prisoners should not lose all their rights once they are admitted to custody. Lawyer and inmate Julius Melnitzer has spent time in correctional institutions at all security levels. In 1995 he wrote a memoir about his experiences. That book, *Maximum, Minimum, Medium*, provides a fascinating look at Canada's correctional system from the inside. Because he has a great deal of experience in the criminal justice system as a lawyer, his analysis of life in Canada's prisons is unique. This chapter, which is drawn from his book, examines the issue of prisoners' rights from the perspective of an actual prisoner—one with a great deal of knowledge of the law.

Julius Melnitzer

> Freedom is not divisible; it disappears from a society as soon as it is denied
> to any member of that society. —Dr. Gabor Maté

After more than 18 years as a trial lawyer in Ontario, including a decade as a criminal lawyer who served for a time as a Provincial Director of the Ontario Criminal Lawyers Association, I went to jail, a criminal serving a nine-year sentence for fraud. As a criminal lawyer, I always believed my job ended with my client's acquittal or sentencing. But two-and-a-half years in maximum, medium, and minimum security federal institutions in Ontario taught me that criminal lawyers who abandon their incarcerated clients should rethink their commitment to their profession and their role in society. Here's why.

The civil rights of prisoners are the lowest common denominator of democracy. In jail, correctional supervisors are the judges in internal disciplinary courts, where their foot soldiers are the prosecutors (one CS [correctional supervisor] convicted a prisoner in the absence of witnesses because "no guard would take the trouble to write out a charge unless it was true"); permission to telephone a lawyer during business hours hangs on the whim of employees of the State; prisoners do not have access to Bell information or telephone books on their ranges; calls are collect only unless written permission is obtained; and telephone discussions with lawyers transpire in a public place or in a CO's (classification officer's) office in the presence of CSC (Correctional Service Canada) staff.

The apathy of all but a few criminal lawyers as well as the Canadian Civil Liberties Association; the reluctance of a cash-starved Legal Aid system to spend its budget on the convicted; the low levels of education and high levels of illiteracy in the system; and CSC's ignorance and disregard of basic procedural fairness in its day-to-day operations all ensure a trampling of prisoners' rights. Ironically, until a recent court case forced authorities to change the practice, CSC forbade the use of the Inmate Welfare Fund, inmates' money, for legal assistance.

The protection of our democratic core lies in the hands of a few committed activists such as the late Order of Canada recipient Claire Culhane and her legacy, the Vancouver-based Prisoners' Rights Group; Ruth Morris from Toronto; Ontario Provincial Court Judges David Cole and Bob Bigelow; prison law practitioners in the Kingston, Ontario bar; and Queen's University's Faculty of Law's Correctional Law Project.

This is not a commentary on the rights prisoners should have: that is for the voters and their elected representatives to decide. Nor is it a denial of the relatively humane conditions under which we warehouse the convicted; rather, it speaks to the disregard of due process that pervades our penal system. As sentences get lengthier, paroles become rarer, and more people spend more time in jail, the prevailing attitude seems to be, "Let's feed them and keep them out of the cold." In a democracy, that will not do; so long as society sees fit to give rights to prisoners, it must protect its values even among its exiles. Our failure to do so says much about our penal system's rehabilitative delinquencies.

CSC's response to the public outcry resulting from my tennis partner, convicted murderer Philippe Clement's assault on a Gravenhurst woman after his escape from minimum-security Beaver Creek was perhaps my starkest experience with civil rights sacrificed on the altar of public opinion and media hype. In the six months following the public outcry, CSC set out to purge the Creek of violent offenders, many of whom were sent to Warkworth, and some of whom opened their files to me. I was appalled at the haste and lack of justification for the majority of the transfers; in no instance was there an immediate threat of escape or violence, yet none of these inmates were given a chance to contact their lawyers before transfer.

My apprehensions about the panic that had set in with Les Judson [a former warden at Beaver Creek] and his superiors were confirmed orally by some Warkworth COs who were now stuck with these men. One CO put her findings in writing:

On December 23, 1992, the subject was transferred to higher security (Warkworth Institution) as the staff at Beaver Creek had information that the subject, along with other perpetrators, had broken into the inmate canteen and stole $3,200 worth of merchandise ...

These suspicions were never confirmed. No charges, either institutional or street, were laid against the subject. There is no evidence tying the subject to this offence. Therefore, there is no valid reason why the security classification on the subject should change. He is still classified as minimum security.

"The subject" was unusually lucky. He was back in minimum within six months. Had his CO been unsympathetic, it would have taken him from 12 to 18 months to have his grievance processed. And likely, "the subject," who was barely literate, would have had to do it on his own: Legal Aid refused his application, and for three months, his collect calls to lawyers went unanswered.

Apart from "the subject," not a single one of the men summarily ejected from Beaver Creek in the fall of 1992 had made it back to minimum one year later. Even those with lawyers were stymied by the delaying tactics of the Crown in Federal Court and the sluggishness of that court's process.

The greatest price of this arbitrary conduct, apart from the diminution in democratic values, is the cost to society. Many of the transferred cons were the system's successes, the most likely candidates for rehabilitation, men who had spent many years fighting institutionalization and their criminal backgrounds and who had been adjudged, step by grudging step, to have the best potential for a productive return to society.

Wade, a very young-looking, intelligent, and self-educated 40-year-old, with two daughters in their twenties and a son in his teens, had fought his way back from tragic alcoholism and drug abuse that led to conviction for two sexual assaults and a 12-year sentence. He had been a model for other prisoners, a star in every therapeutic program he had taken for seven years. At the Creek, he continued his exemplary ways, working in the kitchen, tutoring other inmates, and minding his own business.

Even in the aftermath of the Clement escape, the Parole Board was sufficiently impressed by Wade's record to grant him unescorted three-day passes to a halfway house in Toronto. On his first pass, he dutifully attended the Clarke Institute of Psychiatry for a psychological assessment; there he told the examining psychologist that he had taken one drink almost a year previous, on New Year's Eve.

Wade's honesty was just the excuse Beaver Creek needed to rid itself of another bothersome high-profile case. Wade was summarily advised that the Administration had been "informed"—by parties unmentionable, of course—of "derogatory remarks" Wade had made about the deputy warden. Lacking knowledge of his accusers and without access to counsel, Wade had no opportunity to defend himself and was promptly transferred to Warkworth, where he remained until his statutory release in February 1994. CSC's extraordinary powers made a strong impression on me when I reported for transportation to a Kingston hospital for medical testing. The escorting officers politely told me to undress.

"Am I under suspicion for anything?" I asked.

"No," was the quick reply.

My question was deliberate. I had researched the new prison legislation as it related to searches and discovered that "routine" strip-searches were unlawful in the absence of individualized suspicion, except for some carefully circumscribed exceptions that did not apply here.

"Then you've got no right to search me," I asserted.

The officers resolved their confusion by phoning the security office.

"You can't go if you refuse a search," the senior guard told me as he got off the phone.

"Fine," I replied, "I'll go back to my Block." Visions of medical lawsuits and grievances for damages danced in my head.

"The IPSO [internal preventative security officer] says we have to search you anyway."

"You mean that I'm now under suspicion because I insisted on my rights."

"I don't know," said the guard abashedly, "you're the lawyer. I just do what the keeper tells me."

"What are my choices?"

"Go to the hole. They'll strip-search you there." Previous personal experience told me that a request to call my lawyer would not be well received, serving only to heighten suspicion about my refusal to be strip-searched.

I was in a quandary. If I refused, I'd be in the hole. I tried to imagine the write-up on this incident: by the time the IPSO finished, I would doubtlessly be labelled as "under suspicion," CSC's favourite phrase, of trafficking in something or other. I complied, wondering how many thousands of inmates would be searched in ignorance of their rights.

The "cavity search," a fishing expedition through body orifices, is distinguished from assault only by the mandated presence of a doctor and is a more sublime form of intrusion than a strip-search. If a tactile proctological examination doesn't reveal anything, the doctor may use an instrument best described as an anal crank to have a better look through a larger opening.

Refusal to submit to a cavity search is, in a system where random urinalysis testing is common, a virtual admission to drug trafficking. Being labelled as a trafficker is, in turn, an invitation to unremitting harassment, restrictions on visits, and a practical bar to early parole.

Cavity searches are, however, expensive, time-consuming, and embarrassing when fruitless. CSC prefers the "dry cell," where the toilet can't be flushed by the inmate. In Kingston Penitentiary, the nine-by-four windowless cell contains a bed, an eating surface, a steel toilet, and a sink. The lights are on all day and at night, a bulb strong enough to read by intrudes on sleep, but no books are allowed. The cell is video-monitored 24 hours daily, and patrolling guards have an unobstructed vista through a plastic plate on the ceiling. The cell design allows the guards to watch the prisoner's excretions, which remain with him in the uncovered toilet, until the guards find time to come around and secure the evidence.

Just how far down the human rights scale prisoners have fallen can be demonstrated by comparing the dry cell experience with recent court decisions prohibiting police from detaining suspects until they have a bowel movement, enabling authorities to search stool samples for drugs.

Random urinalysis, recently declared constitutional by the courts, is slowly replacing the cavity search and the dry cell, but the tests are no less intrusive, if somewhat more humane.

To those law-and-order aficionados who cheered their way through the last few paragraphs, I merely point out that these methods are designed to prove guilt. Until and if the shit hits the fan, so to speak, the innocent must pay the price with the guilty. The innocent have no recourse if the suspicions against them prove groundless. The irony is that they therefore have far more incentive than the guilty to submit to these barbaric intrusions.

Occasionally, an activist Inmate Committee chairman tries to help inmates assert their rights. The Inmate Committee exists at the discretion of an institution's warden, but now that CSC is legally required to consult with inmates on all matters affecting them other than security, the Inmate Committee is a handy funnel to the population.

The inmate chairman is elected by the population every six months and appoints his own executive. The chairman's capacity to represent the inmates is severely limited, however, because the chairman is himself a prisoner, whose fate hinges on the whims of his keepers.

While politicization is creeping into institutional politics, wardens tend to deal swiftly and severely with chairmen whom they see as rabble-rousers. Shortly before I got to Warkworth, Greg, a 50-year-old first-timer serving a 14-year-sentence for the attempted murder of his wife, was elected chairman. Greying, fatherly, and somehow tweedy in his prison greens, Greg was educated and clever, with a knack for organization.

Greg set out to enforce the Supreme Court of Canada's declaration, in a precedent-setting decision giving prisoners the right to vote, that inmates were entitled to all civil rights other than those that necessarily accompanied the loss of freedom.

To that end, he first presented the Administration with a scheme for effective inmate representation at the grass-roots level. Censorship was his next target: I helped him draw up a grievance against the Administration's refusal to allow the popular Sharon Stone movie *Basic Instinct* into Warkworth; after months of enduring explicitly violent martial arts movies on prison video, I laughed at the exclusion. Simultaneously, Greg hotly protested against the Administration's control and occasional misuse of the Inmate Welfare Fund. The powers-that-be were most unhappy with him.

"They're going to get me, Julius. They don't want a chairman who does anything," Greg told me.

As the tension rose, Greg desperately tried to get in touch with a lawyer; he wrote both to the Ontario Provincial Criminal Lawyers Association, which continued its historical disregard of those who had already paid their bills, and the Canadian Civil Liberties Association, which must have had more popular fish to fry and didn't bother to answer. I finally called my lawyer, Bob Bigelow, who agreed to see Greg on his next visit to Warkworth.

Before Bob could see Greg, the Administration pounced, blaming him for irregularities in the canteen; without explanation, he was hauled out of a visit with his wife and sent to the hole. Soon afterward, Greg resigned and became a non-presence in short order.

Inmate Committee chairmen are not the only targets of the kind of intimidation Greg experienced. Grant, convicted by an internal disciplinary court of possession of a joint after eight offence-free years in the pen, objected to the severity of the penalties for his minor offence. On the street, he would have been fined lightly, at worst; in prison, he lost his single cell in Warkworth's model non-smoking unit, was transferred back to double-bunked Reception, had his pay cut by four levels, lost his job, and spent a week in the hole awaiting Disciplinary Court.

With the law clerk's certificate he had earned in prison from the American Trial Lawyers Association in hand, and with some guidance from me, Grant filed a claim in the Federal Court challenging the severity and multiplicity of his punishments. The attorney general applied to quash Grant's claim but failed in its summary motion. Grant, who worked in the kitchen, thanked me for my help with a plate of delicately cooked fresh crabmeat that a friendly guard had smuggled in for him.

For a few months I heard nothing more about his case, attributing Grant's silence to the long delays in Federal Court.

"I shut it down," he said six months later, in a hush, averting his eyes.

"Why?" I was sincerely dismayed.

"I've got to do what's right for me. My wife wants me out of here, or at least in camp. I'm on a life beef—they call the shots."

Not yet dislodged from the insulated naïveté of my street days, I had no idea what Grant was talking about.

"They called me in, the unit manager," he went on. "He told me that even if I win, I lose. If I forget it, maybe I get to camp soon."

The threat was not an idle one. And if the unit manager chose to forget his promise once Grant dropped his claim, [the unit manager] could always find new facts to support his change of heart; CSC's power to affect the man's freedom would be as useful in the breaking of the promise as it was in its making.

As I chafed at the injustices, the feelings that drove me as a criminal lawyer came back in spades. In January 1993, I wrote to prison activist Claire Culhane, whose books I had been reading, offering to help in her cause of prisoners' rights. Though my ability to assist was limited by the inaccessibility of research materials, our correspondence continued throughout my incarceration.

CSC's licence to trample human rights stems from its lack of accountability. Politically, the human rights of convicts is hardly an issue with which to blaze to power; an unsympathetic media and public ensure that accountability, where it exists, operates only to inmates' detriment.

Wardens have some discretion in granting passes, escorted and unescorted, as well as work releases. Release[s] in serious cases, the ones in the headlines, are the province of the National Parole Board. Through its case management teams and therapeutic staff, CSC makes highly influential recommendations to the board. Wisdom and insight into the human psyche spout from the mouths of 23-year-old COs barely out of community college, secretarial school graduates who have won the CSC promotion competition, or M.A. students suddenly become "therapists." Their power is frightening and unchecked, often subjective and arbitrary; if quality control or any serious effort at consistency in release decisions and recommendations existed, I couldn't find it in the files I reviewed.

There is little risk for CSC in urging the Parole Board to detain an inmate, but a wrong call for release can have disastrous public relations fallout; thus, it is not surprising that case management teams lean against release. As Jeremiah's CO told him, "Personally, I don't think you should be in here, but I don't want to be the one kicking my lunch bucket down the street." Reid, who had spent 17 years in prison, observed, "When I got in the system, COs tried to help you. Now, they try to find obstacles to keep you in so they can cover their ass."

CSC's materials are essentially unchallengeable before the Parole Board, a body that the late Chief Justice of Canada's Supreme Court, Bora Laskin, called "draconian." The hearings consist of a presentation by the CO, followed by 30 minutes to 5 hours of untrammelled inmate grilling by at least a 2-member board, many of whom are trained only in the fruits of political loyalty and start with the assumption that credibility is not in a criminal's repertoire.

Anything in a CSC report passes for evidence: fact, opinion, hearsay, innuendo, and suspicion—even philosophical musings. Reports are in writing; there is no in-person evidence and no opportunity to cross-examine in the quest for liberty. The inmate's lawyer is reduced to an "assistant," usually sitting by without objection, involved only in procedural matters and ten minutes of final arguments. Where evidence favouring release exists, the Parole Board is notorious for capriciously ignoring it, going so far as to reject, without reasons, recommendations from CSC's own professionals. Homespun psychology is regularly expounded as definitive gospel by politically appointed board members, many of them part time, with little experience and less training: "The offender's response to our questions shows that he has not fully appreciated the consequences of his actions and is not ready for release" are the board's favourite buzzwords.

Always, the spectre of public opinion hangs over the proceedings, twisting the issue of "risk to society"—the fundamental question the Parole Board is empowered to decide—into considerations of "How will it look?" Thus, by ignoring the law, the Parole Board assumes the role of lawmaker, affecting a demagogic juggernaut that tramples on concepts of fundamental justice. These concepts are democracy's triggers of accountability, ever so slight a curtsy to an inalienable right—not to freedom, but to the right to fight for it on even ground.

DISCUSSION QUESTIONS

1. *What is meant by the term "due process," and how does it apply to prisoners?*
2. *Is random urinalysis testing acceptable in prison?*

FURTHER READING

Jackson, M. 2002. *Justice Behind the Walls: Human Rights in Canadian Prisons.* Vancouver: Douglas and McIntyre.

Melnitzer, J. 1995. *Maximum, Minimum, Medium.* Toronto: Key Porter.

CHAPTER 18
The Treatment of Prisoners in Canada

Imprisonment is generally reserved for offenders convicted of the most serious crimes. Offenders sentenced to the longer periods of custody—two years or more—serve their time in a federal penitentiary. The federal correctional system therefore houses the most serious offenders in the criminal justice system in Canada. How should these offenders be treated? Does the fact that they have been convicted of the most serious offences in the *Criminal Code* mean they should be deprived of many of the rights that law-abiding Canadians enjoy? For example, although federal prisoners have the right to vote, is this appropriate?

In this chapter, Shereen Benzvy Miller discusses the issue of prisoners' rights. The chapter reviews the rights that prisoners have and identifies the reasons why these rights should exist.

Shereen H. Benzvy Miller, M.A., LL.B

Canada's *Criminal Code* defines hundreds of activities as crimes because they have offended public values. Offenders convicted of the most serious offences can be sentenced to long periods of custody. What kind of treatment can an offender expect if sentenced to serve a term of imprisonment? Do or should offenders lose all their rights? Should they lose any rights—for example, the right to hold citizenship or to vote in elections? Why should we care about people who have hurt others and who have offended against our values?

Winston Churchill said: "The mood and temper of the public in regard to the treatment of crime and criminals is one of the most unfailing tests of the civilization of any country. A calm, dispassionate recognition of the rights of the accused, and even of the convicted criminal ... measure[s] the stored-up strength of a nation and [is] sign and proof of the living virtue in it." Thus, protecting the rights of individual members of our society is at the core of Canada's constitutional and legal frameworks. And sentenced or not, offenders remain members of the society to which they will return having served their time. The criminal justice system and corrections specifically must balance the rights of the individuals involved and public safety concerns.

HAVEN'T OFFENDERS FORFEITED THEIR RIGHTS?

As noted in Chapter 2 of this text, the rights of all Canadians are set out in and protected by the Constitution and the *Canadian Charter of Rights and Freedoms* (the *Charter*). Canada's commitment to various international human rights agreements[1] has set certain standards and enshrined many of these obligations in legislation and the *Charter*. We retain these rights throughout our lives whether we are hospitalized, serving a sentence of imprisonment, or simply enjoying life (when we are most likely to take them for granted).

Until someone tries to limit your rights, you may not think much about your right to practice the religion of your choice, the right to freedom of expression, freedom of peaceful assembly and association, the right to legal counsel, the right to a fair hearing, the presumption of innocence, freedom from arbitrary detention and imprisonment, the right not to be subjected to cruel and unusual treatment and punishment, and the right not to be subjected to unreasonable search or seizure. However, these rights are fundamental to the quality of life in Canada, and we should be vigilant in requiring our government to respect them.

Offenders retain the rights and privileges of all members of society, except those that are necessarily removed or restricted as a consequence of the sentence of the court. Statutes such as the *Corrections and Conditional Release Act (CCRA)* protect the fundamental right to life and security, fair and just treatment, and protection from discrimination and mistreatment. Other domestic legislation protects the rights of all Canadians, including offenders, such as the *Canadian Human Rights Act;* the *Privacy Act;* the *Access to Information Act;* the *Official Languages Act;* and the *Transfer of Offenders Act.* By their very nature, the principles of administrative law in Canada protect individuals who enter the criminal justice system. Due process, the duty to act fairly, and strictly defined powers and delegations of authority limit what actors may do in the name of the State, be they police, prosecutors, judges, or corrections officials.

You might well ask: What does this really mean in the context of a penitentiary? After all, shouldn't prison be a painful and punitive experience? Shouldn't offenders have thought about the rights they would be losing before committing the crime? If we examine the fundamental rights listed above, it is difficult to find more than one or two that people actually agree should be removed. The argument goes something like this: If we want our communities to be safer, we need to remove criminals from among us. But all offenders except the very few who have committed the most heinous offences will be released back into the community at some point. Thus, if our goal is to maximize safety and if those who have committed crimes will at some point be back living in society, then we must act responsibly toward them during their period of incarceration. This means that although offenders lose the right to liberty, they do not forfeit the entitlement to be treated with dignity and humanity. But what of the right to liberty? Why not incarcerate all offenders for life? Wouldn't that make our streets *really* safe?

WHY NOT SIMPLY "LOCK 'EM UP AND THROW AWAY THE KEY"?

Locking up offenders and throwing away the key might have been the strategy of some penal systems in the past and may still be how some Canadians would prefer that sentences be administered. But we should consider the purposes of sentencing when considering locking people up. These are found in part XXIII of the *Criminal Code*, which defines the purposes of sentencing:

> 718. The fundamental purpose of sentencing is to contribute, along with crime prevention initiatives, to respect for the law and the maintenance of a just, peaceful and safe society by imposing just sanctions that have one or more of the following objectives:
>
> (a) to denounce unlawful conduct;
>
> (b) to deter the offender and other persons from committing offences;
>
> (c) to separate offenders from society, where necessary;
>
> (d) to assist in rehabilitating offenders;
>
> (e) to provide reparations for harm done to victims or to the community; and
>
> (f) to promote a sense of responsibility in offenders, and acknowledgment of the harm done to victims and to the community.

Sending offenders to prison can serve any or all of the purposes outlined above: it can be (a) a way of expressing societal disapproval of the individual and *denouncing* the criminal conduct; (b) a means of deterring the offender and other potential offenders from further offending; (c) a way of *incapacitating* the individual and preventing him or her from committing further crimes in the community, at least during the period of detention; (d) an opportunity to provide treatment and rehabilitative programming to ensure safe *reintegration* of the offender back into the community when the sentence of imprisonment ends; (e) a time to repair the harm caused; and last, (f) a means of ensuring that people are held responsible for their behaviour and actions. It is worth noting that there is no mention of sentencing providing a form of *retribution* or *punishment* for the misdeed. We are not vindictive or retaliatory in our response to crime.

In the context of a sentence that includes imprisonment, rehabilitation or social reintegration is the most difficult goal to accomplish and also the most important. It is hard to help people fit back into a community from which they have forcibly been pulled. For this reason, Canada's Parliament has defined the purpose of incarceration[2] in Section 3 of the *Corrections and Conditional Release Act* (CCRA) as follows:

Purpose of correctional system

3. The purpose of the federal correctional system is to contribute to the maintenance of a just, peaceful and safe society by

(a) carrying out sentences imposed by courts through the safe and humane custody and supervision of offenders; and

(b) assisting the rehabilitation of offenders and their reintegration into the community as law-abiding citizens through the provision of programs in penitentiaries and in the community.[3]

Providing both assistance to and control of inmates is a monumental task when one considers the correctional system's responsibilities on an average day (in 2008–09) in supervising the sentences of 13,287 federally incarcerated offenders and 8,726 offenders in the community.

The Correctional Service of Canada (CSC) manages 57 penitentiaries of different security levels (including treatment centres and annexes within penitentiaries), 16 community correctional centres, and 84 parole offices.[4] In addition to federally-operated facilities, the CSC partners with community-based non-governmental organizations that run approximately 200 community-based residential facilities across the country (i.e. halfway houses). A fundamental value of CSC's work is *respect:* for the dignity of individuals, for the rights of all members of society, and for the potential for human growth and development. CSC assumes that people have the potential to live as law-abiding citizens. These are important assumptions if the goal is safer communities.

Incarceration is expensive, both in fiscal terms and in human terms. Moreover, it is disruptive to families and communities and should only be used when all other options are exhausted or deemed unsafe. Courts therefore do not incarcerate all offenders in perpetuity because it is unnecessary and even counterproductive to promoting the safety of the community. Moreover, it would be dangerous to staff to try to manage people devoid of hope and with nothing to lose because the keys to the cell have been thrown away! The rehabilitation and reintegration of offenders must therefore remain a top priority. Penitentiaries are not "warehouses" for offenders; rather, they are institutions in which a prisoner can receive treatment and participate in education and employment programs. Correctional programs are designed to address factors identified as contributing to their criminal behaviour and to help in ultimately controlling and reducing the risk that these people will present in the future.

WHY LET PRISONERS OUT BEFORE THE ENTIRE SENTENCE IS OVER?

Some members of the public ask why we do not require prisoners to serve every day of their sentence in prison, without being allowed to serve any part of it under supervision in the community. Most prison systems around the world have programs that permit prisoners to serve part of their sentence in the community. *Parole* is the best-known example of such early release programs. Prisoners apply for conditional release from prison, meaning that they serve the last part of the sentence in the community, subject to conditions imposed by the parole authorities. The purpose of conditional release supervision is to further protect society by helping offenders become law-abiding citizens by providing them with a transitional period where they are still being assisted and receiving programs while they adapt to life on the outside. Conditional release is also intended to improve public safety over the long run. Released offenders must adhere to certain standard conditions set out in the release certificate. The releasing provisions in the CCRA allow the parole board to set individually crafted conditions to minimize the risk of reoffending and to increase the likelihood of success in the community. Canada and CSC have invested heavily in research in order to understand the individual needs of offenders. Good correctional practice guides the specific conditions that are imposed in order to help the offender make the adjustment back into society.

For example, offenders must travel directly to their home or to a residential facility upon release and must report regularly to their parole supervisor. The parole board may impose additional conditions. These conditions can include curfews, restrictions on movement, prohibitions on drinking, and prohibitions on associating with certain people (such as children and former victims). CSC parole officers can take action if they believe the offender is violating release conditions or is planning to commit another crime. They can suspend the release and return the offender directly to prison until the risk is reassessed. Some of these offenders may remain in prison. Others may be released again, but under more severe restrictions and only after more supervision or community support services are in place. Research has shown that interventions and supervision are the best ways of promoting successful community reintegration and therefore public safety. One example of a community intervention for offenders serving sentences for sexual assault is Circles of Support and Accountability initiatives.

Circles of Support and Accountability (COSA) Initiatives

The vast majority of sexual offenders receive determinate sentences and will eventually return to the community. The Circles of Support and Accountability initiative has its roots in the public's response to a single incident: the release into the community from a federal penitentiary of a high-risk, repeat, child sexual abuser. This event triggered picketing, angry calls for political intervention, heightened media attention, and 24-hour police surveillance. In response to the offender's pleas for assistance, a Mennonite pastor gathered a group of congregants to offer humane support and to develop a realistic accountability framework. Following a similar intervention with another offender a few months later, the Mennonite Central Committee of Ontario (MCCO) agreed to sponsor a pilot project called the Community Reintegration Project. From this, the Circles of Support and Accountability (COSA) movement was born.

COSA has had a profound effect on all those involved: offenders, community volunteers, affiliated professionals, and the community at large. Ninety percent of parolees reported that in the absence of COSA, they would have had difficulty adjusting to the community, and two-thirds reported that they likely would have returned to crime. COSA volunteers said they believed the community became safer as a result of the initiative.

Professionals and agencies involved in COSA include police officers and social services professionals. They report that COSA increases offender responsibility and accountability. Community safety and support are the focus of the project. In a survey of the community at large, 68 percent of respondents reported they would feel safer if they learned that a high-risk sexual offender in their community belonged to a COSA circle.

Effects on Reoffending Rates

COSA group members reoffend at a much lower rate than their matched counterparts, even though COSA participants have a higher risk profile. In each of the three instances of sexual recidivism in the COSA group, the new offence was less severe than the offence for which the participant had most recently served a sentence. The recidivism results compiled in evaluating the COSA pilot project are very encouraging. Sexual recidivism by COSA participants is 70 percent lower than for the matched comparison sample and less than one-quarter of projected sexual recidivism rates.

The Correctional Service of Canada (CSC) uses COSA and produced a more recent evaluation titled "Circles of Support and Accountability: A National Replication of Outcome Findings" (2008). Its results showed that offenders who participated in COSA had significantly lower rates of any type of reoffending than the matched comparison offenders who did not participate in COSA. Specifically, offenders who participated in COSA had an 83 percent reduction in sexual recidivism in contrast to the matched comparison group (2.1% vs. 12.8%), a 73 percent reduction in all types of violent recidivism (including sexual—8.5% vs. 31.9%), and an overall reduction of 72 percent in all types of recidivism (including violent and sexual—10.6% vs. 38.3%). Overall, COSA participants were responsible for considerably less sexual, violent, and general offending than the matched comparison group.

Finally, it is worth noting that a risk assessment completed upon the release of the first two parolees to participate in COSA indicated a 100 percent chance of reoffending within seven years. But by the time of the COSA evaluation in 2002, both men had reached their 11th anniversary of crime-free life in the community.

— HOW DOES CANADA ENSURE THAT THE FOCUS ON HUMAN RIGHTS REMAINS SHARP?

Many decisions affecting a federal prisoner's life are relegated to someone else's authority, such as that of correctional officers, parole officers, program managers, or institutional heads. A former inmate of Beaver Creek Institution, a minimum-security facility in Ontario, marvelled at CSC's power to affect a prisoner's freedom and what he called "CSC's license to trample human rights" (Melnitzer 2003, 83). Hearing such a statement makes one wonder what mechanisms exist to protect inmates from the immense power of CSC and its 15,000 employees. CSC is accountable to the public for its performance.

CSC's operations are monitored by external bodies that hold it accountable for its operations. As a federal agency, CSC is responsible to the Parliament of Canada, which upholds the rights and freedoms of all Canadians. The Auditor General monitors the proper conduct of government activities and audits CSC's financial accounts. The Information Commissioner investigates complaints from people who believe they have been denied rights under the *Access to Information Act*, which is Canada's freedom-of-information legislation. Like all Canadian citizens, offenders can exercise their right to submit complaints to the Information Commissioner. Another mechanism for external oversight is the Office of the Privacy Commissioner, which advocates for the privacy rights of Canadians.

One of the most active external oversight bodies for CSC is the Office of the Correctional Investigator (OCI). Under the *Corrections and Conditional Release Act,*[5] the Correctional Investigator acts as the Ombudsman for federal offenders. The office's principal function is to investigate and resolve the complaints of individual offenders. As well, the OCI reviews CSC's policies and procedures as they relate to inmates' complaints, and makes recommendations. The OCI publishes an annual report detailing CSC's application or non-application of the recommendations made by the OCI. It records incidents of failure to comply with its governing legislation, policies, and directives, and reports annually to Parliament.

CSC has its critics and its watchdogs. In 1994, on the recommendation of the Solicitor General, the Honourable Justice Louise Arbour was appointed to lead an Inquiry into Certain Events at the Prison for Women in Kingston. In her report, Justice Arbour wrote that CSC did not understand or respect the rule of law. Her report led to a complete reassessment of how CSC provides for women offenders, as well as a great deal of soul searching to ensure that all CSC decisions would be governed thereafter by the rule of law. In 2002, Professor Michael Jackson wrote a book titled *Justice Behind the Walls*[6] about CSC's failure to respect basic human rights in Canada's prisons. In December 2003 the Canadian Human Rights Commission (CHRC) produced a systemic review of human rights in correctional services for the federally sentenced.

The CHRC administers the *Canadian Human Rights Act* and ensures that the principles of equal opportunity and non-discrimination are followed in all areas of federal jurisdiction, including and especially in the criminal justice system. Offenders have access to the CHRC's complaint process. If it cannot resolve a complaint, the commission may investigate the case further; it may ultimately request that the Canadian Human Rights Tribunal hear the case.

In 2004, in a special report titled *Protecting Their Rights: A Systemic Review of Human Rights in Correctional Services for Federally Sentenced Women*, the CHRC wrote that female prisoners[7] continued to face systemic human rights problems in the federal correctional system. It recommended that the correctional system be tailored to the unique needs of, and lower security risks posed by, female offenders. Specifically, it called for the correctional system to take a more gender-based approach to custody, programming, and reintegration for female offenders.

In the autumn of 2009, Professor Michael Jackson and Graham Stewart published a sharp critique of CSC's most recent transformation: "A Flawed Compass: A Human Rights Analysis of the Roadmap to Strengthening Public Safety." In depth, this 200-page treatise explored CSC's history and the importance of individual rights. It reaffirmed that democracy can be served only when imprisonment is humane and respectful.

Some people argue that the media constitute an accountability mechanism because they report on successes and failures throughout the criminal justice system. But the media are not a systemic mechanism for reporting results. The media require a sound bite or an image, and much of CSC's operations cannot be reduced to a brief report. As a result, media coverage has often distorted or sensationalized events in Canada's prisons. For example, the video clip of a tragic 1999 incident in which an inmate died from a seizure in the basement of an isolated institution was played repeatedly on television. The media coverage implied that ominous events were occurring in the institution. Not one reporter asked the more interesting question: How did the video come to exist? No tourist standing on a balcony could have filmed this incident. The answer is that CSC films all "use of force" interventions and strip searches to ensure that these difficult situations can be reviewed later. Instead of hiding this video footage in a vault under the commissioner's desk, CSC sends every tape to the Correctional Investigator for review. In this case, the copy of this video was also shared with the coroner who conducted the inquest into the death.

In addition to external mechanisms, CSC has an Offender Redress system, which is a formal internal mechanism that addresses complaints by individual prisoners or groups of inmates. The system is designed to provide offenders with access to a fair and effective redress mechanism and to recommend corrective action in cases where there is mistreatment or injustice. It helps ensure that offenders' problems and expectations are brought to the attention of personnel across the service by providing grievance-based information on trends and specific issues. There are four levels of appeals in the service, the final level being the Commissioner or his/her designate at National Headquarters (NHQ).

In 2009–10, Offender Redress at NHQ processed 1,850 offender grievances from a total of 28,236 offender complaints (and grievances) at all levels of the process. CSC serves many functions that are handled by myriad agencies and infrastructures in the outside world, from food service and mail delivery to transportation of people and personal effects around the country. When decisions are being made about all aspects of running these small cities, some people will be unhappy with them. Most complaints and grievances do not arise from misconduct or deliberate poor performance. More often, they arise from either misunderstanding a policy, misinterpreting a policy, or disagreement over a decision. The complaint and grievance system provides managers at all levels with valuable feedback on performance as well as comprehension and communication around policies and procedures. The process is also a useful strategic planning tool, in that as concerns and values shift, the complaint and grievance process may be where such shifts are first documented. For example, the emergence of a desire for vegetarian diets based on conscience rather than religion or culture was first seen in the grievance process. A grievance on genetically modified foods, for example, might be harbinger of another value shift.

As Winston Churchill said: "Criticism may not be agreeable, but it is necessary. It fulfils the same function as pain in the human body. It calls attention to an unhealthy state of things." Critics and oversight bodies are critical to the good health of an organization and help ensure respect for rights.

HOW WOULD A DECISION MAKER CONSIDER THE "SPIRIT" OF LAW?

The values underlying the *Corrections and Conditional Release Act* are captured in a statement of principles in Section 4. These principles help decision makers exercise their discretion properly. The most relevant principles include the following:

(d) that the Service will use the least restrictive measures consistent with the protection of the public, staff members, and offenders;

(e) that the offenders retain the rights and privileges of all members of society, except those rights that are necessarily removed or restricted as a consequence of the sentence; and

(g) that correctional decisions be made in a forthright and fair manner, with access by the offender to an effective grievance procedure.

In 2004, CSC's Executive Committee adopted a human rights decision-making model that marries the operational, legislative, and ethical imperatives. Every decision (and CSC makes many pertaining to the 22,000 people who are under supervision on any given day) is tested against three questions:

Can I?
May I? *and*
Should I?

These three questions require all decision makers, when exercising their discretion, to ask themselves whether they can *operationally* do something, whether the *law* allows it, and whether it is *ethically* the right thing to do. When these questions are considered, it is more likely that the decision will respect both the spirit and the letter of law and policy.

DOES THE SYSTEM VIOLATE PRISONERS' RIGHTS?

Rights are not absolute: my right to swing my fist stops at the end of your nose. The Canadian correctional system has a vast of array of law and policy as well as oversight mechanisms and complaint systems aimed at preventing needless (or malicious) limitations of rights. But as in any "people business," much depends on the exercise of judgment by individual actors in a variety of situations. Good training and supervision, strong accountability mechanisms, and a culture that emphasizes sound judgment are important for ensuring that rights are respected.

Some people believe there are systemic problems that need attention. They raise these concerns in a variety of ways, such as through the annual Correctional Investigator (CI's) Report to Parliament. CSC submits its response to this report, along with the CI's Report, to the Minister of Public Safety, who tables both reports together. Special commissions, internal audit systems, Auditor General's audits, and internal investigations help highlight other problems. Moreover, the access-to-information legislation can expose any document produced by CSC. In a typical year, around 500 access-to-information requests occur in the correctional system.

WHY SHOULD CANADIANS CARE?

Canadians should value and protect the rights of all citizens all of the time, not only because it is the moral thing to do, but also because it is good public policy. Respecting rights helps ensure that offenders have the best chance of rehabilitating themselves; this in turn makes the country a safer place. How civilized are Canadians compared to the standards in Churchill's quotation, cited earlier? The answer depends on a culture of respect for the rule of law, to ensure that every Canadian is safe, wherever we find ourselves in whatever circumstances.

DISCUSSION QUESTIONS

1. *One of the prisoner rights that has been hotly contested in recent years is the right to be pardoned. Some people think that sex offenders should not be allowed to apply for a pardon. What is your view?*
2. *The author says that the news media tend to focus on "events" rather than on the day-to-day running of institutions. This means that the public hear about dramatic "bad news" stories but not about the daily success stories. Do you think the media have a responsibility to describe the successful working of the system?*

FURTHER READINGS

Jackson, M., and G. Stewart. 2009. "A Flawed Compass: A Human Rights Analysis of the Roadmap to Strengthening Public Safety." http://www. justicebehindthewalls.net/resources/news/flawed_Compass.pdf

Jackson, M. 2002. *Justice Behind the Walls. Human Rights in Canadian Prisons.* Vancouver: Douglas and McIntyre.

Melnitzer, J. 1995. *Maximum, Medium, Minimum.* Toronto: Key Porter.

REFERENCES

Melnitzer, J. 2003. "Prisoners' Rights." In J.V. Roberts and M. Grossman, eds., *Criminal Justice in Canada.* 2nd ed. Toronto: Thomson Nelson.

Wilson, R., J. Picheca, and M. Prinzo. 2002. *Circles of Support and Accountability: An Evaluation of the Pilot Project in South-Central Ontario.* Ottawa: Correctional Service of Canada.

ENDNOTES

1. These international instruments include the UN's Charter; Universal Declaration of Human Rights; Convention on the Rights of the Child; International Covenant on Civil and Political Rights; International Convention of the Elimination of All Forms of Racial Discrimination; Convention Against Torture and Other Cruel, Inhumane, or Degrading Treatment of Punishment; and Standard Minimum Rules for the Treatment of Prisoners.

2. The *Corrections and Conditional Release Act* applies to offenders who are sentenced to two years or more in a federal penitentiary and who are supervised on conditional release in the community by the Correctional Service of Canada.

3. This statement of purpose was derived from the mission document that CSC developed in 1989, which reads: "The Correctional Service of Canada (CSC), as part of the criminal justice system and respecting the rule of the law, contributes to the protection of society by actively encouraging and assisting offenders to become law-abiding citizens, while exercising reasonable, safe, secure and humane control."

4. CSC also manages an addiction research centre, five regional headquarters and staff colleges, and a national headquarters.

5. See Part 3 of the *Corrections and Conditional Release Act.*

6. The book can be accessed at http://www.justicebehindthewalls.net

7. Female offenders are particularly affected by the experience of imprisonment. They are often the primary caregiver for children, and they have high rates of mental and physical disability, self-destructive behaviour (such as slashing and cutting), depression, and suicide attempts. Eighty percent report prior abuse. They experience significant poverty and have higher unemployment rates than their male counterparts and Canadian women as a whole.

CHAPTER 19
Jury Reviews of Parole Eligibility for Lifers: The "Faint Hope" Clause

One of the most controversial provisions in the *Criminal Code* is colloquially known as the "faint hope" clause. This permits many prisoners convicted of murder and who are serving life sentences to apply for a jury review of their parole eligibility date. The provision is one of the few areas in which members of the public have some input into sentencing and parole. If the prisoner has made great progress in prison, the jury has the power to make the prisoner eligible for parole earlier than would otherwise be the case. The faint hope clause has attracted a lot of criticism over the years. A previous Liberal government introduced amendments to tighten the rules in 1997, and in 2009 the Conservative government introduced a bill to abolish the provision. That bill did not become law, but it was reintroduced in Parliament in April 2010.

This chapter explores the origins, nature, and purpose of this controversial element of criminal justice in Canada.

Julian V. Roberts, University of Oxford

SENTENCING IN CASES OF MURDER

There are two categories of murder in Canada: first and second degree. According to Section 231(2) of the *Criminal Code*, murder is first degree when it is "planned and deliberate." In addition, a number of other circumstances can give rise to a first degree murder charge regardless of whether the murder was planned or deliberate. All murder that is not first degree is classified as second degree. A murder conviction in Canada carries a mandatory sentence of life imprisonment, regardless of whether it is first or second degree. However, the two categories of murder are distinguished by their parole eligibility arrangements. Offenders convicted of first degree murder become eligible to apply for release from prison on parole after they have served 25 years in prison. Offenders convicted of second degree murder become eligible to apply for parole after having served between 10 and 25 years in custody, the exact number of years being determined by the trial judge.

When the categories of first and second degree murder were created (in 1976), the Canadian Parliament simultaneously introduced what has subsequently been referred to as the "faint hope" clause. This provision permits prisoners to apply for a jury review of their parole eligibility date. Since prisoners eligible for this jury review still had to wait until they had spent 15 years in prison before they could file an application, no applications were heard until the mid-1980s. Growing public and political pressure led to significant amendments to the jury review provision in 1996.

Life prisoners in Canada spend significantly longer periods in custody than offenders convicted of murder in other jurisdictions such as the United States, France, England, and Wales (Correctional Service of Canada 1999). In most Western nations, life prisoners spend between 10 and 15 years in prison before being released on parole. For example, in Sweden the average is 12 years. In Canada, prisoners serving life for first degree murder spend more than 20 years, on average, before being released on parole.

Section 745.6 of the *Criminal Code* permits most prisoners serving a life term in excess of 15 years to apply, after having served 15 years in prison, for a jury review of their parole eligibility date. Thus the provision affects all inmates convicted of first degree murder as well as a small percentage of prisoners serving life terms for second degree murder. The purposes behind the provision—known as the "faint hope" clause—were to provide an incentive to rehabilitation for life prisoners and to offer some incentive to inmates serving the longest terms of imprisonment.

PUBLIC INPUT INTO SENTENCING AND PAROLE

One of the unique features of the sentencing regime for murder in Canada is the role of the general public. There are two ways in which community opinion may influence the sentencing and subsequently the administration of life sentences for offenders convicted of murder. First, jurors who have convicted an offender of second degree murder may make a recommendation to the sentencing judge with respect to the number of years the offender must serve in prison before becoming eligible to apply for parole. Second, Section 745.6 of the *Criminal Code* permits a jury review of the parole eligibility date for most persons who have been sentenced to life imprisonment and who have to serve at least 15 years before becoming parole eligible.

Critics of jury reviews of parole dates have argued that they are likely to be invoked routinely by all eligible prisoners once they reach the eligibility period for an application. If this were the case, the correctional and court systems would have difficulty coping with the number of applications. Jury review hearings require months of preparation, consume weeks of court time, and can constitute a considerable drain on legal aid resources. However, the first interesting finding yielded by an analysis of applications to date is that only a small minority of all eligible inmates apply for the review. Within the first 13 years of the application of this provision, 393 life prisoners became eligible for a review. During this time, only 105 (27%) hearings were held—approximately one-quarter of the eligible population. Despite the provision's high profile, it has been subject to almost no scholarly research over the past 30 years. (For an analysis of outcomes under the provision to 2001, see Roberts 2002.) Finally, it is important to note that juries in Canada have the power only to allow the applicant to apply for parole; the decision whether to deny or grant parole remains in the hands of the National Parole Board.

HISTORY OF THE FAINT HOPE CLAUSE

In the mid-1990s a number of factors aligned to provoke the federal government into amending the jury review provision. (For further discussion, see Roberts and Cole 1999.) First, the high rate of successful applications led to criticisms from populist politicians, who argued from the perspective of "truth in sentencing" that a life sentence that meant in reality "only" 25 years was now being reduced by up to 10 years (in cases in which the jury rendered a decision to make the applicant immediately eligible for parole). Second, applications from some high-profile prisoners such as Clifford Olson, one of Canada's most notorious murderers, attracted widespread media attention and critical commentary. Third, a private member's bill was introduced in Parliament for the specific purpose of repealing the provision outright.

The federal government responded by amending the provision in several ways. These amendments tightened the rules, making fewer inmates eligible. Offenders convicted of multiple or serial murders are no longer eligible to apply. Also, the jury must now be unanimous in its decision to grant an earlier parole date. The shift to unanimity and the judicial "pre-screening" were retrospective in application; they applied not just to offenders sentenced after the amendments were proclaimed, but to also to prisoners already in the correctional system. Critics of the retrospective nature of the reforms argued that it violated prisoners' constitutional rights: they had been sentenced under one set of parole rules and now these rules had been changed. However, in 1999 a *Charter* challenge to the retrospective nature of the provisions was rejected by the Ontario Court of Appeal.

Here is how the faint hope clause currently functions.

FAINT HOPE HEARING PROCEDURES

The faint hope provision has two distinct stages. First, a judge reviews the prisoner's application—a form of judicial "pre-screening"—to determine whether he or she has a reasonable prospect of success with the jury. The worst cases—prisoners who have made no efforts to rehabilitate themselves and who have no hope of a positive response from a jury—are thus prevented from applying. This screening prevents prisoners from wasting the time and money it takes to get a faint hope hearing off the ground; it also spares victims the experience of having to relive the trauma as they hear about the crime all over again. Applications that pass this test are allowed to proceed to a jury review.

The hearing must take place in the province in which the offence took place, regardless of where the application is made. The hearings are adversarial in nature: the prisoner is represented by counsel, and applications are usually opposed by a prosecutor. The jury is required to consider the applicant's character, his conduct while serving the sentence, the nature of the offence of conviction, and any information provided by a victim either at the original sentencing hearing or at the time of the judicial review hearing itself, as well as "any other matters that the judge considers relevant" (*Criminal Code*, s. 745.63(1)).

POWERS OF THE JURY

The jury has a number of options with respect to these applications. It can reduce the number of years that the applicant must serve before being eligible to apply for parole (in which case it will specify the number of years reduced); it can make the applicant immediately eligible to apply for parole; or it can decide that the number of years to be served ought not to be reduced. If the application is denied, the jury must set a time—not earlier than two years hence—after which a subsequent application may be made. Finally, the jury can decide that the prisoner cannot make another application under this provision, in which case he or she will have to wait until the statutory point is reached (25 years for first degree murder).

PUBLIC OPINION AND THE FAINT HOPE PROVISION

Over the years it has been argued that the public opposes "early parole" for prisoners convicted of the most heinous crimes. Critics have contended that abolishing the faint hope provision would promote public confidence in the justice system. It is true that most Canadians perceive sentencing as too lenient, and parole as being granted too soon to too many prisoners (see Chapter 1). However, the "public confidence in justice" argument has two fatal flaws. First, the public attitudes just cited are derived from opinion surveys in which people are asked simplistic questions and are given no opportunity to reflect on their answers. Second, the discretion to amend a prisoner's eligibility date resides not with a judge or a parole board, but with members of the public. There is something self-defeating about claims to abolish the provision in order to promote public confidence when the provision actually gives the community *more* input into the justice system. But let's begin by seeing what the polls say about public attitudes toward this provision.

In a national survey conducted in 1987, more than four-fifths of respondents stated that offenders convicted of murder should never be eligible for parole (Roberts 1988). Respondents were also asked how many years a prisoner serving a life term for murder should serve in prison before becoming eligible for parole. Almost half said that these prisoners should *never* receive parole; 39 percent chose a figure between 20 and 30 years. Only 12 percent of respondents favoured a parole eligibility date under 20 years for inmates convicted of murder (see Roberts 1988).

To date, only a single poll has directly asked the public for its views about the provision, and unfortunately, the survey illustrates the deficiencies in public opinion research when poorly constructed questions are used. In June 2009, Angus Reid Global Monitor asked a representative sample of Canadians the following question:

> "The "faint hope" clause allows people convicted of murder to apply for early release after 15 years in prison. The federal government has proposed scrapping the "faint hope" clause, meaning that people convicted of murder would not be eligible to apply for early release. Do you support or oppose scrapping the "faint hope" clause?"

This question fails to provide respondents with sufficient information about the provision. For example, it does not tell them about the restriction on prisoners convicted of multiple counts of murder, the judicial pre-screening, or the fact that very few eligible prisoners have benefited from the provision. Nor does it provide respondents with any information about how the provision has worked in practice.

A wealth of research in the field of public opinion has demonstrated that when respondents are given more time to answer the question, or are given a specific case to consider, they respond less punitively. This phenomenon has emerged with respect to mandatory sentencing, the death penalty, conditional sentencing, parole, and many other punishment-related issues (see Doob and Roberts 1983; Roberts and Hough 2005).

The true nature of public opinion is to be found not in public opinion polls, which require an instant response to a simple question, but rather in the decisions taken by juries. After all, juries are composed of members of the public. The critical difference between a jury and a public opinion poll is that while both involve the public, a jury is sworn to consider all arguments and evidence. That is why trials are decided by juries rather than by a show of hands from the general public.

With public opinion findings such as these, it might be reasonable to assume that members of the public would oppose granting life prisoners the right to apply for parole after "only" 15 years; the results of jury reviews might therefore be a foregone conclusion. In fact, as will be seen, quite the opposite trend emerges from the results of jury reviews conducted to date. Next, let's see what has happened in faint hope applications heard since the provision was created.

RECENT TRENDS

As of June 2008, 169 applications under the faint hope clause have resulted in a completed hearing. Few cases of second degree murder result in a parole ineligibility date in excess of 10 years; accordingly, the vast majority (147, or 87%) of the 169 applications to date have been made by prisoners convicted of first degree murder. Fully 89 percent of the 169 hearings were held in one of four provinces (Quebec, Ontario, British Columbia, Alberta). As can be seen in Table 19.1, fully 83 percent of the hearings—more than four-fifths of the applications—resulted in some reduction in the number of years to be served before parole eligibility.

Clearly, jurors had considerable sympathy for these prisoners. These findings demonstrate again that single-question opinion polls cannot capture the complexities of public opinion (see Zamble and Kalm 1990). The fact that in the actual hearings, jurors were more likely to decide in favour of rather than against the applicant suggests that when provided with adequate information about a specific offender (such as his conduct in prison), members of the public (serving in this context as sworn jurors) can move beyond the instinctually punitive response that most people would have to a request made on behalf of someone convicted of the most serious offence in the criminal code.

Another interesting feature of these jury review outcomes relates to the range of responses from juries. If juries had responded uniformly, by reducing all (or none) of the periods of parole eligibility, this might imply an insensitivity to the nature of the evidence introduced in the hearings; it would suggest that jurors were acting on the basis of their pre-hearing attitudes toward

Table 19.1 *Outcomes of "Faint Hope" Applications to 2008*

Province	Number of applications (and % first degree murder applications)	% of outcomes in which a reduction in parole ineligibility was granted
Quebec	77 (78)	94
Ontario	31 (68)	65
Alberta	21 (100)	76
British Columbia	20 (95)	85
Other provinces	20 (85)	80
Canada total	169 (87)	83

Source: Public Safety Canada. *Corrections and Conditional Release Statistical Overview.* 2008. Table E2. Pg. 106. Found at: *http://www.publicsafety.gc.ca/res/cor/rep/2008-04-ccrso-eng.aspx*

granting parole to life prisoners. However, different cases have received very different reductions in their periods of parole ineligibility. Thus the number of years reduced ranged from the minimum possible (one year) to the maximum possible (ten years). This supports the position that juries offer a responsible, evidence-driven alternative to reviews by the executive, the judiciary, or administrative tribunals such as parole boards.

INTERPROVINCIAL VARIATION

Table 19.2 summarizes outcomes of hearings involving first degree murder applicants to date across all jurisdictions. As can be seen, there is considerable interprovincial variation in outcomes, with the highest success rate in Quebec and the lowest in Ontario. This interjurisdictional variation is hard to interpret without a more detailed study of the case files. It is possible that characteristics of the murder account for the differential success rates—a higher proportion of more serious first degree murder cases, possibly involving child victims, or of multiple victims in cases sentenced before the 1997 amendments. This seems unlikely, however, as there is no reason why more serious cases of first degree murder should be more likely to occur in one province. It is possible that in Quebec, the Crown is less likely to oppose, or opposes applications less rigorously. This, too, may explain the higher success rates of applicants in that province. But this remains only a hypothesis.

A more plausible explanation is that juries in Quebec are more sympathetic to applications than are their counterparts in other provinces. Support for this explanation can be found in the results of the recent poll on the subject: opposition to repealing Section 745.6 was greater in Quebec than in any other province. Only Sixty-six percent of Quebec respondents supported repealing the provision, compared to the national average of 72 percent, support for repeal was highest in B.C. (82% of respondents).

Table 19.2 *Faint Hope Application Outcomes, First Degree Murder Cases*

Jurisdiction	Number of first degree murder applications	Number (%) successful	Number (%) unsuccessful
Quebec	60	57 (95)	3 (5)
British Columbia	19	16 (84)	3 (16)
Alberta	21	16 (76)	5 (24)
Ontario	30	20 (67)	10 (33)
Other provinces	17	13 (76)	4 (24)
Canada total	*147*	*122 (83)*	*25 (17)*

Source: Public Safety Canada. *Corrections and Conditional Release Statistical Overview.* 2008. Table E2. Pg. 106.
Found at: *http://www.publicsafety.gc.ca/res/cor/rep/2008-04-ccrso-eng.aspx*

IMPACT OF FAINT HOPE DECISIONS ON PAROLE RELEASE DECISION

Finally, the statistics on the response of the parole authorities to successful applications demonstrate the important gate-keeping function of the jury in decisions to release prisoners on parole. Of all applications to date in which juries have granted the right to make an early application to the National Parole Board, fully four out of five were granted release on full parole.

It is also perhaps worth noting that of the life prisoners who have been granted parole following a successful review by a jury under this provision, only two individuals have had their parole status suspended or revoked, although many of these prisoners have now been on parole for years. These statistics seldom come to the attention of the public, as the news media focus on parole failures, not successes. An important step in public legal education, therefore, would involve informing the public about the low failure rate of life prisoners on parole. One of the most glaring public misperceptions about parole is that a significant proportion of parolees reoffend. For example, a national survey in Canada found that 79 percent overestimated by a considerable margin the recidivism rate of offenders on parole (see Roberts, Nuffield, and Hann 2000). Whatever the merits of long-term imprisonment, the statistical record clearly shows that releasing a small number of carefully selected life prisoners into the community does not create a risk to the community.

CONCLUSIONS

Several conclusions can be drawn from Canada's experience with jury hearings of parole eligibility dates for life prisoners. First, creation of a jury review provision relating to parole eligibility dates does not necessarily mean creating an automatic review as each prisoner becomes eligible—only a small minority of eligible prisoners apply for a review. Second, the data suggest that whatever opinions members of the public express in response to opinion surveys, when they sit on juries, they can discharge their duties to react as unbiased decision makers, even in cases involving prisoners serving life terms for the most heinous crimes. Jurors' responses to these applications demonstrate that members of the public can modulate their response to the merits of the case and are not overwhelmed by sympathy for the victim, or by antipathy for the offender.

The experience with faint hope hearings makes it clear that the views of the public can reasonably be incorporated into the determination of parole eligibility dates for even the most serious offenders: those serving life terms for planned and premeditated murder. If the review of a life prisoner's parole date were made by a judge or an administrative tribunal, the result would inevitably be additional public criticism of judges or parole boards. There is a clear advantage to letting jurors make this decision rather than criminal justice professionals. When the decision to reduce the time served prior to parole eligibility is made by members of the public, the criticism that the parole system is too lax (and inconsistent with the views of the public) loses much of its power. After all, it is hard to argue that a provision of this kind is inconsistent with community sentiment when the authority to modify parole eligibility dates rests with community members serving as jurors.

DISCUSSION QUESTIONS

1. *If juries have an important impact on the parole eligibility dates for offenders convicted of murder, do you think there is a more general argument that juries should have input into eligibility dates for other offenders as well? Indeed, should juries composed of members of the public have more input into sentencing and parole decisions?*
2. *Do you agree or disagree with the government's proposal to eliminate the faint hope provision?*

FURTHER READING

Roberts, J.V. 2002. "Determining Parole Eligibility Dates for Life Prisoners: Lessons from Jury Hearings in Canada." *Punishment and Society: International Journal of Penology* 4: 103–14.

Roberts, J.V., and D.P. Cole. 1999. "Sentencing and Early Release for Offenders Convicted of Murder." In *Making Sense of Sentencing.* Toronto: University of Toronto Press.

REFERENCES

Correctional Service of Canada. 1999. *Comparison of Time Served in Custody by Life Prisoners in Western Nations.* Ottawa: Correctional Service of Canada.

Department of Justice Canada. 2010. "Backgrounder: Legislation to Repeal the "Faint Hope" Clause." http://www.justice.gc.ca/eng/news-nouv/ nr-cp/2010/doc_32495.html

Doob, A., and J.V. Roberts. 1983. *Sentencing: An Analysis of the Public's View.* Ottawa: Department of Justice Canada.

Roberts, J.V. 1988. "Early Release: What Do the Canadian Public Really Think?" *Canadian Journal of Criminology* 30: 231–39.

——. 2002. "Determining Parole Eligibility Dates for Life Prisoners: Lessons from Jury Hearings in Canada." *Punishment and Society: International Journal of Penology,* 4: 103–14.

Roberts, J.V., and D.P. Cole. 1999. "Sentencing and Early Release for Offenders Convicted of Murder." In *Making Sense of Sentencing.* Toronto: University of Toronto Press.

Roberts, J.V., and M. Hough. 2005. *Understanding Public Attitudes to Criminal Justice.* Maidenhead: Open University Press.

Roberts, J.V., J. Nuffield, and R. Hann. 2000. "Public Knowledge and Attitudes Toward Parole in Canada." *Empirical and Applied Criminal Justice Research* 1, no. 1.

Zamble, E., and K. Kalm. 1990. "General and Specific Measures of Public Attitudes Toward Sentencing." *Canadian Journal of Behavioural Science* 22: 327–37.

CHAPTER 20
Release from Prison: Rick Sauve's Story

In this chapter a life prisoner describes his life in prison and his application for early release on parole as a result of the "faint hope" provision. As noted in the previous chapter, this clause in the *Criminal Code* allows most prisoners sentenced to life imprisonment to apply for a jury review of their parole eligibility date. The provision has been criticized, usually without much discussion of the way it works. Rick Sauve discusses the provision and describes his testimony before a Parliamentary Committee that was considering a government proposal to abolish the jury review. His testimony demonstrates the importance of considering the views and experiences of all parties involved in the justice system when contemplating reform.

Rick Sauve

My name is Rick Sauve, and I am currently serving a life sentence while living in the community. In this chapter I am going to do two things. First, I am going to tell you about my life in prison—how I spent my 17 years inside and how I prepared to make an application under the so-called "faint hope" clause. Second, I am going to describe the testimony that I delivered to the Parliamentary Committee reviewing a government bill that would have eliminated this provision from the *Criminal Code*. I hope to show you that this provision plays an important role in the criminal justice system in Canada—that's why Parliament created it in the first place.

LIFE IN PRISON WHILE PREPARING TO MAKE A FAINT HOPE APPLICATION

When I was sentenced to prison with a life sentence with no parole eligibility for 25 years I decided early on that the only way I could survive the prison experience—both physically and psychologically—was to take control of my environment in a productive way. I was fortunate as I had good family support to supply me with hope and encouragement while serving my sentence. I realized early in my sentence that in order to eventually earn parole I would have to try and remain positive and actively work toward that goal. One of the hurdles I knew I would face was that I refused to accept my conviction and that I was determined to fight it. I maintained my innocence and as a result my case management team constantly told me that the only way I would ever get out of prison was to admit guilt. But how could I admit guilt to an offence I never committed? In the end, all of this actually strengthened my determination to succeed, and to avoid becoming immersed and lost in the prison subculture. I recognized that prison could "eat you up" if you didn't maintain a sense of your identity.

Going to School in Prison

One of the first things I did when I got to Millhaven, a maximum-security prison, was enroll in school. Prior to prison I had not completed my grade ten, so I took the opportunity to begin completing my education. It's not easy getting an education inside prison.

There were a number of benefits to enrolling in school besides achieving an education. First, the school setting itself offered a sense of sanctuary that took me out of the prison environment. At school I was able to see myself as a student rather than just as a prisoner. It also provided me with the opportunity to interact with teachers rather than uniformed institutional staff. Furthermore, it provided me with some sense of control, in the sense that I had a right to deviate from the regimentation of daily prison life. I was able to select the courses I wanted to take. Finally, school allowed me to share these experiences with my family—in particular my daughter. This allowed me to share a normal kind of routine that wasn't necessarily prison related.

After completing my high school requirements, I was accepted into a degree program offered by Queen's University. I completed two courses in psychology from Queen's while serving time at Millhaven. When I applied for a transfer to a medium-security prison, the transfer board had some concerns because I wouldn't admit guilt; nor would I discuss my conviction, because I was still fighting my case. However, because of my good behaviour in prison, my positive attitude, and my educational achievements, I was eventually granted a transfer to Collins Bay, a medium-security prison.

One of the first things I did when I arrived at Collins Bay was to continue with my education. I was determined that I was going to finish my degree.

I also became involved in other activities that took me out of the routine prison environment. One of these was the Exceptional Peoples Olympiad, which was sponsored by prisoners inside the prison walls on an annual basis. I became part of the executive. This allowed me to be productive and also gave me a sense of giving back and being a part of the outside community. Another important step I took was to co-found the Lifers group at the institution. We were an active group of like-minded prisoners serving life sentences who wanted to try and create a more positive environment inside the prison. We became affiliated with faculty members and students from the Criminology Department at the University of Ottawa.

I continued my studies and graduated from Queen's University in 1987 with a B.A. in psychology. That made me the first prisoner from Collins Bay to do so. As a result I was granted permission, with the Solicitor General intervening on my behalf, to attend my graduation ceremonies on an escorted temporary absence. This happened after he was contacted by Mick Lowe, a journalist who had written a book chronicling my case and conviction. Initially the institution had refused to let me attend my own graduation. But after the intervention by the Solicitor General, my application to attend was granted by the National Parole Board.

The next stage in my education came when, with the support of Dr. Robert Gaucher, I was accepted into the graduate studies program in criminology at the University of Ottawa. Thus I became a graduate student—not a bad achievement for someone who had entered prison without grade ten. I had met Robert in my capacity as chairman of the Lifers group, which had become affiliated with some of the faculty and students of the University of Ottawa.

This affiliation became important not only to me but also to the students, faculty, and guests. A symbiotic relationship developed: the students and guests learned first-hand from our prison experiences, while I and the other Lifers were further connected to the community. Together we wrote papers and articles about a variety of criminal justice issues, including sentencing. We regularly invited outside guests ranging from politicians and activists to senior corrections officials. I developed many lasting friendships from this experience, which helped keep me linked to the community.

Voting Rights for Prisoners

It was also at Collins Bay that I launched the court challenge for the prisoners' right to vote case under the *Charter of Rights and Freedoms*. At the time, prisoners in Canada did not have the right to vote in federal elections. The fact that you are serving time should not mean you lose this basic democratic right. If society wants prisoners to rehabilitate themselves, it should encourage prisoners to take part in the electoral process—not exclude them. The case eventually made its way to the Supreme Court of Canada, where the Court ruled that prisoners have the right to vote.

After several years at Collins Bay, I was approached by the warden, who told me that the Commissioner of Corrections wanted to start a pilot program to send Lifers serving a minimum of 25 years to a minimum-security camp, and that I had been selected as one of the first candidates to go. I was then transferred to Frontenac, a minimum-security institution. While there I continued with my graduate studies, completing my honours year and all my course requirements for a Masters degree in criminology.

I also became much more involved in community projects. I organized and chaired the Conwalk, a fundraiser for muscular dystrophy during which one group of prisoners went into communities to collect money to turn over to fire departments for the Muscular Dystrophy Association; meanwhile, a second group walked on a marathon back to the institution, beginning at Parliament Hill in Ottawa. In four years we raised almost $130,000 for this worthy cause. I also became involved in the Ontario Special Olympics. I organized a group of inmates and staff to build bleachers for the event and to provide volunteers to assist.

I also created the Straight Talk program, designed for young offenders and youth at risk. This followed a two-pronged approach. The first part involved going to schools, group homes, and other community organizations to talk about the experience of prison. At two of these events I paired up with the community's police chief to make presentations to students. The other part of the Straight Talk program was more structured—an eight-week program for young offenders that my wife and I developed. We would have the youth come into the prison and, with other Lifers we had trained, we would work on a variety of problem areas affecting their lives. We also encouraged parents and guardians to participate. We ran this program for about four years while I was at Frontenac, and continued some aspects of it after I was released on parole.

My Faint Hope Application

After serving 15 years inside, I became eligible for a "faint hope" hearing. This involved applying to a court for a jury to hear about my life in prison, with a view to determining whether I could apply to the National Parole Board before having spent 25 years in prison. At my faint hope hearing, the kinds of activities I was involved in were presented to the jury for their consideration in determining whether I should be considered eligible to have my parole date changed—from 25 years down to something sooner. I was able to call witnesses to testify about these activities. They included family members, friends, community associates from my volunteer work, one of my professors, and the warden from Frontenac. They all gave evidence under oath before the jury. They were able to paint a picture of who I really was for the jury to consider. I attest here that throughout my sentence I never involved myself in any activities to gain favour for my review or for my eventual parole. I involved myself because I believed I could make a positive contribution to my community both inside prison and beyond its walls. After hearing all the evidence, the jury—composed of members of the public—recommended that

I be considered for parole immediately. This did not mean that I could leave prison—such a jury does not have that power. What it meant was that I could now apply to the Parole Board, which would conduct its own review of my case. As you can see, it is not easy to get released from prison.

Applying for Parole

I still had to appear before the National Parole Board to present my case and to prove to the board's members that I would not pose a risk if I was released into the community. The board decided to initially grant me four unescorted temporary absences over a six-month period. These all went well. I then applied for and was granted day parole to a halfway house. After six months I again appeared before the board, which this time granted me full parole.

LIFE AFTER RELEASE FROM PRISON

After leaving prison I worked for a year as cabinetmaker. I then secured employment as a Child and Youth Worker for the Toronto Boys' Home for three years. There I worked with open detention and open custody youth, many of whom were involved in street gangs. I shared with them my background and experiences, hoping they might gain some insights from what I had been through. While I was employed there I received two promotions and developed a good rapport with both the youth and other staff. I also continued speaking at schools and to groups across the province. For the past 11 years I have been working for Lifeline, going back inside various prisons as an inreach worker. To this day I continue to speak to youth at risk; I also make presentations to schools, victims' groups, and other community groups and conduct many media interviews. I have never hidden the facts of my prison experiences or my journey through the justice system, including my experience with the faint hope clause. Not once has anyone among the thousands of people I have presented to over the years ever implied to me that I should not have been released on parole, or not have been entitled to the faint hope clause. To me that speaks volumes. I believe that when people are properly informed and have a clear understanding of the issues, they are more accepting and understanding of them.

Life Today

Today I am currently working for LifeLine as an inreach worker with St. Leonard's Society of Windsor. LifeLine is a uniquely Canadian concept that was developed by community organizations such as St. Leonard's, the Correctional Service of Canada (CSC), and the National Parole Board. Currently there are 26 in reach workers across the country. We provide institutional services in prisons at all security levels. Our focus is on providing hope to men and women who are serving life sentences. All inreach workers are paroled lifers or long-term prisoners. With periods of incarceration getting longer, it is difficult for many lifers to maintain hope and to develop realistic plans to some day return to the community. We help them in this regard, as we ourselves had to make that transition. To make the adjustment back into the community after 10 to 25 years (often longer) can be overwhelming. We also assist them with their parole hearings. We bring a unique perspective for the Parole Board to consider, as we have worked with our clients for many years in prisons of various security levels. We also assist them with their reintegration plans—for example, by helping them select halfway houses that fit their needs. We know first-hand how difficult that can be, as we ourselves have experienced it.

To give people a better understanding of what prison is like, we also speak at schools, as well as to community groups and the media. We see ourselves as a valuable resource to foster understanding about the system and to break down the myths and misconceptions that surround it. It is not easy for inreach workers to go back into the prisons that they worked so hard to get out of and stay out of. For many of us it is a vocation, not simply a job.

I do a lot of public speaking, especially to youth. I hope that by sharing my experiences I can help them make positive decisions in their lives. Sharing keeps me grounded and helps me make sense of my own life experiences. One of my passions is cabinetmaking. It helps bring balance into my life. After 17 years in prison and five days a week going back into prison, cabinetmaking provides me with the escape from the prison experience that I need. I spend my "free time" at our home in the country enjoying the quiet and solitude.

TESTIFYING BEFORE PARLIAMENT

In November 2010 I had the opportunity to testify before the Parliamentary Standing Committee on Justice and Human Rights. This was with regard to Bill C-36, which would have erased the faint hope provision from the *Criminal Code*. I hoped that the committee members would see me as a credible source. I believed that my experiences would benefit them by helping them understand how the hearings actually worked and their impact on the correctional system. I felt that by answering their questions I would be enlightening them as to the realities of the faint hope provision. I also believed that by sharing my experiences I would be showing them that the faint hope clause does not undermine public safety—indeed, it enhances public safety.

For me, personally, there was a sense of achievement, in that I felt myself to be part of the democratic process by which legislation is produced. I hoped that the committee members would be able to set aside any personal biases and hear my testimony for what it was, as coming from an informed and credible source. Yet I also knew that some of the members were philosophically opposed to the faint hope clause and might well be opposed to parole for anyone serving a life sentence. I knew that some members were entrenched in their positions—that they would not see that this legislation had merit and that those who succeeded in their faint hope applications could make positive contributions to society. The government had long made its intention known to abolish the faint hope clause.

I knew also that some MPs were opposed to parole eligibility for people convicted of murder, which included me. Furthermore, I knew there were some MPs who favoured capital punishment, which, again, would have applied to me. I recognized that because of this, I might well be dismissed as someone who should not have been eligible for faint hope at all and who should never have been released from prison.

I knew that from a personal and professional standpoint, I could provide testimony that covered all perspectives regarding the current legislation as well as the impact of abolishing it. As someone who will be on parole for the rest of his life, who has gone through this procedure, and who currently works within the correctional system with men and women serving life sentences, I knew I had a professional as well as a personal investment.

As a citizen, a parent, a grandparent, and a productive member of the community, I too had concerns about who was coming back into the community. I, too, wanted some assurance that such transitions were balanced with public safety and sound sentencing, which must entail earned reintegration. I hoped that the committee members would recognize this and that my testimony would bring an informed perspective to the debate and put a human face on those affected by this law.

Legislation had been introduced in 1997 that made the faint hope mechanism more restrictive then when I made my application. Those changes had not in my opinion been introduced to enhance public safety. They had been introduced mainly to limit access by a few high-profile prisoners who had absolutely no chance of succeeding with their applications. At the time, it had been suggested—erroneously—that those prisoners who were eligible to apply for the faint hope clause would be eligible to apply for parole after 15 years. This was not correct. That was only the eligibility date at which one could apply for the faint hope clause. Not one person who succeeded in achieving a reduction in parole got out after 15 years. The changes not only have limited who can apply for a hearing but also have made it harder for applications to succeed.

One of the major changes was that the jury's decision now had to be unanimous. When I went through the procedure it was necessary to have a two-thirds majority to change parole eligibility. Another significant change was that someone who had committed multiple homicides would no longer be eligible to apply. These changes were made after Clifford Olson, a serial killer, made an application for a review. There was never the remotest possibility that he would succeed—or, for that matter, that he would ever be released on parole. In my view, that particular change had been a knee-jerk reaction based on emotion rather than logic or reality. Yet even with the new restrictions, some applicants have succeeded (see Chapter 19). This testifies to the strength of our jury system—to how an informed jury views our judicial and correctional system. This is not a weakness or flaw in the system, but rather a strength.

Another myth that was being presented was that this procedure might release a flood of individuals serving life sentences back into the community. In fact, most prisoners who are eligible to apply do not. I know this from personal experience as an inreach worker, and the statistics support me. I have asked many of my clients who are eligible to apply why they don't apply, and I have received a number of responses. One of the main reasons given is that they don't want to put the victims or their own families through the experience of reliving the crime. Many have long come to terms with the impact of their crime and have accepted their sentence. Others, after completing 15 years, are beginning to see some light at the end of the tunnel and believe that if they remain positive they can still at some point achieve parole. Note that release on parole is not automatic and that full parole can take a number of years to achieve. I can attest to this; in my work I have assisted in over 200 parole hearings for lifers at various stages of the releasing process.

From a correctional and rehabilitative perspective, the faint hope clause is sound. It provides hope to those who have received a life sentence. It is hard for many people to comprehend the reality of serving a life sentence with 15 or more years before parole eligibility. There is a commonly held belief that parole is easy to attain and that a life sentence does not mean life; in fact, many prisoners will never be released on parole. For those prisoners who want to change, the faint hope clause serves as a means to approach rehabilitation. It is a valuable tool for prisoners who want to rehabilitate themselves and for the corrections system as a whole. Many of the clients I work with who are just starting out use the faint hope clause in precisely this manner. Over and over again, lifers have told me that if they maintain positive behaviour and complete their correctional treatment programs, they could reintegrate successfully if given the opportunity. But with the prospect of serving 20 years or more, they can't conceive of successful reintegration. I have been working for more than 11 years as an inreach worker and have seen this in hundreds of clients. Lifers cannot imagine what changes will have occurred in the community and how they will find a place in it again after so many years.

I can personally attest to the positive input that ex-prisoners who went through this procedure have provided to our community. By going back into prisons, we demonstrate by example that it is possible to reintegrate successfully.

My Testimony

As the date of my testimony drew near, I had to determine how I could make the greatest impact with my evidence. I had only been given a week to prepare, as the hearings had already ended. I had been given the opportunity to provide a written brief; the question was what to put in it and how best to present it. I could utilize statistics to underscore the merits of the faint hope clause. For example, I could provide data on the number of lifers who are eligible to apply but choose not to. I could present the statistics for those who had applied and the outcomes of those hearings. I could talk about the realities of prison life and the fact that many lifers died inside prison while serving out a sentence. I could point out how many prisoners will likely never be released on parole.

I could discuss the conditions of parole, such as reporting, travel restrictions, and other realities. But I also realized that the current federal government's position was that the facts simply did not matter—they were philosophically opposed to this legislation and were determined to rescind it.

I recognized that for them it was difficult to differentiate between the crime, the criminal, the prisoner, and the rehabilitation process. The concept of change and the very notion of "earning" parole were not part of their philosophy. I knew that for them, life on parole was not serving out one's sentence; it merely illustrated that those who favoured the faint hope clause were soft on crime and that parole was in essence freedom. In the end, I decided not to submit a written brief, for I was certain it would be summarily dismissed. I decided that the best approach would be similar to that of going through the review process: to present myself as I am, to illustrate that I am not a threat to public safety and that I am a contributing member of the community.

The morning of my testimony, I was feeling intimidated at the prospect of testifying on Parliament Hill. I wasn't sure how I would be received. I had stayed the night at my daughter's house and was having breakfast with my grandkids. My eldest grandson (who is 12) asked me to put into terms he could understand why I was testifying and what I would be testifying about. His request helped me decide how I would present. Here is what I said to the Parliamentarians.

Rick's Statement

"I'm pleased to have the opportunity to speak today, but without the faint hope clause, I wouldn't have been able to be here. In preparation for today I was talking to my grandson this morning and he asked me what Bill C-36 was about. He asked me to explain it to him in terms he might understand. He's 12 years old and very bright. I've never hidden from him the fact that I'm serving a life sentence. I'm still serving a life sentence, but now I'm in the community.

"I explained to him that one of the pillars of our justice system is the jury system. I was convicted of first degree murder and sentenced to parole ineligibility for 25 years, after I could make application to go back to the community—the community where I was arrested and where the crime had taken place. It was up to the people from my community, 12 men and women, to make a decision about my parole date after hearing the nature of the offence. They took into account how I served my time in prison, my character, and whether I should be allowed to come back to their community. After a week of hearing evidence about my character and what I had been doing in prison for the past 16 years the jury had to decide whether I should be allowed to apply for parole to come back to that community. They voted yes. The important point though is that it was a jury that made the decision – a jury composed of people from the community.

"We often hear that the community has an interest about who's going to be coming back into their community. They want to feel a part of the process. They want to know who it is that's going to be their neighbour. When I explained that to him my grandson said that it made sense. Why would we change that? I could talk about looking at it from a correctional perspective, that it gives hope, and that it's a good correctional tool for Corrections to assist people in the rehabilitation process. For me, it was about talking to the people from my community and letting them know that they were a part of that decision-making process. I feel that it would be unfortunate if that were removed from them."

That concluded my opening statement.

I chose this approach for a number of reasons. First, I was hoping that the members might get a better understanding of the reality of the process. I was sure the members had read over the current legislation, but I wasn't confident that they clearly understood the process. I had listened to previous speeches by those in favour of scrapping the faint hope clause—speeches that contained misinformation. For example, that "prisoners would be released after serving only 15 years" or that abolishing the faint hope clause would enhance public safety. I thought that by explaining the reality, I might provide clarity as well as present factual information, which might in turn have some impact.

Most important, however, I wanted to get across the point that this process involved input from community members, who were a valued part of the judicial process. It was *their* involvement that determined parole eligibility and who would be accepted back into the community. I had heard the government repeatedly state that its constituents were concerned about public safety and wanted this provision abolished. I believed that by focusing on how the cases were presented to juries, I would be demonstrating that juries—in effect, the community—were willing and able to make informed decisions and that there was value to their involvement.

The questions I faced provided me with a further opportunity to reinforce the reality of the procedures and the impact of parole in general. It also gave me an opportunity to talk about some of the things I have been doing since I got full parole. I was able to inform the committee that I had spoken to hundreds of people about the faint hope clause, the prison system, and the realities of parole, and that not one person had ever told me the legislation should be scrapped or that I should never had been released from prison. It gave me an opportunity to provide them with my own reality: I had exposed myself to the community, and that community had accepted me. Furthermore, I was able to tell them about my current work with Lifeline and about some of what actually takes place in the prison system. I was hoping that they would see the person I was and distinguish me from the crime of which I had been convicted. I did get to present some of what a jury would consider in determining their decision.

One member (Joe Comartin), had obviously had done some research into my background and my experiences, for he quoted many of my accomplishments. "Let me just play devil's advocate for a minute," he said, "to suggest that you're one of the exceptional cases. Do you see yourself that way or are there other individuals whom you've come across? I'm looking for an analysis of where you fit into the overall parameters of the people who apply and are successful in getting out on early release."

I responded: "I would say I'm somewhat exceptional, but that's what this legislation was for. It was for those who do exceptionally well inside a prison environment." I was hoping that with this answer they would see that this was the view that a jury would take in making its decision.

Since my testimony, Parliament has been prorogued and Bill C-36 has died as a result. I am certain, however, that the bill will be reintroduced at some point as part of the current government's tough law-and-order agenda. I can only hope that my testimony will have some impact on how MPs view the correctional system and how they treat those in their care. I believe that my experience has demonstrated the importance of encouraging prisoners to better themselves while inside. And with respect to the faint hope clause, I have proved that the best way to promote reintegration is to give people in prisoner some hope—hence the name of the provision.

DISCUSSION QUESTIONS

1. *In light of what you have learned about the "faint hope" clause, do you believe it is a positive feature of the correctional system in Canada?*
2. *In your view, why has this provision attracted so much public controversy?*

CHAPTER 21
Drugs and the Canadian Criminal Justice System

A significant proportion of the criminal justice budget is consumed by responses to offences involving drugs. Responding to the international drug trade, from cultivation to importation and distribution, has for many years been a major challenge, and not just for Canada. In this chapter the author takes a critical look at the criminal justice response to drugs. He argues that the prohibition-based approach, with its emphasis on punishment and deterrence, has failed and indeed is creating more problems than it resolves.

Eugene Oscapella, Department of Criminology,
University of Ottawa

Governments have many options for dealing with the vast array of mind-altering or "psychoactive," drugs available today. For example, they can decide to impose minimal restrictions on production, sale, and possession, as is largely the case with coffee and tea. Both beverages contain a psychoactive drug—caffeine—yet both are largely unregulated. Anyone, including a child, can purchase coffee, even though a 500 gram package of supermarket coffee contains more than enough caffeine to kill that child or even an adult.

Other drugs are regulated more strictly—for example, by limiting who can produce and buy them and where and when the drugs can be consumed. Alcohol is an example of this stricter regulation. Governments can also regulate advertising (as with alcohol) or prohibit advertising altogether (as with tobacco, which contains nicotine). Governments can tax drugs to discourage their excessive use. Again, alcohol and tobacco are examples. The criminal law comes into play only if, for example, someone drives a car or boat while impaired by alcohol. Governments also regulate drugs such as cold and allergy medications by imposing testing, quality control, and labelling standards. Still other drugs—such as sleeping pills, antidepressants, and strong painkillers— can be sold only in pharmacies and only to those holding a prescription.

Another option is to use the criminal law to prohibit the possession, production, transfer, and import or export of a drug. That is what Parliament has done with heroin, cocaine, cannabis, LSD, ecstasy, amphetamines, and hundreds of other substances. Most of these drugs are prohibited unless sold under prescription. Parliament prohibits these drugs through the *Controlled Drugs and Substances Act* (CDSA). The drugs "controlled" by this criminal law are the focus of this chapter. We commonly call them "illegal" or "illicit" drugs.

A CENTURY OF USING THE CRIMINAL LAW AND "PROHIBITION"

The *Controlled Drugs and Substances Act* came into force in 1997. It continues a century-long tradition in Canada of using the criminal law to prohibit an ever growing range of drugs. Before 1908, when Canada first "criminalized" it, opium was legally available, as were cannabis, cocaine, and many other drugs that Parliament has since prohibited. Parliament prohibited cocaine in 1911, cannabis and heroin in 1923, and hundreds of other substances since then. Using the criminal law to deal with these drugs is largely a phenomenon of the 20th century, one that continues into the 21st. The CDSA prohibits many actions related to the substances it lists. Among the acts it prohibits are possession, sale, sharing, distribution, delivery, production, and import and export. This approach—using the criminal law—is called "prohibition." The CDSA does not forbid drug use itself. The *Criminal Code* lists some crimes relating to drug use, such as driving while impaired by alcohol or a drug, and distributing "drug paraphernalia." But it is the CDSA that contains the bulk of Canada's provisions on "illegal" drugs.

Statistics Canada has reported that the overall rate of police-reported drug offences in Canada has generally been increasing since 1993. In 2007 that rate reached 305 incidents per 100,000 population—the highest point in 30 years. The same report noted that the rising drug offence rate coincided with a decreasing overall crime rate. Most drug offences involved cannabis, consistent with long-term trends. In 2006–7, "about half of all drug-related court cases were stayed, withdrawn, dismissed or discharged. If convicted, youth were most often sentenced to probation. Probation was also the most common sentence for adults convicted of drug possession; however, adults convicted of drug trafficking were more often sentenced to custody" (Statistics Canada 2009).

Penalties under the CDSA vary widely. Possession of a small quantity of cannabis is punishable by up to six months' imprisonment, a fine of up to $1,000, or both. At the other extreme, importing or exporting cannabis, heroin, cocaine, and scores of other substances is punishable by a maximum penalty of life imprisonment. Trafficking, which can include simply sharing a small quantity of a drug with a friend for no money, is punishable by up to life imprisonment for many drugs, including cocaine and heroin. The penalty for trafficking cannabis is a maximum of five years less a day if no more than three kilograms of cannabis is involved, and life imprisonment for larger amounts. However, courts almost never impose these maximum penalties.

The current drug laws contribute significantly to Canada's prison population. For example, in 2005–6, 10 percent of adult admissions to federal custody involved a drug offence as the offender's major offence (Statistics Canada 2008). This figure does not include imprisonment for "acquisitive" offences committed to obtain the money to pay for illegal drugs, nor does it include imprisonment for violent crimes committed by those fighting for a share of the trade in illegal drugs. Nor does it include admissions to provincial custody for drug offences, related acquisitive offences, and drug trade offences. Still, it is clear from even these limited statistics that drug laws are responsible, directly or indirectly, for a significant share of Canada's prisoners.

Criminal penalties are the most serious sanctions that the State can impose. One would expect it to base its decisions to apply these penalties on sound evidence that they will reduce the problematic use of a given drug. One would not expect decision makers to ignore evidence and instead to rely on ideology or other inappropriate considerations. Unfortunately, decisions in Canada (and in other countries) to use the criminal law to deal with a particular drug have often flowed from prejudice, propaganda, political ideology, or historical accident, not from a rational search for ways to reduce the harms associated with the drug.

DOES THE CRIMINAL LAW REDUCE DRUG-RELATED HARMS?

In theory, the prospect of serious penalties for possessing, producing, or distributing drugs should discourage such activities. However, the evidence often points in the other direction—that the criminal law actually *increases* drug-related harms and that prohibition plants the seeds of its own failure. In other words, serious penalties cause many of the very problems they seek to prevent. Below are discussed some of the many reasons why criminal penalties are counterproductive:

Prohibiting the supply of a drug forces users to buy it on the illegal market. The huge profits to be made in this "black" market act as an incentive to produce and sell illegal drugs and to develop new customers. The United Nations Office on Drugs and Crime (UNODC) recently described this illegal market as "of staggering proportions" (United Nations 2009a).

How profitable is the black market created by drug prohibition? UN figures from the mid-1990s indicated that a farmer in Pakistan received about US$90 for a kilogram of opium produced from the poppy plant. Ten kilograms of opium would be processed to yield 1 kilogram of heroin, so someone would pay about $900 for enough opium to produce a kilogram of heroin. The final retail price of that kilogram of heroin in the United States at that time was $290,000 (*Economist* 2001). This final price was more than 320 times the price paid to the farmer. That is an enormous profit and a powerful incentive—just the opposite of what governments want—to produce and sell drugs on the black market. In contrast, the final retail price of a pound of ground coffee beans might be as little as three times the price paid to the farmer who produced the coffee beans (Miron 2003).

The funds generated by the black market help finance criminal, terrorist, and insurgent groups, adding to their power to corrupt and kill. Some RCMP reports have described the black market trade in drugs as a major, if not *the* major, source of income for most criminal groups in Canada. In 2000, RCMP Commissioner Giuliano Zaccardelli warned that for the first time, organized crime groups in Canada had accumulated so much money and power that they were threatening Canada's democratic institutions: "We are seeing signs of criminal organizations that are so sophisticated that they are focusing on destabilizing certain aspects of our society" (*National Post* 2000). Even the UNODC, long an advocate of prohibition and one of the many forces outside Canada's borders that constrain innovative drug policies in Canada, acknowledged the dramatic violence and corruption caused by current "global drug control efforts"—a polite way of saying prohibition:

> Global drug control efforts have had a dramatic unintended consequence: a criminal black market of staggering proportions. Organized crime is a threat to our security. Criminal organizations have the power to destabilize society and Governments. The illicit drug business is worth billions of dollars a year, part of which is used to corrupt government officials and to poison economies. (United Nations 2009b)

Yet the head of the UNODC immediately dismissed the most effective means to destroy the black market in drugs—replacing prohibition with strict regulation. "Legalization," as he simplistically described these alternatives, would be a "historical mistake" (United Nations 2009). Yet he did not explain why, nor did he explain what this historical mistake was. Often, support for prohibition-based approaches to drugs, even at the highest levels, continues to be based on blind faith rather than on reason and evidence.

Criminals fight to the death for control of the black market and its profits. Warring groups in Colombia, often funded by huge profits from drug sales, have killed tens of thousands in the past few decades. More recently, rival drug gangs battling for control of the drug trade in Mexico have killed thousands (*Economist* 2010). And violence is not restricted to battles between drug lords in countries that produce and ship drugs; it reaches the consuming countries as well. A 2008 news report cited a claim in a U.S. Department of Justice report that Mexican drug traffickers posed the biggest organized crime threat to the United States. The report continued that Mexican gangs controlled distribution in most American cities and were gaining strength in areas they did not yet control (BBC 2008). These same gangs will inevitably reach into Canada, bringing further gang violence to this country. Even without the involvement of foreign criminal groups, domestic "turf" wars over control of the drug trade in Canada can be deadly. For example, a 2001 news report cited police sources for a claim that more than 150 people had been murdered in Quebec over the preceding six years in battles between criminal gangs for control of the drug trade there (*Washington Post* 2001).

In an attempt to suppress the drug trade and to confront sometimes well-armed drug gangs, the police arm themselves more heavily and develop a more aggressive style of policing. This increases bystanders' risk of death and injury during police actions. This sort of "militarization" of policing to tackle drug gangs may eventually lead to a militarization of policing generally. Law enforcement may foster violence in another way. A recent study contends that law enforcement practices that seek to disrupt drug markets may unintentionally increase drug market violence. Removing key players from the market may lead others to fight over the turf vacated as a result of the law enforcement action (British Columbia 2010). In addition, the black market leads to significant police and other official corruption, with police and officials sometimes actively involved in the drug trade themselves.

Law enforcement only marginally reduces the supply of drugs. In many countries, police and other government officials regularly admit that they stop only a small percentage of the illegal drugs destined for or produced in their countries. For example, a federal official told a House of Commons committee in 2001 that "law enforcement is able to stop only about 10 percent of the $7 billion to $10 billion annual trade in illegal drugs in Canada" (Connolly 2001). Even that 10 percent reduction may be futile. If there is a local glut of a drug, a 10 percent reduction may not increase prices or reduce availability or use. And even if policing does reduce the availability of one drug, users can simply switch to another of the many other illegal drugs that remain readily available.

Even what appears to be an obvious "success" in enforcing the drug laws—a seizure of a large quantity of drugs—can produce harm. A large seizure may create a shortage and drive up a drug's price locally, in just the same way that a shortage of oil drives up its price. This increases the value of the drug held by the sellers who were not arrested, thereby increasing their profits. The higher price may lure others into selling because of the even greater profits to be made. As well, the now higher price of the drug may force dependent users to commit more crimes to get the extra money they now need to buy the drug. High prices may also lead users to search for more efficient ways of using their drugs, such as by injection. Injection with equipment infected by HIV or hepatitis C—always a possibility in the world of illegal drug use—greatly increases the risk of acquiring these serious diseases. And as noted above, users who cannot afford or get access to the drug may shift to other drugs. Users who are not familiar with these "substitute" drugs are more vulnerable to harm from them.

There is little evidence that the criminal law and criminal justice policies deter people from using drugs. In 2001 the Senate Special Committee on Illegal Drugs heard from Professor Peter Cohen of the University of Amsterdam that the tolerance of access to cannabis in the Netherlands has had little, if any, impact on its use:

> In terms of our national [cannabis consumption] averages, we are in the same league as Germany and France. We are considerably lower than the UK or Denmark, and much lower than the USA. The USA has levels of drug use that are double to triple the levels in the Netherlands. I do not say that this is because of drug policy, because it is my firm opinion that drug policy in itself has very little influence on the number of people who use drugs or who do not use drugs. The incredibly easy availability of cannabis-type drugs in The Netherlands has not at all changed the number of people who want to use it, because the decision to use it is based on the cultural composition of the population, who your friends are, the image of drugs and the economic situation of individuals. It does not matter what the government thinks about these drugs. (Cohen, 2001)

Prohibiting drugs can make their use much more dangerous than it would otherwise be.

Unlike regulated drugs, prohibited drugs have no quality controls or labels indicating their potency. Governments discourage honest drug education for fear of "condoning" drug use. Police, rather than public health workers, often deliver the limited "education" that does occur. Such education provides little, if any, instruction on how to minimize the risks of using certain drugs. Much of the education preaches abstinence, abandoning to ignorance the many who do try illegal drugs.

Drug users may end up in prison for drug offences or related crimes. There, HIV and hepatitis C rates are many times higher than in open society. Users may well continue to use the drugs that are readily available there, but government authorities will not permit them access to some types of equipment, such as syringes, needed to prevent the spread of infection.

Both within and outside Canada, the stigma—indeed, outright hostility—attached to certain drugs has fostered conditions for the explosive spread of HIV and hepatitis C. Globally, millions of people have become infected as a result of government and public inattention, or outright opposition, to means for reducing the risk of disease among drug users. The failure to reduce the spread of such diseases among users will eventually result in their spreading more widely into the general population.

The "war on drugs" mentality has led governments and the public to tolerate troubling violations of rights. Violent police raids of private dwellings, increased powers of search and seizure and surveillance in homes and schools, employee drug testing, calls for long mandatory prison terms, and the encouragement of an "informer society"—once largely the preserve of authoritarian regimes—are all products of this mentality. These State powers are not directed solely at drug users: all society suffers a loss of privacy and other rights. And because these measures do not work, police demand—and governments and the public support—even greater powers of surveillance, control and incarceration.

Conviction for a drug offence results in a criminal record (although an accused person can sometimes obtain an absolute or conditional discharge, which in theory produces no criminal record). A criminal record can result in serious collateral harms—stigma, difficulty in securing a job, complete ineligibility for some jobs, and restrictions on travel to other countries.

Money spent on enforcing drug laws and building and running prisons is not available for other, often more effective programs to reduce problematic drug use. Canada's criminal justice system receives the overwhelming share of federal funds directed at the drug issue. The Auditor General reported in 2001 that "about 95 percent of the federal government's expenditures that address illicit drugs were used for supply reduction (enforcement or interdiction)." This percentage declined over the next few years, but the intention of the present Conservative government to introduce harsher drug penalties and bolster drug law enforcement will require extensive new resources for the criminal justice apparatus. This will leave programs outside the criminal justice system starved of funding to deal with drug issues.

Perhaps the most fundamental flaw of prohibition is that it has failed to address the causes of problematic drug use. Prohibition assumes that the problem is drug availability and that the problem can be solved by reducing availability and by punishing those who use illegal drugs. Such approaches ignore the real issues that often underpin problematic use—alienation, homelessness, physical and sexual abuse, mental illness, other forms of trauma, and so on. The prohibition philosophy pretends that punishment is the answer.

WHERE IS CANADA HEADED?

There have been several attempts to move away from a prohibition-based approach to regulating drugs. In 2002 the Senate Special Committee on Illegal Drugs, focusing primarily on cannabis, recommended a regulatory regime to replace the current prohibitionist model (Senate 2002). Later that same year, the House of Commons Committee on the Non-Medical Use of Drugs called for simple possession of cannabis and production of small amounts to be decriminalized. These activities would remain offences, but not *criminal* offences—those convicted would not receive a criminal record. The Commons Committee also supported a supervised injection facility where users could more safely inject the drugs on which they were dependent, and it recommended projects to provide heroin to severely dependent heroin users (House of Commons 2002).

The Liberal government in power during the first six years of the 21st century did introduce legislation to reduce penalties for simple possession of cannabis and for production of small quantities. However, Parliament never enacted the law. The government did, however, permit a supervised injection facility, known as "Insite," in Vancouver, and it supported heroin maintenance trial projects in Vancouver and Montreal.

The Conservative government elected in 2006 took a much more punitive line. In 2007 it introduced a bill to impose mandatory minimum penalties for several drug offences, ignoring substantial evidence about the ineffectiveness of mandatory minimums (Bill C-26 2007). The government rhetoric accompanying the introduction of the bill signalled a clear intention to get "tough on drugs" despite the demonstrated failure of such approaches around the world—most notably in the United States. That bill died when a federal election was called, but in 2009 the next Conservative government introduced a virtually identical bill (Bill C-15 2009). That bill died when Parliament was prorogued late in 2009. In May 2010 the government revived the bill and gave it a misleading "short" title, the Penalties for Organized Drug Crime Act (Bill S-10 2010). If enacted, and if the courts do not strike its sentencing provisions down as violating the *Canadian Charter of Rights and Freedoms*, the bill will almost certainly result in small-time drug sellers, many of them dependent users, being imprisoned as a consequence of mandatory minimum terms of imprisonment. "Organized crime" leaders will remain as insulated as ever from the reach of the criminal law. The current government has also opposed the Vancouver supervised injection facility, but to date has been unable to close it because of two recent court decisions affirming its right to exist. The government is now seeking to have the Supreme Court of Canada hear an appeal of these decisions.

WHY PERSIST WITH SOMETHING THAT DOESN'T WORK?

Drug prohibition has not worked, is not working, and will not work to reduce drug problems. The prohibitionist system is broken. In May 2010 the head of the U.S. Office of National Drug Control Policy acknowledged this. "In the grand scheme," he said, the "war on drugs" strategy employed in the United States over the previous 40 years "has not been successful ... Forty years later, the concern about drugs and drug problems is, if anything, magnified, intensified" (Associated Press 2010).

Yet the continuing failure of prohibition has not stopped many governments—including successive federal governments in Canada—from calling for more of the same prohibitionist policies. As long as drug policy and drug laws in Canada remain driven by ideology rather than by rational, non-partisan discussion and evidence, it will be exceedingly difficult to mend this broken system. Another serious impediment to reform—perhaps the greatest blockage in practice—is the simple reality that various interests benefit from prohibition, even if it damages society as a whole. These range from "tough on crime" politicians seeking election; to organized crime and terrorist groups; to police organizations, which benefit through increased budgets to "fight drugs"; to others in what Nils Christie has called the "crime control industry."

Instead of relying on Parliament to fix the broken drug-control system, reform advocates have increasingly turned to the courts. The successful—to this point—constitutional challenge to the call by the current Conservative government to shut down the Vancouver supervised injection facility is a case in point. Other constitutional challenges have led several courts to declare the prohibition on cannabis to be unconstitutional and forced the federal government to develop a program for access to medicinal cannabis, although higher courts later overturned some of these decisions.

ALTERNATIVES TO PROHIBITION

Several groups have described regulatory models that could replace prohibition. It is not possible in this brief chapter to explain these models in detail. Prohibition's one virtue—despite its utter failure as a policy—is its structural simplicity: simply prohibit a drug. The regulatory models that would replace prohibition are necessarily more complex, for they seek to take into account the subtleties of human behaviour; the many effects, good *and* bad, of currently illegal drugs; and the most effective ways to reduce the harms of those drugs and to enhance their benefits. Readers who wish for greater detail about regulatory alternatives to prohibition can find this information in the references cited in the following paragraphs.

In 2002 the Senate Special Committee on Illegal Drugs called for an end to the criminalizing of cannabis users. It proposed a "criminal exemption" scheme under which the production and sale of cannabis would be licensed (Senate 2002). It also called for an amnesty for the hundreds of thousands of Canadians with a criminal record for possession of cannabis. Similarly, in 2005 the Health Officers Council of British Columbia rejected many aspects of prohibition—only this time, for all currently illegal drugs, not merely cannabis. The council called for an approach based on public health principles:

> Current conditions are right to enter into serious public discussions
> regarding the creation of a regulatory system for currently illegal drugs in
> Canada, with better control and reduced harms to be achieved by manage-
> ment in a tightly controlled system. The removal of criminal penalties for
> drug possession for personal use, and placement of these currently illegal
> substances in a tight regulatory framework, could both aid implementation
> of programs to assist those engaged in harmful drug use, and reduce sec-
> ondary unintended drug-related harms to society that spring from a failed
> criminal-prohibition approach. This would move individual harmful illegal
> drug use from being primarily a criminal issue to being primarily a health
> issue ...

Part of a public health approach includes harm reduction. Reviews of the evidence show that selected harm reduction strategies do work. Harm reduction strategies such as needle exchanges, safe injection sites and opioid substitution programs have been shown to reduce the spread of infectious diseases and the number of overdose deaths. These programs also act to draw in the otherwise marginalized drug users giving them access to health services and an opportunity to move towards risk-behavior reduction or treatment for the addiction. Harm reduction strategies have not been as effective as possible due to their implementation within the prohibition model. (Health Officers 2005, 2, 15)

Despite the overwhelmingly prohibitionist nature of Canadian drug policy, several harm reduction measures are now established in Canada, among them syringe distribution and methadone maintenance programs and education about techniques for safer drug use. More controversial programs such as heroin maintenance and supervised injection facilities such as Vancouver's Insite stand on shakier ground. As the Health Officers Council noted, operating within a prohibitionist model makes harm reduction efforts less effective than they would otherwise be.

In late 2009 the British drug policy reform group Transform published its proposals for reform in what it called a "Blueprint for Regulation." The Blueprint concluded that "both experience and research suggests that the most effective way of minimizing drug arms is regulation, based upon normative, legal frameworks rather than prohibition." The Blueprint proposed five key models, none involving prohibition, for managing drugs:

Prescription: the most controlling model, this would be an exact equivalent to current prescription models for medical drugs, and some opiate maintenance programmes.

Pharmacy sales: drugs would be made available through pharmacies or pharmacy-like outlets, either on prescription or over the counter.

Licensed sales: vendors would be granted a licence to sell specific drugs under certain, clearly defined conditions, on off-licence like premises.

Licensed premises: vendors would be licensed to manage premises where drugs would be sold and consumed, much like public houses and bars.

Unlicensed sales: certain low risk substances could be managed through food and beverage legislation, as—for example—coffee is currently managed (Transform, 2009, 7–8).

None of alternatives to prohibition discussed above seek to abandon drug users to their fate. Instead, they seek to minimize the harms associated with using these drugs. This may include measures to help problematic users quit. At the same time, these measures avoid the grave harms to users and their societies caused by prohibition.

CONCLUSION

Canada's approach to "illegal" drugs demonstrates one of the sorriest misuses of the criminal law. The criminal law does not address the fundamental questions—why people use drugs, and why some of them use drugs in a way that harms them and those around them. As long as people want to alter their mental states, they will do so, whether through criminal or legal means. As this chapter has argued, the criminal law, instead of controlling problematic drug use, causes profound additional harms. Yet prohibition is so firmly entrenched as a means of dealing with certain drugs that many people and organizations do not even question its worth. As legal philosopher Douglas Husak argues in his discussion of using the criminal law to prohibit drug use, those calling for reform are always challenged to show why change is necessary. But, he says, those who support prohibition have never been called on to provide evidence that prohibition "works":

> Any policy that resorts to punishment requires a justification. We should not assume that what we are doing is right unless someone can prove that it is wrong. We must always be prepared to show why what we are doing is right ... Those who favor punishments for drug users must explain why they think this policy is fair and just. (Husak 2002, 13)

DISCUSSION QUESTIONS

1. *One alternative to prohibition is legalization. The State could legalize the consumption of drugs such as marijuana and then control the sale of the drug— in the same way that alcohol is sold. What advantages or dangers can you see to this approach?*
2. *Do you see any implications of the harm reduction approach for prisons? For example, should the correctional system regulate the provision of drugs to prisoners to prevent the violence associated with drug dealing inside?*

FURTHER READINGS

Alexander, B.K. 2008. *The Globalisation of Addiction: A Study in Poverty of the Spirit.* Oxford: Oxford University Press.

Duke, S.B., and A.C. Gross. 1993. *America's Longest War: Rethinking Our Tragic Crusade Against Drugs.* New York: Putnam.

Maté, G. 2008. *In the Realm of Hungry Ghosts: Close Encounters with Addiction.* Toronto: Random House of Canada.

REFERENCES

Associated Press. 2010. "US Drug War Has Met None of Its Goals." May 13, 2010.

Auditor General of Canada. 2001. *Report of the Auditor General of Canada—2001, chapter 11, Illicit Drugs: The Federal Government's Role*. Ottawa.

Bill C-26. 2007. *An Act to amend the Controlled Drugs and Substances Act and to make consequential amendments to other Acts*. 2nd Session, 39th Parliament, 56 Elizabeth II, 2007.

Bill C-15. 2009. *An Act to amend the Controlled Drugs and Substances Act and to make related and consequential amendments to other Acts*. 2nd Session, 40th Parliament, 57–58 Elizabeth II, 2009.

Bill S-10. 2010. *An Act to amend the Controlled Drugs and Substances Act and to make related and consequential amendments to other Acts*. 3rd Session, 40th Parliament, 59 Elizabeth II, 2010.

BBC News. 2008. "Mexico Drug Gangs 'Top US Threat.'" December 16, 2008.

—— . 2009. "US Ready to Aid Mexico Drug Fight." March 2, 2009.

British Columbia Centre for Excellence in HIV/AIDS, Urban Health Research Initiative. 2010. *Effect of Drug Law Enforcement on Drug-Related Violence: Evidence from a Scientific Review*. Vancouver: University of British Columbia.

Cohen, P. 2001. Testimony before the Senate Special Committee on Illegal Drugs. May 28, 2001.

Connolly, M. 2001. Testimony before the House of Commons Special Committee on Non-Medical Use of Drugs. October 1, 2001.

Economist, The. 2001. "Survey: Illegal Drugs." July 26, 2001.

—— . 2010. "Mexico's Murder Capital: A 'Dying' City Protests." February 18, 2010.

Health Officers Council of British Columbia. 2005. *Discussion Paper: A Public Health Approach to Drug Control in Canada*. Vancouver.

House of Commons, Special Committee on Non-Medical Use of Drugs. 2002. *A Policy for the New Millennium: Working Together to Redefine Canada's Drug Strategy*. Ottawa.

Husak, D. 2002. *Legalize This! The Case for Decriminalizing Drugs*. London: Verso.

Miron, J.A. 2003. *The Effect of Drug Prohibition on Drug Prices: Evidence from the Markets for Cocaine and Heroin*. Cambridge, MA: National Bureau of Economic Research.

National Post. 2000. "Organized Crime Plans to Corrupt Parliament: RCMP Commissioner." September 8, 2000.

Senate of Canada, Special Committee on Illegal Drugs. 2002. *Cannabis: Our Position for a Canadian Public Policy*. Ottawa.

Statistics Canada. 2008. "Adult Correctional Services in Canada, 2005/2006." *Juristat* 28, no. 6.

—— . 2009. "Trends in Police-Reported Drug Offences in Canada." *Juristat*, May 2009.

Transform Drug Policy Foundation. 2009. *After the War on Drugs: Blueprint for Regulation*. Full Report and Executive Summary. Bristol.

United Nations, Department of Public Information. 1998. Press release: "UN Moves to Confront World Drug Problem." April 23, 1998.

United Nations, Economic and Social Council. 2009. "Draft Political Declaration and Plan of Action on International Cooperation towards an Integrated and Balanced Strategy to Counter the World Drug Problem." E/CN.7/2009/L.2. March 10, 2009.

United Nations, Office on Drugs and Crime. 2009a. http://www.unodc.org/drugs/en/security-and-justice/index.html

——. 2009b. *Organized Crime and its Threat to Security: Tackling a disturbing consequence of drug control*. Vienna.

Washington Post. 2001. "Canadian Motorcycle Gangs Gun for Control of Illegal Drug Trade." February 5, 2001.

CHAPTER 22
When Justice Fails: Wrongful Convictions in Canada

A common perception among many members of the public is that the justice system tends to protect the rights of the accused, with the result that guilty parties too often escape conviction. However, the opposite can also occur: innocent accused persons are sometimes convicted of crimes they did not commit. This is especially disturbing when the conviction results in a long prison sentence, as happened with David Milgaard and several other individuals. Criminologists in Canada and elsewhere have explored the causes and consequences of wrongful convictions. In this chapter, two leading Canadian researchers discuss the issue of wrongful convictions.

Kathryn M. Campbell, University of Ottawa, and
Myriam Denov, McGill University

The Canadian criminal justice system is based on the adversarial model, in which two parties—the State and the accused—present their case before an impartial judge. The theory is that as a result of the criminal trial between competing parties, the truth eventually emerges. Numerous procedural safeguards are presumed to protect the innocent from unintentional and/or intentional errors on the part of the police, prosecutors, and judges. Unfortunately, the cases of wrongful conviction in Canada call into question the ability of our criminal justice system to distinguish between the guilty and the innocent. The devastating ordeals of wrongly convicted Canadians, such as Donald Marshall, Jr., David Milgaard, Guy Paul Morin, Steven Truscott, and Jamie Nelson, serve as powerful reminders of the potential for error in the justice system. The media and lobby groups such as the Association in Defence of the Wrongly Convicted (AIDWYC) help in raising awareness about these cases.

This chapter explores the causes and consequences of wrongful convictions, as well as government responses to the problem. It begins by examining the individual and systemic factors that contribute to wrongful convictions. It then explores the effects of wrongful conviction on individuals and their families, based on in-depth interviews with two Canadians who have been wrongly convicted and falsely imprisoned. Finally, it addresses state responses to wrongful conviction, including conviction review, commissions of inquiry, and government approaches to compensation.

THE PREVALENCE OF WRONGFUL CONVICTIONS

A wrongful conviction occurs when an individual has "been arrested on criminal charges [and has] either plead guilty to the charge or [has] been tried and found guilty; and who, not withstanding plea or verdict, [is] in fact innocent" (Huff, Rattner, and Sagarin 1996, 10). While in the past, wrongful convictions were thought to be relatively rare, more recent estimates of the frequency of such miscarriages range from very few cases each year to 20 percent of all convictions (Holmes 2001). A British study conducted at a maximum-security prison for the National Association of Parole Officers revealed that as many as 6 percent of the inmates may have been wrongly convicted. The association believed that this figure was typical of other British prisons (Carvel 1992). An earlier study by Huff, Rattner, and Sagarin (1986) suggests that 0.5 percent of all convictions in the United States could be in error. More recently, Gross and colleagues (2005, 551) found in their study of false convictions in the United States that from 1989 to 2003, any estimate of the number of wrongful convictions in that country would be in the tens of thousands. There is no reason to believe that the rate of wrongful conviction is any lower in Canada.

CAUSES OF WRONGFUL CONVICTION

Research has revealed that wrongful convictions do not occur as a result of one individual making a single grave mistake. Instead, several individual and systemic factors, alone or in concert, contribute to wrongful convictions (Castelle and Loftus 2001). These factors include eyewitness error, erroneous forensic science, false confessions, the use of jailhouse informants, professional and institutional misconduct, and racial bias.

Eyewitness Error

Psychological research shows that due to normal deficiencies in human memory, eyewitness identification is inherently unreliable (Sanders 1984; Wells and Olsen 2003). Eyewitness testimony is often the sole or major source of evidence leading to a conviction; it follows that it is the single most important factor leading to wrongful convictions (Huff, Rattner, and Sagarin 1986). A U.S. National Institute of Justice study of 28 wrongful conviction cases (Conners et al. 1996) found that 24 of those convictions were at least partly the result of erroneous eyewitness identification. In the United States, through DNA testing, the Innocence Project has helped overturn 254 wrongful convictions; eyewitness misidentification was a major contributing factor in 75 percent of those cases (Innocence Project 2010).

Eyewitness errors occur for several reasons, including suggestive police interviewing, unconscious transference, and the malleability of confidence (Castelle and Loftus 2001). *Suggestive police interviewing* occurs when the police communicate information to eyewitnesses that subsequently influences and ultimately contaminates their testimony. In Canada, suggestive police interviewing led to the initial convictions of Donald Marshall, Jr., David Milgaard, and Thomas Sophonow. In each of these cases, witnesses were pressured by police until they abandoned their original testimony and gave false evidence (Anderson and Anderson 1998). *Unconscious transference* is witness confusion between a person seen in one situation and a person seen in another situation (Loftus 1979). The term *malleability of confidence* refers to the pliable nature of a witness's certainty of his or her testimony. Research has demonstrated that witnesses who identify a suspect from a police lineup or group of photos are far more confident of their choice if they receive positive feedback from authorities (cf. Wells and Bradfield 1998).

Because most jurors are unaware of the unreliability of eyewitness identification, they may place unwarranted faith in its accuracy (Sanders 1984). In Canada, defence lawyers are not permitted to call upon experts to discuss the weaknesses of eyewitness identification. While judges are supposed to inform the jury of the limitations of such evidence, they do so infrequently (Bayliss 2002). Moreover, when a judge plays the role of "expert" in such instances, the accused does not have a chance to refute or qualify any instructions and a jury is likely to find any admissions from a judge about a particular issue at trial far more compelling than similar evidence from an expert witness (Bala 2001, 286). The questionable accuracy of eyewitness testimony and the undue weight it receives from criminal justice personnel make eyewitness identifications a significant contributor to wrongful convictions.

Erroneous Forensic Science

Erroneous and fraudulent forensic science has also been cited as a cause of wrongful convictions. In some cases, inadvertent human error, sloppiness, exaggeration, misinterpretation, and bias may work to contaminate evidence, whether in the forensic laboratory or at the crime scene (Castelle and Loftus 2001). More disturbing, however, are those cases in which forensic scientists deliberately tamper with evidence. For example, Stephanie Nyznyk, a laboratory technician working out of the Centre for Forensic Sciences in Ontario, suppressed information that hair and fibre samples used by the prosecution to successfully convict Guy Paul Morin of murder had been contaminated and should not have been entered as evidence (Anderson and Anderson 1998). A further example of this problem is the work of Dr. Charles Smith. While he was the chief paediatric forensic pathologist at the Hospital for Sick Children in Toronto, he made a number of serious errors in more than 40 autopsies of children whose deaths had occurred under questionable circumstances. In 2007 the Goudge Commission of Inquiry into Pediatric Forensic Pathology in Ontario examined the more egregious errors in 20 of Smith's cases, as well as the practice and oversight of paediatric forensic pathology in Ontario. The inquiry revealed that Smith had testified outside his area of expertise; had ignored the testimony of other experts that conflicted with his own; had used unscientific methods in coming to his conclusions; and had functioned more as a "hired gun" for the prosecution instead of presenting unbiased, objective testimony based on the facts. A comprehensive series of recommendations emerged from this inquiry; nonetheless, the lives of those 20 individuals and their families were irredeemably altered by Smith's errors.

False Confessions

A confession is often viewed as the most powerful piece of evidence that the prosecution can bring against an accused. Juries are said to believe a defendant who confesses to a crime, regardless of other evidence pointing to the contrary (Leo and Ofshe 1998). While most people find it difficult to believe that anyone would confess to a crime that he or she did not commit, research indicates that this may not be such a rare phenomenon. Studies in the United States have found that false confessions were the leading or primary cause of wrongful conviction in anywhere from 14 to 25 percent of cases studied (Drizin and Leo 2004, 902). To understand how innocent people can come to confess to crimes they did not commit, it is important to consider the psychology behind police interrogation techniques.

Christopher Bates was wrongly convicted of murder and spent five-and-a-half years in a maximum-security prison after giving a false confession to police. Bates was arrested and charged with the murder of a shopkeeper who had been killed and robbed of $90. While in police custody, Bates was interrogated, threatened, and tormented for 17 hours. Furthermore, he was held without access to food, water, toilet facilities, and legal counsel for 72 hours. He was told that if he did not confess, child protection authorities would take his children away. After many hours of physical and psychological torture, Bates agreed to sign a declaration linking him to the robbery and murder. Bates later explained that extreme fear for his life had led him to sign the declaration. His false confession played a pivotal role in his conviction.

Bates's case illustrates a coerced false confession. Compare this with the case of Romeo Phillion, who in 1972 voluntarily confessed to a crime he did not commit. Voluntary false confessions are normally freely given to the police, with little interrogation or pressure. The literature indicates that these types of confessions are likely the result of a desire for notoriety, attention, or fame; a need to expiate guilt for real or imagined acts; an inability to distinguish between fantasy and reality; or a pathological need for acceptance or self-punishment (Gudjonsson 2002). In Phillion's case, while he was later found to have an intellectual limitation and to suffer from psychological problems, he claimed that he had confessed to killing an Ottawa area fireman because he wanted his partner to collect the reward money. Even though he immediately retracted his confession, he served over 30 years in jail for this murder, and was exonerated only in 2010.

The Use of Jailhouse Informants

The use of jailhouse informants may also play an important role in the conviction of the innocent. Prisoner informants provide information to law enforcement officials in exchange for money, property, or the promise of leniency in sentencing. Use the testimony of such informants as a means of securing convictions. Indeed, the Innocence Project (2010) found that in over 15 percent of more than 250 cases of wrongful conviction overturned by DNA testing, an informant or jailhouse snitch testified against the defendant. Furthermore, jurors give great weight to confessions made to jailhouse informants. American studies indicate that to the average juror, there is not much difference between the manner in which they receive and weigh a confession given to a police officer and a confession given to a jailhouse informant (Cory 2001).

In Canada, the case of Guy Paul Morin illustrates the dangers of relying on jailhouse informants. In 1985, Morin was charged with the murder of a young girl, Christine Jessop. While Morin was jailed without bail, two jailhouse informants who were facing charges of sexual assault and assault came forward claiming that Morin had confessed to the crime. This was the only direct evidence of Morin's guilt (Kaufman 1998, 546). Both informants—who had lengthy criminal histories, as well as histories of psychiatric problems—were desperate to get out of jail and received more lenient sentences as a result of their testimony. Morin was convicted in part because of their testimony, but his conviction was later reversed on appeal. The informants testified again at Morin's second trial, where he was convicted again. Through DNA evidence, Morin was later found to be innocent and was subsequently released from prison.

The risks of relying on jailhouse informants are obvious. In his report on the wrongful conviction of Thomas Sophonow, Justice Cory described jailhouse informants as a "uniquely evil group [who] should as far as it is possible, be excised and removed from our trial process" (Cory 2001). Informants may have much to gain and little to lose by providing false testimony to authorities. It is thus essential that this relatively common practice in the justice system be subject to limited use and that informants be prohibited from testifying. Due in large part to the difficulties revealed by these wrongful conviction cases, several provinces now have safeguards in place, such as In-Custody Informant Registries, which severely circumscribe the use of such informants, as well as committees comprised of attorneys that vet the testimony of jailhouse snitches.

Professional and Institutional Misconduct

Unprofessional conduct on the part of police, the prosecution, and the judiciary is an important factor in wrongful convictions (Huff et al., 1996). As a first point of entry into the criminal justice system, the police play a pivotal role in deciding whom to charge and in collecting evidence to support a charge. In building their case against a suspect, the police may suppress, lose, misinterpret, or overlook evidence that supports the defendant's claim of innocence. Such errors may occur through prejudicial identification lineups, misuse of informants, solicitation of false confessions, or reliance on poor forensic science. This unprofessional behaviour may be motivated by a sincere desire to strengthen the case against a suspect whom professionals are convinced is guilty. This set of process errors is often referred to as *tunnel vision:* a suspect's guilt is assumed, and evidence is then subconsciously manipulated to prove that guilt. Whether the tunnel vision occurs among police officers or the prosecution, the authorities may become so focused on one suspect that they deliberately destroy that individual's alibi and eliminate all other potential suspects from the investigation (MacFarlane 2008).

Professional misconduct can also involve withholding evidence considered favourable to the defence. The Canadian justice system prohibits police and prosecutors from pursuing a prosecution while withholding evidence that supports a claim of innocence. Both case law and policy require prosecutors to disclose to the defence all relevant evidence in their possession, and they face sanctions if they fail to do so (*R. v. Stinchcombe*). This obligation, however, does not apply to the police in the same manner. Withholding evidence raises ethical questions about prosecutorial conduct and may also contribute to wrongful convictions (Rosenberg 2002).

The Canadian case of Donald Marshall, Jr., who was wrongly convicted of the murder of Sandy Seale in Nova Scotia in 1971, shows how the police and the prosecution can fail to disclose information crucial to an accused's defence. Ten days after Marshall's conviction for the murder of Sandy Seale, a witness (Jimmy MacNeil) told police he had seen Roy Ebsary stab Seale, not Marshall. The police failed to thoroughly investigate this assertion. Moreover, according to the Marshall Inquiry (Royal Commission 1989), MacNeil's claim was never disclosed by police to either Marshall's defence counsel or to the Halifax Crown counsel handling Marshall's appeal of his conviction. Had this information been presented to the Court of Appeal, a new trial would likely have been ordered (ibid.). Also, the prosecution failed to inform Marshall's defence counsel of statements from several witnesses whose stories tended to corroborate Marshall's account of the murder (Wall 1992). Marshall spent 11 years in prison for a crime he did not commit. Roy Ebsary was tried and later convicted of manslaughter for the murder of Sandy Seale, but served only one year in jail.

Wrongful convictions also occur in the larger institutional context. Martin (2001) identifies three institutional factors that contribute to convicting the innocent: the high-profile nature of the case, which pressures authorities to make a quick arrest; the marginalized status of the accused (an "outsider"); and the unreliable nature of the evidence. When all three factors are present in the institutional context, authorities are more likely to overlook the initial reluctance of an eyewitness; to believe an unreliable jailhouse informant; to fail to disclose favourable evidence; or to pressure a defendant into a false confession. Any one of these may precipitate a wrongful conviction.

The wrongful 22-year imprisonment of David Milgaard for the rape and murder of Gail Miller in 1970 involved police and institutional misconduct, as well as tunnel vision on the part of prosecutors. The high level of public anxiety over this brutal crime created pressure on the police to make a quick arrest. Milgaard, who had already been labelled an impulsive and marginalized troublemaker, became the target. The case against him was based on questionable evidence obtained through police intimidation. Around six years after Milgaard's release from prison, DNA testing established his innocence. Larry Fisher, a serial rapist living just blocks away from the murder scene, was subsequently convicted of the crime in 1999.

Racial Bias

Racism is a complex set of ideologies, attitudes, and beliefs claiming the superiority of one race over another, sometimes involving racial discrimination and disadvantage for ethnic minorities (Cashmore 1996). Racism is built into economic, political, and legal institutions, where it contributes to differential opportunities and differential treatment of racialized groups. Institutionalized racism makes racial minorities severely vulnerable to miscarriages of justice. Bedau and Radelet (1987) have shown that among 350 cases of documented wrongful convictions in the United States during the 20th century, 40 percent involved a black defendant. Racial discrimination within the criminal justice system is especially evident among blacks and Hispanics in the United States (Parker, Dewees, and Radelet 2001). Several factors, such as institutionalized racism, erroneous cross-racial identification, stereotyping, and extreme social disadvantage, help explain why racial minorities are disproportionately represented among those wrongly convicted.

While little Canadian research has addressed the link between race and wrongful conviction, the prominent case of Donald Marshall, Jr.—a Mi'kmaq wrongly convicted of the murder of Sandy Seale—illustrates the ways in which race is embedded in Canada's criminal justice system. The Royal Commission on the prosecution of Marshall acknowledged that Marshall had been wrongly convicted and imprisoned because, *inter alia,* he was Mi'kmaq:

> The tragedy of the failure is compounded by the evidence that this miscarriage
> of justice could and should have been prevented, or at least corrected quickly,
> if those involved in the system had carried out their duties in a professional
> and/or competent manner. That they did not is due, in part at least, to the
> fact that Donald Marshall, Jr. is a Native. (Royal Commission 1989, 1)

The commission's report stated that a two-tier system of justice existed in Nova Scotia and that it responded differently according to the status, wealth, and race of the person being investigated (ibid.). As a Mi'kmaq, Donald Marshall, Jr., was at the bottom of the second tier (Turpel/Aki-Kwe 1992). The commissioners noted Marshall's second-class treatment and found that his defence counsel had failed to provide him with an adequate standard of professional representation (ibid.). Marshall's lawyers had access to whatever financial resources they required, yet they had conducted no independent investigation, had interviewed no Crown witnesses, and had failed to ask for disclosure of the Crown's case against their client. The Marshall case demonstrates how stereotyping and social disadvantage can contribute to miscarriages of justice.

More recently, William Mullins-Johnson, an Ojibway Canadian, was acquitted of murdering his four-year-old niece, Valin, in 2007; but by then he had already served 12 years of a life sentence in prison. Mullins-Johnson was a victim of the errors of Dr. Charles Smith, a disgraced pathologist who found evidence of child abuse, sexual assault, and murder. Yet it was later revealed that Valin died of natural causes (see Chapter 23).

THE EFFECTS OF WRONGFUL IMPRISONMENT

The negative effects of incarceration on those serving long terms of imprisonment have been well documented. According to Sykes (1958), the "pains of imprisonment" include the following losses: liberty, goods and services, heterosexual relationships, autonomy, and security. However, not all prisoners experience these deprivations in the same way. This section draws upon in-depth interviews with two Canadians who were wrongly convicted. Jamie Nelson was wrongly convicted of a sexual assault that never actually occurred and served more than three years in prison; Christopher Bates served more than five years for a murder he did not commit. These interviews suggest that the negative effects of incarceration are often exacerbated by a miscarriage of justice.[1]

Identity

A prison sentence constitutes a "massive assault" on the identity of the person who is imprisoned (Berger 1963). This assault is said to be especially strong for first-time inmates, who must contend with the sudden and abrupt shift in their social situation (Schmid and Jones 1991). To protect themselves and their identity, prisoners are often compelled to adopt a provisional or "suspended identity" during the period of their incarceration (ibid.). Jamie Nelson explains how it was important for him to take on a new identity in prison to ensure his survival:

> I had to build up that extra protection in prison. The other layer of Jamie wasn't there ... I couldn't be Jamie. I had to be someone that I'm not, somebody that will fight, somebody that will push, somebody that doesn't give a f---. I had to wear certain hats to survive.

Many inmates attempt to suspend their pre-prison identity and formulate a provisional identity while incarcerated. However, the situation becomes highly complex for those wrongly convicted. Not only are these individuals forced to take on a prison identity that defines them as criminals when they are in fact innocent, but they may also be compelled to create a further identity, given the nature of their conviction. Jamie Nelson, who was wrongly convicted of a sexual assault, explains:

> I developed a second story right away. I certainly didn't want anybody to know I was in custody for violently raping a woman. My second story was "I beat somebody up that was trying to break into my house." I had to create a good enough lie that could explain away me going to prison for 5 to 7 years ... so, it was a pretty grisly tale. I kicked him in the head a few times with steel boots, you know, I beat him up bad. That was my second story.

Nelson maintains that he could only show his true identity as an innocent man in the presence of the Parole Board members who were to determine his fate:

> I had to wear a different hat when I was with the people that made the difference [prison administration]. That's when I wore the Jamie hat—when I was in front of the panel [Parole Board]. I never once deviated from my claim of being innocent. And that was the only time that I got to wear that hat ... I could be Jamie, behind that door, because they could not release anything to the population. I knew I was safe in that room, in that environment. It was when I was living in the community as an inmate that I ... needed to wear those different hats.

Resistance

Being wrongly imprisoned appears to produce an unfaltering resistance to all aspects of prison life. Throughout their incarceration, both Nelson and Bates resisted being labelled as criminals and maintained their innocence to the prison administration. Their constantly declaring themselves to have been wrongly convicted was often perceived by the authorities as an inability to adapt to the prison environment and as a denial of their offence. As Bates notes:

> I was obsessed about my case ... I was wrongly convicted. [My case manager] kept on making reports "the guy just denies and denies and denies, he keeps talking to you about his case ..." My classification officer told me, "Jesus, you've got to stop doing this, you're never going to get out ... The parole board takes this as if you're denying the crime ... that you're not healed ... you're not fixed ... You have to admit to the crime in order to fix your problems." Sorry! I'm not guilty! I'm not denying. I'm just telling you the truth.

This unwavering resistance often created further difficulties. Nelson, who was wrongly convicted of sexual assault, maintained his credibility and status as an innocent man by refusing to apply for parole and by refusing to participate in prison programs for sexual offenders. He explains:

> I was clinging to my innocence ... I started to get myself in trouble because I wouldn't even apply for parole. You don't have to apply, it's a damn privilege last time I looked at it. I didn't want it, because I'd have to be that guilty man. So I wouldn't even apply, but then that started to go negatively against me. [They would say to me] "What are you hiding?

As a result of his refusal to self-identify as a sex offender and to participate in prison sex offender programs, he was eventually placed in segregation:

> [The administration] told me that I was going to the sexual behaviour program ... and I said, no, I wasn't. I made it clear to them that the only way that they would have me go to that program was that somebody had to drag me to it. So they ended up keeping me in the hole six months.

Loss of Freedom and Consequences for the Prisoner's Family

The losses experienced by the wrongly convicted can be profound. For Jamie Nelson, these included loss of freedom and the loss of a sense of self: "I lost me, is what I lost ... my identity, who I am ... The way I viewed life." But the most significant loss appears to be the loss of family. Three of Nelson's four children were taken by child protection authorities when his wife suffered a breakdown during his incarceration. He explains the devastation of losing his family:

> What it affected was my nuclear family—wife and my children, my family. It completely devastated that. We lost our home ... I lost my kids ... I lost the care and guidance and companionship of my dad. We were extremely close ... the hardest part about being an inmate was the loss of the family.

Furthermore, the hardships that accompany losing one's family through incarceration also affect the family itself. Its members are deprived of the emotional support of their loved one and are forced to deal with the reality of having a family member in prison. They may also be deprived of an essential source of income (Ferraro et al. 1983). As Nelson explains:

> [My wife] was left living with the reality of being single, with four children, a mortgage, hydro, the groceries and other accoutrements that go with having four young children: one in school, needing to work, needing to deal with baby-sitters and, oh yeah, my husband's in prison.

It is clear that the effects of a wrongful conviction and imprisonment are devastating for the individual and his or her family. In response, the State has proposed several methods of redress, which are outlined in the next section.

STATE RESPONSES TO WRONGFUL CONVICTION: ISSUES OF REDRESS AND COMPENSATION

When a miscarriage of justice has occurred, a number of policy responses can be instigated—by the individual *or* by the State—to rectify the miscarriage of justice. These include conviction review through the *Criminal Code*, commissions of inquiry, and financial compensation. However, none of these are automatically applied in cases of wrongful conviction. In addition, all occur many years after the fact and require considerable financial and emotional resources to pursue.

Conviction Review

Currently, Sections 696.1 to 696.6 of Canada's *Criminal Code* allow individuals who maintain that they have been wrongly convicted to ask the federal Minister of Justice to review the circumstances of their case in order to ascertain whether a miscarriage of justice "likely" occurred. This remedy is also available for reviews of the dangerous offender designation. Canada relies on the Criminal Conviction Review Group (CCRG) in the Department of Justice to undertake such reviews. The criteria of eligibility regarding application for a conviction review are quite narrow. First, while this right is available to all who have been convicted of an offence, it is considered to be an extraordinary measure (Campbell 2005). Second, these individuals must have exercised all of their rights of appeal through the various courts—a process that can take many years. Finally, there must be new matters of significance that were not previously considered by the courts or that arose after the conventional avenues of appeal had been exhausted. The review process can take many years. Once all of the relevant information has been compiled and investigated, the Minister of Justice receives legal advice before making a decision. The minister does not make decisions regarding guilt or innocence, but if satisfied that a miscarriage of justice has occurred, he or she can make one of the following recommendations: (1) decline to make a remedy; (2) order a new trial or hearing; (3) order a new appeal proceeding; or (4) refer any question to the court of appeal for its opinion.

Few applications are made each year to the Minister of Justice. For example, in 2008–9, the minister's office received a total of 25 applications: 6 preliminary assessments are under way; 2 investigations are under way; 3 decisions were made, with 2 files closed because there was no basis for the investigation; and 1 application was granted by the minister, who ordered a new trial (Department of Justice 2009). One reason for these small numbers may be the arduous application process involved. Moreover, some wrongfully convicted individuals have questioned whether it is appropriate to apply to the government for "mercy." As David Milgaard asked: "Why ask the Canadian government to give you mercy for something that you haven't done? I refuse." (Milgaard 2002).

The *Criminal Code* was amended in 2002 to clarify the ministerial review process as well as to expand the minister's investigative powers. At the same time, an independent senior individual from outside the Department of Justice, Bernard Grenier, a retired Quebec Provincial Court judge, was appointed to work with the CCRG. His role is to review all CCRG decisions, to screen applications at the assessment stage, and to provide separate advice to the minister on the merits of applications that make it as far as the investigation stage. Criticisms of the conviction review process remain: it is long and costly; it is conducted mainly in secrecy; the principle of finality in law may encourage reluctance on the part of the minister and the appeal courts to interfere with a conviction; established rules of procedure are lacking; and conflicts of interest are possible (Braiden and Brockman 1999).

As a means of redress, conviction review has limited application and may still be inaccessible to many. In recent years there have been a number of calls to establish an independent commission of inquiry, detached from the Department of Justice, similar to Britain's Criminal Cases Review Commission. One reason put forward for establishing an independent commission is that leaving the power to revisit convictions in the hands of the Minister of Justice amounts to a clear conflict of interest (Zellick 2006, 556). However, successive Canadian governments have resisted the pressure from lobby groups for such a commission. Prior to the last amendments to the power of ministerial review to the *Criminal Code* in 2002, one of the reasons given for not establishing such a commission was that "the Canadian experience with cases of wrongful conviction bears little resemblance to that of the United Kingdom" (*Canada Gazette* 2002). Presumably, counsel was referring to the prosecution system in the United Kingdom, which differs from the Canadian system. In Britain, a head prosecutor serves the entire country; whereas in Canada, each province has an Attorney General and its own Court of Appeal.

Commissions of Inquiry

Historically, as a result of the work of various Royal Commissions or commissions of inquiry, the Canadian judiciary and public have become aware of flaws to the criminal justice process. To date, six commissions of inquiry have addressed the circumstances surrounding wrongful convictions. The Marshall Inquiry of 1989 resulted from the wrongful conviction of Donald Marshall, Jr., and had a broad mandate to review and assess the administration of criminal justice in Nova Scotia and to "make recommendations" to help prevent such tragedies in the future (Royal Commission 1989). The report contained findings of fact as well as specific recommendations that addressed the role of the police and Crown attorneys; ways to ensure more equitable treatment of blacks and Aboriginals in the criminal justice system; and new mechanisms to deal with future wrongful convictions (ibid.).

The Kaufman Inquiry of 1998 in Ontario (into the wrongful conviction of Guy Paul Morin) and the Sophonow Inquiry in Manitoba (into the wrongful conviction of Thomas Sophonow) examined police and forensic investigations and criminal proceedings that can lead to wrongful convictions. Together, these two inquiries recommended changes to police procedures regarding evidence gathering and jailhouse informants; they also called for enhanced disclosure of evidence to the defence. The Lamer Inquiry of 2006 addressed the wrongful conviction and imprisonment of three individuals in Newfoundland in the 1990s. According to its terms of reference, the inquiry was meant to investigate the administration of criminal justice regarding the arrests and prosecutions of Gregory Parsons and Randy Druken, as well as the lengthy delay experienced by Ronald Dalton with respect to the appeal of his conviction. The Commission of Inquiry into Certain Aspects of the Trial and Conviction of James Driskell took place in 2007 in Manitoba; the Saskatchewan Commission of Inquiry into the Wrongful Conviction of David Milgaard took place in 2008. These successive inquiries indicate that various provincial governments have been compelled to ascertain and address the factors that make it possible for wrongful convictions to occur in the first place. However, one must question the extent to which recommendations stemming from such commissions can realistically affect policy, since implementation of the recommendations is sporadic at best.

Compensation

When a wrongful conviction occurs, individuals often seek financial compensation for the harm they have suffered. The awarding of compensation is an attempt by the government to rectify a miscarriage of justice; unfortunately, such awards are small consolation for the devastation to family, credibility, livelihood, and mental health that a wrongful conviction entails. With some wrongful convictions, compensation was awarded by the courts in the absence of a commission of inquiry. David Milgaard's case is one example: he served 22 years in prison for a murder he did not commit and in 1999 received $10 million in compensation from the Saskatchewan and federal governments for pain and suffering, lost income, out-of-pocket expenses, and legal fees. In recognition of the impact that wrongful convictions have on family members, Joyce Milgaard, David's mother, received $750,000 in compensation.

To date, various provincial governments have awarded from $105,000 to $10 million. The amount seems to be based largely on the number of years an individual has spent in prison and the amount of time he or she has waited for compensation. Many individuals have had to wait an inordinate amount of time for compensation, with extremes at both ends of the continuum. The average period has been 11.7 years from date of the original conviction.

In these cases, provinces have recognized errors in the administration of justice and have awarded compensation. However, these awards are difficult to obtain and come only after many years of legal and political wrangling. Even so, Canada has an obligation to provide compensation to the wrongly convicted. Besides its obligations under national laws, Canada has a binding obligation under international law, having ratified the International Covenant on Civil and Political Rights in 1976. Moreover, Canada in 1988 adopted a set of federal–provincial guidelines for compensation, conditions of eligibility, and criteria for quantum of compensation (Campbell 2005). Problems regarding the kinds of cases deemed deserving of compensation as well as the amount of compensation deemed appropriate plague this process. Ultimately, financial compensation, regardless of the amount, does little to rectify the emotional, social, and financial damages wrought by a wrongful conviction.

CONCLUSION

Both individual and systemic factors contribute to errors that result in wrongful convictions in Canada. Moreover, the State's existing responses to rectify these wrongs seem unable to adequately confront and tackle these issues. For example, the most recent amendments to the *Criminal Code*'s conviction review process fall short of achieving their stated goals of enhanced transparency and accountability. Commissions of inquiry, which seek to address the issue of prevention, are often disappointing, since their recommendations are rarely implemented in full. From time to time, the media draw attention to the issue of wrongful conviction through highly controversial and publicized cases; however, this attention is often fleeting and fails to result in long-term change. Piecemeal reforms introduced to address individual errors are insufficient. There must be greater accountability among agents of the criminal justice system as a whole. Programs of education in law schools and in police academies will allow these individuals to become more aware of how their actions can contribute to wrongful convictions. A report by the Department of Justice regarding the prevention of miscarriages of justice offers some hope in this regard (Department of Justice 2005). As well, the voices of the wrongly convicted themselves need to be heard. Only by listening to their accounts and experiences will Canadians understand the true extent and impact of the problem.

DISCUSSION QUESTIONS

1. *Parole authorities often require a prisoner to accept responsibility for "their" crime before parole is granted. Do you see the problem that this creates for prisoners serving time for crimes they did not commit?*
2. *In light of what you have read in this chapter, do you think the Canadian criminal justice system does enough to prevent wrongful convictions?*

FURTHER READINGS

Anderson, B., and D. Anderson. 1998. *Manufacturing Guilt: Wrongful Convictions in Canada*. Halifax: Fernwood.

Huff, C.R., A. Rattner, and E. Sagarin. 1996. *Convicted but Innocent: Wrongful Conviction and Public Policy*. Thousand Oaks: Sage Publications.

Westervelt, S., and J. Humphrey, eds. 2001. *Wrongly Convicted: Perspectives on Failed Justice*. New Jersey: Rutgers University Press.

REFERENCES

Anderson, B., and Anderson, D. 1998. *Manufacturing Guilt: Wrongful Convictions in Canada*. Halifax: Fernwood.

Bayliss, D. 2002. "The Impact of Canadian Inquiries into Wrongful Conviction." Paper presented at the Conference on Wrongful Conviction: Experiences, Implications, and Working Towards Justice, University of Ottawa.

Bala, N. 2001. "*R. v. D.(D.)*: The Supreme Court and Filtering of Social Science Knowledge About Children." *Criminal Reports (5th)*, 36: 283–90.

Bedau, H.A., and M. Radelet. 1987. "Miscarriages of Justice in Potentially Capital Cases." *Stanford Law Review* 40: 21–179.

Berger, P. 1963. *Invitation to Sociology: A Humanistic Perspective*. Garden City: Doubleday Anchor.

Braiden, P., and J. Brockman. 1999. "Remedying Wrongful Convictions Through Applications to the Minister of Justice under Section 690 of the *Criminal Code*." *Windsor Yearbook of Access to Justice* 17: 3–34.

Campbell, K. 2005. "Policy Responses to Wrongful Conviction in Canada: The Role of Conviction Review, Public Inquiries, and Compensation." *Criminal Law Bulletin* 41: 145–68.

Canada Gazette. 2002. *Regulations Respecting Applications for Ministerial Review— Miscarriages of Justice*. Part 1, vol. 136, no. 39. Ottawa: Queen's Printer.

Carvel, J. 1992. "Many Prisoners Could Be Wrongly Jailed." *Guardian Weekly*, April 5.

Cashmore, E. 1996. *Dictionary of Race and Ethnic Relations*. London: Routledge.

Castelle, G., and E. Loftus. 2001. "Misinformation." In S. Westervelt and J. Humphrey, eds., *Wrongly Convicted: Perspectives on Failed Justice*. New Brunswick: Rutgers University Press.

Conners, E., T. Lundregan, N. Miller, and T. McEwan. 1996. *Convicted by Juries, Exonerated by Science: Case Studies in the Use of DNA Evidence to Establish Innocence After Trial*. Washington: National Institute of Justice.

Cory, P. 2001. *Commission of Inquiry Regarding Thomas Sophonow*. Winnipeg: Manitoba Justice.

Department of Justice Canada. 2005. "Report on the Prevention of Miscarriages of Justice." Federal/Provincial/Territorial Heads of Prosecution Committee Working Group, Ottawa.

——— . 2009. "Applications for Ministerial Review: Miscarriages of Justice." Annual Report 2009, Minister of Justice. http://www.justice.gc.ca/eng/pi/ccr-rc/rep09-rap09/index.html

Drizin, S., and R. Leo. 2004. "The Problem of False Confessions in the Post-DNA World." *North Carolina Law Review* 82, no. 3: 892–1007.

Ferraro, K.J., J.M. Johnson, S.R. Jorgensen, and F.G. Bolton. 1983. "Problems of Prisoners' Families: The Hidden Costs of Imprisonment." *Journal of Family Issues* 4: 575–91.

Gross, S., K. Jacoby, D. Matheson, N. Montgomery, and S. Patil. 2005. "Exonerations in the United States: 1989 Through 2003." *Journal of Criminal Law and Criminology* 95: 523–60.

Gudjonsson, G. 2002. *The Psychology of Interrogations and Confessions: A Handbook.* Chichester: Wiley.

Holmes, W. 2001. "Who Are the Wrongly Convicted on Death Row?" In S. Westervelt and J. Humphrey, eds., *Wrongly Convicted: Perspectives on Failed Justice.* New Brunswick: Rutgers University Press.

Huff, C.R., Rattner, A., and E. Sagarin. 1986. "Guilty Until Proven Innocent: Wrongful Conviction and Public Policy." *Crime and Delinquency* 32: 518–44.

——— . 1996. *Convicted but Innocent: Wrongful Conviction and Public Policy.* Thousand Oaks: Sage.

Innocence Project. http://www.innocenceproject.org

Kaufman, F. 1998. *Commission on Proceedings Involving Guy Paul Morin: Executive Summary and Recommendations.* Toronto.

Leo, R., and R. Ofshe. 1998. "The Consequences of False Confessions: Deprivation of Liberty and Miscarriages of Justice in the Age of Psychological Interrogation." *Journal of Criminology and Criminal Law* 88· 429–96.

Loftus, E. 1979. *Eyewitness Testimony.* Cambridge: Harvard University Press.

MacFarlane, B. 2008. "Wrongful Convictions: The Effect of Tunnel Vision and Predisposing Circumstances in the Criminal Justice System." Paper prepared for the Goudge Inquiry.

Martin, D. 2001. "The Police Role in Wrongful Convictions: An International Comparative Study." In S. Westervelt and J. Humphrey, eds., *Wrongly Convicted: Perspectives on Failed Justice.* New Brunswick: Rutgers University Press.

Milgaard, D. 2002. "The Voices of the Wrongly Convicted: Innocents Behind Bars." November 16, 2002. Conference presentation available from Association in Defence of the Wrongly Convicted.

Parker, K., M. Dewees, and M. Radelet. 2001. "Racial Bias and the Conviction of the Innocent." In S. Westervelt and J. Humphrey, eds., *Wrongly Convicted: Perspectives on Failed Justice.* New Brunswick: Rutgers University Press.

R. v. Stinchcombe, [1991] 3 S.C.R. 326.

Rosenberg, M. 2002. *Public Inquiries: The Process and the Value.* Paper presented at the Innocents Behind Bars Conference, Ottawa, November 17, 2002, available from Association in Defence of the Wrongly Convicted.

Royal Commission on the Donald Marshall Jr. Prosecution. 1989.
Commissioners' Report. Halifax.

Sanders, R. 1984. "Helping the Jury Evaluate Eyewitness Testimony: The Need
for Additional Safeguards." *American Journal of Criminal Law* 12: 189–220.

Schmid, T., and R. Jones. 1991. "Suspended Identity: Identity Transformation
in a Maximum Security Prison." *Symbolic Interaction* 14: 415–32.

Sykes, G. 1958. *The Society of Captives.* Princeton: Princeton University Press.

Turpel/Aki-Kwe, M. 1992. "Further Travails of Canada's Human Rights
Record: The Marshall Case." In J. Mannette, ed., *Elusive Justice: Beyond the
Marshall Inquiry.* Halifax: Fernwood.

Wall, B. 1992. "Analyzing the Marshall Commission: Why It Was Established
and How It Functioned." In J. Mannette, ed., *Elusive Justice: Beyond the
Marshall Inquiry.* Halifax: Fernwood.

Wells, G., and A. Bradfield. 1998. "Good, You Identified the Suspect: Feedback
to Eyewitnesses Distorts Their Reports of the Witnesses' Experience."
Journal of Applied Psychology 83: 360–76.

Wells, G., and E. Olsen. 2003. "Eyewitness Testimony." *Annual Review of
Psychology* 54: 277–95.

Zellick, G. 2006. "Facing Up to Miscarriages of Justice." *Manitoba Law Journal*
31: 555–64.

ENDNOTES

1. Both Jamie Nelson and Christopher Bates gave us permission to reveal
their identities and their stories.

CHAPTER 23

Innocent but Presumed Guilty: The Wrongful Conviction of William Mullins-Johnson[1]

Chapter 22 discusses the phenomenon of wrongful conviction, drawing upon the research that has accumulated on this subject over the past few years. This chapter provides insight into the causes and consequences of wrongful conviction from the perspective of one individual. In 1992, Bill Mullins-Johnson was convicted of the murder of his four-year-old niece, Valin. Following an evening during which Bill babysat her, Valin was found dead in her bed the next morning. Bill quickly became the sole suspect in her murder. After being convicted almost entirely on flawed forensic evidence, he served 12 years in prison before being released and exonerated by the Ontario Court of Appeal in 2007. Bill was a victim of forensic errors made by Dr. Charles Smith, who testified to finding evidence of sexual assault and strangulation where none actually existed. Ultimately it was established that Valin had died of natural causes. In this chapter, Bill describes his experience of wrongful conviction, imprisonment, release, and subsequent exoneration.

Kathryn M. Campbell, University of Ottawa

FACTORS THAT INFLUENCED HIS WRONGFUL CONVICTION

In my own case, I believe one factor was my cultural heritage. You see, I'm Aboriginal—I'm Ojibway. I was raised most of my life on the reserve. That's my home, that's where I'm from. I don't like the word racism, myself. But that's what happens sometimes. I'm sure that this was a factor in my case—not the only factor but I'm sure it was one of them.

People in the community were angry and emotional. What I was charged with raised a lot of emotions here. People had blind faith in what they were being told in the press and by the police. The fact that I had a previous conviction for robbery in 1989 had an impact too, it had been in the news at the time. Being arrested for a crime involving a child victim made things much worse and the community reaction at the time was significant. I was arrested in the midst of the Bernardo[2] trial. Bernardo and Homolka were the big story at the time—everybody was up in arms about that. But at the time here in the Sault there were three very high-profile cases going on,[3] including mine. We were all Aboriginal and they were all high profile, front page, every one of us. So I can see how the public anger boiled over. Whether people want to admit it or not, what happens in the courtroom is sometimes influenced by public opinion. There was a rush to judge me and immediately upon my arrest, I began receiving death threats. It's not merely just one thing that results in a wrongful conviction, but many factors.

ARREST

They arrested me less than 12 hours after we found Valin. We found her body that morning and the cops and paramedics came and the coroner was there, too. They took her away and then everybody left. It was only the family in the house, and just before noon the cops came back and told everybody to leave except for Pauly (Valin's father, Bill's brother), Kim (Valin's mother, Bill's sister-in-law), and myself. They stationed two uniformed cops with us and we weren't allowed to leave the house. The police took statements from us that morning and they took me to the police station that night. That's where I spent the night, in a holding cell, and the interrogation room. The day that I was arrested and the day that they did that postmortem, all their conclusions were made. They were made over the phone with Charles Smith. In the police notes it shows that they had me targeted at about 8:30 that morning.

Dr. Charles Smith is a disgraced pathologist whose errors became the subject of the Inquiry into Pediatric Forensic Pathology in Ontario. In 2007 the inquiry, chaired by the Honourable Stephen T. Goudge, examined the practice and oversight of paediatric forensic pathology in Ontario, and after systemic review and assessment made a series of recommendations. The inquiry came about as a result of the Chief Coroner's Review into 45 homicide cases in which Dr. Smith had been involved. In 20 of those cases reviewers took issue with either his findings or his testimony or both.

When they told me I was arrested for Valin's murder, I didn't have the words to express what that news did to me. I think I went into an immediate mental breakdown. To tell you the truth, I still suffer from it. I suffer from sleeplessness, restlessness, and anxiety attacks where I think I am about to die. My throat closes up, I can't breathe, and I think I'm dying—I can't even describe the level of distress. It would even wake me up at night. That's how much I would panic, and it was like that for years after my arrest.

Over the years, people have asked me: "How did you handle all that stress and pressure?" Well, when I was arrested I'd like to think it's the human spirit, that everybody would do this. But the arrest was so wrong to me, there was no way I was backing down from it, even if that meant I ended up serving life in prison. It was just so wrong that it changed the person that I was forever, and I knew it at the time.

BAIL

I wasn't released on bail after my arrest, it wasn't even a consideration. I didn't even ask for bail. I figured that I was safer in prison because of the death threats that I had received. I was safer in the "the hole" (administrative segregation), for my own safety.

MY FAMILY

In the beginning my family alternated between believing I was guilty or believing I was innocent—they went back and forth. But most of the time, the family closed ranks on my mom and myself. Only my mom came to visit me in prison. Whether I was waiting for trial, or doing my sentence, my mom was pretty much the only one who came and saw me. The family started closing ranks the day I was arrested. Maybe it was because of our conservative upbringing, the church influence and believing in what the authorities tell you, that kinda thing.

After I was convicted, anything I heard about family was through mom. She would write to me every week and I called her every week, and she would come down four or five times a year. For mom's sake I maintained that contact with her just to let her know that I was still alive and kicking, but really I didn't want any contact from the street after a while.

CHARGED WITH FIRST DEGREE MURDER

Because of the alleged assault the charge became first degree murder. They said I had an extra charge of alleged aggravated sexual assault. But I was never convicted of that—it was pretty much withdrawn, yet they still used it, so they could get the conviction.

THE TRIAL

The trial lasted about three weeks in Sault St. Marie, Ontario. There was a judge and jury but there were no Indian people on my jury. There was an agreement between the defence and the Crown that anyone on the jury could not know anyone on the witness list. This meant that pretty much every Aboriginal person in the area was excluded, as they all knew either me or my family. It's my feeling that I was convicted by a segment of society that views me as inferior, and so you're going to have very little chance of getting a fair trial. As a matter of fact, I asked my lawyers to get a change of venue[4] because of that, just to have some Aboriginal people on the jury, but the answer was no. At the trial, there was so little evidence against me, everyone was surprised I was convicted, and as the trial went on, people started seeing that I wasn't guilty of this crime.

Dr. Smith's Testimony

Smith testified and his testimony basically was that when I killed her, I was molesting her. But he didn't perform an autopsy—he never looked at anything, just some photographs. There were two pathologists on each side and the majority of them (because of the sexual nature of the crime), deferred to Smith. But none of them could agree on the time of her death—or even if she had been molested. Since Smith was the big guy in the field, he was the star expert witness. They all deferred to him and that's pretty much why I was wrongfully convicted. Smith never had the qualifications for that job, yet his bosses didn't even look into what his training was—they propped him up to be this star guy and they protected him.

> Dr. Charles Smith testified at Bill's trial, as well as at the trials of 19 other individuals, and serious errors were found with respect to his testimony on autopsies regarding the cause and time of death of children. The Goudge Commission of Inquiry found that among other things, Smith testified outside his area of expertise, ignored conflicting expert testimony, was chronically late with his findings, lost evidence, misinterpreted findings, and used unscientific methods. The inquiry produced 169 recommendations regarding how deaths that occurred in "questionable circumstances" should be investigated. It also called for an overhaul of the entire autopsy system. Bill's case was the only one where a wrongful conviction and imprisonment occurred. In a number of the other cases, charges were laid and subsequently dropped, but not until after months and sometimes years of pre-trial detention, as well as the removal of other children in the family by child protection services. So far, none of these victims have received compensation. In 2008 the Attorney General for Ontario set up a team

to consider the matter of compensation for some 40 victims of Smith's errors. It was to report in May 2010 but has not yet done so. Shortly after the inquiry, Bill launched a civil suit for $13 million in compensation against Smith and his two supervisors: former chief coroner Dr. James Young and his deputy, Dr. James Cairns.

CONVICTION

The jury went out about 2:30 in the afternoon. They came back at about 9:00 p.m. to ask a question to confirm something. They then went back in and came back about an hour later. They told the judge that they didn't think they would be able to come to a verdict, but he sent them back to continue their deliberations. An hour later, they returned with a verdict: "guilty of first degree murder." Maybe they felt pressured to come up with a verdict.

When I heard the verdict, I thought "I'm dead." I'm a dead man. I thought somebody would kill me. Because of the hierarchy of crimes in the prison population, where some crimes are targeted because of their nature, I knew that this crime of murdering a child would mark me once I was in prison. That's how I felt inside, really. When they came down with that verdict, my lawyer didn't want me to stand up for the verdict. I told him "F--- you, I'm going to stand up for this." It's a good thing I was holding on to the edge of the prisoner's box because when they came back with that verdict, I thought I was going to collapse, like my insides had been ripped out.

I heard my mom break out in hysterics on my left. Someone else cried out "No," and someone cried out "yeah," you know, so response was mixed. But I did make eye contact with Pauly (Bill's brother, the father of Valin) at the back of the courtroom that day. He looked right back at me and told me later that he almost attacked me right there in the courtroom. You know how certain things happen in your life that you will never forget? That was one of mine—and probably one of Pauly's. Well, I knew it wasn't me that killed her, so I had to keep looking at Pauly.

IMPRISONMENT

They sent me to Millhaven, a maximum-security prison. It was a very rough joint, but I didn't get punched out or anything like that. I guess my own character pulled me through all the years I was in there. But nobody came at me or anything like that. It was a good experience. It's weird to say that, and it's not that I felt comfortable in there, by any stretch, but the guys around me kinda helped me through. It's odd what I experienced, but I made new friends when I was there.

I was transferred to Joyceville (a minimum-security prison) just before Christmas 1994. And by that spring I was sitting back in the hole waiting to get transferred again. I got bounced out of the Joyceville population because they were going to kill me. Two guys approached me and told me that the order had been sent down. But they were willing to give me a chance to walk out of Joyceville. They told me if I was still there in the general population of the prison the next day, there was nothing anybody could do. I was going to get killed the next day. So they sent me to Warkworth, a PC (Protective Custody) joint. The majority of the prisoners there were sex offenders. I spent 10 straight years there. There were guys in there that would love to have stabbed me. But my size, I think, kinda helped me out. I'm 250 pounds right now, but at my peak I was 260 pounds of solid muscle, 6 feet 4 inches, with 20-inch arms. I was a big man, a muscular man. And fit, and with a rage in me that could bring down a mountain.

There were times, over the years, when I was nose-to-nose with guards who threatened me with violence, and I'd be inviting them to do it right on the spot. And doing this in front of other convicts too, you know, and other guards. I don't know what it is with me—I just wouldn't back down from them. That's how wrong it was, I just felt that it was so wrong that I was there and that I wasn't about to let them turn me into something I wasn't.

COPING

I did many things to cope. I tried to occupy my mind as much as I could, with something, so it turned into a lot of "some-things." I would find something that could get my attention, get momentum, a little bit of doing something, and I would ride that momentum as far as I could until I thought of something else.

In the environment I was now in I had to understand that with all the violence, my life was now in danger. Once I understood the environment I was in, I was able to respond to it better. I didn't go through this process analytically at the time I was arrested because my emotions were shot. When I was first arrested I was in hysterics. So it wasn't a matter of sitting down and rationally thinking this through, not at all. It was a very sporadic, very unpredictable environment that I was in. And so the only thing I could do was understand that if somebody came at me, I would have to defend myself to whatever end.

My mainstay was the guitar. I taught myself to play guitar while I was in. I got involved with different groups. I was chairman of the Native Brotherhood a number of times. I was also involved with the Warkworth Literacy Council. I was vice-chairman there and helped organize symposiums. I tutored two Aboriginal high school courses. I stayed quite busy. I gardened and helped start a garden project for the brotherhood. We grew corn and other grains. We had a tree farm in there too. Five hundred trees were donated to street projects, neighbourhood beautification, landscaping for old folks' homes. I had my own computer and some guys helped teach me. I kinda taught myself too, just how to do basic programs. I taught myself how to use spreadsheets, and databases and PowerPoint and Word. But my escape was really games, computer games. I got into the gaming world in a big way.

Getting exonerated did occupy my mind and my time. But I was now deep in the justice system, so I had to come back out through the same processes that got me in there in the first place. It was just a matter of filing documents properly, and going to the right people to help me. But I didn't spend days and days worrying about this or that at all. I just got an appeal lawyer, filed my appeals, lost them, and then got a hold of AIDWYC. Lawyers from AIDWYC dug and dug, and finally got me out. But it really didn't occupy my time the way it did for others.

AIDWYC is the Association in Defence of the Wrongly Convicted. Based in Toronto, it is a pro bono, grassroots organization that fights for the release and exoneration of the wrongly convicted and that lobbies for criminal justice reform. It has a dual mandate: to prevent and rectify wrongful convictions. It was established in 1993, having grown out of the Justice for Guy Paul Morin Committee. At the present time, AIDWYC only investigates murder convictions where the accused is "factually innocent" and where proof exists (through DNA or other means) that the person was not involved in any way with the murder. AIDWYC has over 30 lawyers, who work pro bono, mainly in Ontario, and believes that it fills the place of an "independent" review body for claims of innocence. Where warranted, AIDWYC's lawyers will prepare an application for ministerial review for the Criminal Conviction Review Group (see Chapter 22).

I guess I understood the situation I was in: I was a lifer. I kinda accepted it. In a way I was fighting to get out. But I understood that I was a lifer now, regardless of what I say for the rest of my life. So in these small, confined boundaries I had to find happiness for myself somehow. So that's why I did so many activities. They didn't force me to take any programs. I did do some Aboriginal programs throughout the years, but there were many times when I told them I would not take their sexual behaviours program. They would say, "Well you're going to have to, because you have been convicted of a sexual crime." I said: "You show me on my file where I'm convicted of sexual assault." My corrections officer told me once, "Well, it's not there," then "F--- you" I would say. As far as I knew, that charge had been dropped because it's not on my file, being convicted of sexual assault.

I knew by refusing the program I was going to be in for the rest of my life, and I understood that. The consequence for me was that I was going to die in prison, and I understood that. But I wasn't going to give up any of the person that I was in this matter. I was an innocent man—as I told them so many times over the years that I was in prison. I would sometimes get into an argument with the guards and my parole officer and I would tell them: "I'm an innocent man in prison." But they never believed me.

The biggest myth about prison is that every convict claims to be innocent. They might for a while, but your own conscience gets you and the behaviour shows that they've accepted their own guilt. But I just refused to give in. I would not let them turn me into what they wanted me to be—a child molester, and a child killer. I was furious, I still am. I was suicidal for some time. But I learned how to deal with it better through disciplining the mind, disciplining the body, disciplining the spirit. Once I was released I cut loose a little bit, and did some partying. When I was inside I smoked pot and all that kinda stuff, but I didn't drink. I exercised a lot. I jogged, I ran, and doing weights helped me discipline my mind. You have to concentrate on doing weights rather than what's going on around you—it helps you discipline your mind. Running does the same thing.

EXONERATION

I got a hold of AIDWYC for the first time in 1994 and they told me I had to go through the appeals process first before they would get involved. So I did. I lost my Supreme Court appeal in 1998 and then I got a hold of AIDWYC again and they started slowly looking into my case and according to them, they were immediately convinced there was merit to my case. But they had to go through everything again and they reviewed it and they kinda hit a wall so to speak—they didn't know where to go after that. You know they went down [the path] ... "Well if it wasn't Bill then it must have been Paul" ... but that was a dead end. Maybe there was no murder at all. The last resort was to check the science in the case. That's when they started running into roadblocks from Smith's office and trying to find those slides, those tissue boxes—they had to fight with Smith for two years. When they finally got the tissue samples in early 2005, they nailed him.

An AIDWYC lawyer came and saw me. I think he was sent there to test my resolve in some ways. He had my trial transcripts open and everything, he was asking and angering me, he was pushing me about stuff. And I finally told him, "You show me in them f---ing files right there ... You show me where it says I'm guilty of this ... like one piece of evidence that substantially says I did this." And he said, "Well, there's none." And I said, "Then what am I doing in prison?" I said, "If you're going to help me, then help me—if not get the hell out of my life and don't ever talk to me again." And that's what convinced him that I was innocent.

I got out in September 2005 but had to wait a couple of years to get my date in the Court of Appeal. Then in October of 2007 I finally got cleared. I was in shock, I was happy, mind you—I was elated, but I was still shocked to think "I'm cleared!"

DR. SMITH APOLOGIZES

During the Goudge Inquiry, James Lockyer (Bill's lawyer) asked Dr. Charles Smith to apologize to Bill Mullins-Johnson. The following is their exchange:

Dr. Charles Smith:

Sir, I don't expect that you would forgive me, but I do want to make it—I'm sorry. I do want to make it very clear to you that I am profoundly sorry for the role that I played in the ultimate decision that affected you. I am sorry.

Mr. William Mullins-Johnson:

For my healing, I'll forgive you but I'll never forget what you did to me. You put me in an environment where I could have been killed any day for something that never happened. You destroyed my family, my brother's relationship with me and my niece that's still left and my nephew that's still living. They hate me because of what you did to me. I'll never forget that but for my own healing I must forgive you. (Goudge Commission of Inquiry, Executive Summary, 5).

LIFE AFTER RELEASE

Since I've been out, it's been kind of a rollercoaster, but all in all, not too bad. I struggled a bit with drug abuse. I finally got my own place and it's comfortable. I was uptown last week and walking around and people are starting to acknowledge me more and more. That day about 15 people stopped me to wish me well and welcome me home. No one can believe what I've been through. Everybody I talk to is in such shock about it still. It's been almost five years since I've been out now, but everybody's still in shock, saying things like "how in the hell did that happen to you?" A few people still don't talk to me, but overall it's healing—it's just going to take some time.

I'm not working at present. Because no matter what way I expand it on my CV, there is a 12-year gap in my life that I'm going to have to explain over and over again. Even building relationships, like dating for example. I don't have to spell it out to everybody all the time, but if I start getting close to somebody, I'm going to have to explain things. It's not possible to leave it behind me now, largely because I don't want to leave it in the past right now. I want to get my story out there. I want to tell people not to be so ready to believe the first thing they hear about somebody, especially an accusation as serious as the one against me. This has affected my life in ways that I don't even know yet. And I'm still in counselling because of it. I'd like to see somebody from the Attorney General's office charge the people responsible. They should have done a better investigation, to say "You know what? This little girl died of natural causes." In the end, there isn't going to be any justice for me or the other people caught up by Smith.[5] We were criminally wronged and there is nobody stepping up to protect us under the law. There's nobody representing our interests or the public's interest of equal protection and benefit of the law.

DISCUSSION QUESTIONS

1. *In your view, how should the criminal justice system compensate people like Bill who have spent years in prison for a crime they did not commit?*
2. *What steps can the justice system take to ensure that wrongful convictions become less likely?*

ENDNOTES

1. Thanks to David J. D'Intino for research assistance.
2. Paul Bernardo was a notorious serial killer and rapist and was convicted for two murders and two aggravated sexual assaults in 1995. He is currently serving a life sentence and has been designated a dangerous offender. All of his victims were young teenaged girls. Karla Homolka, his wife, was also implicated in the two murders and struck a controversial plea bargain with the prosecution, garnering a 12-year sentence for manslaughter even though evidence unearthed following the plea bargain implicated her to a much greater degree.
3. At that time there were three other Aboriginal persons accused of killing someone in Sault Ste. Marie; one was charged with attempted murder, the other two with first degree murder (one of these was charged with killing a police officer).
4. A motion for a change of venue involves asking a trial court to determine whether a case should be heard where it is filed or in a court in another city, county, or province. In cases where a change of venue is granted by a judge, it is normally for the sake of convenience, or—when a case is highly publicized—to ensure a fair trial.
5. He is referring to the 20 people whose cases were examined in detail at the Inquiry into Pediatric Forensic Pathology in Ontario in 2007.

Chapter 24
Why Say Sorry When I Didn't Do It? Remorse and the Dilemma of the Wrongfully Convicted

Most people expect wrongdoers to express remorse for their transgressions; it seems a natural way to make amends to the victim. When offenders do express remorse, it is appreciated by the victim as well as by the community in general. For this reason, the corrections system tends to be more punitive toward offenders who fail to express remorse. The criminal law reflects this attitude toward offenders by imposing more lenient sentences on remorseful offenders, such as those who plead guilty in court.

But what happens when the person charged with an offence is innocent? These people can hardly be expected to express remorse for crimes they did not commit. A dilemma arises for persons who are wrongfully convicted and who then enter the correctional system. They are expected to express remorse, yet they remain adamant in their claims of innocence. As a result, they are treated more harshly by correctional authorities, who perceive them in negative terms simply because they refuse to accept responsibility and express remorse. Drawing on examples from Canada and the United States, Richard Weisman explores the question of remorse and the wrongfully convicted individual.

Richard Weisman, York University

On June 19, 1998, a young man (Mr. W.) left a party with twice the legal limit of alcohol in his blood. He got behind the wheel of his car, having refused a friend's offer to drive him home. After driving westbound on eastbound lanes for several kilometres, he collided with another vehicle, despite frantic attempts to get his attention. Three of the four passengers in the other car died and the other was critically injured (*Toronto Star* May 29, 2001). A jury convicted Mr. W. of three counts of criminal negligence causing death, criminal negligence causing bodily harm, impaired driving causing bodily harm, and exceeding the legal blood alcohol limit. When Mr. W. appeared in court to be sentenced, the Assistant Crown Attorney described him as unremorseful—"He expressed no remorse at any time throughout these proceedings"—and asked the court to sentence Mr. W. to 8 to 12 years in prison. Counsel for the defence asked for 3 to 5 years.

Before imposing sentence, the judge asked Mr. W. if he had anything to say. The reply was "No." The judge noted that the sentence was determined partly by the fact that Mr. W. had not shown "any remorse during the course of the trial." He added that when given the opportunity to make a statement, Mr. W. had refused to say anything: "Mr. W. is not inarticulate. He's a well-spoken gentleman who could say he was sorry. But he didn't." After that preamble, the judge imposed a sentence of 9 years, to be served in a federal penitentiary.

But, unexpectedly, just after the judge had finished speaking, Mr. W. stood up and faced those who were in attendance, declaring, "I want to address the families and friends of the deceased." The Crown attorney told him to face the other way so that the court reporter could take down his words. Mr. W. refused, saying, "I'm not interested in what you guys put on the record. What I have to say is for the families." He then made the following statement:

> I've chosen to give my statement after the judgment because it was the only way I had to show you I meant what I was saying. Despite what has been said in prior hearings, it has never been my intention to deny the accident took place nor my part in the horrific and tragic loss of lives. I have no right to request your understanding, nor do I have the right to ask for your forgiveness. But I do ask that someday you search your hearts and find that I did not intend for this to happen. I would surely surrender my life if this could return your brother, your father, your husband, your friend, your son. I'm so very sorry for the grief and sorrow I have caused your family and friends. I am truly ashamed of my actions, and all I have to offer are these words: I'm sorry.

The reporter who witnessed these events described the reaction of those who were present: "Silence ... And as everyone else in the courtroom sat stunned, unsure of what to do, a young man broke the silence. 'Thank you,' he said" (Clairmont 2001).

IMPORTANCE OF REMORSE IN CRIMINAL JUSTICE

I recount this remarkable vignette for two reasons. First, it reveals the importance that both the courts and the media place on expressions of remorse or their absence. People who show remorse are viewed as deserving of compassion and as entitled to mitigation in the form of a more lenient punishment. Those who, like Mr. W., do not show remorse (prior to being sentenced) are viewed more harshly and denied the benefits of mitigation. Second, because expressions of remorse are linked to mitigation, it is difficult to decide whether offenders say they are sorry because they mean it or because they want to obtain a more lenient sentence. Mr. W. went to great lengths to solve this problem by deliberately withholding his expression of remorse until he could not possibly obtain any benefit from it.[1]

Long before their vindication (if vindication ever occurs), the wrongly convicted are designated as persons who lack remorse, and they are separated from those who are characterized as having remorse. Just as in the case of Mr. W., they are perceived as not acknowledging responsibility for their crime and as not having any feelings of sorrow or empathy for their victim(s). This chapter examines the impact of this designation on the identity and treatment of those who have been wrongly convicted. People who have been wrongly convicted often assert their innocence and, not surprisingly, refuse to express remorse for crimes they did not commit. This chapter explores the consequences of failing to express remorse. For the purposes of this analysis, I will draw on both Canadian and American data.

The most widely publicized instances in which remorse makes a difference have involved the life-or-death decisions of jurors in capital trials in the United States. In 2003, in a trial that attracted international attention, a jury was charged with deciding whether John Muhammad, convicted of six murders—the so-called "sniper" killings—should be executed. One juror was quoted in explaining why he had voted for the death penalty: "I tried to pay attention to his demeanor the whole time. I looked for something in him that might have shown remorse. But I never saw it." The jury foreman agreed that "the lack of emotion, his [Muhammad's] failure to even acknowledge what he had done, had played into" his decision to support the death penalty as well (Dao and Bacon 2003.) A continuing research project set up in 1993—the National Capital Jury Project—used a sample of 1,155 real jurors from 340 capital trials in 14 states to establish that the offender's remorse is one of the most important determinants of whether a jury will decide in favour of death rather than a life sentence in capital trials (Sundby 1998).

The social preoccupation with remorse is also illustrated in the public response to offenders who commit offences that shock the sensibilities of their communities. No aspect of the execution of Timothy McVeigh—the man convicted of the notorious Oklahoma City bombing that resulted in 168 deaths—was more thoroughly scrutinized than whether he had shown remorse prior to his death. A search through Canadian newspapers using Factiva shows a similar interest when it comes to high-profile offenders—for example, Karla Homolka, regarding whether she felt remorse for participating in the murder of her sister and of two other teenage girls, who were also raped by her husband. Thousands of news items appearing each week in the North American mass media focus on whether the convicted offender showed remorse for his or her wrongdoing. How people feel about their wrongful acts is as important to the courts and to the public as *why* they did it or *that* they did it.

WHY BE MORE LENIENT TOWARD PEOPLE WHO EXPRESS REMORSE?

One reason for this interest in remorse-related cases is that expressions of remorse tell us whether those who have violated the community's norms feel the same way about their misdeeds as would those who are law-abiding. Social psychologists have demonstrated that groups respond with empathy and compassion if they believe that a wrongdoer is sorry for his or her misconduct. People are likely to be far more punitive if they perceive that wrongdoers feel indifferent to the harm they have caused. In this sense, when judges denounce offenders who fail to show remorse while showing mercy to those who do, they are reflecting and affirming values that are shared by the community as a whole.

Another reason why courts pay so much attention to remorse is the widespread belief that offenders who feel remorse are less likely to offend again. Judges as well as members of the public tend to view remorse as revealing one's true character. If at the deepest level of feeling, offenders condemn their own actions, then it is possible that the emotional pain they experience may help deter them from further misconduct. Also, many correctional authorities regard the expression of remorse as the first step toward rehabilitation.

These justifications for leniency lose their force if the expression of remorse is strategic or insincere rather than genuine. Hence, judges and juries are interested not just in the expression of remorse but also in whether, in their view, what is shown corresponds to what is felt. Since very few offenders are prepared to act as unstrategically as Mr. W., with all the risks this entails, most expressions of remorse leave room for doubt as to whether appearance corresponds to reality.

As we shall see below in the case of the wrongly convicted, this potential gap between appearance and reality can also work the other direction. Just as a claim to feel remorse can be discredited if it seems rehearsed or unfelt, so also can a claim not to feel remorse be invalidated by what are perceived as underlying feelings of guilt or shame.

THE PROBLEM OF REMORSE FOR THE WRONGLY CONVICTED

There is much at stake in a wrongful conviction even apart from the rupture of the innocent person's life. As Huff, Rattner, and Sagarin (1996) have observed, wrongful convictions often involve a multiplicity of errors and occasional wrongdoings that may implicate different levels of the criminal justice system in "the ratification of error." Well-known Canadian cases over the past

30 years have shown that the eventual unravelling of a wrongful conviction that restores the reputation of the innocent may also challenge the credibility of those police, defence and Crown attorneys, judges, witnesses, jurors, correctional staff—even high-ranking political officials—who contributed to or condoned the injustice that led to the wrongful conviction. At the root of every wrongful conviction is a contest of credibility between an individual who asserts a claim of innocence and whose reputation and potential liberty depend upon this claim, and the justice system which claims that a conviction and the punishment that followed were justified.

Remorse is one of the issues that will determine whose definition of the situation will prevail. For the authorities, an assertion of innocence after conviction calls into question the credibility of the entire system of criminal justice; whereas a show of remorse is an affirmation that the institutions that imposed punishment did so with just cause. But for the person who has been convicted, any show of remorse subverts the claim to innocence. Even the momentary abandonment of this claim is enough to cast a lingering doubt as to its validity and thus compromise later attempts at exoneration—should the opportunity arise. The net effect of this clash of purposes is to trigger a process in which correctional staff and other officials intensify their efforts to elicit a show of remorse from the individual, while those who wish to advance a claim of wrongful conviction must embark on a project of long-term resistance.

However, this contest is decidedly unequal. Wrongly convicted persons who maintain their innocence are likely to be placed in the category of the unremorseful and to be subjected to the same deprivations as others who have been designated as lacking in remorse.[2] These deprivations are evident both in the sentencing process and in the way that the sentence is administered. Those who plead guilty to an offence are already credited with the most elemental demonstration of remorse—namely, they have acknowledged their responsibility for the commission of the offence. Those who claim innocence but are nonetheless found guilty are not allowed this credit.

These presumptions pervade all forms of sentencing, from the least to the most severe of penalties. The person who pleads guilty is officially entitled to mitigation even though the absence of remorse (as reflected in a plea of not guilty) should not result in a harsher sentence (*R. v. Ambrose*). When it comes to sentencing, pleading guilty translates into measurable and tangible reductions in the severity of sentences. More recently, it has also come to fulfill what appears to be an emerging requirement for a conditional sentence of imprisonment (served in the community) and for sentencing by sentencing circles. Because remorse in the form of acknowledgment of responsibility is taken as a first step toward rehabilitation and toward renunciation of the offending criminal conduct, those who maintain their innocence after conviction are perceived as not having accepted responsibility for their actions and, therefore, as more likely to reoffend, more dangerous, and more of a risk to the community.[3]

Moreover, the reluctance to express remorse, whatever its source, has deep cultural connotations in our society from which the law is not insulated. Individuals define themselves as members of a shared moral community to the extent that their feelings of remorse affirm the seriousness that others attach to moral transgressions. The findings of the Capital Jury Project show that jurors are more likely to impose a death sentence on persons who deny guilt on grounds of factual innocence or reasonable doubt (Sundby 1998); moreover, jurors' responses indicate a strong negative characterization of the persons who raise these defences. Especially in cases involving the death of the victim, there is a cultural expectation that those perceived as perpetrators will experience regret commensurate with the gravity of the offence. Those who do not—even on the impeccable moral ground that they were wrongly convicted—risk adverse characterization as "cold-hearted" or "utterly without feeling."[4] The moral career of the wrongly convicted thus begins not just with a harsher sentence but with the ascription of qualities that define them as more of a risk than others similarly situated and as lacking the moral sentiments—the inner emotional life—that other members of the community share.

In the context of this asymmetrical struggle for credibility, it becomes possible to better understand the pressures placed on the wrongly convicted to show remorse and the tenacity with which these pressures are often resisted. The most obvious pressures consist in deprivations, which are likely to be far greater for wrongly convicted persons who have been incarcerated than for other inmates. The annals of the wrongly convicted in Canada point to denials of parole and temporary absence because of continued assertions of innocence.[5] Even evidence that would normally favour a positive outcome, such as acquiring a skill, being active on committees, or having a record of no institutional violence, fails to outweigh the negative impact of a denial of guilt.

The pressures to show remorse are also likely to be indirect. Programs of therapy that enhance a person's eligibility for parole and other benefits typically require as a first sign of rehabilitation that the prisoner admit responsibility for the crime, even though fulfilling such a condition negates a claim of innocence. The result is that the wrongly convicted tend to accumulate a record that attests not only to their denial of guilt but also to their nonparticipation in programs designed to make them safe to return to the community.

LACK OF REMORSE VIEWED AS PSYCHOPATHOLOGY

However, no occasion touches more directly on issues of credibility than the psychological assessment and treatment of those who maintain their innocence. Here the assertion of innocence is approached less as a factual claim to be contested or rejected than as a symptom that requires therapeutic intervention. From the standpoint of the specialists—be they psychiatrists, psychologists, parole officers, or others who favour this perspective—the unwillingness to take responsibility for the crime is less a matter of defiance than of denial. An excerpt from the *Royal Commission on the Donald Marshall, Jr. Prosecution* offers a revealing glimpse into how this framework was applied during Marshall's wrongful incarceration for the murder of Sandy Seale. In the following exchange, the commission was exploring a memo in which a parole officer had denied Marshall's request for a temporary absence "as it [was] felt that in light of his unstableness at the present time, he presents too high a security risk" (Hickman 1989, 110):

Q. What was his unstableness?
A. This was a period of time when his behaviour in the institution was extremely aggressive towards the staff, towards myself, and towards the other members of the case management team where in one case he threw a chair at one of the staff members.

Q. Are you able to offer any insight as to what provoked that aggressiveness?
A. I suspect that it had a lot to do with the issue of whether he was guilty or innocent of the crime. Although I was not (putting) a lot of pressure on him to admit that he was guilty, some people were.

Q. Who would these people have been?
A. Some of the other people were members of his case management team who had contact with him far more frequently than I did on a daily basis.

Q. Was it your sense that his frustration in maintaining his innocence in the face of the response that he was guilty was causing this aggression to a degree?
A. In retrospect, yes. At the time, my belief was that he was coming close to admitting that he was involved in the crime and that it was starting to come out.

Because the officials presume guilt, they seek underlying disturbances that show a gap between appearance and reality in the expression of remorse and that undermine the claim of innocence. Just as overt claims of remorse can be challenged by inconsistencies between words and feelings or feelings and deeds, so also can a claim of innocence be invalidated by involuntary displays of conscience whether in the form of "aggression" or emotional turbulence.[6]

Similarly, the therapeutic approach used on Stephen Truscott during his wrongful conviction for the murder of Lynne Harper also involved a search for "abnormal" reactions. When Truscott failed to break down and admit guilt even after being administered sodium pentothal and several doses of LSD over an extended period, the psychiatric notes read as follows: "He is so controlled, so pleasant, and so objective that certainly there must be in his subconscious a tremendous control for commanding details" (Sher 2001, 376). In another log entry, the psychiatrist observed: "If he's guilty and is not admitting guilt, then this implies that there is a complete repression of the problems involved" (ibid., 395).

Yet paradoxically, the absence of these same "abnormal" reactions does not lead experts in forensic psychiatry to conclude that the person's claim of innocence may be credible. In one well-known American case of wrongful conviction, the prisoner's absence of affect resulted in the psychiatrist diagnosing the defendant as "a sociopathic personality disorder" because of "the absolute absence of any type of guilt or remorse" (Adams 1991, 129). In another Canadian case in which the person incarcerated had long asserted his innocence, the psychologist performing the assessment observed that the defendant's "calm, confident, and remorseless exterior was consistent with the reaction of an innocent man" (Harris 1996, 397–98); but then added: "A similar presentation associated with heinous and egregious behaviour would represent a powerful indicator of psychopathy." It would seem that there is no psychological model of what would be a normal reaction to a wrongful conviction.

Biographies and interviews reveal how the wrongly convicted resist these pressures to weaken their resolve. Despite maintaining their claims of innocence, most did attempt at some point to fashion a measure of relief from the restrictions, deprivations, and adverse characterizations to which they were being subjected. These actions illustrate the challenge of meeting official expectations without forfeiting one's credibility. In one instance, a man who had been wrongly convicted of sexual assault agreed to attend therapy sessions directed at sex offenders while refusing to sign a document admitting guilt (Liptak 2002, 4). Donald Marshall, after unrelenting attempts by the authorities to elicit a show of remorse, achieved a compromise of sorts when he agreed to admit to his parole officer, after being asked, that, even if he may not have committed the murder for which he was convicted, "he was the sort of individual who could have committed a murder ... a condition with which Marshall complied in hopes of improving his situation" (Harris 1990, 285).

Similarly, Stephen Truscott eventually produced a generalized statement in his application before a parole board in which he neither asserted his innocence nor explicitly claimed responsibility for the crime. This was in an effort to win freedom without negating the original claim of innocence (Sher 2001, 372). Years later, even this isolated incident would have to be explained and accounted for in the application to the Minister of Justice for his case to be reconsidered (s. 690 application for retrial between Her Majesty the Queen and Steven Truscott, November 28, 2001, 115.) Not until August 28, 2007, was Trustcott's appeal heard and an acquittal substituted for the conviction entered almost 50 years before, in 1959 (*R. v. Truscott* 2007).

The demand that all persons who are convicted of crimes demonstrate remorse by accepting responsibility for their offences has unintended consequences for those who have been wrongly convicted. The self-same efforts to maintain one's integrity in opposition to external pressures—actions that in other circumstances might well be viewed as virtuous—result in what Goffman (1961) referred to as the *mortification of the self*—the process by which the self is stripped of its social and psychological supports so that a new identity can replace the identity that has been lost. The treatment of the wrongly convicted illustrates this process, in which the force of criminal justice and corrections is directed toward recasting the truths claimed by those who are innocent as pathology at best and defiance at worst.

DISCUSSION QUESTIONS

1. *What is the solution to the problem identified by the author? Should the justice system ignore expressions of remorse and treat all people charged or convicted of a crime in the same way, whether they are remorseful or not?*
2. *Victims often state that they appreciate the expression of remorse from the offender. Is this a good justification for imposing less severe punishments when the offender says he or she is sorry?*

FURTHER READINGS

Medwed, D. 2008. "The Innocent Prisoner's Dilemma: Consequences of Failing to Admit Guilt at Parole Hearings." *Iowa Law Review* 93: 491.
Weisman, R. 2009. "Being and Doing: The Judicial Use of Remorse to Construct Character and Community." *Social and Legal Studies* 18, no. 1: 47–69.

REFERENCES

Adams, R. (with W. Hoffer and M. Hoffer). 1991. *Adams v. Texas*. New York: St. Martin's.
Clairmont, S. 2001. "'Unrepentant' Drunk Driver Utters a Stunning Last Word." *Toronto Star*, May 29, A5.
Dao, J., and L. Bacon. 2003. "Death Sentence for Muhammad: Sniper Jury Cites Lack of Sorrow." *New York Times*, November 25, A1.
Davis, S. 1997. "The Rape That Wasn't." *Alberta Report*, June 2, 30.
Finkle, D. 1998. *No Claim to Mercy*. Toronto: Penguin.
Goffman, E. 1961. *Asylums: Essays on the Social Situation of Mental Patients and Other Inmates*. New York: Doubleday Anchor.
Harris, M. 1990. *Justice Denied: The Law Versus Donald Marshall*. Toronto: HarperCollins.
——. 1996. *The Judas Kiss*. Toronto: McClelland and Stewart.
Her Majesty the Queen and Steven Truscott, s. 690 Application for Retrial, November 28, 2001
Hickman, A. 1989. *Royal Commission on the Donald Marshall, Jr. Prosecution*, vol. 1, Findings and Recommendations. Halifax: Province of Nova Scotia.
Huff, C., A. Rattner, and E. Sagarin. 1996. *Convicted but Innocent: Wrongful Conviction and Public Policy*. Thousand Oaks: Sage Publications.
Karp, C., and C. Rosner. 1991. *When Justice Fails: The David Milgaard Story*. Toronto: McClelland and Stewart.

Liptak, A. 2002. "Not at All Remorseful but Not Guilty Either." *New York Times,* November 3, 4.

Makin, K. 2001. "Man Jailed 29 Years Had Alibi but Police Buried It." *Globe and Mail,* November 8, 1.

——. 2008. "Baltovich Goes Free." *Globe and Mail,* April 22, 1.

Myers, L. 1997. "An Appeal for Clemency: The Case of Harold Lamont Otey." In H. Bedau, ed., *The Death Penalty in America.* New York: Oxford University Press. 361–83.

O'Hear, M. 1997. "Remorse, Cooperation, and 'Acceptance of Responsibility': The Structure, Implementation, and Reform of Section 3e1.1 of the Federal Sentencing Guidelines." *Northwestern University Law Review* 91: 1507.

Sher, J. 2001. *"Until You Are Dead" Stephen Truscott's Long Ride Into History.* Toronto: Knopf Canada.

Sundby, S. 1998. "The Capital Jury and Absolution: The Intersection of Trial Strategy, Remorse, and the Death Penalty." *Cornell Law Review* 83: 1557.

Vandersnick, L. 1998. "Lack of Remorse Versus Persistence of Innocence." *Illinois Bar Journal* 86: 692.

Weisman, R. 1999. "Detecting Remorse and Its Absence in the Criminal Justice System." In A. Sarat and P. Ewick, eds., *Studies in Law, Politics, and Society* 19.

Williamson, L. 2001. "A Canadian Tragedy: Money Can Never Right the Wrongs of the Thomas Sophonow Case." *Calgary Sun,* November 10, 15.

Young, N. 1989. *Innocence Regained.* Annandale: Federation.

CASES CITED

R. v. Allard (1999) 43 W.C.B. (2nd) 296.

R. v. Ambrose (2000) 271 A.R., 164.

R. v. A.G.W. (1994) 117 Nfld. & P.E.I.R., 233.

R. v. Baltovich (1992) 18 W.C.B. (2nd) 215.

R. v. Baltovich (2000) 47 O.R. (3rd) 761.

R. v. Layte (1983) 38 C.R. (3rd) 205.

R. v. Parent (1999) O.C.J. Lexis 47.

R. v. Taylor (1997) 122 C.C.C. (3rd) 376.

R. v. Truscott(2007) 225 C.C.C.(3rd) 321

R. v. Wood (2005) 196 C.C.C.(3rd) 155

Riggins v. Nevada (1992) 112 S. Ct. 1810.

ENDNOTES

1. Paradoxically, Wood did appeal his sentence partially on the grounds that the judge erred in principle in using his lack of remorse as one of the factors contributing to his relatively severe sentence. The court declined the appeal, ruling that the sentence was fit. (See para. 24 in *R. v. Wood* (2005) 196 C.C.C.(3rd) 155).

2. Many wrongful convictions begin with a false confession rather than with a plea of not guilty. For purposes of this analysis, I am assuming that whether or not wrongfully convicted persons maintain their innocence from the outset, at some point they will have to assert their innocence in order to pursue the claim. Once they do so, they will experience the disadvantages arising from an assertion of innocence.

3. The equation of an absence of remorse with dangerousness is commonplace in Canadian and American judgments. See, for example, *R. v. Allard*, [1999] (B.C.C.A.) at para. 5: "The trial judge was quite properly concerned with protection of the public, and hence the extent to which the applicant constituted a continuing danger to those he had harmed and threatened to harm, as well as to others. For that purpose, the appellant's apparent lack of remorse was relevant ..."

4. One example is the reaction of the court to Robert Baltovich's assertion of innocence after he was convicted of murder in 1992. See *R. v. Baltovich*, [1992]18 W.C.B. (2nd) 215 at para. 25: "The record shows a cold, calculating person, and that person killed a person who had loved and trusted you"; or at para. 26: "You have high intelligence, but you are totally devoid of heart and conscience." Sixteen years later, Baltovich's conviction was overturned on appeal, a new trial was ordered, and the prosecution withdrew its case against him, resulting in a directed verdict of acquittal in 2008 (Makin 2008, 1).

5. Examples include the following: Thomas Sophonow, wrongly convicted of second degree murder, who was refused parole and temporary absences (Williamson 2001, 15); Wilfred Beaulieu, who was wrongly convicted of sexual assault and denied temporary absence to attend the funerals of his brother and sister (Davis 1997, 30); David Milgaard, wrongly convicted of sexual assault and murder, who was turned down for parole and temporary absences many times during his 23 years in prison (Karp and Rosner 1991, 129); Donald Marshall, wrongly convicted of murder, who was refused parole for the same reasons (Harris 1990, 266). Romeo Phillion, who served nearly 35 years for a conviction that was successfully challenged and whose requests for parole were also consistently denied, was not altogether mistaken when he was quoted as saying that "parole is for the guilty, not for the innocent." (Makin 2001, 1). Subsequently, the Ontario Court of Appeal decided 2–1 to overturn Phillion's conviction on March 5, 2009, and to order that a new trial be held. However, in July 2009, the Attorney General of Ontario chose to withdraw charges, leaving Phillion in a legal limbo: neither convicted nor acquitted. Currently, Phillion is appealing to the Supreme Court of Canada to ask that a new trial be ordered so that his name might be cleared.

6. Interestingly, from this vantage point, those family members and others who believe the claim of innocence are viewed as supporting the underlying pathology; hence, continued contact is seen as problematic. Thus, one of Marshall's parole officers included in his appraisal: "There still

remains the problem of Marshall himself denying his guilt and being supported in this by an overprotective mother" (Harris 1990, 283). In the case of David Milgaard, one case worker at Stony Mountain wrote: "This writer questions how constructive familial support is. First, if the subject is guilty, familial belief in his innocence provides a firm block to subject even admitting to or working through intrapsychic aspects of offence" (Karp and Rosner 1991, 130).

CHAPTER 25

The Changing Face of Youth Justice: Impact of the Youth Criminal Justice Act

For many years, crime by young people has been a cause of great public concern in Canada as well as in many other Western nations (Roberts 2004a) This concern has generated many different approaches to youth crime around the world (see Tonry and Doob 2004). The *Youth Criminal Justice Act* (YCJA), which came into force in 2003, was the federal government's attempt to improve the justice response to offending by young persons. This reading reviews the YCJA, with particular focus on issues related to diversion from court, the use of custody, and youth crime trends. (For a more detailed discussion of the YCJA and its sentencing provisions, see Bala and Anand 2009.) The chapter summarizes some of the key provisions of the new law and analyzes statistical data from the first five years under the YCJA.

Nicholas Bala, Queen's University,
Peter J. Carrington, University of Waterloo, and
Julian V. Roberts, University of Oxford

REDUCING USE OF COURTS AND CUSTODY

Prior to the introduction of the YCJA, the use of juvenile custody in Canada was higher in Canada than in most other Western nations (e.g., Bala 2003; Doob and Cesaroni 2004). The high use of courts and custody is generally acknowledged to be a more pressing issue at the juvenile level than for adults, as involvement in the formal justice system and the imprisonment of adolescents can have more profound and negative effects than for adults. Community-based responses are often the most cost-effective way to deal with juvenile offenders, especially those who have committed less serious offences and who do not have an extensive history of offending. Imprisonment can often be a more punitive sentence for juveniles than for adults because young people are less able to cope with prison and may be more susceptible to the adverse effects of the inmate subculture (Cesaroni and Peterson-Badali 2005; Cesaroni in this volume).

Furthermore, even though there is generally a greater emphasis on rehabilitation in youth custody facilities, imprisonment deprives adolescents of the social support on which they depend for their moral and psychological development. While there is a need to imprison the most serious adolescent offenders, the inappropriate use of custody is expensive, ineffective, and inhumane; indeed, imprisonment may contribute to a cycle of juvenile reoffending. Thus one of the goals of any youth justice system—reducing reoffending—can be undermined by the use of more intensive forms of intervention such as custody. This conclusion is consistent with research on youth justice in other countries such as Scotland (e.g., McAra and McVie 2007). Accordingly, in 2003 the federal government set as a primary goal of its juvenile justice reform a reduction in the number of juveniles being sentenced to imprisonment.

GENERAL PRINCIPLES OF THE YCJA

Preamble

The YCJA includes a preamble that makes clear the intent of Parliament that Canada should 'have a youth criminal justice system that reserves its most serious interventions for the most serious crimes and reduces the over-reliance on incarceration for non-violent young persons."

Purpose and Nature of the Youth Justice System

The "Declaration of Principle" (s. 3) of the YCJA provides that the criminal justice system for youths "must be separate from that of adults." This declaration establishes the overall purpose of Canada's youth justice system, with Section 3(1)(a) stating that:

the youth criminal justice system is intended to
  (i) prevent crime by addressing the circumstances underlying a young person's offending behaviour,

  (ii) rehabilitate young persons who commit offences and reintegrate them into society, and

  (iii) ensure that a young person is subject to meaningful consequences for his or her offence,
in order to promote the long-term protection of the public[.]

Thus rehabilitation is as important as preventing crime and imposing meaningful consequences. Furthermore, the *long-term protection* of the public is seen as the *consequence* of rehabilitation and accountability, rather than as an independent objective of the youth justice system. This statement directs judges to impose sentences that facilitate the rehabilitation of young offenders, rather than custodial sentences that will merely incapacitate them.

Limited Accountability

The Declaration of Principle of the YCJA articulates a set of principles for responding to youthful offenders that places the greatest emphasis on the proportionality of the response, with Section 3(1)(c) emphasizing that "fair and proportionate" accountability is *the* central principle for responding to youth offending. The principles recognize, however, that it is to be limited accountability in comparison to adults, "consistent with the greater dependency of young persons and their reduced level of maturity."

Diversion from Youth Court by Extrajudicial Measures

The YCJA encourages the diversion of cases from youth court, providing for both "extrajudicial measures" and "extrajudicial sanctions." "Extrajudicial sanctions" are noncourt, community-based programs that may result in responses such as restitution to a victim or family group conferencing. The concept of "extrajudicial measures" is broader, including extrajudicial sanctions as well as oral warnings or written cautions by the police.

The YCJA clearly is intended to reduce the number of youths appearing in youth court, particularly first offenders and juveniles accused of minor offences, as indicated by the presumption in Section 4(c): "Extrajudicial measures are *presumed* to be adequate to hold a young person accountable for his or her offending behaviour if the young person has committed a non-violent offence and has not previously been found guilty of an offence" (emphasis added). Furthermore, there is a direction in the act that a police officer "shall" consider whether to invoke an extrajudicial measure prior to commencing judicial proceedings against a young person (s.6). The YCJA affirms the importance and stresses the range of application of extrajudicial measures, recognizing in Section 4(a) that "extrajudicial measures are often the most appropriate and effective way to address youth crime."

In a growing number of communities across Canada, extrajudicial sanctions programs have been established for minor violent youth offences (such as assaults in schools). Such programs include victim–offender reconciliation and family group conferencing. Either may result in an apology to the victim, restitution, and/or community service or counselling for the offender (Bala 2003). Section 10 of the YCJA provides that extrajudicial sanctions may be used only if a youth "accepts responsibility" for the offence that is alleged to have been committed and consents to the imposition of the sanction. A youth who denies responsibility for the offence or who objects to a specific sanction should be referred to youth court. In an attempt to prevent the application of these interventions to cases in which the young person is not at risk of a judicial proceeding, Section 10(2)(f) states that an extrajudicial sanction may be used only if there is sufficient evidence to prosecute a case in youth court. If the youth complies with the conditions of the extrajudicial sanction, the case against the young person cannot proceed to youth court. The record of having received an extrajudicial sanction is not technically a finding of guilt, but if in the two years following the imposition of the sanction the youth is found guilty of an offence in youth court, the existence of the prior extrajudicial sanction may be used by the youth court as a justification for imposing a more severe sentence.

The YCJA has resulted in a significant drop in the number of youth charged by police, as well as an increase in the use of various methods of police diversion. In Figure 25.1, the rates of youth charged and cleared otherwise are summarized in one statistic. The charge ratio, or percentage of chargeable youth who were charged, indicates the relative degree to which police are clearing cases by charge rather than by alternatives to charging. This indicator declined gently from 1991 to 2002. In 2003—the year that the YCJA was introduced—it dropped sharply from 56.4 to 44.6 percent charged: a relative change of 21 percent in one year. This means that the YCJA has reduced the use of formal charges at the youth justice level. Next we turn to a second important area of youth justice affected by the YCJA: sentencing.

Figure 25.1 *The Proportion of Chargeable Youth Who Were Charged, Canada, 1986–2007*

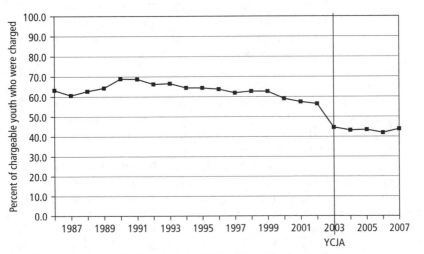

Source: Statistics Canada. Canadian Centre for Justice Statistics, *Uniform Crime Reporting Survey.*

PURPOSE AND PRINCIPLES OF SENTENCING

Purpose of Sentencing in Youth Court

The YCJA articulates the *purpose* of sentencing in youth court and then sets out specific principles of youth sentencing. Section 38(1) states that "[t]he purpose of [youth court] sentencing ... is to hold a young person accountable for an offence through the imposition of just sanctions that have meaningful consequences for the young person and that promote his or her rehabilitation and reintegration." The omission of any reference to deterrence in the YCJA statement of sentencing purpose likely contributed to a reduction in the number of custodial sentences imposed in youth court (Cesaroni and Bala 2008). Its absence in the act suggests that deterrence, be it general or specific, is *not* a goal when young persons are sentenced, although this objective is relevant for adult offenders (for a comparison of the sentencing provisions for young and adult offenders, see Roberts 2004b) have now accepted that deterrence is not a sentencing factor in youth courts (see R. V. B. W. P., 2006, S.C.C.27).

Sentencing Principles

For those youths who proceed to youth court and who are ultimately sentenced, the YCJA provides a detailed set of sentencing principles for judges to apply. Two of these principles reflect the concept of restraint with respect to imprisonment. Thus Section 38(2)(d) states that "all available sanctions other than custody that are reasonable in the circumstances must be considered." Furthermore, Section 38(2)(e) requires that, subject to the requirement that sentences be proportionate to the offence, "the sentence must be the least restrictive sentence that is capable of achieving the purpose [of sentencing]." Both these general principles also apply to the sentencing of adults. However, the YCJA emphasizes the *limited* accountability of youth compared to adults convicted of the same offence; and it has had a much greater impact on youth incarceration than the general statements on sentencing for adults in the *Criminal Code*. Having provided youth courts with these general sentencing principles, the legislation then prescribes specific criteria that must be met before a young offender can be committed to custody.

Criteria for Imposition of a Custodial Sanction

Under the previous youth justice law (the Young Offenders Act), a judge could not commit a young offender to custody unless the court considered "a committal to custody to be necessary for the protection of society having regard to the seriousness of the offence and the circumstances in which it was committed, and having regards to the needs and circumstances of the young person" (s. 24(1)). This vague provision offered little real guidance as to when youths should be imprisoned. This and other similarly vague provisions in the YOA were responsible for the fact that adolescent custody rates in Canada were among the highest in the world.

At the adult level in Canada there are no specific offence-based criteria that must be met before an adult offender is imprisoned. In contrast, the provisions in the YCJA relating to the imposition of a custodial sentence in youth court are far more restrictive, with Section 39(1) establishing four "gateways" to custody:

> A youth justice court shall not commit a person to custody ... unless
>
> (a) the young person has committed a violent offence; [or]
> (b) the young person has failed to comply with non-custodial sentences; [or]
> (c) the young person has committed an ... offence for which an adult would be liable to imprisonment for a term of more than two years and has a history that indicates a pattern of findings of guilt ... or
> (d) in exceptional cases where the young person has committed an indictable offence, the aggravating circumstances of the offence are such that the imposition of a non-custodial sentence would be inconsistent with the purpose and principles set out in section 38.

Thus there are only four circumstances in which a young offender may be committed to custody. As we shall demonstrate later in this chapter, this section has resulted in a substantial reduction in the use of custody since under the previous youth justice law there were significant numbers of young offenders who were imprisoned but who fell outside any of the four conditions now prescribed by the YCJA.

Additional Restrictions Regarding the Use of Custody

If the case before a youth court satisfies one of the four conditions in Section 39(1), a number of other custody-related principles must still be considered before a court can imprison the young offender. The first restriction is a clear reminder to judges in Section 39(2) of the principle of restraint with respect to the use of custody, even if one of the conditions of Section 39(1) is satisfied: "if [one of the criteria for custody] apply, a youth justice court *shall not impose a custodial sentence* ... unless the court has considered all alternatives to custody raised at the sentencing hearing that are reasonable in the circumstances, and determined that there is not a reasonable alternative, or combination of alternatives, that is in accordance with the purpose and principles [of sentencing at the youth court level]" (emphasis added).

A second principle to be observed before a custodial sentence is imposed is designed to discourage judges from escalating the severity of the sentence in response to subsequent offending. Having imposed an alternative to custody for one offence, some judges may impose a custodial sentence if a youth reappears before the court, reasoning that the first sentence was insufficiently severe to discourage the offender. Section 39(4) attempts to constrain this judicial practice, providing that "[t]he previous imposition of a particular non-custodial sentence on a young person does not preclude a youth justice court from imposing the same or any other non-custodial sentence for another offence." While this provision does not prohibit judges from following the "step principle" logic at sentencing, the provision means that the same alternative sanction may be imposed on consecutive occasions.

A third principle that restricts the use of custody is more clearly binding on youth court judges: Section 39(5) explicitly states that a youth court "shall not" use custody as a substitute for a child protection, mental health, or other social measure. Under the previous law, a common justification for imposing a custodial sentence on troubled adolescents was that the judge could see no other way to provide the necessary social intervention for an adolescent at risk. Under the YCJA this justification for the imposition of custody is prohibited.

While the YCJA emphasizes community-based responses for the majority of youth who commit less serious offences, violent or persistent offenders may receive youth sentences of up to 3 years in custody (and up to 10 years for murder). Also, for the most serious adolescent offenders there is the possibility of an adult sentence being imposed.

Creation of New Community-Based Sentences

To encourage judges to sentence fewer youths to custody, the YCJA created a number of community-based sanctions at the youth court level. Some of these new sentences, such as attendance centres and intensive supervision and support, are intended to provide youth with more supervision and support in the community, though they can only be imposed by a court if the province decides to provide the programs.

The most significant new community-based sentence is the "deferred custody and supervision order" (DCSO), which can be imposed by the court even without special programming being introduced by a provincial government. This sentence, analogous to the conditional sentence of imprisonment available at the adult level, allows the court to permit the youth to remain in the community for the duration of the order, subject to supervision by probation officers. In the event of an apprehended breach of the terms of release, the youth may be placed immediately in custody for the balance of the sentence without the need for another court hearing. This sentence, which can be imposed only if the youth has not committed a serious violent offence, has a maximum duration of six months. This new sanction represents the last opportunity for the court to spare the offender committal to custody, and it has been used quite frequently.

To summarize the sentencing provisions, the YCJA contains a number of provisions designed to discourage youth courts from imposing a term of custody on a young offender. These provisions were enacted specifically to reduce the use of imprisonment in youth courts across the country (see Introduction).

Figure 25.2 shows changes over time in the use of custodial sentences in youth court, as indicated by two statistics. The rates per 100,000 show the number of custodial sentences, standardized by population, and reflect any changes in the number of cases coming to court, in the proportion of cases with a finding of guilt, and in sentencing patterns. The proportions of sentenced cases show the use of custodial sentences, standardized by the total number of sentences handed down, and reflect only changes in custodial sentencing itself. Both indicators show a drop when the YCJA came into force in 2003–4.

The rate of custodial sentences dropped by 35 percent in 2003–4 and by a further 36 percent over the next three years. The proportion of sentenced cases receiving a custodial disposition dropped from 27 percent in 2002–3 to 22 percent in 2003–4—a drop of just under one-fifth in one year. It fell by a further 5.4 percent over the following three years, with the result that in 2006–7 only 16.6 percent of youth court cases resulted in a custodial sentence. The observed reduction in the proportion of custodial sentences is strong evidence for the effectiveness of those provisions of the YCJA which restrict the use of custodial sentences.

As a result of the decrease in the volume of cases coming to youth court and in the proportion of cases with a finding of guilt that ended in a custodial sentence, the per capita rate of youth admitted in sentenced custody in Canada decreased dramatically after the YCJA came into force in 2003: by 60 percent from 2001–2 to 2003–4 and by a further 11 percent to 2005–6 (see Figure 25.3).

Figure 25.2 *Rates and Proportions of Custodial Sentences in Youth Court, Canada, 1991/92–2005/06*

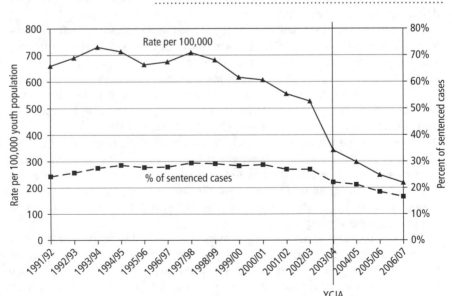

Source: Statistics Canada. Canadian Centre for Justice Statistics. *Youth Court Survey and Integrated Criminal Court Survey.*

Figure 25.3 *Rates of Young Persons Admitted in Sentenced Custody, Canada, 1997/98–2005/06*

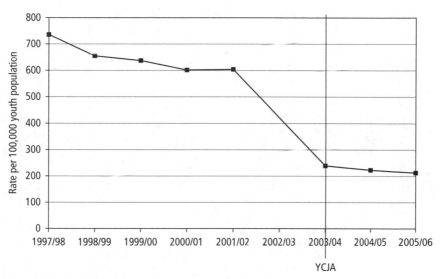

Source: Statistics Canada. Canadian Centre for Justice Statistics. *Youth Custody and Community Services Survey.* Table 251-0010.

In 2005–6 the rate of admissions to sentenced custody was only 35 percent of the rate in 2001–2.

Finally, it is important to note that this reduction in the use of custody for young offenders has not resulted in any increase in the crime rate by young people across Canada. Critics of the previous youth justice system argued that a tougher law was needed, one that promoted rather than constrained the use of custody for young offenders. However, as can be seen in Figure 25.4, the youth crime rate across Canada has not increased, even though the rate of youth brought to court has declined, as has the use of custody (see Bala, Carrington and Roberts (2009) for further discussion).

CONCLUSIONS

The pre-court diversion and sentencing provisions of the YCJA have brought about a major change in the youth justice system in Canada. The implementation of the new law was accompanied by professional education and program changes, as well as by transitional federal funding that undoubtedly reinforced the effects of the YCJA, but it is apparent that enacting a clear, new legislative regime has had a significant effect. The data from the first five years under the new legislation demonstrate that the act has had a significant impact on both recourse to youth court and the use of custody as a sanction.

Figure 25.4 *Recorded Youth Crime Rate (Rate of Young Persons Apprehended by Police), Canada, 1986–2007*

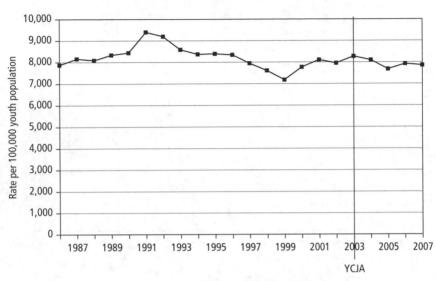

Source: Statistics Canada. Canadian Centre for Justice Statistics. *Uniform Crime Reporting Survey.*

The YCJA has resulted in a very significant reduction in the use of courts and custody for adolescent offenders in Canada; hence, it has allowed for a significant reduction in spending on youth courts and custody facilities, generally accompanied by a shifting of resources to community-based programs. In this sense, the YCJA represents a genuine success story in criminal justice in Canada.

DISCUSSION QUESTIONS

1. *The authors note that general deterrence is not considered an objective of the sentencing of young offenders—but is an objective for adults. Why would Parliament not consider general deterrence to be relevant to punishing young offenders?*
2. *How would you respond to a member of the public who argues that young people should be treated the same as adults when they are convicted of a crime? In other words, why do we have a separate law for the punishment of young people?*

FURTHER READINGS

Bala, N., and S. Anand. 2009. *Youth Criminal Justice Law.* 2nd ed. Toronto: Irwin Law.

Barry, M., and F. McNeill. 2009. *Youth Offending and Youth Justice.* London: Jessica Kingsley.

Doob, A.N., and J. Sprott. 2004. "Changing Models of Youth Justice in Canada." In M. Tonry and A. Doob, eds., *Youth Crime and Youth Justice.* Chicago: University of Chicago Press.

REFERENCES

Bala, N. 2003. "Diversion, Conferencing, and Extrajudicial Measures for Adolescent Offenders." *Alberta Law Review* 40: 991–1027.

Bala, N., and S. Anand. 2009. *Youth Criminal Justice Law.* 2nd ed. Toronto: Irwin Law.

Bala, N., P. Carrington, and J.V. Roberts. 2009. "Evaluating the Youth Criminal Justice Act After Five Years: A Qualified Success." *Canadian Journal of Criminology and Criminal Justice* 51: 131–68.

Cesaroni, C., and N. Bala. 2008. "Deterrence as a Principle of Youth Sentencing: No Effect on Youth, but a Significant Effect on Judges." *Queen's Law Journal* 39: 447–81.

Cesaroni, C., and M. Peterson-Badali. 2005. "Young Offenders in Custody: Risk and Adjustment." *Criminal Justice and Behavior* 32: 251–77.

Doob, A., and C. Cesaroni. 2004. *Responding to Youth Crime in Canada.* Toronto: University of Toronto Press.

McAra, L., and S. McVie. 2007. "Youth Justice? The Impact of System Contact on Patterns of Desistance from Offending." *European Journal of Criminology* 4: 315–45.

Roberts, J.V. 2004a. "Public Opinion and the Evolution of Juvenile Justice Policy in Western Nations." In M. Tonry and A. Doob, eds., *Youth Crime and Youth Justice.* Chicago: University of Chicago Press.

——. 2004b. "Harmonizing the Sentencing of Young and Adult Offenders: A Comparison of the Youth Criminal Justice Act and Part XXIII of the Criminal Code." *Canadian Journal of Criminology and Criminal Justice* 46, no. 2: 301–26.

Tonry, M., and A.N. Doob, eds. 2004. *Crime and Justice: A Review of Research.* Chicago: University of Chicago Press.

CHAPTER 26
The Consequences of Incarceration for Young Offenders

INTRODUCTION

Canada, like many countries, has provisions in its youth justice legislation suggesting that imprisonment should be used sparingly and only for very specific purposes. As noted in the previous chapter of this volume, the *Youth Criminal Justice Act* (YCJA) places important restrictions on the use of custody by a youth court, much greater than any restrictions in adult court. For example, youth court judges must overcome special "hurdles" before sentencing a youth to custody, whereas adult court judges simply follow a general principle that prison should be used only when no other sanction is appropriate.

Why should Canada be reluctant to send young offenders to prison? Historically, one of the main rationales for establishing a separate youth justice system and separate custodial facilities was a belief that youth are more vulnerable than adults. Young people's special needs, their vulnerabilities, and their need to avoid stigmatization were the original impetus for the establishment of youth custody facilities in Canada. The principal reason however, is that imprisonment carries more adverse consequences for young offenders. Indeed, there is agreement around the world that custody affects young offenders more than it does adults and that it is a more severe sanction for youth. However, this belief needs to be substantiated by documented research, since many Canadians feel that judges should not sentence young people differently from adults.

This chapter by Carla Cesaroni explores the effects of incarceration on young offenders. It considers the unique challenge that custody poses for young people and the kinds of young people who end up in custody.

Carla Cesaroni, University of Ontario Institute of Technology

Research evidence suggests that young people experience custody in a unique way. Age is one of the most consistently established correlates of interpersonal violence in prison; for example, compared to adults, young prisoners are more likely to be involved in disciplinary infractions, including assaults on other inmates and staff (MacKenzie 1987). Younger inmates are also less able to cope with the stress of imprisonment. They tend to experience much higher levels of anxiety as a result of being deprived of their families and social networks. Research suggests that custody ranks high among traumatic lifetime stressors for young people, right after the death or divorce of parents (Frydenberg 1997). The suicide risk among older prisoners is often related to psychiatric illnesses; in contrast, the suicide risk among young prisoners is usually a function of their inability to cope with the prison environment itself (Liebling 1999).

For many young offenders, incarceration is the first significant period that they have spent away from their family, friends, and home community. A custodial sentence may increase disengagement from family, pro-social peers, and familial/social values at a critical stage of the young offender's development. In addition, custody removes youth from local schools and therefore may affect young people who already have little commitment to their school. This may place them at risk for reoffending, delinquency, and other problem behaviours (Wasserman et al. 2003).

Adolescence itself challenges a young person's physical, intellectual, emotional, and social development. These challenges become more difficult with the prospect of a custodial sentence. For example, establishing a stable, integrated identity is a central task of adolescent development. It is not hard to imagine the negative impact of an onerous and highly restrictive institutional environment on the development of personal identity.

In addition, peers play a much more important role in the life of an adolescent than in the life of an adult. Given the importance of peer relationships to adolescent development, it is not surprising that the friendships a young person makes while in custody are strong predictors of later adjustment. However, relationships among adolescent peers in custody tend to be volatile. Research suggests that the friendships made by delinquents involve more arguments, more aggressive and impulsive behaviours, and greater conflict and instability than other adolescent friendships (Markus 1996). In addition, studies of delinquents' friendships suggest that delinquents are more likely to ridicule, gang up on, or reject their friends (Claes and Simard 1992).

The criminological literature on youths in custody focuses on *bullying*—the victimization of inmates by their peers (Connell and Farrington 1996). Bullying is a common activity in young offender detention centres. Between 20 and 45 percent of prisoners in young offender institutions report they have been victimized during the course of their sentence (O'Donnell and Edgar 1999).

In addition, youth in custody have difficulty dealing with negative peer relationships. Of course, peer victimization can also occur in schools and local neighbourhoods; but peer abuse within custody centres differs significantly from peer abuse in other settings because it is much more difficult for youth in custody to escape their tormentors. Adolescents are also generally less likely than adults to solicit support directly and are more likely to use help-seeking behaviours that are more indirect and disguised (Gottlieb 1991). Often they are afraid of damaging their reputation with their peers or appearing foolish (ibid.). In addition to the "adolescent code," imprisoned youth often have an "inmate code" to follow. In a study of incarcerated young offenders (Peterson-Badali and Koegl 2001), half the sample reported that if something bad happened, there was an adult/staff/professional inside or outside the institution they could ask for help. However, most said they would be unwilling to do so for fear of being labelled a "rat."

To summarize, a custodial sentence represents a difficult challenge for any young person. The loss of freedom that custody entails and some of the other consequences that are an inevitable part of "doing time"—such as missing family and friends—may be felt more acutely by youth than by adult inmates. Experiencing custody is particularly difficult for youth who are already vulnerable.

TYPES OF YOUNG OFFENDERS IN CUSTODY

Compared to other adolescents, youth in custody are vulnerable because of high levels of psychiatric problems and difficult family backgrounds. There is a high prevalence of psychiatric disorders in the incarcerated youth population (Ulzen and Hamilton 1998). These disorders include unipolar and bipolar depression, alcohol dependence, attention deficit hyperactivity disorder, conduct disorder, post-traumatic stress disorder, and separation anxiety disorder (ibid.). Several studies have attempted to estimate the prevalence rates of psychiatric diagnoses among young offenders in the youth justice system, but the results so far are highly variable (Kazdin 2000). However, even the most conservative results suggest that the prevalence rate of mental disorder is much higher among young offenders than in community samples (ibid.). In addition, research has demonstrated that up to 75 percent of incarcerated young offenders may have a learning disability (Henteleff 1999). Young offenders are also likely to have been involved with the child welfare system prior to custody (Doob, Marinos, and Varma 1995). Moreover, many forms of family adversity are associated with youth incarceration, including physical abuse, family breakup, and violence between parents (Goldson 2005).

Studies of male youth in custodial institutions in Ontario (Cesaroni and Peterson-Badali 2005, 2009, 2010) suggest that over half the youth in custody have had contact with child welfare authorities at some point during their child-hood. This confirms previous research that found significant overlap between youths who are brought to court for offending and those with previous contact with child welfare or mental health agencies. These same Ontario studies sug-gest that substantial numbers of youth in custody had been removed from their family of origin by a Children's Aid Society (almost one-third). Many youth (almost one-quarter) have also spent time in a group home. These findings are noteworthy, since they suggest a strong relationship between placement in foster or group care and subsequent risk of incarceration for criminal behaviour.

There is also evidence that youth in custody have a high exposure to vio-lence both within the home and in their neighbourhood (ibid.). This includes witnessing physical violence between the parents. The violence that youths wit-ness outside the home varies considerably. For some youths, it is the "normal" violence of youths beating up other youths (albeit sometimes with baseball bats and pipes). Others witness a variety of forms of violence, including shootings, stabbings, and beatings in the course of drug deals or other criminal activities.

The last decade has witnessed an increase in gang violence and gang activity in Canada. Correctional staff have identified the increasing challenge of managing rival gang members within youth custody facilities. Anecdotal evi-dence from staff suggests that this has meant more "stand-offs" between youth and staff, more behavioural incidents/reports, and a higher need for lockdowns.

CANADIAN RESEARCH FINDINGS

Canadian research suggests that custodial sentences carry unique risks for young offenders. A great deal of research on youth in custody has been done in the context of official reports or inquiries into the conditions of confine-ment in Canadian youth custody facilities (see Doob 1999; Law Commission of Canada 2000; Office of Child and Family Service Advocacy 2003). Many of these inquiries were responses to specific incidents in custodial facilities, including allegations of excessive use of force by staff and, in one extreme case, the death of a young person at the hands of another youth. These reports are useful because they include qualitative data that describe the youths' experi-ences in their own words. For example, youth who were interviewed about their first experiences in institutional facilities often spoke of "overwhelming sadness, fear of the unknown, anger, and a lack of information about what was happening to them" (Office of Child and Family Service Advocacy 1998, 8). In the words of another young person: "I cried at night, felt kind of lost" (ibid., 9). Government reports and inquiries are also useful because they describe treatment by staff, and living conditions, that many youth may find stressful. They illustrate how the challenges of custody experienced by youth differ from those of adult inmates, particularly in regard to young offenders' relationships with and treatment by adult staff.

The physical environment of youth custody facilities has been an area of concern since the youth justice system was first established. Some modern facilities for youth do not approximate even the "standard" that was set out in the 1908 *Juvenile Delinquents Act*. That act stated that "the care and custody and discipline of a juvenile delinquent shall approximate as nearly as may be that which should be given by his parents" (s. 38). Today's youth agencies, both government-operated and privately run, often house young people in run-down, decrepit buildings. Concerns have also been raised repeatedly regarding the quality and quantity of food in youth facilities (often a cause of bullying), the lack of access to proper health care, and inconsistent and substandard educational programming. Besides concerns about basic needs and necessities, concerns regarding institutional risks have also been raised. These risks relate to peer-on-peer violence, physical restraint, and placement in isolation. Peer abuse and inmate-on-inmate violence seem to be frequent features of custodial life for incarcerated youth.

Abuse in youth detention centres is not necessarily restricted to peer abuse. Certainly, the use of extraordinary control measures with youth in custody is necessary at times to protect staff, restrict the movement of youth, stop a youth from acting in a dangerous or aggressive manner, or confirm suspicions about contraband. Intrusive procedures may include manual restraint, mechanical restraint, isolation, and personal searches. At a minimum, youth see these incidents as "scary," "unsafe," and "unfairly applied." However, it is important to note that youth frequently report injuries; incidents have been documented of youth being kicked, dragged, smashed against the floor or a table, choked, punched, or hit with batons or brooms while immobilized.

A review of reports on conditions in Canadian institutions confirms the high frequency of peer-on-peer victimization in youth facilities. These findings are consistent with research from other Western countries. Peer-on-peer violence can occur in the context of intimidation, extortion, stealing, destruction of personal possessions, and/or verbal abuse. Youth in custody confirm the presence of several types of peer violence, including degrading activities involving bodily fluids. Descriptions of peer-on-peer violence in youth facilities are distressing, descriptions of staff involvement in that violence even more so. One researcher concluded: "From the perspective of those youth who found themselves in [these] secure facilities in Ontario, there not only is a fair amount of violence, but there is also a fair amount of staff involvement in creating or allowing this violence to occur" (Doob 1999, 30). According to youth questioned in one survey, staff involvement in violence included putting inmates at risk by "letting bad things happen" (reported by 46% of the sample), putting an inmate's safety in jeopardy (47%), and bribing inmates to "discipline" other inmates (31%).

Inappropriate treatment of youth inmates by custodial staff is a disturbingly common aspect of institutional life, one that may be linked to the power dynamic inherent in adult–youth relationships. Certainly, there is a power dynamic between guards and inmates in most adult facilities; but in youth facilities, there is the additional power dynamic of *adult* guard supervising an *adolescent* inmate. Being relegated to a childlike status during the age of individuation, independence, and control may create additional conflict for youth inmates with their adult guards, as it does between adolescents and their parents.

THE IMPACT OF CUSTODY ON YOUNG OFFENDERS

Custody remains the most punitive means of holding a young person accountable for his or her offences. Although many Canadians believe in "holding youths accountable" for their actions through imprisonment, it is not clear that the public would want youths to leave a correctional facility in worse condition than when they entered. In fact, many Canadians believe that assisting in the rehabilitation of a young offender is extremely important (Doob et al. 1998). Moreover, they would generally want youths not to suffer any long-term harm as a result of their time in custody. But as Steinberg, Chui, and Little (2004) argue, a rehabilitative perspective on young offenders provides challenges to both practitioners and policy makers because many custodial systems expose young offenders to harmful experiences (e.g., violence or trauma) that create more problems for youths than they had when they entered (ibid.).

Furthermore, the peer- or staff-induced harm that youth experience in custody has implications for institutional adjustment and for the likelihood of reoffending. Wasserman and colleagues (2003, 314) argue that maladjustment to confinement may make rehabilitation much more difficult: "An untreated mental disorder or emotional impairment resulting from a negative reaction to confinement might result in poorer adjustment during confinement that would negatively affect both discipline and a youth's capacity to take advantage of available programs."

What are the key predictors of adjustment to custody? Previously, authorities responsible for young inmates tended to attribute maladjustment to the "weakness" of individual youth (Goldson 2005). Contemporary approaches generally conclude that the characteristics of the individual *and* of the setting are important determinants of behaviour. Studies of youth in custody in Ontario demonstrate that those young people who entered an institution with a higher number of vulnerabilities (e.g., child welfare involvement, problems in school, delinquent peers, instability in the home) were more likely to experience subsequent difficulties with adjustment and psychological well-being (Cesaroni and Peterson-Badali 2005, 2009, 2010).

In addition, risk factors associated with institutional life appear to have an impact on adjustment. Prison stresses (e.g., missing freedom as well as family and friends) are aspects of adjustment to custody that the institution cannot necessarily control. As most front-line staff are likely aware, many youth get used to the common difficulties associated with entry to custody (Cesaroni and Peterson-Badali 2010). There are, however, two important predictors of prison adjustment over which staff do have some control.

First, staff can control the level of fear a youth experiences in an institution as a result of bullying or the possibility of being bullied. The consequences for the victims include not only physical injury but also psychological distress, which manifests itself in insomnia, escape attempts, and—in extreme cases— suicide (Leschied, Cunningham, and Mazaheri 1997). A study by McCorkle (1993) suggests that a youth's level of fear is an extremely important predictor of his or her general well-being: high levels of fear in prison often undermine the correctional system's efforts to treat, educate, and train offenders. He argues that personal security is an essential requirement in any program designed to effect changes in prosocial attitudes or behaviours.

Second, staff internal support can affect a youth's adjustment. Having friends in an institution is important to a youth inmate for a number of reasons, not the least of which is knowing that there are friends in the institution who will "watch your back" (Maitland and Sluder 1996; Office of the Child and Family Advocacy of Ontario 2003). One government inquiry concluded that young prisoners who are friendless within an institution are at serious risk of victimization (ibid.). One youth from that same inquiry suggested: "Alliances and friendships make you safe. Having no friends makes you unsafe" (ibid., 35).

Feelings of fear may be related to the turnover of youth in custody facilities and to the constant renegotiation of alliances and friendships and of "sizing each other up." Many correctional facilities in Canada have a high turnover of youth because of the number of short sentences imposed. Although some of the violence experienced by youth in custodial institutions is staff-related, dedicated staff can play an important role in the adjustment process by providing internal support to youths in custody. Perhaps the most vital role that staff play is that of creating a climate in custody that fosters positive social interactions, a sense of stability, and a secure environment. Perhaps custodial facilities can learn from successful schools: some schools have been very successful in reducing student victimization and fostering positive relationships by developing a positive and supportive organizational climate.

LONG-TERM CONSEQUENCES OF YOUTH CUSTODY

Any psychological distress that a young person experiences while in custody could be considered relatively transient, with no long-term implications for the youth's well-being. Although relatively few studies have explored the long-term psychological consequences of the custodial experience on the life of a young person, some evidence points to long-term developmental effects. Sampson and Laub's (1997) reanalysis of the natural histories of 500 delinquents found that imprisonment had significant negative effects on job stability at ages 25 to 32. According to this study, "the structural disadvantages accorded institutionalized adolescents are so great (e.g., through dropping out of high school, record of confinement known to employers) that the influence lingers throughout adult development" (p. 149). Incarceration appears to cut off opportunities for employment later in life, and this in turn may increase the likelihood that the young person will turn to crime.

CONCLUSION

In light of the short- and long-term implications of custody on a young person's future, custody should be imposed only with great restraint. The slogan "Do the crime, do the time" is often used to argue that youths should receive the same sentences as adults convicted of the same criminal behaviour (see Roberts 2004). However, because of the impact of custodial sentences on youths, for young people custody is in fact *more* punishing than it is for adults. This conclusion provides an additional justification for treating youths differently from adults. This was undoubtedly the spirit behind the establishment of the first youth custody facilities in Canada and, indeed, for the criteria for custody contained in the current youth justice law.

Canada has taken an important step with the YCJA in reducing the use of custody for youth in conflict with the law (see Chapter 25). However, ensuring the reduction of the use of custody may not be sufficient for the YCJA to completely fulfill its mandate. Some youth will continue to be admitted to custody. Directing how youth will do their time, not just how many, is clearly critical to the success of the youth justice regime in Canada.

DISCUSSION QUESTIONS

1. *Some youth justice advocates argue that young offenders should only be imprisoned if they commit the most serious crimes such as murder. Is this a realistic position to take?*
2. *You may have heard of military-style "boot camps" for young offenders, which are used in several American states. Do you think these kinds of institutions would be better than the correctional institutions currently in use here in Canada?*

FURTHER READINGS

Doob, A.N. 1999. *The Experiences of Phase II Male Young Offenders in Secure Facilities in the Province of Ontario.* Toronto: Canadian Foundation for Children, Youth and the Law.

Frydenberg, E. 1997. *Adolescent Coping: Theoretical and Research Perspectives.* New York: Routledge.

REFERENCES

Cesaroni, C., and M. Peterson-Badali. 2005. "Young Offenders in Custody: Risk and Adjustment." *Criminal Justice and Behavior* 32: 251–77.

—— . 2009. Understanding the Experiences of Incarcerated Male Youth: The Importance of a Developmental Framework." In A. Renshaw and E. Suarez, eds., *Prisons: Populations, Health Conditions and Recidivism*. New York: Nova Science.

—— . 2010. "Understanding the Adjustment of Incarcerated Young Offenders: A Canadian Example." *Youth Justice: An International Journal* 10, no. 2: 1–19.

Claes, M., and R. Simard. 1992. "Friendship Characteristics of Delinquent Adolescents." *International Journal of Adolescence and Youth* 3: 287–301.

Connell, A., and D. Farrington. 1996. "Bullying Among Incarcerated Young Offenders: Developing an Interview Schedule and Some Preliminary Results." *Journal of Adolescence* 19: 75–93.

Doob, A.N. 1999. *The Experiences of Phase II Male Young Offenders in Secure Facilities in the Province of Ontario*. Toronto: Canadian Foundation for Children, Youth and the Law.

Doob, A.N., V. Marinos, and K.N. Varma. 1995. *Youth Crime and the Youth Justice System in Canada*. Toronto: Centre of Criminology, University of Toronto.

Doob, A.N., J.B. Sprott, V. Marinos, and K.N. Varma. 1998. *An Exploration of Ontario Residents' Views of Crime and the Criminal Justice System*. Toronto: Centre of Criminology, University of Toronto.

Frydenberg, E. 1997. *Adolescent Coping: Theoretical and Research Perspectives*. New York: Routledge.

Goldson, B. 2005. "Child Imprisonment: A Case for Abolition." *Youth Justice* 5, no. 2: 77–90.

Gottlieb, B.H. 1991. "Social Support in Adolescence." In M.E. Colten and S. Gore, eds., *Adolescent Stress: Causes and Consequences*. New York: Aldine de Gruyter.

Henteleff, Y. 1999. *The Learning Disabled Child-at-Risk: Why Youth Service Systems have So Badly Failed Them*. Paper presented at the Working Together for Children: Protection and Prevention Conference, Ottawa.

Juvenile Delinquents Act, R.S.C. 1970, c. J-3.

Kazdin, A. 2000. "Adolescent Development, Mental Disorders, and Decision Making of Delinquent Youths." In T. Grisso and R. Schwartz, eds., *Youth on Trial: A Developmental Perspective on Youth Justice*. Chicago: University of Chicago Press.

Law Commission of Canada. 2000. *Restoring Dignity: Responding to Child Abuse in Canadian Institutions*. Ottawa.

Leschied, A.W., A. Cunningham, and N. Mazaheri. 1997. *Safe and Secure: Eliminating Peer-to-Peer Violence in Ontario's Phase II Secure Detention Centres*. North Bay: Ministry of Solicitor General and Correctional Services.

Liebling, A. 1999. "Prison Suicide and Prison Coping." In M. Tonry and J. Petersilia, eds., *Prisons: Crime and Justice: A Review of Research*. Chicago: University of Chicago Press.

MacKenzie, D. 1987. "Age and Adjustment in Prison: Interactions with Attitudes and Anxiety." *Criminal Justice and Behavior* 14: 427–47.

Maitland, A., and R.D. Sluder. 1996. "Victimization in Prisons: A Study of Factors Related to General Well-Being of Youthful Inmates. *Federal Probation* 60: 24–31.

Markus, Robert F. 1996. "The Friendships of Delinquents." *Adolescence* 31: 145–58.

McCorkle, R.C. 1993. "Living on the Edge: Fear in a Maximum Security Prison." *Journal of Offender Rehabilitation* 20: 73–91.

O'Donnell, I., and K. Edgar. 1999. "Fear in Prison." *Prison Journal* 79: 90–99.

Office of the Child and Family Service Advocacy. 1998. *Voices from Within: Youth in Care in Ontario.* Toronto.

——. 2003. *Review of Toronto Youth Assessment Centre (TYAC).* Toronto.

Peterson-Badali, M., and C.J. Koegl. 2001. "Juveniles' Experiences of Incarceration: The Role of Correctional Staff in Peer Violence." *Journal of Criminal Justice* 29: 1–9.

Roberts, J.V. 2004. "Public Opinion and the Evolution of Juvenile Justice Policy in Western Nations." In M. Tonry and A. Doob, eds., *Youth Crime and Youth Justice: Comparative and Cross-National Perspectives: Crime and Justice.* Chicago: University of Chicago Press.

Sampson, R.J., and J.H. Laub. 1997. "A Life-Course Theory of Cumulative Disadvantage and the Stability of Delinquency." In T.P. Thornberry, ed., *Developmental Theories of Crime and Delinquency.* New Brunswick: Transaction.

Steinberg, L., H. Chui Len, and M. Little. 2004. "Re-entry of Young Offenders from the Justice System: A Developmental Perspective. *Youth Violence and Juvenile Justice* 2: 21–38.

Ulzen, T., and H. Hamilton. 1998. "Psychiatric Disorders in Incarcerated Youth." *Youth Update* 16: 4–5.

Wasserman, G.A., et al. 2003. "Risk and Protective Factors of Child Delinquency." *Child Delinquency Bulletin Series.* April. Washington: Office of Juvenile Justice and Delinquency Prevention, U.S. Department of Justice.

CHAPTER 27
Responding to Intimate Partner Violence

Violence against intimate partners has become one of the most important problems that the criminal justice system is attempting to address. Only in recent years, with the creation of victimization surveys such as the "Violence Against Women" survey conducted by Statistics Canada, have Canadians come to appreciate the full scope of the problem. Until the advent of victimization surveys, the true extent of domestic violence was unknown, since only a small proportion of incidents were ever reported to the police. Devising appropriate responses to intimate partner violence has proved challenging for all systems of criminal justice. Canada's inheritance of the British common law included the 1784 dictum of Lord Blackstone that a man may beat his wife provided that he use a stick no wider than his thumb. Fortunately, contemporary Canadian law has come a long way in asserting and protecting women's human rights.

In this chapter, two experts in the field of law and sociology review the principal criminal and civil law responses to this grave social problem.

Gillian Blackell, Department of Justice Canada,[1] and
Holly Johnson, University of Ottawa

Intimate partner violence affects a substantial number of victims each year in Canada and commands the attention and resources of the criminal justice, health, and social service systems. For the purposes of this chapter, *intimate partner relationships* refer to marital or common law spousal as well as dating relationships, including same-sex relationships. In 2004, through a national telephone survey on crime victimization, Statistics Canada estimated that 196,000 women and 174,000 men had been victims of spousal violence in that year alone (spousal violence does not include violence in dating relationships) (AuCoin 2005). Approximately 653,000 women and 546,000 men reported violence by a spouse (common law or marital partner) in the preceding five-year period. In addition, between 1991 and 2004, 929 women and 238 men were murdered by an intimate partner in Canada. Police recorded a history of family violence in 55 percent of spousal homicides against women and 72 percent of spousal homicides against men (Johnson 2006).

Although women and men report similar prevalence rates of spousal violence committed against them, the impacts and consequences differ sharply for women and men (ibid.). Women were twice as likely as men to be injured, six times as likely to require medical attention, five times as likely to be hospitalized, and three times as likely to fear for their lives. They were also more likely to experience ten or more assaults and to take time off from paid or unpaid work as a result of the violence.

The risk of violence remains higher for Aboriginal women than for non-Aboriginal women. For example, according to the 2004 victimization survey, 24 percent of Aboriginal women reported being the victim of spousal violence over the previous five-year period, more than three times the rate for non-Aboriginal women (7%) and higher than the rate for Aboriginal men (18%). Moreover, Aboriginal women experience more severe violence and more serious consequences: spousal homicide rates are almost eight times higher for Aboriginal women than for non-Aboriginal women (4.6 and 0.6 per 100,000 population, respectively; ibid.).

Public awareness of intimate partner violence dates back to the 1970s. Domestic violence and sexual assaults in intimate relationships were historically viewed as private matters that did not necessarily warrant intervention by the criminal justice system. Over the past few decades, however, a wide range of interventions—including legislation, policies, and services—have been implemented by federal, provincial, and municipal governments as well as by community organizations in Canada to respond to the problem of intimate partner violence. These include shelters and other supports for victims, treatment for abusive partners, interagency collaboration at the community level, prevention and public awareness campaigns, specialized court processes, changes to both the criminal and the civil law, pro-charging policies for police, and pro-prosecution policies for Crown prosecutors (Johnson and Dawson 2010). Without exploring the full range of interventions to address intimate partner violence, this article summarizes some of the means by which the criminal and civil laws have been utilized to improve the legal response to intimate partner violence.

CRIMINAL LAW RESPONSES

While the *Criminal Code* does not contain a specific offence called *domestic* or *intimate partner violence*, a wide range of criminal offences cover violence within relationships. These include the offences of assault, sexual assault, homicide (murder, manslaughter), criminal negligence, forcible confinement, uttering threats, and criminal harassment. In 1983 the crimes of rape and indecent assault were replaced by the current three-tiered sexual assault provisions (ss. 271, 272, 273). The same reforms repealed spousal immunity from sexual assault charges. In addition to substantive offences, the *Criminal Code* provides procedural protections, preventative measures, and sentencing principles applicable in spousal violence cases.

ADDRESSING CRIMINAL HARASSMENT

The offence of *criminal harassment*, commonly known as *stalking*, was enacted in 1993 following several heinous incidents of estranged male partners harassing and stalking female victims, eventually leading to their death. Although prior to 1993 police were able to charge stalkers for other offences (such as mischief, uttering threats, or making harassing phone calls), the new offence captured seemingly innocuous acts, such as watching someone's place of residence or leaving unwanted gifts on someone's doorstep. In the context of stalking, such acts can be highly threatening for the victim and often serve as precursors to physical violence. Thus, the criminal harassment offence under Section 264 of the *Criminal Code* enables police to intervene if the behaviour is repetitive or threatening and causes the victim to fear for his or her safety or that of someone known to him or her. This offence was modelled on similar offences in the United States (California was the first state to criminalize stalking, in 1990).

The offence is particularly relevant in circumstances of intimate partner abuse, where the risks of violence or the escalation of violence are often heightened during or immediately following separation. For example, according to Statistics Canada's 2004 victimization survey, half the women who were assaulted by a past partner said that the violence occurred after the couple separated; and in one-third of post-separation assaults, the violence began or became more severe after the separation. Moreover, women have a heightened risk of spousal homicide after marital separation; ex-marital partners are responsible for 26 percent of all spousal homicides perpetrated against women but for only 10 percent of homicides perpetrated against men (Johnson 2006).

Additional protections for stalking victims have been introduced since 1993. First, a 1996 amendment to the *Criminal Code* included a lifetime prohibition of firearms after a conviction for criminal harassment. Then, a 1997 amendment made a conviction for criminal harassment while under a restraining order an aggravating factor that should be reflected in sentencing (s. 264(5)); and a homicide committed in conjunction with the commission of an offence of criminal harassment became first degree murder, regardless of whether the murder was planned and deliberate (s. 231(6)). In addition, in 2002 the maximum penalty for criminal harassment upon indictment was doubled from five to ten years. As a result, offenders convicted of criminal harassment offences can be subjected to the dangerous offender application under Section 759 of the *Criminal Code*. Finally, amendments to the *Code* in 2005 enhanced the provisions facilitating testimony by children and other vulnerable persons, including victims of criminal harassment (see below).

Estimates of the number of women and men who have been stalked over a five-year period are available through Statistics Canada's 2004 national crime victimization survey. This survey found that 11 percent of women and 7 percent of men had been stalked over the previous five-year period. Women were twice as likely as men to report being stalked by an intimate partner (current or former spouse or boyfriend): 21 percent of female victims compared to 11 percent of male victims. A strong association between stalking and intimate partner violence and homicide has been found in other research studies (Tjaden and Thoennes 1998; McFarlane et al. 1999). In the 2004 Statistics Canada study, three-quarters of women who were stalked by an ex-partner had also been physically or sexually assaulted by that partner. Ex-partner stalkers were also found to be more dangerous and threatening than other categories of stalkers. Higher proportions of ex-partner stalkers intimidated, threatened, grabbed, or attacked their victims. Sixty percent of women stalked by an ex-partner feared their lives were in danger (Johnson 2006).

In addition to the traditional means of harassment is the relatively recent phenomenon of *cyberstalking*—criminal harassment conducted through the Internet or other electronic means, such as harassing e-mail communications, the posting of offensive or threatening information about the victim on the Internet, or sabotaging the victim's computer. Some cyberstalkers even incite others to harass the victim by posting personal advertisements or images in the victim's name. While some of this conduct falls under the criminal harassment offence, some does not. Other offences, such as the *unauthorized use of a computer* (s. 342.1) or *mischief in relation to data* (s. 430 (1.1)), might be applicable. The difficulties of combating cyberstalking are multiple; they include the anonymity and lack of accountability of the perpetrator as well as cross-jurisdictional barriers.

BATTERED WOMEN AND SELF-DEFENCE

Sections 34 to 37 of the *Criminal Code* set out the statutory law on self-defence. According to these provisions, a person who is attacked is not criminally responsible for using a reasonable or proportionate amount of force to repel his or her attacker. A person can also use defensive force against an apprehended assault or attack because a threat to apply force also constitutes an assault under the *Code*. In addition, the law permits the use of reasonable force to defend someone else from harm or death. A successful claim of self-defence results in an acquittal for the assault or homicide. However, in all cases, the law does not permit the use of excessive or unreasonable force.

Prior to the Supreme Court of Canada's (SCC) groundbreaking decision in *R. v. Lavallée*, [1990] 1 S.C.R. 854, the law of self-defence in Canada was difficult to apply successfully in cases where battered women killed their abusive partners in self-defence. Lyn Lavallée was charged with the murder of her violent common law partner, Kevin Rust, who had regularly subjected her to physical abuse. She shot him in the back of the head as he was leaving the room after he beat her and told her that if she didn't kill him, he would kill her when their guests left. Expert evidence was introduced to demonstrate that Lavallée had been terrorized by Rust and that as a battered woman, her actions were based on a "reasonable" belief that she had no other option but to shoot him. In order to explain the perspective of the accused, the expert referred to the "battered woman syndrome," which is based on the work of Dr. Lenore Walker (1979).

Walker identified three phases of the cycle of domestic violence. The first phase, known as the *tension building phase*, is characterized by a series of minor assaults and verbal abuse. During the second phase, known as the *acute battering phase*, the batterer is unable to control the rage and severely beats the woman. This is followed by the third phase, the *kindness and contrite loving behaviour phase*, during which the batterer behaves kindly toward the woman, asking her forgiveness and promising never to repeat the violence. This final phase provides the woman with positive reinforcement for staying in the relationship. To explain why women remain in violent relationships after the cycle has been repeated more than once, Walker argued that battered women are psychologically paralyzed because they have learned from the repeated beatings that they cannot control their circumstances. This is known as "learned helplessness." Based on the battered woman syndrome, Walker testified that Lavallée's actions constituted the final desperate act of someone who sincerely believed that she would be killed that night. The jury acquitted Lavallée. The decision was appealed to the Supreme Court of Canada, which decided unanimously to acquit her of the charge of murder.

The *Lavallée* ruling was significant for a number of reasons: (1) it made admissible expert evidence related to *battered women's syndrome*, which in turn helped dispel myths about why battered women remain in violent relationships; (2) this evidence affected the *imminency requirement* (the requirement that the risk of attack must be imminent); and (3) the Court accepted that women's experiences and perspectives in relation to self-defence may be different from those of men and that courts must now make their judgments based on the "objective" standard of the actions of a "reasonable person," rather than on the actions of the traditional legal standard, the "reasonable man" (*R. v. Malott*, [1998] 1 S.C.R 123).

While the *Lavallée* decision was initially lauded by those who work with abused women, some feminist scholars have expressed concern that it might lead to the "syndromization" of women's experiences, as has been the case in the United States (Boyle 1990; Grant 1991; Comack 1993; Noonan 1993; Shaffer 1997; Sheehy 2001). The concerns regarding the battered women's syndrome included the risk that this would portray battered women as dysfunctional, deviant, and even pathological. Likewise, concerns were also expressed regarding the creation of a new stereotype of the "authentic" battered woman, thereby restricting the applicability of the syndrome evidence to women who fought back or did not otherwise fit the passive victim profile. While some authors indicate that cases subsequent to *Lavallée* have fallen prey to the syndromization of battered women (Shaffer 1997; Sheehy 2001), the Supreme Court was careful in both *Lavallée* and in *Malott* (another battered women's syndrome case) to indicate that the battered women's syndrome is not a defence in itself, but rather a tool for understanding the "reasonableness" of a battered woman's actions. The *Lavallée* ruling has contributed significantly to raising awareness of the realities of battered women among the judiciary and other criminal justice personnel and is regularly cited in court decisions.

Following *Lavallée*, in October 1995 the Minister of Justice and the Solicitor General of Canada established the Self Defence Review (SDR) to discover whether any women who had been convicted prior to or after *Lavallée* should have benefited from a self-defence claim. The SDR, under the lead of Judge Ratushny, reviewed the cases of women convicted of murdering an intimate partner. The SDR Final Report, released in July 1997, recommended relief in seven cases and included recommendations for reforming the self-defence provision in the *Criminal Code*. In the end, redress was granted in just five of the cases examined; however, no woman was actually released from jail as a result of the SDR (Trotter 2001).

PREVENTIVE MEASURES

A number of provisions in the *Criminal Code* can be used to help prevent intimate partner violence. For instance, Section 810 allows a Justice of the Peace or a judge to issue *recognizances* (peace bonds or protective court orders) to protect someone from a possible criminal offence. Recognizances require alleged offenders to adhere to conditions, such as staying away from the victim's residence or place of work, as well as surrendering any firearms they may possess. Although the standard of proof is a civil standard—meaning that only that on a balance of probabilities, there may be future violence—a breach of conditions is an offence under the *Criminal Code*. In 1995 these provisions were amended to facilitate the obtaining of peace bonds, to make those peace bonds more effective, and to increase the maximum penalty for a breach from six months to two years (Section 811). In light of pro-charging policies in domestic violence cases, peace bonds are generally not used if there are reasonable and probable grounds to arrest the abuser for a criminal offence.

In addition to peace bonds, the *Criminal Code* allows the justice or judge at a bail hearing to make recognizance orders or undertakings with conditions to prevent the accused from communicating with or harassing the victim or witness, in addition to other relevant conditions. In response to concerns regarding violent occurrences during the 24-hour period between arrest and the bail hearing in domestic violence cases, the *Code* was amended in 1999 to permit a justice of the peace who remands arrested persons into custody to order the person not to communicate with any witness or other person between the time he or she is detained and his or her first bail hearing. A 1999 amendment also requires police officers and judges to consider a victim's safety in all bail decisions. The *Code* was further amended in 2008 to reverse the onus in bail hearings to the accused to demonstrate why bail should be granted for offences involving a firearm.

Following the mass killings at the École Polytechnique in Montreal on December 6, 1989, public pressure to update gun control legislation significantly increased. In 1991, screening checks and safety courses for those applying for a Firearms Acquisition Certificate (FAC) were established for these certificates. Then in 1995, the federal government introduced the *Firearms Act*, which established the requirement for a licence for the possession of a firearm, a national registration system for all firearms, and a mandatory minimum sentence of four years of prison and a lifetime prohibition against the possession of restricted or prohibited firearms upon conviction of specific violent offences, including sexual assault with a weapon and aggravated sexual assault. The registration of firearms enables police to be alerted to the presence of firearms at scenes of family violence. Moreover, FACs ensure that the risk factors associated with incidents of family violence are considered, especially through the requirement of spousal consent.

PROTECTIVE PROCEDURAL MEASURES

It is trite to say that the criminal trial process can be gruelling for both the accused and the victim or witness. Concerns about the potential for revictimization of victims of intimate partner violence have led to the introduction of many protective procedural measures over the past two decades. In order to protect sexual assault complainants from having irrelevant evidence of prior sexual activity admitted at trial, revised *rape shield* legislation was introduced in 1992. These amendments to the *Criminal Code* included a definition of consent for the purposes of the sexual assault provisions. The amendments clearly state that the defence of mistaken belief in consent cannot be used if the belief stemmed from the accused's drunkenness, recklessness, or willful blindness, or if the accused did not take reasonable steps to determine whether the victim was in fact consenting.

The Criminal Code also contains a number of provisions to facilitate the testimony of vulnerable victims and witnesses. For example, a court can exclude some or all of the members of the public from the proceedings; as well, it can prohibit the publication or transmission of information that could identify a victim in cases where the victim is under 18 years of age and in cases where such a ban is deemed necessary for the proper administration of justice

(s. 486). Moreover, victims or witnesses under the age of 18 or those who suffer from mental or physical disabilities may be permitted to give evidence by way of a video recording (ss. 715.1, 715.2).

In addition, a wide range of testimonial aids are available to allow victims to testify, including closed circuit television and screens (so that the accused cannot be seen). Also, the victim can be accompanied by a support person at trial. While many of these testimonial aids have been available since 1999 for young victims and witnesses of specified violence and sexual offences, in 2005 they were made available upon application for adult victims of spousal abuse and sexual assault (s. 486). The new Subsection 486.3(4) specifically provides for the presumptive appointment of a lawyer for cross-examination of the victim in criminal harassment cases where the accused is self-represented.

For sentencing in spousal assault cases, the *Criminal Code* provides for victim impact statements and requires that these statements be considered by courts. Moreover, in 1995, the sentencing provisions of the *Criminal Code* were amended to provide that where an offender, in committing the offence, abuses his spouse or child or any position of trust or authority, this shall be considered an aggravating factor for sentencing purposes. Since 2007, conditional sentences (including "house arrest") are no longer available for those convicted of a serious personal injury offence that carries a maximum penalty of ten years or more, including sexual assault. Amendments have also been made to the restitution provisions of the *Code* to entitle a victim to seek restitution for actual and reasonable expenses for moving out of the offender's home to avoid bodily harm.

DOMESTIC VIOLENCE POLICIES AND COURTS

A cornerstone of the criminal justice response to intimate partner violence has been the implementation since the 1980s in all provinces and territories of directives or guidelines for police and Crown prosecutors. These are referred to as *pro-charging* or *pro-prosecution* policies. They generally require police to lay charges in cases of domestic violence where there are legal grounds to do so. Some policies require Crown prosecutors to prosecute domestic violence cases regardless of the victim's stated desire to withdraw charges. The original aim of these directives was to send a message to abusers that spousal violence is a crime and to ensure that victims are supported and offenders treated seriously by the criminal justice system.

Then in September 2000 the Federal-Provincial-Territorial (F/P/T) Ministers Responsible for Justice requested a review of these policies, the first comprehensive review since their inception, in order to assess the effectiveness of these policies and their application and to strengthen the government response to domestic violence. The resulting 2003 report recommended the retention of pro-charging and pro-prosecution policies in spousal abuse cases, as well as the development and enhancement of supporting programs, services, and structures, including a multisectoral response to spousal violence.

In addition, in order to improve the justice system's response to partner violence, several jurisdictions have instituted domestic or family violence courts, which provide a range of specialized services, such as advocacy and support for victims and their children, specially trained Crown prosecutors, translation services, and treatment for abusers. The first specialized family violence court was established in Winnipeg in 1990. Since 1996 the Ontario government has introduced a domestic violence court program in all 54 court sites in the province. Dedicated court processes and specially trained prosecutors can also be found in Yukon, Saskatchewan, Alberta, New Brunswick, and Newfoundland and Labrador. The Domestic Violence Treatment Option (DVTO) Court in Yukon is somewhat different in that it provides a therapeutic court-based alternative to formal criminal court for responding to domestic violence crimes.

The primary goals of these courts are to expedite court processing, to increase victim cooperation and improve conviction rates, to provide better support to victims throughout the criminal justice process, and to provide appropriate sentencing, such as treatment for abusers. There is some evidence of success with these goals. A comparison of the Family Violence Court (FVC) in Winnipeg prior to and following specialization shows increases in victim reporting rates, conviction rates, and the proportion of convictions resulting in probation supervision, jail sentences, and court-mandated treatment for perpetrators (Ursel and Hagyard 2008). Treatment has usually been imposed as a condition of probation, and those sentenced to jail also receive mandatory treatment. However, arrest, conviction and treatment have not been shown to be an effective deterrent for all violent partners: 10 percent of convicted offenders were charged again with assaulting a partner within one year, and 40 percent were charged again at least once over the ten years covered by this study (ibid., 113).

Feminist scholars have raised important questions regarding the potential for mandatory charging and prosecution policies to disempower victims by removing control of the situation from them once a report is made to police (Currie 1990; Snider 1998). The primary need of victims who call the police is to receive protection and to stop the violence from continuing. For many reasons, including financial, emotional, or child-related ones, the victim may be reluctant to have the abuser arrested and incarcerated. But regardless of the victim's wishes, calling the police puts in motion the weight of the entire criminal justice process. To deal with this difficulty, the Winnipeg Family Violence Court has changed its culture to ensure that the process does not revictimize victims and that it gives them some power over case outcomes (Ursel 2002).

One important development in spousal abuse cases is a shift away from the notion that success in a spousal abuse case requires a conviction. Rather than defining success on this single event, prosecutors have begun to place greater emphasis on the process and on providing a service to victims. Victims are encouraged and supported when testifying against an abusive spouse;

but the Crown does not proceed with the prosecution without the victim's cooperation, except in cases where there is a serious risk to the victim or the community. Reluctant victims are encouraged to consider testifying at another time.

In some ways, family violence does not fit the traditional model of criminal justice. Ursel (ibid., 58) argues that the high rate of stays of proceedings in Family Violence Courts is a result of the "single-incident framework" of the criminal justice system. Some spousal violence cases can appear several times as stays in court statistics, but one conviction can be based on an accumulation of charges over time. She argues that it is important for the victim to know that the system is there to help her and that she will be taken seriously and treated with respect if she reports to the police and charges are laid in the future. This follows more closely the philosophy of shelters for battered women, where the focus is on providing support and where efforts are not considered failures when these women return to an abusive partner. This degree of flexibility is absent in many court locations, however, and the lack of choice for women who wish to halt prosecution continues to be debated.

CIVIL LAW RESPONSES

In addition to criminal sanctions that apply across Canada, several remedies for intimate partner violence are available through the civil law. Civil remedies are provided for either through legislation or through the common law. Although historically tort was not applicable between spouses due to the doctrine of unity during marriage, torts such as assault, battery, trespass, and nuisance could now apply to a claim for damages from intimate partner violence. Tort law has not been applied often to domestic violence cases in Canada due in part to victims' fear of their aggressors (Christopher 2009). In addition to remedies for damages through the common law, many jurisdictions have criminal compensation recovery laws to which victims can turn following the conviction of the offender.

Civil Domestic Violence Legislation

Nine provinces and territories have introduced civil legislation to better protect victims in situations of domestic violence: Saskatchewan (enacted in 1995), Prince Edward Island (1996), Manitoba (1999), Alberta (1999), Yukon (2003), Nova Scotia (2003), Northwest Territories (2005), Newfoundland and Labrador (2006), and Nunavut (2008). These civil statutes are intended to complement the criminal law process, and jurisdictions are encouraged to proceed with criminal charges where applicable. The civil remedies available include emergency protection orders, orders providing temporary exclusive possession of the family home, civil restraining orders, and other provisions necessary for the protection of victims and their children. The primary value of civil domestic violence legislation is the immediacy of protection and the practical intervention it offers through remedies to victims and their children. Although the orders are civil, a violation of an order can result in a criminal charge under Section 127 of the *Criminal Code* in the absence of a specified penalty for a breach in the civil legislation.

THE IMPACT OF INTIMATE PARTNER VIOLENCE ON CUSTODY AND ACCESS OF CHILDREN

A considerable body of clinical research has identified the negative impact on children of witnessing spousal abuse (Jaffe, Crooks, and Bala 2006). Currently in five jurisdictions (Newfoundland, Northwest Territories, Nunavut, Alberta, and Ontario), family law legislation lists domestic or family violence as a factor in determining the best interests of the child for the purposes of custody and access (called *parenting orders* in Alberta). Yet even in the absence of specific legislative references, the courts generally consider evidence of family violence to be a relevant factor in post-separation or post-divorce custodial arrangements. Researchers have indicated that child access is often used as a window of opportunity for a partner to continue to intimidate, harass, or continue the violence against a former partner (Jaffe, Lemon and Poisson 2003).

Exposing a child to spousal violence may summon child protection authorities to intervene on the grounds of emotional harm or a risk of emotional harm to the child (Wilson 2003). Moreover, child protection legislation in seven jurisdictions explicitly identifies exposure to domestic violence as a factor to be considered when determining whether a child is in need of protection. Child protection orders supersede custody and access orders in a divorce or separation proceeding (ibid., §3.73); therefore, exposure to post-separation violence could have an impact on the ability of a victimized parent to retain custody of his or her child. However, according to the Canadian Incidence Study of Reported Child Abuse and Neglect (CIS-2003), only 2 percent of cases involving exposure to domestic violence in 2003 resulted in a child welfare placement. An additional 2 percent resulted in informal kinship care placement (Black et al. 2005).

CONCLUSIONS

Over the past 20 years, Canada's legal system has witnessed a form of dialogue among feminists and community organizations, the courts, researchers, and governments concerning the harms of intimate partner violence. To address intimate partner violence effectively requires multiple interventions from health, social, community, and justice service providers. As indicated in this chapter, intimate partner violence continues to be a persistent and pervasive problem in Canada, and the responses of the criminal and civil law continue to evolve as they adapt to the growing body of social science research and case law on this important social problem.

DISCUSSION QUESTIONS

1. *Do you think that the reforms to the law described in this chapter are likely to increase the level of confidence that victims have in the criminal justice system?*
2. *Can you think of any other steps that the justice system can take to more effectively respond to the problem of violence between intimates?*

FURTHER READINGS

Johnson, H. and M. Dawson. 2010. *Violence Against Women in Canada: Research and Policy Perspectives.* Toronto: Oxford University Press.

McKenna, K., and J. Larkin. 2002. *Violence Against Women: New Canadian Perspectives.* Toronto: Inanna Publications and Education.

Vallée, B. 2007. *The War on Women: Elly Armour, Jane Hurshman, and Criminal Violence in Canadian Homes.* Toronto: Key Porter.

REFERENCES

Ad Hoc Federal-Provincial-Territorial Working Group Reviewing Spousal Abuse Policies and Legislation. 2003. *Final Report of the Ad Hoc Federal-Provincial-Territorial Working Group Reviewing Spousal Abuse Policies and Legislation Prepared for Federal-Provincial-Territorial Ministers Responsible for Justice.* Ottawa: Department of Justice Canada.

AuCoin, K. 2005. *Family Violence in Canada: A Statistical Profile, 2005.* Cat. no. 85-224-XIE. Ottawa: Statistics Canada.

Bala, N., and E. Ringseis. 2002. "Review of Yukon's Family Violence Prevention Act." Under contract with the Canadian Research Institute for Law and the Family for the Victim Services Office of the Department of Justice, Yukon.

Black, T., N. Trocmé, B. Fallon, B. MacLaurin, C. Roy, and J. Lajoie. 2005. "Children's Exposure to Domestic Violence in Canada." *CECW Information Sheet #28E.* Montreal: McGill University, School of Social Work.

Boyle, C. 1990. "The Battered Wife Syndrome and Self-Defence: *Lavallée v. R.*" *Canadian Journal of Family Law* 9: 171–79.

Christopher, C. 2009. *Law of Domestic Conflict in Canada.* Toronto: Carswell.

Comack, E. 1993. "Feminist Engagement with the Law: The Legal Recognition of Battered Woman Syndrome." *The CRIAW Papers.* Ottawa: Canadian Research Institute for the Advancement of Women.

Currie, D. 1990. "Battered Women and the State: From the Failure of Theory to a Theory of Failure." *Journal of Human Justice* 1: 77–96.

Department of Justice Canada. 2004. Criminal Harassment: A Handbook for Police and Crown Prosecutors. Ottawa.

Feder, L., and L. Dugan. 2002. "A Test of the Efficacy of Court-Mandated Counseling for Domestic Violence Offenders: The Broward Experiment." *Justice Quarterly* 19: 343–75.

Grant, I. 1991. "The 'Syndromization' of Women's Experience." *University of British Columbia Law Review* 25: 51–59.

Jaffe, P., C. Crooks, and N. Bala. 2006. Making Appropriate Parenting Arrangements in Family Violence Cases: Applying the Literature to Identify Promising Practices. *Research Report, 2005-FCY-3E*. Ottawa: Department of Justice.

Jaffe, P., N. Lemon, and S. Poisson. 2003. *Child Custody and Domestic Violence*. Thousand Oaks: Sage Publications.

Johnson, H. 2006. *Measuring Violence Against Women: Statistical Trends, 2006*. Cat. no. 85-561-MWE. Ottawa: Statistics Canada.

Johnson, H., and M. Dawson. 2010. *Violence against Women in Canada: Research and Policy Perspectives*. Toronto: Oxford University Press.

McCallum, T. 2000. "Ontario Domestic Violence Courts Initiative." In V. P. Bunge and D. Locke, eds., *Family Violence in Canada: A Statistical Profile, 2000*. Cat. no. 85-224-XPE. Ottawa: Statistics Canada.

McFarlane, J., J. Campbell, S. Wilt, C. Sachs, Y. Ulrick and X. Xu. 1999. "Stalking and Intimate Partner Femicide." *Homicide Studies* 3: 300-16.

Noonan, S. 1993. "Strategies of Survival: Moving Beyond the Battered Woman Syndrome." In E. Adelberg and C. Currie, eds., In *Conflict with the Law: Women and the Canadian Justice System*. Vancouver: Press Gang.

Pottie Bunge, V. 2002. "National Trends in Partner Homicides, 1974–2000." *Juristat* 22, no. 5, Cat. no. 85-002-XIE. Ottawa: Statistics Canada.

R. v. Lavallée (1990), 1 S.C.R. 852-9000.

Sampson, F. 2001. "Mandatory Minimum Sentences and Women with Disabilities." *Osgoode Hall Law Journal* 39: 589–609.

Shaffer, M. 1997. "The Battered Women Syndrome Revisited: Some Complicating Thoughts Five Years After *R. v. Lavallée*." *University of Toronto Law Journal* 47: 1–33.

Sheehy, E. 2001. "Battered Women and Mandatory Minimum Sentences." *Osgoode Hall Law Journal* 39: 529–55.

Snider, L. 1998. "Struggles for Social Justice: Criminalization and Alternatives." In K. Bonnycastle and G. Rigakos, eds., *Unsettling Truths: Battered Women, Policy, Politics, and Contemporary Research in Canada*. Vancouver: Collective Press. 145–55.

Tjaden, P., and N. Thoennes. 1998. *Stalking in America: Findings from the National Violence Against Women Survey*. Washington: U.S. Department of Justice.

Trotter, G.T. 2001. "Justice, Politics and the Royal Prerogative of Mercy: Examining the Self-Defence Review." *Queen's Law Journal* 26: 339–95.

Ursel, J. 2002. "'His Sentence Is My Freedom': Processing Domestic Violence Cases in the Winnipeg Family Violence Court." In L. Tutty and C. Goard, eds., *Reclaiming Self: Issues and Resources for Women Abused by Intimate Partners*. Halifax: Fernwood.

Ursel, J., and C. Hagyard. 2008. "The Winnipeg Family Violence Court." In J. Ursel, L.M. Tutty, and J. Lemaistre, eds., *What's Law Got to Do with It?*

The Law, Specialized Courts, and Domestic Violence in Canada. Toronto: Cormorant. 95–119.

Walker, L. 1979. *The Battered Woman.* New York: Harper Perennial.

Wilson, J. 2010. *Wilson on Children and the Law.* Markham: Butterworths.

ENDNOTES

1. The views expressed in this chapter represent those of the authors and do not necessarily reflect the views of Justice Canada.

CHAPTER 28
Crime Victims and the Justice System

For many years, crime victims were overlooked by the criminal justice system. More recently they have come to play an increasingly important role in the criminal process. This is true in Canada as well as in other common law jurisdictions, such as England, Wales, and New Zealand, and at the level of international criminal justice. Federal, provincial, and territorial governments in Canada have introduced legislation and improved services to provide victims with more "voice" in the criminal justice system.

In this chapter, Michelle Grossman, Susan McDonald, and Catherine Kane, all of whom have worked in the area of victims policy and practice for many years, explore ways in which the Canadian criminal justice system has created a role for victims.

Michelle G. Grossman, University of Oxford,
Susan McDonald, Research and Statistics Division, Department of Justice Canada, and
Catherine Kane, Criminal Law Policy Section, Department of Justice Canada[1]

In recent years, federal, provincial, and territorial levels of government in Canada have made significant efforts to improve the experiences of crime victims in the criminal justice system. Despite several advances, many issues related to victims' needs and expectations in the criminal justice system require additional attention. This chapter explores several key issues relating to crime victims and the criminal justice system in Canada by examining relevant Canadian legislation as well as findings from empirical research.[2]

While this chapter does not address the impact of victimization, it is important to recognize that people react differently to crimes committed against them (for more information on impacts, see AuCoin and Beauchamp 2007; Hill 2007, 2009). For example, some victims may be fearful or traumatized following the theft of a car; others will only feel annoyed and inconvenienced and will seek information from the police and others. More serious and personal violence offences have far greater impacts on victims, and longer term consequences for them. Victims are thrown into an unfamiliar justice system where they do not have a clearly articulated or understood role. For a judge or Crown attorney, a victim may be simply one more "case" or one more "witness"; but for the victim, this case will likely have affected his or her life in a myriad of ways.

When asked to identify the "players" in the criminal justice system, people often identify the police, the Crown attorney or prosecutor, the defence counsel, judge, and probation or parole officers. In legal proceedings, be they criminal, civil, or other, the people involved are generally referred to as the "parties" to the proceeding. In civil proceedings (e.g., a claim for damages for negligence), the parties are referred to as the "plaintiff" (the person "complaining" or alleging a wrong and seeking damages) and the "defendant" (the person accused of committing the alleged wrong). In criminal proceedings, the parties are the Crown and the accused. The Crown is complaining on behalf of the State or society about a wrong (i.e., a crime) allegedly committed by the accused. The roles or duties of all these "parties" are clear and defined. The victim (the person who actually suffered because of this wrong) is not a party in the proceedings.

THE EVOLUTION OF VICTIM "RIGHTS" IN CANADA

In Canada, the emergence of victims' voices and recognition of their concerns dates back to the early 1970s. Criminal injuries compensation programs, which provide financial awards to victims of crime, originated in some jurisdictions in the context of compensating police officers injured in the course of their duties; they then expanded to provide limited compensation from the State (i.e., the province) to other eligible victims of violent crime. To encourage the development of such programs in all provinces, the federal government began funding them and established minimum criteria for them. Federal support for these programs, which benefited some victims, coincided with government funding for legal aid programs, which benefited some accused persons.

By the early 1980s, all Canadian provinces and territories had criminal injuries compensation programs. These programs varied in terms of eligibility and the scope of financial awards. By the early 1990s, many provinces and territories were examining the effectiveness of these programs when it came to meeting the needs of victims. Most victims who qualified found the financial assistance beneficial; however, many victims were ineligible, and many other needs of crime victims were not receiving attention. Even more important than statutory reforms were services for victims of crime, such as emergency or crisis response services, shelters, counselling, victim/witness assistance programs, and specialized services for children and for sexual assault survivors.

The current victim-related provisions in the *Criminal Code* and in the *Corrections and Conditional Release Act* (CCRA) are set out below. Keep in mind the distinction between the role of the federal government and that of the provincial and territorial governments. The federal government is responsible for *enacting* the criminal law; the provinces are responsible for *enforcing* the criminal law, *prosecuting* offences, and *administering* justice, which includes providing services to victims. In the territories, the federal government, through the Public Prosecution Service of Canada, is responsible for prosecuting offences as well as for court-based victim services.[3] All provinces and territories have enacted victim-related legislation addressing matters of provincial/territorial responsibility. For example, Manitoba— the first province to enact comprehensive victim legislation, in 1986—has *The Victim's Bill of Rights*, which defines a victim's rights and specifies the obligations of the police, the Crown, and other criminal justice professionals with regard to victims.

At the federal level, the development of victims' rights in the *Criminal Code* has occurred largely since 1988, though the *Criminal Code* has, since the 1950s, contained provisions that permit restitution orders. In addition, significant reforms to Canada's sexual assault laws in the early 1980s recognized that sexual offence complainants require special consideration. Since Canada's sponsorship of the *UN Declaration of Basic Principles of Justice for Victims of Crime* and its endorsement of the *Canadian Statement of Basic Principles of Justice for Victims of Crime,* the federal, provincial, and territorial governments have pursued victim-specific legislative reforms. The descriptions of key *Code* provisions below follow the stages of the criminal process—pretrial, preliminary inquiry, trial, sentencing, and post-sentencing.

CRIMINAL CODE PROVISIONS OF BENEFIT TO VICTIMS

Definition of Victim

In the *Criminal Code*, a crime victim is broadly defined as "the victim of an alleged offence." The definition is nonexhaustive and makes no distinctions among primary victims (i.e., the actual victim), secondary victims (e.g., spouse, parent, coworker), and indirect victims of crime. It only clarifies that the term may properly be used even when the crime is still alleged—in other words, the term "victim" does not presume the guilt of the accused.

Consideration of Victim's Safety in Bail Decisions

When a suspect is arrested, a determination must be made as to whether the suspect should be detained in custody or released with a promise to appear for trial, sometimes with conditions (commonly referred to as *bail*). In some cases, police make these decisions; in others, a justice of the peace or a judge makes them. Regardless of who makes the decision, most victims want to know the outcome and seek assurance that their safety has been taken into account in the bail decision.

Amendments to the *Criminal Code* enacted in 1999 require the decision maker to ensure "the safety and security of any victim of or to the offence" at various points in the criminal justice process. In Canada, as in some other countries such as the United States, Australia, and New Zealand, risk assessment tools have been developed to assist police, judges, and justices of the peace in this decision-making process (see Millar 2009 for an inventory). Decision makers must consider the following factors:

- The responsible judicial officer (officer in charge, justice of the peace, or judge) must consider the safety and security of the victim.
- Where an accused is released pending trial, the judge must consider whether to make as a condition of bail that the accused abstain from any direct or indirect communication with the victim, as well as any other condition necessary to ensure the safety and security of the victim.
- The judge must consider particular concerns of the victim and highlight them in decisions when imposing special bail conditions, including in firearms prohibitions and criminal harassment measures.

Facilitating Testimony

For some victims and witnesses, judicial proceedings can be intimidating or even frightening. The *Criminal Code* contains several provisions for assisting victims and reducing their anxiety. Amendments to the *Code* and to the *Canada Evidence Act* that came into force on January 1, 2006, make testimonial aids available for all child victims, for witnesses under the age of 18, and for vulnerable adult victims and witnesses on application, unless such aids would interfere with the proper administration of justice. For example, these provisions:

- provide discretion for the judge to exclude members of the public from the courtroom when necessary for the proper administration of justice;
- allow a victim or witness who is under 18 years of age, or who may have difficulty communicating the evidence by reason of mental or physical disability, to testify outside the courtroom or behind a screen or device that prevents a view of the accused;
- allow the admission of videotaped testimony of the victim or witness who is under the age of 18 in specified proceedings, including sexual offences;

- permit a support person to accompany a witness or victim who is disabled or young (under 14 years of age); *and*
- restrict personal cross-examination of young sexual offence victims and personal violence offence victims (under 18 years of age) by a self-represented accused (e.g., the Crown can apply for an order appointing counsel to conduct the cross-examination of the victim).

Other vulnerable victims and witnesses, such as victims of spousal abuse and sexual assault or those with a disability, may apply for a testimonial aid, provided that the person can show that in the circumstances (including the nature of the offence and any relationship between the victim/witness and the accused), he or she would not be able to provide a full and candid account without the aid.

Publication Bans

While the general rule is that all criminal proceedings against an accused are held in open court, the *Criminal Code* sets out several exceptions to facilitate victims' or witnesses' participation and to protect their privacy (see Cameron 2004). Sexual offence complainants, young victims, and young witnesses are the primary beneficiaries of these special provisions. A judge can order a publication ban on the identity of a victim or witness and on any information that could disclose that person's identity, if the judge is satisfied that the order is "necessary for the proper administration of justice." The victim, witness, or Crown can apply to the court for a publication ban, stating why the order is required. The hearing to determine whether the publication ban should be granted may be held in private. In addition, a judge must order a publication ban (on application) to protect the identity of all victims of sexual offences and of all witnesses of sexual offences who are under 18 years of age. In these cases, the judge advises the victim, witness, or Crown attorney/prosecutor in advance that he or she may request this protection. In cases of child pornography, a publication ban order must be made.

Provisions for Sexual Offence Victims

Legislative reforms recognize the unique nature of sexual assault offences, the trauma suffered by victims of these offences, and the revictimization often caused by participating in the criminal justice system in such cases. The *Criminal Code* provides a clear and commonsense definition of *consent* for the purpose of sexual assault offences. Any nonconsensual sexual activity is a sexual assault; hence, proof of lack of consent is an essential element of the offence. The *Code* defines *consent* as the voluntary agreement of the complainant to engage in the sexual activity in question. Conduct short of a voluntary agreement to engage in sexual activity does not constitute consent as a matter of law. For greater certainty, the *Code* sets out specific sections where there is no consent in law. Amendments made to the *Code* in 2008 raised the legal age at which youths can consent to nonexploitative sexual activity from 14 to 16. The same amendments provided a number of exceptions to the "consent as no defence" provisions, including a "close-in-age" exception that permits 14- and 15-year old youths to engage in consensual, nonexploitative sexual activity with a partner who is less than five years older.

Sections of the *Criminal Code* protect the complainant from undue interrogation about the complainant's other sexual activity. The *Code* makes it clear that evidence that a complainant has engaged in sexual activity with others is not admissible to suggest that the victim was more likely to have consented to the sexual activity that is the subject matter of the current charge. The provisions restrict the admissibility of evidence to specific instances of sexual activity—those relevant to an issue at trial—and to evidence that has "significant probative value which is not substantially outweighed by the danger of prejudice to the administration of justice." In making this determination, the judge is required to consider a range of factors set out in the *Code*. The *Code* also sets out the procedure to be followed and includes provisions to safeguard the victim's privacy, including provisions for an *in camera* (closed) hearing, noncompellability of the victim at the hearing, and a publication ban on the proceedings. These provisions are sometimes referred to as the *rape shield* laws.

Finally, sections of the *Code* protect sexual offence victims and witnesses from requests for personal records. These provisions place the onus on the accused to establish that the records sought are likely to be relevant to an issue at trial. In addition, the trial judge is required to carefully scrutinize applications and make a decision in accordance with a two-part procedure that balances the accused's right to a defence with the victim's privacy and equality rights. This procedure is set out in the *Code* and includes safeguards for the victim's privacy; these safeguards include an *in camera* hearing, noncompellability of the victim at the hearing, a publication ban on the proceedings and the contents of the application, editing of the records (where ordered to be produced) to delete irrelevant personal information, and the imposition of other appropriate conditions (see McDonald and Wobick 2006 for case law on this provision).

SENTENCING

Reforms to the sentencing provisions of the *Criminal Code* enacted in 1996 defined the purposes and principles of sentencing. Judges are directed to consider a number of objectives when sentencing offenders. Two of these objectives are directly relevant to the interests of victims:

- to provide reparations for harm done to victims or to the community; *and*
- to promote a sense of responsibility in offenders and acknowledgment of the harm done to victims and to the community.

Victim Impact Statements

Although there are only two parties in a sentencing hearing—the offender, represented by defence counsel, and the State, represented by the Crown—the victim of the crime nevertheless has a role to play. Most countries permit the crime victim to submit a statement to the court detailing the impact that the crime has had upon his or her life. Some U.S. states go even further and allow victims to make sentencing recommendations to the court. This is not permitted in Canada. In 1988 the *Criminal Code* was amended to permit the court to consider *victim impact statements* (VISs). Since 1995 the *Code* has required the court to consider a VIS at the time of sentencing. The VIS describes the harm done to or loss suffered by the victim of the offence. The 1999 amendments to the *Criminal Code* did the following to improve the usefulness of VISs:

- ensure that the victim is permitted to read a VIS at the time of sentencing if he or she wishes to do so;
- require the judge to ask, before imposing a sentence, whether the victim has been informed of the opportunity to prepare a VIS;
- authorize adjournments to permit a victim to prepare a statement or to submit other evidence to the court about the impact of the crime;
- require that VISs be considered by courts and review boards following a verdict of not criminally responsible on account of mental disorder; *and*
- clarify that oral or written information may be provided by a victim at any proceeding to determine whether an offender sentenced to life in prison should have an earlier parole eligibility date.

Federal Victim Surcharge

The *federal victim surcharge* is an additional financial penalty automatically imposed on offenders at the time of sentencing (unless the accused seeks an exception owing to undue hardship). In addition to the *federal victim surcharge*, a similar provincial/territorial surcharge exists that is automatically imposed. The federal and provincial/territorial victim surcharges are collected and retained by the provincial and territorial governments and are used to help fund programs, services, and assistance to victims of crime within the jurisdiction. The *federal victim surcharge* was included in the 1988 amendments to the *Criminal Code* and proclaimed in 1989. Amendments in 1999 fixed the amount of the surcharge and provided for automatic imposition upon conviction, although the judge may waive the surcharge in cases of undue hardship on the offender or the offender's family. The surcharge is 15 percent of any fine imposed on the offender. If no fine is imposed, the surcharge is $50 in the case of an offence punishable by summary conviction and $100 in the case of an offence punishable by indictment.

Restitution

The court may order the offender to pay restitution in addition to any other sentence. Restitution may be ordered by the court on its own motion or on application by the Crown or victim to cover easily ascertainable monetary damages, including those resulting from bodily injury (but not for pain and suffering). In 2010 a provision was added to the *Criminal Code* to allow for an order that the offender make restitution to a victim of identity theft or identity fraud for the expenses associated with rehabilitating the victim's identity. In terms of enforcement, if the restitution order is tied to a probation order or a conditional sentence, the probation officer or community corrections officer will work with the offender to ensure that he or she complies with the order, whether through a one-time payment or a schedule of monthly payments. In the case of stand-alone orders, the enforcement of restitution is the victim's responsibility. The victim may file the restitution order as if it were a judgment in civil proceedings and pursue civil remedies.

VICTIMS AND THE CORRECTIONAL SYSTEM

The *Corrections and Conditional Release Act* governs Correctional Service Canada (CSC), which is responsible for supervising offenders sentenced to more than two years in custody, as well as the National Parole Board (NPB), which determines whether to release offenders into the community. This act contains specific provisions authorizing the release of some offender-related information to victims who register with CSC and request information.

Anyone can request publicly available information, such as a description of the offence for which an offender was convicted, the sentence length, and eligibility dates for temporary absences, day parole, or full parole. But victims of crime, as defined in the *CCRA*, may register and request additional information, which may include the penitentiary where the offender is serving the sentence; the date of a Parole Board hearing; the nature of the conditions attached to any work release, parole, statutory release, or temporary absences; and whether the offender is in custody. Victims may request ongoing information and must ensure that CSC and the NPB have their current address for this purpose.

When victims request information from CSC and the NPB, victim liaison officers within CSC generally receive those requests and provide the information. Victims may request to attend Parole Board hearings as observers and may also have access to the NPB's decision registry. Victims may prepare and submit VISs to the Parole Board describing the physical, emotional, and financial impact of the offence upon them. NPB policy permits victims to read or otherwise present the VIS at the hearing. Victims can apply to the Department of Justice Canada for funding to attend the parole hearing.[4]

Victims and Life Sentences

Offenders convicted of murder are sentenced to imprisonment for life; however, most become eligible for parole after serving part of their sentence. In many cases, victims and/or their families want to know when the offender becomes eligible for parole or has a parole hearing. Most prisoners serving a life sentence with no parole for at least 15 years are eligible to apply for a jury review of their parole eligibility date. The provision in the *Code* that permits such an application is sometimes referred to as the *faint hope clause*. The family of a murder victim often expresses a desire to know when the offender in their case makes an application under this provision. To ensure that information is provided to victims about life sentences, the *Criminal Code* requires a judge to state, for the record and for the benefit of surviving victims, that an offender convicted of murder who has received a life sentence may apply for a reduction in the waiting period before his or her parole application may be made. In addition, at proceedings to determine whether an offender should have his or her parole ineligibility period reduced (known as *faint hope clause* hearings), oral or written information may be provided by the victim.

RESEARCH ON VICTIMS IN THE CRIMINAL JUSTICE SYSTEM

Legislative reforms have addressed some victim needs, and while further reforms are necessary, these reforms should be supported by research that examines both the effectiveness of the existing legislation and the broader needs of victims. An exhaustive review of all the research relating to victims of crime is beyond the scope of this chapter. Provided below is a *selection* of key research issues that are intended to inform policy, programs, and legislative reforms relating to crime victims. References for further reading are provided at the end of the chapter.

Victim Needs

The needs of crime victims range from the general to the specific and often depend on the type of victimization experienced and on the characteristics of the individual victim (see, e.g., Egbo 2009; Federal Ombudsman for Victims of Crime 2009; Fraser and McDonald 2009). Victims frequently identify financial needs, emotional needs, practical needs, and needs related to personal safety and security to varying degrees and in varying circumstances. Research indicates that the need for information is one of the most critical and universal needs expressed by victims of crime (e.g., Meredith and Paquette 2001; Wemmers and Canuto 2002; McDonald 2010). For many people the criminal justice process is both unfamiliar and complex, and victims often do not know how to navigate through the system. The information needs of victims and their families fall into three main categories:

1. information about the criminal justice system in general;
2. information about their specific case and their rights; *and*
3. information about services to address their other needs, such as for housing, emotional support, and financial or medical services.

For the most part, accused persons will have defence lawyers to represent them and to explain the details of the case before the trial and as it unfolds. Many victims mistakenly believe that the Crown attorney/prosecutor is their personal lawyer; in fact, the Crown acts on behalf of the State, not the victim. As victims do not generally have their own lawyers to protect their interests or to assist them as the case proceeds through the system, they must rely on criminal justice system officials to provide appropriate information about how their case is proceeding and progressing. This is where victim services providers can play an important role in addressing the information needs of victims/witnesses and their families.

Child Victims/Witnesses

Children and youth have specific needs in relation to the criminal justice system. It has long been recognized that children are particularly vulnerable to retraumatization if they go through the criminal justice system as witnesses. Research (Sas 2004) has documented the cognitive development of children and addressed how the criminal justice system must adapt to ensure that children can participate effectively in the process. Testimonial aids, such as screens, support persons, or giving evidence via closed circuit television, are intended to facilitate testimony. Ongoing research continues to assess how these provisions are working in practice across the country (Northcott 2009).

Plea Negotiations

Plea negotiations (or plea bargains) may not seem like a topic related to victims; however, such negotiations have a significant impact on crime victims. *Plea bargaining* is defined as a "negotiation between the Crown prosecutor, defence counsel, and the accused to determine which charge will be laid or what sentence will be recommended. Typically, this negotiation is undertaken in an effort to have the accused plead guilty and avoid the need for a trial" (Drislane and Parkinson 2005, 106). Plea bargaining is important since about 90 percent of criminal cases are resolved through guilty pleas, many of which are the direct outcome of plea negotiations between Crown and defence (Verdun-Jones and Tijerino 2002). However, as Verdun-Jones and Tijerino note, victims in Canada have almost no role in plea bargaining, even though the results of a plea bargain may have direct consequences for them. These researchers go on to explain that although plea negotiations play an integral role in the criminal justice process in Canada, they in fact "have no formal legal status and are not subject to direct judicial regulation" (2002, 5).

A victim's exclusion from plea bargaining may well affect his or her perception of the criminal justice process. Agreements made between the Crown and the defence without the input or—at a minimum—the knowledge of the concerned crime victim may contribute directly to a victim's dissatisfaction with the criminal justice system. On the other hand, a guilty plea means that victims do not need to participate in trial proceedings—an activity that crime victims may find traumatizing.

In 1987 the Canadian Sentencing Commission made several recommendations related to the issue of plea negotiations, a number of which address victim involvement in the process; however, to date, none of these recommendations have been implemented (Verdun-Jones and Tijerino 2002).

The recommendations included simple steps such as informing victims of the plea negotiation before it takes place, as well as representing a victim's views via the Crown at the time of the plea negotiation. Both these recommendations may serve to satisfy the wishes of many crime victims regarding plea bargaining.

Restitution

Little research has been undertaken in Canada on court-ordered restitution. National data from Statistics Canada show that restitution orders are made primarily in relation to property crimes (80%). The Department of Justice Multi-Site Survey (Prairie Research Associates 2006) included questions on restitution, with criminal justice respondents noting that the main problem is enforcement. The reason given for this is the offender's inability to pay. Research in Saskatchewan, which has the country's only Restitution Coordinator, who works with both offenders and victims, found that victims wanted more information and assistance with respect to all aspects of restitution—what they could request of the court, what happened once an order was made, and how they could enforce the order in civil court (McDonald 2010). In addition, the research found that when victims did not receive the money owed to them, this affected their confidence in the entire justice system.

Federal Victim Surcharge

Research has been undertaken to better understand how the Federal Victim Surcharge (FVS) is working in different jurisdictions. For example, Law and Sullivan (2008) found in their research in New Brunswick that the FVS was being waived in 66 percent of all cases province-wide and in 96 percent of cases with a custodial disposition. These findings were similar to those in the Northwest Territories (Warrilow and McDonald 2008), where the FVS was being waived in 70 percent of all cases territory-wide and in 94 percent of cases with a custodial disposition. As noted earlier, the FVS is collected by the provinces and territories and the revenues collected pay for services for victims. As such, it was important that the research also examined collection rates for the FVS that were not waived at sentencing. In New Brunswick, 83 percent of FVSs were being collected; similarly, 84 percent of all FVSs were being collected in the Northwest Territories. An offender's inability to pay was consistently cited by respondents in these studies as the reason for waiving the FVS.

Victim Impact Statements

Sociolegal research on VISs has been undertaken in Canada since the early 1980s, so there is a significant body of work examining how they are working from both victims' perspectives and from the perspectives of other criminal justice professionals (see Roberts 2008 for a summary). To mark the 20th year since their introduction into the *Criminal Code* (Bill C-89 in 1988), Roberts

(2008) reviewed and synthesized the body of research on VISs and noted the following in terms of lessons learned:

1. Only a minority of victims submit impact statements.
2. Few victims request oral delivery of their VIS, but those who do find it beneficial.
3. Obstacles remain regarding the systematic use of statements.
4. Most victims who submit a VIS report being more satisfied with sentencing.
5. It is important to avoid creating expectations that cannot be fulfilled.
6. The mode of delivery of any VIS program is important to its success.
7. Victims require appropriate information about the purpose and nature of VISs.
8. VISs sometimes include extraneous material.
9. Judges report finding VISs useful, particularly for sentencing offenders convicted of crimes of violence.
10. Little evidence exists that VIS have adverse effects on sentencing process.

CONCLUSION

The criminal justice system needs to consider justice proceedings from the perspective of individual victims. While the role that crime victims play in this system is not as clear as those of other participants in the criminal justice process, crime victims need to be considered. Although the involvement of victims in the justice system has received increased attention in the research literature as well as in policy and legislation, more work remains. Further exploration of the needs and concerns of victims, through appropriate policy research, is necessary, as are continuing efforts to evaluate the benefits of the progress already made (or initiatives already taken) to improve the criminal justice system with respect to victims of crime.

DISCUSSION QUESTIONS

1. *Do you think that the legislative provisions described in the chapter provide an adequate level of involvement for victims, or should the role of the victim be further expanded?*
2. *Some victims' rights advocates suggest that crime victims should be able to include a recommendation about the sentence in their victim impact statement. Others respond that this would only lead to more variability in sentencing. What do you think?*

FURTHER READINGS

Prairie Research Associates. 2006. *Multi-Site Survey of Victims of Crime and Criminal Justice Professionals Across Canada*. Ottawa: Department of Justice Canada, Policy Centre for Victim Issues.

Roach, K. 2010. *Due Process and Victims' Rights: The New Law and Politics of Criminal Justice,* 2nd ed. Toronto: University of Toronto Press.

Roberts, J.V. 2010. "The Role of the Victim at Sentencing and Corrections." In K. Reitz and J. Petersilia, eds., *The Oxford Handbook of Sentencing and Corrections.* New York: Oxford University Press

REFERENCES

AuCoin, K., and D. Beauchamp. 2007. "Impacts and Consequences of Victimization," GSS 2004. *Juristat.* Statistics Canada, cat. no. 85-002-XIE, 27, no. 1.

Canadian Sentencing Commission. 1987. *Sentencing Reform: A Canadian Approach.* Ottawa: Supply and Services Canada.

Cameron, J. 2004. *Victim Privacy and the Open Court Principle.* Ottawa: Department of Justice Canada.

Drislane, R., and G. Parkinson. 2005. *Nelson Criminology Dictionary.* Toronto: Thomson Nelson.

Egbo, R. 2009. *Memorializing the Victims of Terrorism.* Ottawa: Department of Justice Canada.

Federal Ombudsman for Victims of Crime. 2009. *Every Image, Every Child: Internet-Facilitated Child Sexual Abuse in Canada.* Ottawa: Office of the Federal Ombudsman for Victims of Crime.

Fraser, C. and S. McDonald. 2009. *Identifying the Issues: Victim Services Workers' Experiences Working with Victims with Fetal Alcohol Spectrum Disorder.* Ottawa: Department of Justice Canada.

Hill, J.K. 2007. *Victims' Response to Trauma and Implications for Interventions: A Selected Review and Synthesis of the Literature.* Ottawa: Department of Justice Canada.

——. 2009. *Working with Victims of Crime: A Manual Applying Research to Clinical Practice.* 2nd ed. Ottawa: Department of Justice Canada.

Law, M., and M.A. Sullivan. 2008. *Federal Victim Surcharge in New Brunswick: An Operational Review.* Ottawa: Department of Justice Canada.

McDonald, S. 2009. "Understanding Restitution." *Victims of Crime Research Digest* 2: 10–16. Ottawa: Department of Justice Canada.

——. 2010. "'Explain please!' Working with Victims and Restitution." *Victims of Crime Research Digest* 3: 9–14, Ottawa: Department of Justice Canada.

McDonald, S., and A. Wobick. 2006. *Bill C-46: Records Application Post-Mills, A Case Law Review.* Ottawa: Department of Justice Canada.

Meredith, C., and C. Paquette. 2001. *Summary Report on Victim Impact Statement Focus Groups.* Ottawa: Department of Justice Canada.

Millar, A. 2009. *Inventory of Spousal Violence Risk Assessment Tools Used in Canada.* Ottawa: Department of Justice Canada.

Northcott, M. 2009. "Facilitating Testimony for Child Victims and Witnesses." *Victims of Crime Research Digest* 2: 17–23. Ottawa: Department of Justice Canada.

Prairie Research Associates. 2006. *Multi-Site Survey of Victims of Crime and Criminal Justice Professionals Across Canada.* Ottawa: Department of Justice Canada.

Roberts, J.V. 2008. "Victim Impact Statements: Lessons Learned and Future Priorities." *Victims of Crime Research Digest* 1: 3–16. Ottawa: Department of Justice Canada.

Sas, L. 2002. *The Interaction Between Children's Developmental Capabilities and the Courtroom Environment: The Impact on Testimonial Competency.* Ottawa: Department of Justice Canada.

Verdun-Jones, S., and A. Tijerino. 2002. *Victim Participation in the Plea Negotiation Process in Canada: A Review of the Literature and Four Models for Law Reform.* Ottawa: Department of Justice Canada.

Warrilow, L., and S. McDonald. 2008. "A Summary of Research into the Federal Victim Surcharge in New Brunswick and the Northwest Territories." *Victims of Crime Research Digest* 1: 21–4. Ottawa: Department of Justice Canada.

Wemmers, J., and M. Canuto. 2002. *Victim's Experiences with, Expectations and Perceptions of Restorative Justice: A Critical Review of the Literature.* Ottawa: Department of Justice Canada.

ENDNOTES

1. The views expressed in this chapter are those of the authors and do not necessarily represent those of the organizations with which they are affiliated.
2. Statistics Canada publishes a number of reports each year on the nature and extent of victimization using data from the General Social Survey on Victimization, and on services for victims using the Victim Services Survey, and the Transition Home Survey. For more information see: http://www.statcan.gc.ca. Research from the Research and Statistics, division Department of Justice Canada, referenced in this chapter can be accessed at http://www.justice.gc.ca
3. All three territories also provide community-based victim services.
4. For more information on financial assistance for victims to attend National Parole Board hearings see: http://www.justice.gc.ca/eng/pi/pcvi-cpcv/fund-fond/app-dem.html

CHAPTER 29
Restorative Justice

The traditional model of criminal justice in Canada is largely *retributive* in nature. *Retributive justice* focuses on punishing offenders in proportion to the seriousness of their crimes. But an alternative model, called *restorative justice*, is becoming popular in many countries. Under a restorative justice model, the goal is not to punish offenders but rather to seek reconciliation between the offender and the victim and to restore the offender to the community. The emphasis is on achieving some tangible benefit for the victim rather than simply punishing the offender. The restorative response to crime is therefore said to be more victim-oriented than the conventional criminal justice system, in which victims' interests are often neglected.

In this chapter, Liz Elliott discusses the nature of restorative justice and describes some specific restorative justice programs.

Liz Elliott, Simon Fraser University

In many countries around the world, a new paradigm has emerged to compete with the traditional criminal justice model. Restorative justice is a concept with several different meanings. One common perspective is that restorative justice is a program, one that diverts nonviolent, first-time lawbreakers from jail to community-based measures. However, this kind of restorative justice is based on the same assumptions as those of the retributive justice system and is invariably little more than an "add-on" program to that system. Practitioners who begin with this understanding of restorative justice may eventually develop an appreciation for the more inclusive and egalitarian processes of these programs. But without a shift in our framework of understanding crime itself, we lose the opportunity to develop new ways of understanding problems and developing solutions. Howard Zehr (1990), one of the leaders of the late twentieth-century restorative justice movement, suggests: "The framework: it makes a difference. How do we interpret what has happened? What factors are relevant? What responses are possible and appropriate? The lens we look through determines how we frame both the problem and the 'solution'" (177–78). Without this change of lens, appreciations of valuable aspects of restorative processes remain limited to the realm of conventional criminal justice systems. In this chapter I make a case for restorative justice based on such a paradigm shift. I also provide an overview of restorative process models found in current practice.

RESTORATIVE JUSTICE AS PEACEMAKING

When seen through the retributive lens, justice focuses on identifying which laws have been broken, proving who the perpetrators are, and then punishing them according to the seriousness of the crimes. The "justice as scales" metaphor conveys the idea of balancing, equalizing, and measuring. From this perspective, equality in the relationship between the parties (e.g., victim, accused, Crown, legal counsel) affected by a crime is generally sought through punishment (Llewellyn and Howse 1999). Punishment "intends inflicting pain, suffering or loss" (Haan 1990, 112) on an offender; its purpose in inflicting harm on the offender is to "equalize" the harm suffered by the victim. Justice is achieved through the finding of guilt, the imposition of a proportionate sentence, and its subsequent implementation.

This kind of justice system revolves around images of police, courtrooms and lawyers, jails and prisons, and parole officers. Justice is the domain of professionals and institutions acting on behalf of the people involved in the conflict, criminal or otherwise. This institutionalization of justice appears to have increased the dependency of citizens on professionals to solve conflicts, thereby undermining the ability of communities to handle their own personal and local problems. In contrast, justice viewed through a restorative lens replaces the metaphorical image of the scales of retributive justice with the image of a circle. Through the restorative lens, justice begins with a focus on harms suffered by victims, then attends meaningfully to the needs of all the affected parties and tries to restore and/or build relationships among the parties themselves, their families and friends, and the community at large. There is no definable "end" or destination in a circle, just as there is no definable beginning. Restorative justice can be understood as an ongoing process of righting relationships damaged by the harm and entails the pursuit of peaceful relations.

Restorative justice proponents who operate from a peacemaking perspective often find themselves in a similar position to Aboriginal people whose traditional ways conflict with the formal legal system. Familiarity with the conventional criminal justice system and the tendency to include some restorative justice programs within that system make the task of developing values-based restorative processes a challenging one. Moreover, values-based restorative justice needs to avoid the fate of the many alternatives to incarceration developed in the 1980s, all of which simply helped widen the formal criminal justice system. Restorative justice approaches can still operate within the formal system, as long as the integrity of the processes is not compromised by conventional expectations.

RESTORATIVE JUSTICE AS SOCIAL JUSTICE

Criminological theory and research from the beginning of the 1900s has attempted to define the factors that contribute to harm-producing behaviours. The factors affecting criminal actions have been considered historically by theorists such as Sutherland (1947) and Hirshi (1969), who spoke of the influence of social learning, labelling, and basic social arrangements (such as the family). More recently, Canada has improved crime prevention through the reduction of opportunities (see Brantingham and Brantingham 1990) and through social development. Prevention is considered to be in the best interests of the individual, the community, and society at large.

However, the capacity of the criminal justice system to prevent crime is limited. Classical theory holds that people will be deterred from committing crimes by the fear and anticipation of punishment. For this deterrent effect to occur, however, the punishment must be swift and certain. In reality, sentences are imposed long after the crime was committed, and there is considerable uncertainty regarding the nature of the sentence that will be imposed. The problem of trial delays is also a common criticism of the legal system. Apart from the general difficulty in enumerating how many people are, in fact, deterred from crimes, there is also the difficulty of demonstrating exactly what prevents people from committing crimes: Is it the fear of punishment or their own values? The only certain crime prevention function of the criminal justice system is the incapacitation of detected offenders for the duration of their incarceration; but even this notion is undermined by the argument that the prison experience itself often exacerbates criminal behaviour.

A justice system that is only mandated to intervene *after* the commission of crimes is unlikely to prevent many crimes. Moreover, since most crime prevention through social development is likely to occur *outside* the criminal justice system, these programs generally do not receive criminal justice funding. For example, the connections among criminal justice, public schools, the family, and social welfare are often obscured by discrete departmental mandates that inhibit collaboration of agencies toward crime prevention. Particularly troubling is the focus on the needs of the offender only, with minimal attention to the needs of the victim.

In restorative justice processes, the obligations and needs of both the offender and the victim are given full attention. The active involvement of community members—as supporters of both victims and offenders, as professionals, or as interested parties—extends the understanding of these obligations and needs, case after case, into the community itself. The *experience* of restorative values can further shift the community culture. The community has its own needs as well, primarily the need for a restored sense of safety (Sharpe 1998). As an important source of informal social controls, the community also plays a key role in crime prevention (Clear and Karp 1999, 37–57). Restorative processes focus on what is not working in the community, thus creating opportunities for its members to remedy specific deficits and to continue supporting certain community assets. These processes can also help build the capacity of individual members to address conflicts in peaceful ways without the intervention (and expense) of large governing institutions.

By focusing on needs, restorative justice increases the community's awareness of its social problems. These problems—which typically include substance abuse, family violence, sexual abuse, and the neglect and abandonment of children—require remedies within the community itself. If a community begins to recognize child neglect, for example, it can then determine the extent of that problem in that community and develop strategies to respond to it. Governments are a necessary part of that process; but it takes the community, neighbour by neighbour, to attend to the needs of neglected children.

While the social problems revealed by criminal justice processes are generally interpreted as the problems of the individual offender, restorative justice processes look for deeper causes. Restorative justice can be useful in helping individuals explore their own behaviour as part of crime prevention (Haley 1996); but they have much greater potential to explore aggregate problems as symptoms of larger social injustices, such as poverty, racism, and sexism. The greater the community involvement in responding to conflict and harm, the greater the awareness of social justice issues present within the community itself. Crime prevention, then, is not merely about erecting more streetlights and reporting suspicious behaviour, but also about attending to deeper social inequities that are reflected in individual acts of harm. For example, youth gang violence might be viewed as a symptom of a larger problem of racism in high schools. Thus, community members involved in such cases may be motivated to develop strategies in local schools to address the roots of racism.

FROM PHILOSOPHY TO PRACTICE: EXAMPLES OF RESTORATIVE JUSTICE PRACTICES

There are three basic models of restorative justice practice: *victim–offender meetings, family group conferences,* and *circle peacemaking* (Zehr 2002). All of these models include an encounter between the victim and the offender and many also extend to key participants, such as family and community members (Amstutz 2008). The processes are led by volunteer or professional facilitators trained to organize and run the encounters in ways that balance the concerns of everyone involved. These models generally include three discussion components: the facts about the crime (what happened?), the way the parties felt as a result of the crime (how was everyone affected?), and possible resolutions that might be pursued to meet the obligations created by the harm (what can be done?). The parties involved create agreements, which are expected to respect the healing mandate of restorative justice.

Victim–Offender Reconciliation Programs

Victim–offender meetings were first used in Canada in Kitchener-Waterloo, Ontario, as part of the Victim–Offender Reconciliation Program (VORP). This model involves a face-to-face meeting between a victim and an offender that is mediated by a trained community volunteer (Gilman and Bowler 1995). VORP is a pioneer restorative program that has inspired formalized consideration of restorative justice theory in Canada. While the Kitchener-Waterloo program used it exclusively for property crimes, British Columbia extended the VORP concept to include victims and offenders of serious personal crimes. Under the title of Victim Offender Mediation Program (VOMP), the B.C. restorative process began in 1991 as a pilot project of the Correctional Service of Canada (CSC) for federal offenders and their victims. VOMP and VORP differ in some ways, especially regarding the seriousness of the offences that each program deals with and the amount of preparation and aftercare necessary. Given VOMP's success and the growing demand from other provinces, CSC, together with the Community Justice Initiatives Association in Langley, B.C., developed the Restorative Opportunities Program (RO) in 2003. Modelled on VOMP's program, RO has made victim–offender mediation services available across Canada since 2004 and has developed to the point where an experienced team of 14 mediators provide services across the country (CSC 2009, http://www.csc-scc.gc.ca/text/rj/vom-eng.shtml#1).

Victim–offender encounters are used for healing and reconciliation. The process begins when the mediator receives a referral and contacts the victim and the offender to hear their stories. If the victim and offender agree to meet, the mediator arranges an encounter, but only when the mediator senses that an encounter will be helpful to both parties. The amount of time needed for pre-meeting counselling varies with the needs of the parties, because the needs of victims and offenders in serious cases are usually greater than those in minor cases. For example, a meeting between the victim of a car theft and the teenage boy who stole the car might require a few weeks of preparation; whereas a meeting between a victim of serious sexual assault and her assailant may take several months or years to arrange. This time lag can pose problems for cases that are constrained by court schedules; but in general, violent offence mediations occur soon after the offender has been sentenced.

Family Group Conferencing

Family group conferencing was developed in New Zealand through the *Children, Young Persons and Their Families Act* (1989). Family group conferences deal with both child protection cases and youth justice cases and include the youth in question as well as family members and community professionals (Hassall 1996). Family group conferencing is based on restorative justice values such as respect and sensitivity, with a particular criminal justice emphasis on victim inclusion and offender accountability. Australia adapted the family group conference model into a program developed by the police, one that uses a scripted model of facilitation that pays particular attention to the restorative and rehabilitative power of shame (Zehr 2002).

A similar model was developed in Canada by the RCMP in 1995, when RCMP and Crown counsel implemented a process in Sparwood, B.C., that later became known as *community justice forums* (CJFs) (Shaw and Jané 1999). The RCMP officially adopted this model in 1997; and by the end of 1998, it had trained about 1,700 police officers across Canada to use the program (Chatterjee and Elliott 2003). Also called *conferencing*, this process brings together the victim, the offender, their supporters, and other community stakeholders to talk about the harm resulting from the crime and possible solutions to it. This model often relies on a script that guides the facilitators through the process. The offenders are usually young, and the outcomes generally involve material restitution as well as an agreement to deal with certain presenting problems, such as substance abuse or truancy. In Newfoundland and Labrador, pilot conferencing projects have even been used in cases of domestic violence (Shaw and Jané 1999), which helps bring the problem to the community's attention. For example, a study has shown that a model of family group conferencing, such as the Family Group Decision Making Project in Newfoundland and Labrador, can be an effective approach to resolving family violence (Pennell and Burford 2002). Similar programs exist in schools, generally in place of conventional disciplinary penalties, such as detentions and suspensions (Wachtel and Mirsky 2009).

Circle Peacemaking

Circle peacemaking is strongly rooted in indigenous cultures and came to the broader North American society from northern Canadian cultures. In a circle program, participants sit in a circle and pass a "talking piece" to ensure that each person has an opportunity to speak. There is a strong emphasis in circle peacemaking on values such as integrity and truth telling (Pranis, Stuart, and Wedge 2002). The circle includes not only the victim, the offender, and their supporters, but also other community members. In criminal justice programs, circles are used for sentencing (*sentencing circles*) as well as for healing and general community dialogue.

Interest in circles began when judges recognized the limited impact of the conventional process in northern Aboriginal communities. As a result, they adapted circles to the demands of the formal court system for these cultural groups. In circle sentencing, the community and the victim have active roles in the offender's hearing in order to build connections to and within communities (Stuart 1996). Circles have been very effective for discussing public planning issues as well as for encouraging community participation in dealing with common issues (see Ball, Caldwell and Pranis 2010). In cases where the victim's safety is compromised by the offender's liberty, imprisonment may be a component of a sentencing outcome. When carefully deployed, the circle process may be useful in cases of domestic violence, where the community can take stringent measures to deal with power imbalances in intimate relationships. Circle sentencing is used for a range of offences, generally in cases where the offender pleads guilty.

A program example of a circle process that begins after a guilty plea is the Collaborative Justice Program (CJP; see http://www.collaborativejustice. ca/about_e.php). The CJP, which is located in the Ottawa courthouse, accepts cases in which the person charged with a criminal offence pleads guilty. The CJP staff then work with the accused and their victims, if they are willing, to come to some resolution about how to respond to the harm, before formal sentencing by the court. The cases taken on by the CJP can be serious, such as drunk driving causing death, and can take some time to process. However, when presented with the results of the circle process, judges are usually agreeable to accepting the group's decision.

COMMON FEATURES OF RESTORATIVE PROCESSES

Regardless of the specific restorative process model, all restorative justice programs share several characteristics. First, referrals come through negotiated agreements with partnering agencies, such as the police, the courts, schools, or social service agencies; or they may come directly from the community itself. Decisions about whether to accept a case for restorative intervention vary according to mandates, agreements, the specific factors of the case, and the particular circumstances of the main parties to the conflict. These variations depend on the parameters of the restorative resolution service itself; for example, police-run programs may be restricted to minor criminal cases, while school programs may only address disciplinary cases where the conflict is noncriminal. A common distinction is made between services that work with youth only (Morris and Maxwell 2003) and those that accept cases with primary stakeholders of all ages.

Second, all restorative models begin with preparatory casework, which receives attention that varies with the model and the nature of the cases accepted. Victim–offender mediation processes emphasize pre-mediation meetings with each party to the conflict; as Umbreit (1994) notes: "Having the mediator meet with both [parties] individually before even scheduling the mediation is extremely important. It tends to humanize the justice process and results in a higher 'getting-to-the-table' rate of actual mediation participation" (7–8). Given its wider capture of "stakeholder" input, family group conferencing entails pre-conference meetings with a larger number of participants, often constrained by court schedules and legal imperatives. These meetings generally focus on the purpose and process of the conferencing; they also assess the offender's acceptance of responsibility and willingness to participate (Hudson et al. 1996). In circle processes, the referral and pre-encounter stages may take the form of circles, particularly when the key parties need support people. In these preparatory circles, the facilitators ensure that the victim and offender support groups are balanced, that both have received relevant resources, and that both are working on healing plans (Pranis, Stuart, and Wedge 2003).

Restorative processes are also characterized by a post-encounter phase. All models include a subsequent monitoring phase during which either volunteers or professionals assess the agreements created in the encounter phase of the process to ensure that the parties act on the recommendations. The depth and breadth of these interventions generally depend on the seriousness of the offence and the needs of the participants involved. In Canada, conferencing agreements and those generated by relatively minor victim–offender mediation cases tend to be more simple and time-constrained. Post-sentence victim–offender mediation, as well as circle processes for serious crime cases, may involve open-ended, evolving supervision and facilitation of agreements. This often depends on the objectives of the restorative justice process: some are mandated by criminal justice and are concerned with clearing cases; whereas others focus mainly on the healing of those affected by the harm. Whatever the model, several principles must guide the process. These are itemized in Mika and Zehr's "Signposts of Restorative Justice" (see Figure 29.1). A summarizing adage might be to "do no harm" in restorative endeavours, whether in criminal justice or the schools, whether for minor disputes or major crimes.

Figure 29.1 *Signposts of Restorative Justice*

1. Focus on the harms of crime rather than on the rules that have been broken.

2. Show equal concern and commitment to victims and offenders, involving both in the process of justice.

3. Work toward the restoration of victims, empowering them and responding to their needs as they see them.

4. Support offenders while encouraging them to understand, accept, and carry out their obligations.

5. Recognize that while obligations may be difficult for offenders, those obligations should not be intended as harms; moreover, they must be achievable.

6. Provide opportunities for dialogue (direct or indirect) between victim and offender as appropriate.

7. Find meaningful ways to involve the community and to respond to the community bases of crime.

8. Encourage collaboration and reintegration of victims and offenders, rather than coercion and isolation.

9. Give attention to the unintended consequences of your actions and program.

10. Show respect to all parties—victims, offenders, and justice colleagues.

Source: Mika and Zehr, 1998.

CHALLENGES AND CONCERNS

Seasoned practitioners of restorative justice have noted several areas of concern that require attention as restorative justice programs become more popular. One major issue is the role of victims and the attention paid to their needs. For example, conferencing tends to focus on the offender, with victims often used simply as a means of dealing with the offender (albeit in ways that are more inclusive than the formal criminal justice system). Certainly, research shows that victims who participate in restorative justice processes are more satisfied with the results than are victims who participate in the formal criminal justice processes (Strang 2002; Daly 2005; Dignan 2005). Even in cases of serious offences, final results of an evaluation have shown that almost all program participants were highly satisfied with the restorative approach, especially when compared to participants in the traditional criminal justice procedures (Rugge, Bonta, and Wallace-Capretta 2005). However, restitution agreements may offer only material compensation for victims (which can be sufficient in some cases), without meaningful attention to the victim's personal healing needs (Herman 2004). This concern is particularly strong in restorative processes that are "add-ons" to the formal criminal justice system, as opposed to programs that operate autonomously.

Another concern relates to the potential for coercion and the consequent lack of safety for participants. While safety may be a concern for offenders, the problem for victims may often be more subtle and potentially more dangerous. The problem of victim safety was raised first in Canada by practitioners and advocates working with victims of familial violence, where power imbalances in close intimate relationships can hide the vulnerability of victims from proper scrutiny (see Ptacek and Frederick 2009). While restorative justice has been used effectively in cases of domestic violence (Mills 2006; van Wormer 2009) and child abuse (Pennell and Burford 1996), there are many situations where restorative processes are not appropriate for these kinds of offences. For example, Aboriginal women and children in isolated communities may be silenced by the local political leadership and by unhealthy kinship relationships (Stewart, Huntley, and Blaney 2001). Some advocates argue that sexism in Aboriginal communities prevents safety for women and children in restorative processes, and recommend that restorative practices be discontinued until further research is conducted (Cameron 2006). Furthermore, some argue that responding to domestic violence is an important limit to the restorative justice model (Busch 2002).

A final important concern expressed by many is the impact of restorative justice on the offender's human rights (Morris 2002; Skelton and Frank 2007). Ashworth (2002) argues that the State must maintain a fundamental role in the administration of justice to ensure that proper procedural standards are met. Hence, it is important that restorative justice initiatives respect certain safeguards—namely, they must be led by an independent and impartial person; receive legal advice before and after any restorative justice process; and respect certain principles of proportionality, such as the offender's ability to pay the amount to restore the victim. More recently, Ward and Langlands have studied the question empirically. They argue that while a restorative justice approach can contribute to the protection of certain individual rights, it can also clash with certain of those rights. They propose a model that attempts to minimize the degree of conflict by ensuring that human rights are respected in the pursuit of communitarian aims and the repair of relationships (Ward and Langlands 2008).

CONCLUSION

Can restorative justice ever replace the existing punitive justice system? The question is probably premature. Current efforts in restorative justice are more concerned with preventing its absorption into the existing justice system. Perhaps in time, restorative justice will become the first option for criminal justice interventions, with the conventional system playing a backup role. A more likely scenario is for restorative justice processes to become established alongside traditional justice systems, as an option for offenders who want to take responsibility for their actions and for victims who want a restorative encounter as part of their own healing. The few evaluations of the effectiveness of restorative justice programs to date have been promising (e.g., Umbreit 1994; Flaten 1996). Restorative justice challenges Canadians to consider what we want from justice and what kind of world we want to live in. If the purpose of justice is peace and safety in our communities, then we need to find the means to get us there. To do so requires us to challenge primary concepts about criminal justice, such as punishment. Perhaps the simple availability of other response options to harm-doing afforded by restorative justice will help broaden this perspective. If the only tool we have is a hammer, every problem looks like a nail.

DISCUSSION QUESTIONS

1. *In your view, what is the most important advantage of restorative justice over the conventional criminal justice system?*
2. *Critics of the restorative justice movement have identified a number of problems associated with this new paradigm. Do you see any difficulties with the restorative response?*

FURTHER READINGS

Braithwaite, J. 1999. "Restorative Justice: Pessimistic and Optimistic Accounts." In M. Tonry, ed., *Crime and Justice: A Review of Research.* Chicago: University of Chicago Press.

Roach, K. 2000. "Changing Punishment at the Turn of the Century: Restorative Justice on the Rise." *Canadian Journal of Criminology* 42: 249–80.

Roberts, J.V., and K. Roach. 2003. "Restorative Justice in Canada: From Sentencing Circles to Sentencing Principles." In A. von Hirsch, J.V. Roberts, A. Bottoms, and K. Roach, eds., *Restorative Justice and Criminal Justice.* Oxford: Hart.

REFERENCES

Amstutz, L.S. 2008. *Little Book of Victim Offender Conferencing: Bringing Victims and Offenders Together in Dialogue*. Intercourse: Good Books.

Ashworth, A. 2002. "Responsibilities, Rights, and Restorative Justice." *British Journal of Criminology* 42: 578–95.

Ball, J., W. Caldwell, and K. Pranis. 2010. *Doing Democracy with Circle: Engaging Communities in Public Planning*. St. Paul: Living Justice.

Braithwaite, J. 1989. *Crime, Shame, and Reintegration*. New York: Cambridge University Press.

Brantingham, P., and P. Brantingham. 1990. "Situational Crime Prevention in Practice." *Canadian Journal of Criminology* 32: 17–40.

Busch, R. 2002. "Domestic Violence and Restorative Justice Initiatives: Who Pays if We Get It Wrong?" In H. Strang and J. Braithwaite, eds., *Restorative Justice and Family Violence*. Cambridge: Cambridge University Press. 223–48.

Cameron, A. 2006. "Stopping the Violence: Canadian Feminist Debates on Restorative Justice and Intimate Violence." *Theoretical Criminology* 10: 49–66.

Chatterjee, J., and L. Elliott. 2003. "Restorative Policing in Canada: The Royal Canadian Mounted Police, Community Justice Forums, and the *Youth Criminal Justice Act*." *Police Practice and Research* 4: 347–59.

Clear, T., and D. Karp. 1999. *The Community Justice Ideal: Preventing Crime and Achieving Justice*. Boulder: Westview.

Daly, K. 2005. "A Tale of Two Studies: Restorative Justice from a Victim's Perspective." In E. Elliott and R. Gordon, eds., *New Directions in Restorative Justice: Issues, Practice, Evaluation*. Portland: Willan.

Dignan, J. 2005. *Understanding Victims and Restorative Justice*. New York: Open University Press.

Flaten, C. 1996. "Victim-Offender Mediation: Application with Serious Offences Committed by juveniles." In B. Galaway and J. Hudson, eds., *Restorative Justice: International Perspectives*. Monsey: Criminal Justice Press.

Gilman, E., and C. Bowler. 1995. *Victim Offender Mediation Training Program: Training and Resource Manual*. Rev. ed. Langley: Fraser Region Community Justice Initiatives Association.

Haan, W. 1990. *The Politics of Redress: Crime, Punishment, and Penal Abolition*. Boston: Unwin Hyman.

Haley, J. 1996. "Crime Prevention Through Restorative Justice: Lessons from Japan." In B. Galaway and J. Hudson, eds., *Restorative Justice: International Perspectives*. Monsey: Criminal Justice Press.

Hassall, I. 1996. "Origin and Development of Family Group Conferences." In J. Hudson, A. Morris, G. Maxwell, and B. Galaway, eds., *Family Group Conferences: Perspectives on Policy and Practice*. Monsey: Criminal Justice Press.

Herman, S. 2004. "Is Restorative Justice Possible Without a Parallel System for Victims?" In H. Zehr and B. Toews, eds., *Critical Issues in Restorative Justice*. Monsey: Criminal Justice Press.

Hirshi, T. 1969. *Causes of Delinquency*. Berkeley: University of California Press.

Hudson, J., B. Galaway, A. Morris, and G. Maxwell. 1996. "Introduction." In J. Hudson, A. Morris, G. Maxwell, and B. Galaway, eds., *Family Group Conferences: Perspectives on Policy and Practice*. Monsey: Criminal Justice Press.

Llewellyn, J., and R. Howse. 1999. *Restorative Justice: A Conceptual Framework*. Ottawa: Law Commission of Canada. http://www.lcc.gc.ca

Mika, H., and H. Zehr. 1998. "Fundamental Principles of Restorative Justice." *Contemporary Justice Review* 1: 47–55.

Mills, L. 2006. *From Insult to Injury: Rethinking Our Responses to Intimate Abuse*. Princeton: Princeton University Press.

Morris, A. 2002. "Critiquing the Critics: A Brief Response to Critics of Restorative Justice." *British Journal of Criminology* 42: 596–615.

Morris, A., and G. Maxwell, eds. 2003. *Restorative Justice for Juveniles: Conferencing, Mediation, and Circles*. Portland: Hart.

Pennell, J., and G. Burford. 2002. "Feminist Praxis: Making Family Group Conferencing Work." In J. Braithwaite and H. Strang, eds., *Restorative Justice and Family Violence*. Cambridge: Cambridge University Press. 108–27.

Pranis, K., B. Stuart, and M. Wedge. 2003. *Using Peacemaking Circles in the Justice System*. Minnesota: Living Justice.

Ptacek, J., and L. Frederick. 2009. "Restorative Justice and Intimate Partner Violence." National Online Resource Centre on Violence Against Women. http:// www.vewnet.org

Rugge, T., J. Bonta, and S. Wallace-Capretta. 2005 *Evaluation of the Collaborative Justice Project: A Restorative Justice Program for Serious Crime*. Ottawa: Public Safety Canada.

Sharpe, S. 1998. *Restorative Justice: A Vision for Healing and Change*. Edmonton: Edmonton Victim Offender Mediation Society.

Shaw, M., and F. Jané. 1999. *Family Group Conferencing with Children Under Twelve: A Discussion Paper*. Ottawa: Department of Justice Canada.

Skelton A., and C. Frank. 2007. "Human Rights and Restorative Justice." In G. Johnstone and D.W. Van Ness, eds., *Handbook of Restorative Justice*. Cullompton: Willan. 580–97.

Stewart, W., A. Huntley, and F. Blaney. 2001. *The Implications of Restorative Justice for Aboriginal Women and Children Survivors of Violence: A Comparative Overview of Five Communities in British Columbia*. Ottawa: Law Commission of Canada.

Stuart, B. 1996. "Circle Sentencing: Turning Swords into Plowshares." In B. Galaway and J. Hudson, eds., *Restorative Justice: International Perspectives*. Monsey: Criminal Justice Press.

Strang, H. 2002. *Repair or Revenge: Victims and Restorative Justice*. Oxford: Clarendon.

Sutherland, E. 1947. *Criminology*. 4th ed. Philadelphia: Lippincott.

Sykes, G. 1958. *The Society of Captives: A Study of a Maximum Security Prison*. Princeton: Princeton University Press.

Umbreit, M. 1994. *Victim Meets Offender: The Impact of Restorative Justice and Mediation*. Monsey: Criminal Justice Press.

van Wormer, K. 2009. "Restorative Justice as Social Justice for Victims of Gendered Violence: A Standpoint Feminist Perspective." *Social Work* 54, no. 2: 107–16.

Vold, G., T. Bernard, and J. Snipes. 2002. *Theoretical Criminology*. 5th ed. New York: Oxford University Press.

Wachtel, T., and L. Mirsky. 2009. *Safer Saner Schools: Restorative Practices in Schools in Education*. Bethelhem: International Institute of Restorative Practices.

Ward, T., and R.L. Langlands. 2008. "Restorative Justice and the Human Rights of Offenders: Convergences and Divergences." *Aggression and Violent Behavior* 13, no. 5: 355–72.

Zehr, H. 1990. *Changing Lenses*. Waterloo: Herald.

——. 2002. *The Little Book of Restorative Justice*. Intercourse: Good Books.